DARWINISM
AND THE
DIVINE

DARWINISM
AND THE
DIVINE

EVOLUTIONARY THOUGHT AND NATURAL THEOLOGY

THE 2009 HULSEAN LECTURES
UNIVERSITY OF CAMBRIDGE

ALISTER E. McGRATH

A John Wiley & Sons, Ltd., Publication

This edition first published 2011
© 2011 Alister E. McGrath

Blackwell Publishing was acquired by John Wiley & Sons in February 2007. Blackwell's publishing program has been merged with Wiley's global Scientific, Technical, and Medical business to form Wiley-Blackwell.

Registered Office
John Wiley & Sons Ltd, The Atrium, Southern Gate, Chichester, West Sussex, PO19 8SQ, United Kingdom

Editorial Offices
350 Main Street, Malden, MA 02148-5020, USA
9600 Garsington Road, Oxford, OX4 2DQ, UK
The Atrium, Southern Gate, Chichester, West Sussex, PO19 8SQ, UK

For details of our global editorial offices, for customer services, and for information about how to apply for permission to reuse the copyright material in this book please see our website at www.wiley.com/wiley-blackwell.

The right of Alister E. McGrath to be identified as the author of this work has been asserted in accordance with the UK Copyright, Designs and Patents Act 1988.

Wiley also publishes its books in a variety of electronic formats. Some content that appears in print may not be available in electronic books.

Designations used by companies to distinguish their products are often claimed as trademarks. All brand names and product names used in this book are trade names, service marks, trademarks or registered trademarks of their respective owners. The publisher is not associated with any product or vendor mentioned in this book. This publication is designed to provide accurate and authoritative information in regard to the subject matter covered. It is sold on the understanding that the publisher is not engaged in rendering professional services. If professional advice or other expert assistance is required, the services of a competent professional should be sought.

Library of Congress Cataloging-in-Publication Data
McGrath, Alister E., 1953–
Darwinism and the divine : evolutionary thought and natural theology / Alister E. McGrath.
    p.   cm.
  Includes bibliographical references and index.
  ISBN 978-1-4443-3343-5 (hardback) – ISBN 978-1-4443-3344-2 (paperback)
1. Natural theology.   2. Faith and reason.   3. Evolution (Biology)   4. Evolution (Biology)–Religious aspects–Christianity.   5. Darwin, Charles, 1809–1882. On the origin of species.   6. Paley, William, 1743–1805. Natural theology.   I. Title.
  BL183.M335 2011
  231.7′652–dc22
                                                                    2010039893
A catalogue record for this book is available from the British Library.

Set in 10/12pt Sabon by SPi Publisher Services, Pondicherry, India

1   2010

*For the Principal, Fellows, and Staff
of Harris Manchester College, Oxford*

Contents

List of Figures   x
Preface   xii
Acknowledgments   xv

Introduction   1

**Part I   Conceptual Clarifications:
On the meaning of terms**   9

1 Natural Theology: A Deeper Structure to the Natural World   11
   Natural Theology in the Classical Tradition   13
   The Conceptual Fluidity of Natural Theology   15
   The Eternal Return of Natural Theology   18

2 Darwinism: A Narrative of Evolution   27
   Darwinism: A Defensible Term?   28
   Darwinism as an Ideology   32
   The Metaphysical Inflation of Evolutionary Thought   36
   Conclusion to Part I   40

**Part II   Historical Exposition: Darwin and the
English natural theology tradition**   47

3 English Natural Theology of the Augustan Age, 1690–1745   49
   The Emergence of English Natural Theology   50
   Newtonian Physics and Natural Theology   53
   The Protestant Assumptions of English Natural Theology   56
   A Foundation for Consensus: The Doctrine of Creation   61
   Physico-theology: The Appeal to Contrivance   63
   Natural Theology and the Beauty of Nature   72

The Problem of Development within Nature 74
Assessing Evidence: Changing Public Perceptions 75

4 A Popular Classic: William Paley's *Natural Theology* (1802) 85
Introducing Paley's *Natural Theology* 85
Paley's Source: Bernard Nieuwentyt's *Religious
  Philosopher* (1718) 88
The Watch Analogy: The Concept of Contrivance 91
Paley on Intermediary Causes within Nature 97
The Vulnerability of Paley's Approach 99

5 Beyond Paley: Shifts in English Natural Theology, 1802–52 108
The Impact of Geology upon Paley's Natural Theology 110
Henry Brougham: A Natural Theology of the Mind 112
Evidence, Testimony, and Proof: A Shifting Context 115
A New Approach: The Bridgewater Treatises 119
John Henry Newman: The Theological Deficiencies of Paley 127
Robert Browning's "Caliban Upon Setebos":
  A Literary Critique of Paley 130
English Natural Theology on the Eve of the
  Darwinian Revolution 133

6 Charles Darwin, Natural Selection, and Natural Theology 143
The Development of Darwin's Views on Natural Selection 146
Problems, Prediction, and Proof: The Challenge
  of Natural Selection 150
Natural Selection and Natural Theology: An Assessment
  of Darwin's Impact 155
Conclusion to Part II 171

Part III   Contemporary Discussion: Darwinism
           and natural theology 183

7 A Wider Teleology: Design, Evolution, and Natural Theology 185
Directionality within the Natural World 187
Teleology: Introducing an Idea 188
  Chance, Contingency, and Evolutionary Goals 191
The "Wider Teleology" of Evolution 194
The Inference of Design and Natural Theology 197
Suffering, Evolution, and Natural Theology 202

8 The Concept of Creation: Reflections and Reconsiderations 217
The Seventeenth Century: The Regnant Theology of Creation 218

Creation as Event and Process: Augustine of Hippo   222
Evolution and an Emergent Creation   230
God's Action within the Evolutionary Process   233

9   Universal Darwinism: Natural Theology as
     an Evolutionary Outcome?   247
     The Darwinian Paradigm and Cultural Development   249
     The God-Meme: Natural Theology and Cultural Replicators   254
     Religion: Evolutionary Adaptation or Spandrel?   262
     Natural Theology and Evolutionary Theories
        of the Origins of Religion   265
     Conclusion to Part III   267

Part IV   Conclusion   277

10   The Prospects for Natural Theology   279
     Natural Theology and the Human Evolutionary Past   281
     Natural Theology, Observational Traction,
        and the Best Explanation   283
     A Community of Discernment: The Church
        and Natural Theology   285
     In Quest of Meaning   288

Index   294

List of Figures

2.1 Engraving of Charles Robert Darwin (1809–82) in old age.   28

2.2 Frontispiece of the *Origin of Species* by Charles Darwin, published in 1859.   30

2.3 Daniel C. Dennett, University Professor and Austin B. Fletcher Professor of Philosophy, and Director of the Center for Cognitive Studies at Tufts University, photographed in his office at Tufts, November 28, 2005.   36

2.4 British evolutionary biologist, philosopher, and author Richard Dawkins listens to a question during a press conference on the occasion of his being granted an honorary doctorate by the Universitat de Valencia, March 31, 2009.   36

3.1 Isaac Newton (1642–1727), English physicist and mathematician. Among other things, Newton discovered the ability of a prism to separate white light into its composite colors.   53

3.2 John Wilkins (1614–72), English mathematician and founder of the Royal Society, c. 1655, in an engraving of 1708.   64

3.3 A meeting of the Royal Society in Crane Court, Fleet Street, where it had rooms from 1710 to 1782. Isaac Newton is in the President's chair. Artist's reconstruction. Wood engraving c. 1880.   67

4.1 English writer and theologian William Paley (1743–1805), c. 1790.   86

4.2 Movement view of a gold open-faced, quarter repeating, perpetual pocket watch. No. 3 (or No. 33) by Abraham-Louis Breguet. Paris c. 1790.   89

5.1 The Central Court and Arcades of the Oxford University Museum. This engraving shows the interior of Oxford University's Museum of Natural History in 1860.

The collection was arranged along the lines suggested
by William Paley's *Natural Theology* in 1836.   109
5.2   Portrait of the British polymath William Whewell
(1794–1866).   114
5.3   Cardinal John Henry Newman, c. 1870.   128
5.4   Lithographed portrait of Robert Browning, c. 1880.   130
6.1   Engraving of HMS *Beagle*, the ship that carried
Charles Darwin during the voyage that inspired
his theory of evolution.   144
6.2   Daguerreotype of Anne Elizabeth Darwin (Annie), 1849.   158
6.3   Asa Gray (1810–88), American botanist. Photograph, 1880s.   163
6.4   Queen Victoria's favorite pets. Sir Edwin Landseer
(1803–73): *Hector, Nero and Dash with the parrot, Lory,*
1838, oil on canvas, 120.2 × 150.3 cm. Commissioned
by Queen Victoria.   170
7.1   Engraving of English biologist Thomas Henry Huxley
(1825–95), in 1874.   186
9.1   American paleontologist Stephen J. Gould, January 1982.   255

Preface

Natural theology is enjoying a renaissance, catalyzed as much by the intellectual inquisitiveness of natural scientists as by the reflections of Christian theologians and biblical scholars. It offers an important conceptual framework for the exploration of Christian theology as a rational enterprise, and a clarification of how the inner logic of the Christian faith relates to scientific rationality. Natural theology, in the full sense of the term, mandates a principled engagement with reality that is rigorously informed, both theologically and scientifically. It has the potential to open up new vistas of understanding and critical yet positive dialogue between scientific and religious cultures and communities.

There remains, however, a widespread perception that Charles Darwin's theory of natural selection marked and continues to mark the end of any viable natural theology, particularly as it had been given classic formulation in the writings of William Paley (1743–1805). Paley's theory is often interpreted as marking the apex of Christian thinking, which is thus portrayed as having been comprehensively routed and discredited by Darwin's theory of natural selection. As it happens, Paley's approach is the late, popular flowering of a relatively recent and distinctively *English* approach, the origins of which can be traced back to the late seventeenth century, and which was already in some difficulty at the time when Darwin's theory of natural selection was developed. Natural theology may have developed in new directions after Darwin; if so, it was merely deflected from some of its seventeenth-century implementations, rather than defeated in its intellectual vision. It was not the Christian enterprise of natural theology that was discredited by Darwin, but a specific form of such a theology, which emerged in England after 1690 and was already rejected by many Christian theologians by 1850. The Darwinian debates about science and religion were, in one sense, thoroughly English, reflecting local approaches to natural theology, rather than those of the Christian tradition in general.

There is clearly a need for an extended and detailed examination of the implications of evolutionary thought for natural theology, both at the time of Darwin himself and in more recent times. *Darwinism and the Divine* sets out:

1 to identify the forms of natural theology that emerged in England over the period 1690–1850 and how these were affected by the advent of Darwin's theories; and
2 to explore and assess twenty-first-century reflections on the relation of evolutionary thought and natural theology.

This book is an expanded version of the six 2009 Hulsean Lectures at the University of Cambridge, marking the 200th anniversary of Darwin's birth, and the 150th anniversary of the publication of his *Origin of Species*. Cambridge was an ideal location at which to explore these issues. Both Charles Darwin and William Paley were students at Cambridge University; indeed, they are believed to have occupied the same student room at Christ's College, Cambridge. These lectures built on the renewed interest in Darwin and the theory of evolution, making use of this welcome opportunity to reopen the whole question of the relation of evolutionary thought and natural theology, both as historical and contemporary questions. I have always taken the view that there is much to be gained from the creative yet principled encounter between evolutionary science, conscious of its own limits, and a self-critical theology, rooted in an awareness of the ultimate mystery of its subject matter. I hope that this work will stimulate further discussion of their themes, even if it cannot hope to resolve them.

I owe thanks to the Hulsean Electors of the University of Cambridge for their kind invitation to deliver these lectures, and the large audience that turned out to hear the lectures for their perceptive comments and questions, which were invaluable in redrafting the material. In particular, I would like to thank my Cambridge colleagues Professor Eamon Duffy, Professor David Ford, Dr Peter Harland, and Dr Fraser Watts for their warm hospitality throughout my visits. I also acknowledge the kindness of the John Templeton Foundation in supporting the substantial research underlying this work.

The detailed engagement with primary sources of the seventeenth, eighteenth, and nineteenth centuries, which is such a significant feature of the second part of this work, was carried out primarily in the Bodleian Library, Oxford, and the Tate Library of Harris Manchester College, Oxford. I am immensely grateful to both institutions for the help rendered. Even though many of the relevant primary sources became available online at the time of writing this work, there is still no substitute for the experience of physically handling ancient works, and enjoying a sense of physical solidarity with their chains of readers down the centuries.

In the end, research depends upon the support and encouragement of a community of scholars. I thus take great pleasure in dedicating this work to the Principal, Fellows, and Staff of Harris Manchester College, Oxford. I had the privilege of becoming a Senior Research Fellow at the college while serving as Professor of Historical Theology at Oxford University. It is a privilege to remain part of its fellowship, and I acknowledge the collegiality, warmth, and generosity of this vibrant college community with gratitude and admiration.

Alister E. McGrath
King's College London
May 2010

Acknowledgments

The editors and publisher gratefully acknowledge the permissions granted to reproduce the copyrighted material in this book.

Figure 2.1   Science Photo Library.
Figure 2.2   Science Photo Library.
Figure 2.3   © Rick Friedman/Corbis.
Figure 2.4   © Kai Foersterling/epa/Corbis.
Figure 3.1   © Bettmann/Corbis.
Figure 3.2   SSPL/Getty Images.
Figure 3.3   World History Archive/TopFoto.
Figure 4.1   Rischgitz/Getty Images.
Figure 4.2   Horologicam/TopFoto.
Figure 5.1   © Illustrated London News Ltd/Mary Evans Picture Library.
Figure 5.2   Science Photo Library.
Figure 5.3   © Hulton-Deutsch Collection/Corbis.
Figure 5.4   © Chris Hellier/Corbis.
Figure 6.1   Science Photo Library.
Figure 6.2   © English Heritage Photo Library, Down House, Kent.
Figure 6.3   © Bettmann/Corbis.
Figure 6.4   The Royal Collection © 2010, Her Majesty Queen Elizabeth II.
Figure 7.1   Science Photo Library.
Figure 9.1   © Wally McNamee/Corbis.

Introduction

The natural sciences throw up questions that insistently demand to be addressed; unfortunately, they often transcend the capacity of the scientific method to answer them. The sciences raise questions of the greatest interest and importance, which by their very nature often go beyond the realms in which science itself is competent to speak. One group of such questions is traditionally addressed by what is generally known as natural theology. Might the natural world be a sign, promise, symbol, or vestige of another domain or realm? Might the world we know be a bright shadow of something greater?

There is resistance to discussion of such questions within some sections of both the scientific and religious communities. Some natural scientists, for example, fear that such metaphysical reflections might erode the distinctive identity of the natural sciences. Without necessarily denying the validity of such metaphysical questions, some scientists would nevertheless regard them as inappropriate, given the specific remit and limits of the scientific method. The "demarcation problem" remains at least as significant in the early twenty-first century as it was in the late nineteenth century. Many natural scientists attribute certain specific characteristics to the practitioners, assumptions, methods, and values of the sciences, in order to construct a social boundary that distinguishes the sciences from other intellectual activities.[1] Boundaries must be drawn and respected. Scientists, like all other professionals, are strongly territorial and resent intrusion on their territory by those who are not members of the guild. Natural theology, some of their number would maintain, represents such a scholarly trespass, opening the door to intellectual contamination.

Darwinism and the Divine: Evolutionary Thought and Natural Theology, First Edition.
Alister E. McGrath.
© 2011 Alister E. McGrath. Published 2011 by Blackwell Publishing Ltd.

There is an important point about intellectual authority and competency under consideration here, which unfortunately can easily degenerate into a cultural turf war. While it may indeed remain important for certain purposes to maintain an absolute separation of the sciences from other disciplines, there are many – including myself – who hold that science is at its most interesting when it engages in dialogue with other disciplines – including theology, religion, and spirituality.

Yet misgivings about natural theology are not limited to the scientific community. Some religious thinkers also have reservations about enhanced levels of dialogue with the natural sciences. Might a growing scientific understanding undermine core religious beliefs? Might a scientifically accommodated version of a religion emerge, standing at some considerable distance from its more traditional forebears? Psychologist Paul Bloom gently hinted at this possibility in a recent article, suggesting that increasing scientific understanding inevitably leads to erosion of traditional religious beliefs, and hence the gradual secularization of a religious perspective. "Scientific views would spread through religious communities. Supernatural beliefs would gradually disappear as the theologically correct version of a religion gradually became consistent with the secular world view."[2]

Bloom may have a point. As we shall see in the next chapter, during the late seventeenth century English natural theology shifted away from the "signs and wonders" approach of earlier generations, and focused on the rationality and order of the natural world. Such a natural theology bears little relation to the vision of God as an active, transforming power found, for example, in modern Pentecostalism. Might this represent the kind of scientific accommodation that Bloom has in mind? However understandable this development may have been within the cultural context of the English scientific revolution, it inevitably meant a move away from a notion of a God who is experienced as active in history toward that of a God whose past imprint may be reasonably discerned within the structures of nature.

Darwinism and the Divine sets out to explore the impact of Darwinism on the generic enterprise of natural theology, whether this is described (for its variety of interpretations are such that it cannot be *defined*) in terms of the "proof" of God's existence from the natural world, or the exploration of the degree of intellectual resonance between the Christian vision of reality and what is actually observed in nature. The term "natural theology" is open to multiple interpretations, and does not designate a single narrative or program.[3] Although the term is routinely paraphrased as "proving God's existence from nature," this is only one way of conceptualizing the enterprise. Nevertheless, a significant degree of "family resemblance" can be discerned between these various approaches, most notably their engagement with the natural world with the expectation that it may, in some manner and to some extent, disclose something of the divine nature. Natural theology is about maximizing the intellectual traction between the Christian vision of reality and observation of the natural world.

This work seeks to explore the impact of evolutionary thought on Christian natural theology, reflecting partly the historical importance of the issue, and partly the need to evaluate competing notions of natural theology in the light of their capacity to accommodate such thinking. Elsewhere, I have developed and defended the notion of natural theology, considered not as an attempt to prove the existence or character of God from nature, but as a Trinitarian direction of gaze toward nature.[4] On this approach, natural theology is the understanding of the natural world that arises when it is seen through the interpretative lens of the Christian faith, allowing its rich Trinitarian ontology to illuminate both the status of the natural world and the human attempt to make sense of it. This, however, is only one of many approaches. An evaluation of their capacity to provide theological maps of the evolutionary landscape is potentially an important indication of their adequacy.

The first major part of this work attempts to achieve some degree of clarification of the multiple meanings of both "natural theology" and "Darwinism," noting how issues of definition are central to any evaluation of their relationship. Particular emphasis is placed upon the uneasy and often unexamined relationship between Darwinism considered as a provisional scientific theory, and Darwinism considered as a universal theory – what some would call a worldview or metanarrative.

The second part of the study deals with a specific family of approaches to natural theology that emerged within England during the seventeenth century and continued to be of major religious and cultural significance into the late nineteenth century. The historical analysis presented in this part of this work cannot be regarded as an unnecessary diversion from the real business of the book. Today's debates about the impact of evolution upon religious thought invariably make historical assumptions, draw implicitly upon historical analysis, and make theological judgments shaped by memories of the past. Today's discussions of these themes are often subtly shaped by the lengthening shadows of earlier debates, not always accurately recounted or assessed.

This substantial part of the study consists of a critical re-reading of the tradition of natural theology that developed in England during the later seventeenth and eighteenth centuries, and a review of its role in shaping the theological dimensions of public discussion of Darwin's theory of natural selection. The analysis opens with a study of the types of natural theology to emerge in England during the "Augustan age" (1690–1745). This is followed by a re-evaluation of the approach of William Paley, particularly in his classic *Natural Theology* (1802), and the reception and revision of this approach in England until the eve of the publication of Darwin's *Origin of*

Species (1859). These chapters, based on a critical and close reading of primary sources, highlight the need to re-evaluate some traditional judgments about the types of natural theology that developed in England during this period, and their role in shaping the reception of Darwin's theories.

I had been concerned for some time that certain reflexive habits of thought appeared to have developed in some of the secondary literature, especially in relation to Paley's classic *Natural Theology* (1802). I therefore decided to read the primary sources once more – especially the core writings of John Wilkins (1614–72), John Ray (1627–1705), William Derham (1657–1735), William Paley (1743–1805), and William Whewell (1794–1866) – in chronological order, taking care to contextualize these works against the intellectual culture of their day. For obvious reasons, this approach also had subsequently to be extended to the works of Darwin and his close associates, particularly Thomas H. Huxley (1825–95). I did not undertake this close reading of Darwin and his circle until I had completed reading and assessing works of English natural theology up to 1837, in order that I could read Darwin in the light of the conceptual nets thrown over the interpretation of nature by these various styles of natural theology, rather than retrojecting more modern assessments and opinions onto his age. By the end of this critical re-reading, it was clear that some traditional judgments concerning Darwinism and natural theology – including several that I myself had adopted even in the recent past – could not be sustained on the basis of the evidence.

The most obvious, and perhaps most important, such conclusion is that it cannot be maintained that Darwin's theory caused the "abandonment of natural theology."[5] The enterprise may have been refined and redirected; it was certainly not abandoned, in England or elsewhere. Furthermore, Darwin's writings, when seen in this context, cannot be said to have "abolished" the notion of teleology. Not only are Darwin's writings on evolution marked by implicit and explicit teleological statements; it is clear that his approach demands not the abolition of teleology but its reform and restatement – the "wider teleology" of which Huxley correctly spoke.

This extended historical analysis considers how the English tradition of natural theology was shaped by its English intellectual and cultural context. In particular, it shows how certain features of English Protestantism of the seventeenth century – specifically, its implicit "disenchantment" of nature, and its explicit commitment to belief in the cessation of miracles within nature on the one hand, and the providential guidance of the natural world on the other – led to the emergence of approaches to natural theology that emphasized its sense-making capacities, and focused on evidence of apparent design in the biological realm. Paley's *Natural Theology*, which is considered in some detail within this section, is to be seen as a late flowering of this approach.

These distinctively English forms of natural theology proved to be of defining importance for the German *Aufklärung*. Thus Johann August Eberhard's influential *Vorbereitung zur natürlichen Theologie* (1781), which served as an important source for Immanuel Kant's views on natural theology,[6] explicitly identifies a series of English writers as major influences on the reshaping of natural theology in response to the new intellectual currents of the eighteenth century.[7] Kant's impact upon German-language discussions of natural theology was considerable. Indeed, it may be suggested that Karl Barth's critique of the generic notion of "natural theology" is actually and unwittingly an indirect critique of this specifically English approach.

Yet by the time Victoria came to the British throne in 1837, shifts in English culture were forcing revision of such approaches to natural theology. Changing public attitudes toward the assessment of evidence, evident in parliamentary debates over criminal justice in the 1830s, pointed toward more inferential approaches to evidence. The celebrated Bridgewater Treatises of the 1830s adopted a more nuanced approach to natural theology, often accentuating the harmony or consonance between the Christian faith and the scientific observation of nature.

It is against this complex and shifting intellectual background that Darwin's theory of descent with modification through natural selection is to be set. The leading features of Darwin's theory are here considered within their intellectual and cultural context, and their implications for prevailing forms of English natural theology assessed. It is impossible to avoid the conclusion that this is a peculiarly English debate. The theological context, which established the conceptual frameworks that would give rise to potential tensions between Darwin's theory and natural theology, was distinctively English, reflecting the assumptions and debates that had defined the emergence of English natural theology from the seventeenth century onwards. Although the American biologist Asa Gray (1810–88) played no small part in assessing the relation of Darwin's theory to natural theology, Darwin's dialogue partners in this discussion are predominantly English. If Darwin's theory had developed against a theological background shaped by alternative approaches to natural theology, such as those characteristic of the Greek patristic tradition, a somewhat different outcome would have resulted.

Having explored the historical background to the relation of evolutionary thought and natural theology in some detail, I then turn to consider the contemporary evaluation of this relationship. The third part of this work focuses on the most significant challenges, issues, and opportunities for natural theology that arise from contemporary scientific understandings of the development of biological life. What does it mean to speak of "creation"? How does the suffering and waste of the Darwinian process fit into a theistic worldview? Can one consider evolution to be a providentially directed process? Can one speak of belief in God itself as the outcome of an evolutionary process? A concluding chapter offers some reflections on both the future of natural theology as an intellectual enterprise, and which of its possible forms might be best adapted to both the challenges and the opportunities it now faces.

Evolutionary thought, like all aspects of the scientific enterprise, is to be considered as a work in progress. There is, inevitably and rightly, a significant degree of provisionality implicit in scientific theorizing, including evolutionary thought. This study is therefore to be seen as an exploration of the present-day understanding of a series of important questions bearing on the relation of evolutionary theory to natural theology. It is essential to emphasize that future generations may understand and assess the relation of "Darwinism and the Divine" in quite different manners.

Since this book sets out to explore the relation between natural theology and evolutionary thought, it is inevitable that we must begin our analysis by considering some questions of definition and approach, attempting to achieve at least some degree of clarification over how the terms "natural theology" and "Darwinism" are to be used. As already noted, the term "natural theology" denotes a family of approaches, rather than a specific method or set of ideas. The use of the term "Darwinism" also turns out to be a little problematic, and requires closer attention. There is a significant debate taking place at present within the evolutionary biology community about whether the term should be retained, and if so, what it should be understood to designate. There is a similar ambiguity about the term "Darwinism." It is impossible to proceed further without exploring both notions in greater detail.

We therefore begin our explorations by reflecting on what is meant by the phrase "natural theology."

Notes

1   For this issue, see Gieryn, Thomas F., "Boundary-Work and the Demarcation of Science from Non-Science: Strains and Interests in Professional Ideologies of Scientists." *American Sociological Review* 48 (1983): 781–95; Gieryn, Thomas F., *Cultural Boundaries of Science: Credibility on the Line*. Chicago: University of Chicago Press, 1999, 1–35.

2   Bloom, Paul, "Is God an Accident?" *Atlantic Monthly* (December 2005): 1–8, see especially 8.

3   As noted by Fergusson, David, "Types of Natural Theology." In *The Evolution of Rationality: Interdisciplinary Essays in Honor of J. Wentzel Van Huyssteen*, ed. F. Le Ron Shults, 380–93. Grand Rapids, MI: Eerdmans, 2006. A failure to grasp the multiplicity of conceptual possibilities designated by "natural theology" has impeded theological discussion in recent years: note, for example, the somewhat restricted concept of natural theology discussed in Gunton, Colin E., "The Trinity, Natural Theology, and a Theology of Nature."

In *The Trinity in a Pluralistic Age*, ed. Kevin Vanhoozer, 88–103. Grand Rapids, MI: Eerdmans, 1997.

4   See McGrath, Alister E., *The Open Secret: A New Vision for Natural Theology.* Oxford: Blackwell, 2008, 1–20; McGrath, Alister E., *A Fine-Tuned Universe: The Quest for God in Science and Theology.* Louisville, KY: Westminster John Knox Press, 2009, 21–82.

5   This assertion mars the analysis of the American situation in Russett, *Darwin in America*, 43. Russett's discussion of Paley's contribution (32–6) is also very weak. See Russett, Cynthia Eagle, *Darwin in America: The Intellectual Response, 1865–1912.* San Francisco: W. H. Freeman, 1976. For an important corrective, see Roberts, Jon H., *Darwinism and the Divine in America: Protestant Intellectuals and Organic Evolution, 1859–1900.* Madison, WI: University of Wisconsin Press, 1988, 117–45.

6   Kant's pre-critical essay "Untersuchungen über die Deutlichkeit der Grundsätze der natürlichen Theologie und der Moral" is of interest here. This lecture, delivered in 1762 and published in 1764, primarily concerns itself with the relation of mathematical and metaphysical truth. For comment, see Engfer, Hans-Jürgen, "Zur Bedeutung Wolffs für die Methodendiskussion der deutschen Aufklärungsphilosophie: Analytische und synthetische Methode bei Wolff und beim vorkritischen Kant." In *Christian Wolff, 1697–1754: Interpretationen zu seiner Philosophie und deren Wirkung*, ed. Werner Schneiders, 48–65. Hamburg: Meiner, 1986.

7   For Kant's annotations on this work, see Kant, Immanuel, *Gesammelte Schriften.* 30 vols. Berlin: Reimer, 1902, vol. 28, 491–606.

Part I
Conceptual Clarifications

On the meaning of terms

1

Natural Theology: A Deeper Structure to the Natural World

"It is not too much to say that the Gospel itself can never be fully known till nature as well as man is fully known."[1] In his 1871 Hulsean Lectures at Cambridge University, F. J. A. Hort (1828–92) set out a manifesto for the theological exploration and clarification of the natural world. These words are a fitting introduction to the themes of this work. How can God be known through a deepening knowledge of nature itself, as well as of human nature? The delivery of Hort's lectures coincided with the publication of Charles Darwin's *Descent of Man*,[2] thus raising the question of how the debates about both the natural world and human nature resulting from Charles Darwin's theory of descent with modification through natural selection affect our knowledge of God.

So are the structures and symbols of the observed world self-contained and self-referential? Or might they hint at a deeper structure or level of meaning to the world, transcending what can be known through experience or observation? Christianity regards nature as a limiting horizon to the unaided human gaze, which nevertheless possesses a created capacity, when rightly interpreted, to point beyond itself to the divine. The philosopher and novelist Iris Murdoch (1919–99) used the term "imagination" to refer to a capacity to see beyond the empirical to discern deeper truths about the world. This, she argued, is to be contrasted with "strict" or "scientific" thinking, which focuses on what is merely observed. An imaginative engagement with the world builds on the surface reading of things, taking the form of "a type of reflection on people, events, etc., which builds detail, adds colour, conjures up possibilities in ways which go beyond what could be said to be strictly factual."[3]

Murdoch's point here is that the imagination supplements what reason observes, thus further disclosing – without distorting – a richer vision of reality. If we limit ourselves to a narrowly empirical account of nature,

Darwinism and the Divine: Evolutionary Thought and Natural Theology, First Edition.
Alister E. McGrath.
© 2011 Alister E. McGrath. Published 2011 by Blackwell Publishing Ltd.

we fail to appreciate its full meaning, value, or agency.[4] The Christian faith is also able to offer an approach to nature that is grounded in its empirical reality, yet possesses the ability to discern beyond the horizons of the observable. It provides a lens through which questions of deeper meaning may be explored and brought into sharp focus.

Although some limit the meaning of the term "natural theology" to an attempt to prove the existence of God on the basis of purely natural arguments, this is only one of its many possible forms.[5] The field of "natural theology" is now generally understood to designate the idea that there exists some link between the world we observe and another transcendent realm. The idea possesses a powerful imaginative appeal, inviting us to conceive – and, in some of its construals, to anticipate inhabiting – a world that is more beautiful than that which we know, lacking its pain and ugliness.

Yet the appeal of the notion is not purely emotional or aesthetic; it has the potential to offer a framework for intellectual and moral reflection on the present order of things. A Christian natural theology is fundamentally hospitable toward a deeper engagement with reality. It provides an intellectual scaffolding that enables us to understand our capacity to engage with the world, and reaffirms its objectivity.[6] For example, the mathematical awareness implanted within us enables us to discern and represent the rational patterns of the universe we inhabit, just as the moral awareness implanted within us allows us to orientate ourselves toward the good that lies at its heart. A robust Christian natural theology allows believers to pitch their tents "on the boundary between the manifest and the ineffable."[7] It is a cumulative enterprise,[8] weaving together observation and reflection on the deep structures of the universe and the particularities of human experience.

One of the most familiar statements of this approach is found in the Hebrew Psalter, where the observation of the wonders of nature is explicitly connected with a deeper knowledge of the covenant God of Israel as the ultimate transcendent reality:[9]

> The heavens are telling the glory of God;
> and the firmament proclaims his handiwork (Psalm 19:1).

The basic affirmation here is that the glory of the God whom Israel already knew through the Law was further displayed within the realm of nature. The specific God who is already known to Israel through self-disclosure is thus known at a deeper level through the natural world. This passage does not suggest that nature proves or implies the existence of God; rather, it affirms that nature attests, declares, and makes manifest this known God.

A similar line of thought, without any necessary presumption of theistic entailment, is found in Plato's theory of Forms, perhaps the most familiar philosophical account of this notion. Plato's theory can be argued to arise from philosophical reflection on the imperfection of the sensible world.[10] Experience discloses imperfect exemplifications of beauty, in a world of shadows. Plato holds that there exists a world of Forms, in which true beauty exists, contrasting with its shadowy and imperfect manifestations in the world of human experience. There is a connection between these two worlds, even if Plato is generally thought to have failed to construct a secure bridge by which one might be entered from the other.[11]

So what reasons might be given for believing in the existence of such a transcendent realm, when it is not capable of being observed directly? For many writers of the classical age, the answer lay in the deep structure and apparent design of the natural world. Such writers regularly proposed that the observation of the world pointed to a divine creator.[12] The Jewish wisdom tradition, for example, affirms a reverence and fascination for the natural world, while pointing out that this admiration should be transferred from the created order to the one who created it:[13]

> For all people who were ignorant of God were foolish by nature; and they were unable from the good things that are seen to know the one who exists, nor did they recognize the artisan while paying heed to his works; but they supposed that either fire or wind or swift air, or the circle of the stars, or turbulent water, or the luminaries of heaven were the gods that rule the world. If through delight in the beauty of these things people assumed them to be gods, let them know how much better than these is their Lord, for the author of beauty created them. And if people were amazed at their power and working, let them perceive from them how much more powerful is the one who formed them. For from the greatness and beauty of created things comes a corresponding perception of their creator (Wisdom 13:1–5).

The fundamental argument here is that the arc of reasoning that should lead from nature to God has been disconnected and misdirected, leading to the attribution of divinity to the created order, rather than its wise artificer.[14] This line of reasoning did not involve an appeal to the naturally inexplicable, or to effects whose origins were declared to lie outside the course of nature. Rather, the appeal is made to nature itself and its ordinary operations – operations whose "power and working" were seen as reflecting and embodying the power and wisdom of God.

Natural Theology in the Classical Tradition

Such themes find wide acceptance throughout the Mediterranean world of the classical era. In his *De natura deorum*, Marcus Tullius Cicero (106–45 BC) argued that it was virtually impossible to believe that the order of the world and the heavens came about by chance. Cicero argued that nature's providential care for both animals and human beings, the complex design of the human and animal bodies, and the intricate interdependency of all parts of nature pointed to the existence of some artificer or designer.[15] Cicero himself suggested that analogies might be drawn with certain mechanisms – such as water-clocks or sundials – to point toward the conclusion of apparent design entailing the existence of a designer.[16]

A similar approach was developed by Dio Chrysostom (c. 40–c. 120) in his *Olympic Oration*, delivered at the Olympic Games probably around the year 107.[17] Chrysostom here asserts that humanity developed its idea of divinity through reflection on the wonders of the natural world. Awe-inspiring or wonder-evoking sights in the heavens (such as the sun, moon, and stars) and on earth (such as the winds and woods, rivers and forests) pointed to the existence of the divine powers who brought them into being, and who could be known through them.[18] Chrysostom saw the power of natural forces, as much as the beauty and ordering of nature, as indicators of their divine origination and signification.

Yet other classical writers were more cautious, noting the ambiguity of the natural world. Although Virgil's *Georgics* (written in 29 BC) exult in the beauty of the natural world, finding great pleasure in its richness and diversity, his nascent natural theology confronts without mastering the darker side of nature – such as the constant threat of attack by wild animals, or fear of the untamable forces of nature that could destroy life and render agriculture impossible.[19]

Given this aesthetic and moral ambivalence of nature in general, it is perhaps not surprising that others chose to focus on more promising aspects of the natural world – such as the intricacies of the human body. The imperial physician Galen of Pergamum (129–c. 200) saw the construction of human muscles as offering strong evidence of design, and devised a teleological account of the created order on the basis of his physiological insights. Galen's physiological and anatomical works are often dominated by the idea that every single part of the human body had been purposively designed as the best possible instrument for carrying out the functions of human existence. There is thus a strongly teleological aspect to Galen's account of the complexity of human anatomy, as set out in his *De usu partium*.[20] At times, Galen attributes this agency of design to nature itself; at others, to a Demiurge.[21] Christian apologists were quick to use substantially the same argument, but attributing such teleological dimensions of the human body to God, perhaps most notably in the case of Lactantius's *De opificio Dei* (written around 303).[22]

Early Christian writers lent support, implicit and explicit, to such lines of reasoning. The first letter of Clement, widely believed to date from around 97, reaffirms that God's wisdom and power are to be seen in the regular workings of the universe.[23]

The heavens orbit in quiet submission to [God]. Day and night run the course God has ordained for them, without interfering with the other. Sun, moon, and the dancing stars orbit in harmony at God's command, none swerving from its appointed course. Season by season, the earth bears fruit in fulfilment of God's provision for the needs of people, beasts, and all living things upon its surface.

An appeal to the harmony of nature was an important element of Celtic Christianity, which recognized the creative hand of God manifested in both the harmony and power of the natural world.[24] The hymn often known as the "Deer's Cry" or the "Lorica," traditionally ascribed to Patrick, patron saint of Ireland, offers an excellent example of such a vision of nature.[25]

> I arise today, through the strength of Heaven:
> light of Sun, brilliance of Moon, splendour of Fire,
> speed of Lightning, swiftness of Wind, depth of Sea,
> stability of Earth, firmness of Rock.

The relation between our everyday world and a proposed transcendent realm is traditionally discussed using the category of "natural theology." The origins of this phrase are pre-Christian, and can be located in the writings of Marcus Terentius Varro (116–27 BC).[26] Varro set out a threefold taxonomy of approaches to theology: "mythical theology (*theologia fabulosa*)," "civil theology (*theologia civilis*)," and "natural theology (*theologia naturalis*)."[27] Varro's preference clearly lay with "natural theology," understood as a rational attempt to discern God within the natural world by philosophers.

This approach had a significant impact on the manner in which Augustine of Hippo (354–430) chose to develop his own notion of natural theology.[28] We see this hinted at in a famous statement in his *Confessions*: "Then I really saw your invisible things, which are understood through those which are created. Yet I was not able to keep my gaze fixed."[29] The fundamental theme, once more, is that human reflection itself, including human reflection on the natural order, is capable of disclosing at least something concerning the realm of the divine. The origins of the notion of "natural theology" lie outside the Christian tradition. Nevertheless, Christian theologians found this to be a helpful notion, not least in that it facilitated apologetic engagement with late classical culture.[30] A secular notion was thus baptized and found its way into the service of Christian apologetics.

The Conceptual Fluidity of Natural Theology

The concept of natural theology became well established within Christian theology by the early modern period. Natural theology is a conceptually fluid notion, and always has been resistant to precise theological definitions, even though the term is now generally used in a rather prescriptive manner in the philosophy of religion to denote "the enterprise of providing support for religious beliefs by starting from premises that neither are nor presuppose any religious beliefs."[31] Four broad approaches to natural theology can be identified in recent theological works, all with significant historical pedigrees.[32]

1   A movement of the human mind toward God, grounded in humanity's being made with an innate capacity or longing for God. The classic "argument from desire," as found in the writings of C. S. Lewis and others,[33] can be placed in this category. This view holds that humanity is a "being with an intellectual destiny orientated God-ward,"[34] and thus rests on a particular view of human nature and destiny.
2   An argument from essentially "naturalistic premises" to religious beliefs. This might refer to theological beliefs drawn from the interpretation of nature, or to a theology based on deduction from *a priori* principles, rather than based upon divine revelation. An example of this would be the cosmological argument, as traditionally stated, which makes no religious assumptions in drawing its conclusions. This is probably the best-known form of natural theology, which has unfortunately led some to conclude that it is its only and defining form.
3   A "theology of nature," which offers an interpretation of nature that is conducive to, or consistent with, religious belief. Here, a set of beliefs derived from revelation or the Christian tradition is used as a framework for developing a particular way of interpreting the natural world.[35] This is not understood as an argument from nature to God, but rather as an "attempt to show that the theological categories of thought are adequate to the interpretation of nature and the natural sciences."[36] Natural theology thus affirms the resonance or consonance of the Christian faith and the natural world, without claiming that this observed resonance *proves* the truth of the Christian faith.
4   The exploration of perceived correspondences between "natural and evangelical experience." The existence of an "analogy between the realm of grace and the realm of nature" – that is, between religious and physical experience – leads us to trace them back to the same ultimate source.[37]

Some accounts of the development of natural theology have prematurely and improperly made adjudications concerning which of its forms is to be regarded as normative. The history of natural theology makes it clear that the term designates a variety of approaches, whose appeal is determined partly by cultural considerations, and partly by theological and philosophical pre-commitments. Every style of "natural theology" is embedded in a social matrix, consisting of a series of assumptions, often better intuited rather than demon-strated, which gives such a natural theology its distinctive plausibility.[38] As John

Hedley Brooke and other historians have stressed,[39] there is no single master narrative of natural theology within the Christian tradition. Rather, what we observe is a complex, shifting set of approaches, adapted to the envisaged contexts and audiences for any specific natural theology.

There are good reasons for proposing a direct link between natural theology and the natural sciences in the late Renaissance,[40] including the imaginatively powerful notion of the scientist as a priest in God's temple of nature.[41] A fascination with the wonder of nature is an integral element of European culture throughout the Renaissance and early modern periods.[42] The beauty, complexity, and order of nature were the subject of both admiration and speculation for many medieval and Renaissance writers, not least on account of the widespread assumption that the natural world was somehow emblematic of its creator. Bonaventura of Bagnoregio (1221–74) was representative of a much wider tradition, which held that the wonders of nature should be seen as "shadows, echoes and pictures" of God its creator, and that these "are set before us in order that we might know God."[43]

Yet these intuitions of divinity were explored and expressed in a diversity of manners. Far from being codified in some formal system of "natural theology," they represent different modes of engagement with, and levels of representation of, the perceived religious significance of nature. Some are clearly cognitive in style; others are more imaginative, appealing to the beauty of nature. Some exult in the beauty of nature as observed; others argue for the need for a deeper level of engagement, if nature's deeper structures and beauty are to be fully appreciated. Natural theology became an increasingly significant motivation for natural science in the early modern period.

The rise of natural theology in the early modern period was not without its debates and difficulties. The culturally dominant interpretation of the intrinsically polyvalent term "natural theology" began to shift. Where once natural theology was generally understood to affirm the consonance of reason and the experience of the natural world with the Christian tradition, it increasingly came to designate the attempt to demonstrate the existence of God by an appeal to reason or to the domain of nature.[44] Although initially this development was seen as strongly supportive of faith in the late seventeenth and early eighteenth centuries, anxieties began to emerge,[45] leading many to question whether the enterprise of natural theology was apologetically useful, or theologically defensible.

The main difficulty was that this form of natural theology seemed to point toward an impoverished conception of God, which was not worthy of the Christian tradition. Nature revealed a divine watchmaker – a divine mechanic, who seemed to fall far short of the Christian notion of a transcendent, glorious personal God.[46] Furthermore, natural theology often seemed to result in a form of Christian belief which was not merely religiously inadequate, but potentially heretical.[47] Even those who pursued the route of natural theology in the eighteenth century were aware that it could incline the mind to atheism as much as to religious belief.[48]

More recently, the entire enterprise of natural theology has fallen under a cloud of suspicion within many sections of Protestant theology.[49] A distinct sense of nervousness attends any discussion of the theme;[50] to speak of "natural theology" is to tread on confessional eggshells. The theological ascendancy of Karl Barth (1886–1968) has led to natural theology being seen as subversive of divine revelation, and erosive of theological distinctiveness.[51] For Barth, natural theology undermines the necessity, uniqueness, and distinct character of God's self-revelation. If knowledge of God can be achieved independently of God's self-revelation in Christ, then it follows that in principle humanity can dictate the place, time, and means of its knowledge of God. Natural theology, for Barth, represents an attempt on the part of humanity to understand itself apart from and in isolation from revelation, amounting to a deliberate refusal to accept the necessity and consequences of revelation.

A response may certainly be made to these concerns, most notably by proposing that natural theology abandon its pretensions to epistemological independence and move away from any attempt to conceive itself as offering proofs of God's existence, independent of divine revelation.[52] There is no reason why natural theology should not be reconceived as the affirmation of the consonance or resonance of reason and the experience of the natural world with the Christian tradition. Yet the Barthian critique remains a concern for many, and it needs to be addressed.[53]

Yet despite these and other concerns, natural theology appears to be enjoying a renaissance in the early twenty-first century. Why?

The Eternal Return of Natural Theology

Natural theology has a persistent habit of returning, even when its death notice has been extensively and repeatedly published.[54] The question of the imaginative potential of nature to point beyond itself remains alive, continuing to possess the power to captivate the human mind and imagination,[55] appealing to our yearning for truth, beauty, and goodness.[56] For William James, natural theology is a means of appeasing the "craving of the heart" to believe that there is something of ultimate significance beyond the empirical world of nature.[57] As the philosopher John Cottingham points out, a Christian natural theology[58]

> ... provides a framework that frees us from the threats of contingency and futility that lurk beneath the surface of supposedly self-sufficient and autonomous secular ethics. It offers us not a proof, but a hope that the "cave" of our human world (to use Plato's image) is not utterly sealed and closed, but that our flickering moral intimations reflect the ultimate source of all goodness.

When properly grounded on a robust and intellectually fertile Trinitarian foundation, natural theology offers ontological stability to what might otherwise be little more than happenstance intuitions, longings, and aspirations.

Among the cultural shifts that are creating, or have the potential to generate, a new interest in natural theology, we may note the following.

1   There is growing interest in natural theology emerging within the natural sciences. Many natural scientists are coming to the conclusion that their disciplines raise fundamentally theological and metaphysical questions, the pursuit of which constitutes a legitimate extension of the scientific method.[59] There is growing sympathy for the view that natural theology can provide a deeper understanding on fundamental issues such as the fine-tuning of the universe, where the natural sciences can raise questions that point beyond its intellectual horizons, and transcend its power to answer.[60] In my 2009 Gifford Lectures at the University of Aberdeen,[61] I explored how a Christian natural theology appears to be able to accommodate "anthropic" phenomena in an intellectually satisfying manner, noting how contemporary scientific thinking about cosmic origins and development resonates with a Trinitarian theological vision. This is not understood to prove the Christian faith; merely to indicate its capacity for observational accommodation, which might reasonably be taken as an indication – but certainly not a *demonstration* – of its truth.

2   Despite the secularization of western culture, empirical research shows that there remains a significant level of public interest in the notion of the transcendent.[62] Even though western culture is often asserted to be secular, there is widespread evidence of continuing interest in transcendent experiences, in which people form the impression that there is "something there"; or that they were in contact with – to use Rudolf Otto's luminous phrase – "the wholly other";[63] with something boundless, limitless, and profoundly different, which was resistant to precise definition; which was not necessarily associated with any religious institutions or authorities; which they could not fully grasp; and which utterly surpassed the human capacity for verbal expression. This sense of a heightened awareness of the transcendent is often linked with a transformative encounter with nature, both in the past (as in the writings of the Romantic movement) and in the present.[64]

3   Recent years have seen the resurgence of various forms of paganism, which often emphasize the spiritual importance of nature. Neopaganism began to emerge in Germany during the period of the Weimar Republic (1919–33), and is often cited as a growing influence on contemporary German culture.[65] The new forms of paganism are not monolithic, and represent a wide range of beliefs and practices, some of which represent reappropriations of pre-Christian ideas (such as Druidism), others of

which are better understood as postmodern constructions reflecting a growing cultural interest in nature and spirituality.[66] Yet underlying most, if not all, of these new forms of paganism is a strong sense of nature as a sacred entity, capable of disclosing its secret wisdom to those who are able to discern its deeper levels of meaning.

Such considerations, to which others might easily be added, point to the need to renew a vision for natural theology within the academy and church, not least as the basis for a sustained intellectual engagement with contemporary culture. The recognition of the importance of such an undertaking is not, of course, new. In 1934, for example, Emil Brunner famously declared the need for his generation to rediscover a proper understanding of natural theology, able to engage with the concerns of the age. "It is the task of our theological generation to find its way back to a proper natural theology."[67]

Brunner's attempt to reconstruct such a natural theology did not find wide support at the time, nor subsequently. Yet while Brunner's specific approach to natural theology might be problematic, I believe that he was completely correct in identifying the importance of natural theology in his own cultural situation, and that its importance has, if anything, increased since then. Brunner bequeathed to his successors a task, rather than its solution. We still need to find our way back to a workable natural theology that is rooted in Scripture, as well as defensible theologically and usable apologetically.

However, any meaningful attempt to develop a viable "natural theology" must now face the challenges raised by Charles Darwin and his legacy. It is often suggested that the publication of Darwin's *Origin of Species* (1859) marked the end of any defensible natural theology, causing the curtain to fall on this once-great enterprise of Christian theology. Yet is this actually the case? Was this the judgment of Christian theologians at the time of Darwin? Or need it be the judgment of Christian theologians today? Given these questions, it seemed entirely appropriate to consider the complex yet fascinating legacy of Charles Darwin for natural theology in my 2009 Hulsean Lectures at Cambridge University, marking both the 200th anniversary of his birth, and the 150th anniversary of the publication of his landmark work.

The impact of Darwin's theory of descent with modification through natural selection was shaped by its intellectual context in Victorian England, within which certain approaches to natural theology had become dominant at the level of the popular imagination. As events made clear, this specific form of natural theology proved to be especially vulnerable at critical points. At least to some minds, the erosion of the intrinsic plausibility of certain specific approaches to natural theology, whether through internal incoherency or a failure to engage adequately with the external world, discredited the enterprise of natural theology in general.

Yet we have already made frequent reference to the importance of Darwinism, without offering any clarification of what this term might mean. In the following chapter, we shall explore the many facets of this complex notion.

Notes

1 Hort, F. J. A., *The Way, The Truth, The Life: The Hulsean Lectures for 1871.* 2nd edn. London: Macmillan, 1894, 83.
2 Hort's Hulsean Lectures, though delivered in 1871, were not written up for publication until twenty years later. His personal journals record much anxiety about the quality and delivery of the lectures: Hort, Fenton John Anthony, and Arthur Hort, *Life and Letters of Fenton John Anthony Hort.* 2 vols. London: Macmillan, 1896, vol. 2, 52–4; 148; 161. In some letters written in 1860, Hort commented that he regarded Darwin's theory, as set out in the *Origin of Species*, as "unanswerable": Hort, *Life and Letters*, vol. 1, 414; 416.
3 Murdoch, Iris, "The Darkness of Practical Reason." In *Existentialists and Mystics*, ed. Peter Conradi, 193–202. London: Chatto, 1998, 198.
4 See the discussion in Smith, Barbara Herrnstein, *Natural Reflections: Human Cognition at the Nexus of Science and Religion.* New Haven, CT: Yale University Press, 2009. Smith argues that a new "natural theology" emerges through the naturalizing of religion on the one hand, and the theologizing of natural science on the other.
5 Fergusson, David, "Types of Natural Theology." In *The Evolution of Rationality: Interdisciplinary Essays in Honor of J. Wentzel Van Huyssteen*, ed. F. Le Ron Shults, 380–93. Grand Rapids, MI: Eerdmans, 2006.
6 For what follows, see Cottingham, John, *Why Believe?* London: Continuum, 2009, 44–7.
7 Cottingham, *Why Believe?*, 47.
8 It is important to note that reflections on "design" are only one strand in such a cumulative approach: see the important points made by Geivett, R. Douglas, "David Hume and a Cumulative Case Argument." In *In Defense of Natural Theology: A Post-Humean Assessment*, ed. James F. Sennett and Douglas Groothuis, 297–329. Downers Grove, IL: InterVarsity Press, 2005.
9 On the dating and leading themes of this Psalm, see Vos, Cas J. A., *Theopoetry of the Psalms.* Pretoria: Protea Book House, 2005, 92–116. See further Collins, John J., "The Biblical Precedent for Natural Theology." *Journal of the American Academy of Religion* 45 (1977): B35–B67; Barr, James, *Biblical Faith and Natural Theology.* Oxford: Clarendon Press, 1993, 81–101.
10 Fine, Gail, *On Ideas. Aristotle's Criticism of Plato's Theory of Forms.* Oxford: Clarendon Press, 1993, 97–100.
11 Devereux, Daniel T., "Separation and Immanence in Plato's Theory of Forms." *Oxford Studies in Ancient Philosophy* 12 (1994): 63–90. For the resolution of this problem in Middle Platonism, see Cox, Ronald R., *By the Same Word:*

Creation and Salvation in Hellenistic Judaism and Early Christianity. Berlin: De Gruyter, 2007, 28–55.

12   As noted by Vidal, Fernando, and Bernard Kleeberg, "Knowledge, Belief, and the Impulse to Natural Theology." *Science in Context* 20 (2007): 381–400.

13   For the importance of this tradition in relation to the quest for God within and through nature, see Lefebure, Leo D., "The Wisdom Tradition in Recent Christian Theology." *Journal of Religion* 76 (1996): 338–48; Burkes, Shannon, "Wisdom and Apocalypticism in the Wisdom of Solomon." *Harvard Theological Review* 95 (2002): 21–44; Fiddes, Paul S., "'Where Shall Wisdom Be Found?' Job 28 as a Riddle for Ancient and Modern Readers." In *After the Exile: Essays in Honor of Rex Mason*, ed. John Barton and David Reimer, 171–90. Macon, GA: Mercer University Press, 1996; Dell, Katharine J., *The Book of Proverbs in Social and Theological Context*. Cambridge: Cambridge University Press, 2006, 125–54.

14   For a similar argument in Paul's letters, especially the opening chapters of Romans, see Dunn, James D. G., *The Theology of Paul the Apostle*. Grand Rapids, MI: Eerdmans, 2006, 38–49.

15   Cicero, *De natura deorum*, II.34. "An, cum machinatione quadam moveri aliquid vedemus, ut sphaeram ut horas ut alia permulta, non dubitamus quin illa opera sint rationis."

16   Gerson, Lloyd P., *God and Greek Philosophy: Studies in the Early History of Natural Theology*. London: Routledge, 1994, 155–60.

17   Klauck, Hans-Josef, "Nature, Art, and Thought: Dio Chrysostom and the *Theologia Tripertita*." *Journal of Religion* 87 (2007): 333–54, especially 341–50.

18   Betz, Hans Dieter, "God Concept and Cultic Image: The Argument in Dio Chrysostom's Oratio 12 (Olympikos)." *Illinois Classical Studies* 29 (2004): 131–42.

19   Boyancé, Pierre, "La Religion des 'Géorgiques' à la lumière des travaux récents." *Aufstieg und Niedergang der Römischen Welt* II.31.1 (1980): 549–73.

20   Cosans, Christopher E., "The Experimental Foundations of Galen's Teleology." *Studies in History and Philosophy of Science* 29 (1998): 63–80.

21   For the form of natural theology this approach envisaged, see Lindberg, David C., *The Beginnings of Western Science: The European Scientific Tradition in Philosophical, Religious, and Institutional Context, Prehistory to AD 1450*. 2nd edn. Chicago: University of Chicago Press, 2007, 129–31.

22   Lactantius, *De opificio Dei*, 2–13. Lactantius here seems to make indirect use of Galen.

23   1 Clement 20:1–4.

24   Newell, J. Philip, *The Book of Creation: An Introduction to Celtic Spirituality*. New York: Paulist Press, 1999, 51–64.

25   Stokes, Whitley, and John Strachan, *Thesaurus Palaeohibernicus: A Collection of Old-Irish Glosses, Scholia, Prose, and Verse*. 2 vols. Cambridge: Cambridge University Press, 1901, vol. 2, 354–8. The hymn is generally dated to the seventh century, although it reflects older ideas.

26   See Lehmann, Yves, *Varron théologien et philosophe romain*. Brussels: Latomus, 1997, 193–225.

27 Or "tripartita." See Lieberg, Godo, "Die 'Theologia Tripartita' in Forschung und Bezeugung." *Aufstieg und Niedergang der römischen Welt* 4 (1973): 63–115; Lieberg, Godo, "Die Theologia Tripartita als Formprinzip antiken Denkens." *Rheinisches Museum für Philologie* 125 (1982): 25–53.

28 Dihle, Albrecht, "Die Theologia Tripertita bei Augustin." In *Geschichte – Tradition – Reflexion: Festschrift für Martin Hengel zum 70. Geburtstag*, ed. Hubert Cancik, 183–202. Tübingen: Mohr Siebeck, 1996.

29 Augustine of Hippo, *Confessions* VII.xvii.23. See also VII.xx.26 and X.vi.10. Note the implicit reference to Paul's statements in Romans 1.

30 See the account in Pelikan, Jaroslav, *Christianity and Classical Culture: The Metamorphosis of Natural Theology in the Christian Encounter with Hellenism.* New Haven, CT: Yale University Press, 1993, 22–39.

31 Alston, William P., *Perceiving God: The Epistemology of Religious Experience.* Ithaca, NY: Cornell University Press, 1991, 289.

32 I here broadly follow the analysis of Casserley, J. V. Langmead, *Graceful Reason; The Contribution of Reason to Theology.* London: Longmans, Green, 1955, 1–8. Other frameworks of analysis could easily be developed: for example, see Fergusson, "Types of Natural Theology." The fundamental point here is the historical diversity of approaches to natural theology.

33 See especially Kreeft, Peter, "C. S. Lewis's Argument from Desire." In *G. K. Chesterton and C. S. Lewis: The Riddle of Joy*, ed. Michael H. MacDonald and Andrew A. Tadie, 249–72. Grand Rapids, MI: Eerdmans, 1989.

34 Casserley, *Graceful Reason*, 2.

35 This is the kind of approach that I myself develop in a number of works, most notably McGrath, Alister E., *The Open Secret: A New Vision for Natural Theology.* Oxford: Blackwell, 2008, 1–20; McGrath, Alister E., *A Fine-Tuned Universe: The Quest for God in Science and Theology.* Louisville, KY: Westminster John Knox Press, 2009, 21–82. However, my own approach goes beyond this, holding that such a theology of nature leads naturally into the notion of a human quest for God, rather than seeing natural theology as a mode of reasoning distinct from a theology of nature.

36 Casserley, *Graceful Reason*, 3. This approach, framed in terms of the demonstration of the "consonance" between Christian theology and the scientific observation of the world, plays an important role in the thought of John Polkinghorne: see particularly Irlenborn, Bernd, "Konsonanz von Theologie und Naturwissenschaft? Fundamentaltheologische Bemerkungen zum interdisziplinären Ansatz von John Polkinghorne." *Trierer Theologische Zeitung* 113 (2004): 98–117; Stenke, Johannes Maria, *John Polkinghorne: Konzonanz von Naturwissenschaft und Theologie.* Göttingen: Vandenhoeck & Ruprecht, 2006.

37 Casserley finds this view in the writings of Joseph Butler (1692–1752), especially his *Analogy of Religion, Natural and Revealed* (1736): see Casserley, *Graceful Reason*, 3–6. See further Rurak, James, "Butler's Analogy: A Still Interesting Synthesis of Reason and Revelation." *Anglican Theological Review* 62 (1980): 365–81.

38 The issue here is that of "plausibility structures," a term introduced by sociologist Peter Berger to refer to a "structure of assumptions and practices which

determine what beliefs are plausible and what are not." See Berger, Peter L., *A Far Glory: The Quest for Faith in an Age of Credulity*. New York: Free Press, 1992, 125–6.

39   See especially Brooke, John Hedley, "Natural Theology and the Plurality of Worlds: Observations on the Brewster–Whewell Debate." *Annals of Science* 34 (1977): 221–86; Brooke, John Hedley, "Science and the Fortunes of Natural Theology: Some Historical Perspectives." *Zygon* 24 (1989): 3–22; Brooke, John Hedley, and Geoffrey Cantor, *Reconstructing Nature: The Engagement of Science and Religion*. New York: Oxford University Press, 2000, 141–206.

40   Ogilvie, Brian W., "Natural History, Ethics, and Physico-Theology." In *Historia. Empiricism and Erudition in Early Modern Europe*, ed. Gianna Pomata and Nancy G. Siraisi, 75–103. Cambridge, MA: MIT Press, 2005.

41   Harrison, Peter, " 'Priests of the Most High God, with Respect to the Book of Nature': The Vocational Identity of the Early Modern Naturalist." In *Reading God's World*, ed. Angus Menuge, 55–80. St Louis, MO: Concordia, 2004.

42   For the wider background, see Daston, Lorraine, and Katharine Park, *Wonders and the Order of Nature, 1150–1750*. Cambridge, MA: MIT Press, 1998.

43   Bonaventure, *Itinerarium Mentis in Deum*, 2.

44   Such rationalist approaches to natural theology can be found in the writings of Benedict Spinoza (1632–77), Gottfried Wilhelm Leibniz (1646–1716), and Christian Wolff (1679–1754): see Corr, Charles A., "The Existence of God, Natural Theology and Christian Wolff." *International Journal for Philosophy of Religion* 4 (1973): 105–18; Webb, Mark O., "Natural Theology and the Concept of Perfection in Descartes, Spinoza and Leibniz." *Religious Studies* 25 (1989): 459–75.

45   See the classic study of Odom, Herbert H., "The Estrangement of Celestial Mechanics and Religion." *Journal of the History of Ideas* 27 (1966): 533–58.

46   This point was made repeatedly by late Victorian writers, such as Aubrey Moore, alarmed at the deficient notion of God found in William Paley's natural theology: Moore, Aubrey, "The Christian Doctrine of God." In *Lux Mundi: A Series of Studies in the Religion of the Incarnation*, ed. Charles Gore, 57–109. London: John Murray, 1890.

47   See Brooke, John Hedley, and Ian Maclean, eds., *Heterodoxy in Early Modern Science and Religion*. Oxford: Oxford University Press, 2005.

48   Buckley, Michael J., *Denying and Disclosing God: The Ambiguous Progress of Modern Atheism*. New Haven, CT: Yale University Press, 2004, 38–43.

49   For the significant challenges to natural theology that arose within the Protestant tradition during the nineteenth and twentieth centuries, see Kock, Christoph, *Natürliche Theologie: Ein evangelischer Streitbegriff*. Neukirchen-Vluyn: Neukirchener, 2001, 295–412.

50   Jüngel, Eberhard, "Das Dilemma der natürlichen Theologie und die Wahrheit ihres Problems." In *Entsprechungen: Gott – Wahrheit – Mensch*, 158–77. Tübingen: Mohr Siebeck, 2002, 158–9.

51 Szekeres, Attila, "Karl Barth und die natürliche Theologie." *Evangelische Theologie* 24 (1964): 229–42; Kapper, Michael, "'Natürliche Theologie' als innerprotestantisches und ökumenisches Problem? Die Kontroverse zwischen Eberhard Jüngel und Wolfhart Pannenberg und ihr ökumenischer Ertrag." *Catholica* 49 (1995): 276–309.

52 An approach defended by a number of writers, including myself: see McGrath, *The Open Secret*, 171–216.

53 Anderson, Ray S., "Barth and a New Direction for Natural Theology." In *Theology Beyond Christendom: Essays on the Centenary of the Birth of Karl Barth*, ed. John Thompson, 241–66. Allison Park, PA: Pickwick, 1986.

54 A point often made about the related field of natural law: see Rommen, Heinrich, *Die ewige Wiederkehr des Naturrechts*. Leipzig: Hegner, 1936.

55 McGrath, Alister E., "'Schläft ein Lied in allen Dingen'? Gedanken über die Zukunft der natürlichen Theologie." *Theologische Zeitschrift* 65 (2009): 246–60.

56 Most notably, see McGrath, *The Open Secret*, 221–313.

57 James, William, "Is Life Worth Living?" In *The Will to Believe and Other Essays in Popular Philosophy*, 32–62. New York: Longmans, Green, 1897, 40. For a critique of James's views on natural theology, see Hauerwas, Stanley, *With the Grain of the Universe: The Church's Witness and Natural Theology*. London: SCM Press, 2002, 43–86.

58 Cottingham, *Why Believe?*, 47.

59 See, for example, Barrow, John, and Frank J. Tipler, *The Anthropic Cosmological Principle*. Oxford: Oxford University Press, 1986; Gingerich, Owen, "Is There a Role for Natural Theology Today?" In *Science and Theology: Questions at the Interface*, ed. M. Rae, H. Regan, and J. Stenhouse, 29–48. Edinburgh: T. & T. Clark, 1994; Conway Morris, Simon, *Life's Solution: Inevitable Humans in a Lonely Universe*. Cambridge: Cambridge University Press, 2003.

60 Polkinghorne, John, "Where Is Natural Theology Today?" *Science and Christian Belief* 18 (2006): 169–79.

61 McGrath, *Fine-Tuned Universe*, 111–202.

62 Hay, David, *Something There: The Biology of the Human Spirit*. London: Darton, Longman & Todd, 2006; McGrath, *The Open Secret*, 23–40.

63 Otto, Rudolf, *Das Heilige, über das Irrationale in der Idee des Göttlichen und sein Verhältnis zum Rationalen*. 17th edn. Munich: C. H. Beck, 1931, 13–74.

64 Weiskel, Thomas, *The Romantic Sublime: Studies in the Structure and Psychology of Transcendence*. Baltimore, MD: Johns Hopkins University Press, 1986; Faulconer, James E., ed., *Transcendence in Philosophy and Religion*. Bloomington, IN: Indiana University Press, 2003; Richards, Robert J., *The Romantic Conception of Life: Science and Philosophy in the Age of Goethe*. Chicago: University of Chicago Press, 2002.

65 For example, see Faber, Richard, and Renate Schlesier, eds., *Die Restauration der Götter: Antike Religion und Neo-Paganismus*. Würzburg: Königshausen & Neumann, 1986; Schnurbein, Stefanie von, *Göttertrost in Wendezeiten: Neugermanisches Heidentum zwischen New Age und Rechtsradikalismus*. Munich: Claudius Verlag, 1993; Figl, Johann, *Handbuch Religionswissenschaft:*

Religionen und ihre zentralen Themen. Innsbruck: Verlagsanstalt Tyrolia, 2003, 207–21.

66 Hutton, Ronald, *The Triumph of the Moon: A History of Modern Pagan Witchcraft*. Oxford: Oxford University Press, 2001, 398.

67 Brunner, Emil, "Natur und Gnade: Zum Gespräch mit Karl Barth." In *Ein offenes Wort. Vorträge und Aufsätze 1917–1934*, ed. Rudolf Wehrli, 333–75. Zürich: Theologischer Verlag, 1981, 375. For reflections on this controversy, see Gestrich, Christof, *Neuzeitliches Denken und die Spaltung der dialektischen Theologie: Zur Frage der natürlichen Theologie*. Tübingen: Mohr, 1977, 158–69; 342–50.

2

Darwinism: A Narrative of Evolution

It is widely agreed that Charles Darwin's theory of descent with modification through natural selection had a significant impact on humanity's understanding of its own identity and place in the universe. Sigmund Freud (1856–1939) declared that humanity had been the subject of three "narcissistic wounds" in the modern age, each of which challenged the human sense of self-importance.[1] The first such wound, Freud argued, was inflicted by the Copernican revolution, which showed that human beings did not stand at the center of the universe, but were actually located at its periphery. The second was the Darwinian demonstration that humanity did not even have a unique place on planet earth. The third, Freud somewhat immodestly suggested, was his own demonstration that humanity was not even the master of its own limited realm, being the secret prisoner of subconscious psychological forces. According to Freud, each of these revolutions added to the pain and wounds inflicted by its predecessor, forcing a radical re-evaluation of the place and significance of humanity within the universe.

Our concern is with the second of these "wounds," whose significance Freud saw as lying in the erosion of the distinctive biological position of humanity.[2]

> We all know that, only a little more than half a century ago, the research of Charles Darwin, his collaborators and predecessors, put an end to this presumption of mankind. Man is not different from, or better than, the animals; he is himself the outcome of an animal series, related more closely to some, more distantly to others. His latest acquirements have not been able to efface the evidences, in both his physical structure and his mental dispositions, of his equality with them.

Darwinism and the Divine: Evolutionary Thought and Natural Theology, First Edition.
Alister E. McGrath.
© 2011 Alister E. McGrath. Published 2011 by Blackwell Publishing Ltd.

Freud was explicit in his view that Darwin's theory of evolution was laden with theological implications, not least in relation to the status of humanity. Some of these themes will be developed in the present work, most notably the complex associations and history of the "natural" world, which earlier generations saw as generally unproblematic.

So what exactly is this "Darwinism," whose implications for human thought about God are to be investigated? Is the continuing use of the term "Darwinism" as a virtual synonym for evolutionary thought defensible?

Darwinism: A Defensible Term?

Many scientific theories are initially known by the names of their originators or chief advocates. "Darwinism" is an obvious example of this phenomenon, deriving its name from Charles Darwin (1809–82), whose works set out the theory of descent with modification through natural selection,[3] more generally (though much less accurately) known simply as "the theory of evolution."[4] We shall consider the development of Darwin's views later in this work (143–70), paying particular attention to the intellectual context within which they emerged. Yet such theories subsequently undergo change and development over time, so that the practice of naming them after their founders may be of only historical interest, clarifying their lineage and ancestry, yet not necessarily illuminating their present core beliefs.

So is it legitimate to use the term "Darwinism" to refer to contemporary theories of biological evolution? Some writers would certainly defend the continued use of the term in this sense. Jean Gayon is an excellent example of a writer taking this position.[5]

Figure 2.1 Engraving of Charles Robert Darwin (1809–82) in old age.

The Darwin–Darwinism relation is in certain respects a causal relation, in the sense that Darwin influenced the debates that followed him. But there is also something more: a kind of isomorphism between Darwin's Darwinism and historical Darwinism. It is as though Darwin's own contribution has constrained the conceptual and empirical development of evolutionary biology ever after.

A case can certainly be made for arguing that "Darwinism" designates a "research tradition," "research program," or "scientific practice." On this understanding, at any given moment in its history, Darwinism can be thought of as a family of theories related by a shared ontology, methodology, and goals, which generate a lineage of theories that, although increasingly distant from their founder's approach, chronologically and conceptually, continue to draw inspiration from it.

Others, however, find the use of the term "Darwinism" deeply problematic.[6] Why should contemporary thinking about evolution be described in this manner? After all, the term "Copernicanism" is not used to refer to contemporary thinking about the solar system, tending to be used in a specifically *historical* sense to refer to the particular way of thinking about the solar system developed in the sixteenth century by Nicolaus Copernicus (1473–1543) and his immediate followers. The term "Copernicanism" is generally held to be historically defensible, not least because it marked a decisive challenge to the hitherto regnant geocentric way of thinking, invariably designated as the "Ptolemaic" model.[7]

Copernicus developed a theory of the solar system which supplemented its primary heliocentric hypothesis with a subsidiary hypothesis that the movements of all planetary and lunar bodies must be circular and uniform. The term "Copernicanism" therefore refers to a theory which incorporates both the *correct* central heliocentric assumption, and the *incorrect* subsidiary assumption that all the planets orbit the sun in perfect circles at constant speeds. The former assumption was subsequently affirmed, just as the second was subsequently corrected, by Johannes Kepler (1571–1630).[8]

The term "Copernicanism" thus designates a particular model of the solar system, which includes some elements now considered to be correct, and others that are recognized as being wrong. The same applies to the term "Darwinism." Darwin's theory about the origins of species consists of a number of elements, of which two are of especial significance: the idea of "evolution" itself, namely the belief that living things have descended with modifications from common ancestors; and a proposed mechanism by which this development took place, which Darwin designated as "natural selection." It is impossible to make sense of the historical process of evaluation and reception of Darwin's ideas without distinguishing these two elements, which are clearly capable of being decoupled, both conceptually and historically. For example, studies of the reception of Darwin's ideas following the publication of the *Origin of Species* suggest that the idea of descent with modification achieved relatively wide support within the British scientific community within a decade. The idea of natural selection, in marked contrast, was seen as deeply problematic, not least because of the genetic problem of "blending," which we shall consider later (151–2). "Darwinism" is a composite notion, referring to a network of interlocking ideas on the origins and development of species, including – but not being restricted to nor uniquely defined by – the core notion of natural selection.

"Darwinism" could thus be said to designate a cluster of ideas originating within Darwin's writings, not simply the notion of the evolution of

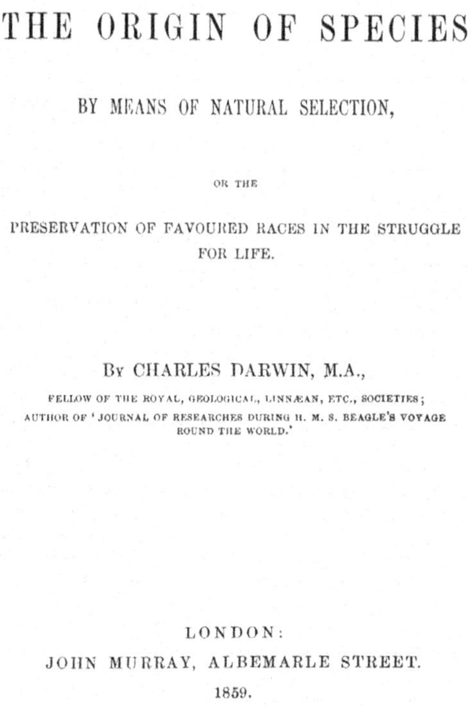

THE ORIGIN OF SPECIES

BY MEANS OF NATURAL SELECTION,

OR THE

PRESERVATION OF FAVOURED RACES IN THE STRUGGLE
FOR LIFE.

By CHARLES DARWIN, M.A.,

FELLOW OF THE ROYAL, GEOLOGICAL, LINNÆAN, ETC., SOCIETIES;
AUTHOR OF 'JOURNAL OF RESEARCHES DURING H. M. S. BEAGLE'S VOYAGE
ROUND THE WORLD.'

LONDON:
JOHN MURRAY, ALBEMARLE STREET.
1859.

Figure 2.2 Frontispiece of the *Origin of Species* by Charles Darwin, published in 1859.

species itself. But can the term be used as a form of shorthand for "evolutionary thought"? A significant body of opinion now holds that it cannot, and should not. On this view, "Darwinism" is an essentially historical term, to be used properly only to refer to the ideas that Darwin himself developed. As is well known, modern evolutionary biology has developed a range of ideas which are decidedly non-Darwinian – that is to say, ideas of which Darwin knew nothing. To speak of Darwinism is thus "grossly misleading," suggesting that Darwin was "the beginning and the end, the alpha and omega, of evolutionary biology," and that the subject changed little since the publication of the *Origin of Species*.[9] A series of developments has moved the discipline far beyond the intellectual landscape originally envisaged by Darwin.[10]

The modern approach to evolutionary theory, though grounded in Darwin's theory of natural selection, was initially supplemented with Mendelian genetics in the 1930s and 1940s, and subsequently by the development of mathematical systems allowing the modeling of evolution in populations in the 1940s and 1950s, and the emergence of an understanding of the molecular basis of evolution through the structures and function of RNA and DNA.[11] Continuing to talk about "Darwinism," some suggest, merely fosters the inaccurate and unfortunate perception that the field stagnated for 150 years after Darwin's own day.

One possible solution to the dilemma is to use the label "Neo-Darwinism," thus indicating both the origins of some core themes of modern evolutionary biology, while at the same time acknowledging their significant modification and amplification through subsequent research. Yet this is only one such way of designating this modification of Darwin's ideas; others that have achieved wider currency – such as the "evolutionary synthesis," the "modern synthesis," the "modern evolutionary synthesis," or the "new synthesis" – avoid mentioning Darwin by name. As pressure grows for modification of at least some of the elements of this evolutionary synthesis,[12] the value of the term "neo-Darwinism" seems increasingly fragile.

Modern evolutionary biologists now tend to use the term "Darwinism" rarely, except in a historical sense to designate Darwin's formative ideas.[13] A survey of the literature suggests that most modern biologists, when speaking about present-day understanding of evolutionary biology, tend to speak about "the theory of evolution" or "evolutionary biology," rather than "Darwinism." It is certainly true that Darwin's three core principles of variation, inheritance, and selection remain significant to modern evolutionary theories; nevertheless, these are now supplemented with additional notions.[14]

Furthermore, it is now widely agreed that there are significant difficulties with the central concept of "natural selection," which is a single term that enfolds what is now recognized to be a network of mechanisms. Darwin introduced the notion to explain evolutionary change;[15] the idea, however, is better seen as an explanation of the maintenance of adaptation. This "dynamic stabilization" does not explain the origin of species or adaptations, though it is unquestionably helpful in accounting for their spread.[16] A series of non-Darwinian processes – such as autopoiesis, self-organization, epigenetic mechanisms, and symbiosis – are now realized to play a significant role in the evolutionary process, considered as a whole.[17]

The use of the term "Darwinism" to refer to modern evolutionary biology thus seems to some to be about as useful as "Copernicanism" to refer to contemporary cosmology. The terms both designate important turning points in the history of the disciplines, in the course of which at least some elements of today's thinking were developed. These have, of course, been supplemented (and modified) by many others since then. So why not abandon the term "Darwinism," in favor of one of the many superior alternatives? There seems no obvious scientific reason for retaining it. As time passes, it is inevitable that increasing historical distance from Darwin will weaken the links between his specific formulation of the evolutionary process and contemporary understandings of the field.[18] The use of "Darwinism" to refer to evolutionary biology as this is presently understood would seem at least unnecessary, and probably unwise.

Yet even the historical use of the term "Darwinism" to designate the evolutionary thought of the later nineteenth century is being challenged. The predominance of English-language scholarship has led to Darwin being given a position of privilege that marginalizes, often to the point of ignoring, the significant pre-Darwinian discussions in France, Germany, and Italy, which helped bring about the revolutionary change in thinking from a static understanding of biological organisms, to the dynamic, evolutionary viewpoint that is now taken for granted.[19] Darwin was unquestionably a major influence in bringing about this revolution; he cannot, however, be seen as its sole originator.

While the convenience of using the term "Darwinism" to refer to evolutionary thought in general cannot be denied, the historical implications of such a practice must be questioned. The casual visitor to the Jardin des Plantes in Paris can hardly overlook the 1908 statue of Jean-Baptiste Lamarck (1744–1829), inscribed with the words "Fondateur de la doctrine de l'évolution." It is tempting to dismiss this as Gallic arrogance; it is, nevertheless, an important corrective to any narrative of the development of evolutionary thought which refuses to place Darwin in his proper historical context. Darwin may have corrected contemporary evolutionary narratives; he could not have done so, however, without standing on the shoulders of those who had preceded him.

The title and subtitle of this work reflect, without endorsing, this complex situation. The main title – "Darwinism and the Divine" – is intended to pick up on the continuing conversation about the deeper cultural significance of Darwin's ideas, including the more extreme viewpoint that "Darwinism" designates a grand narrative that necessarily excludes such notions as transcendence, purpose, and above all belief in God. The more neutral subtitle – "Evolutionary Thought and Natural Theology" – makes it clear that I intend to challenge and correct what I consider to be metaphysically inflated approaches to evolutionary biology,[20] thus allowing a more balanced and appropriate exploration of the genuine significance of evolutionary thought for natural theology.

Darwinism as an Ideology

The real problem, of course, concerns the use of the term "Darwinism" in the twenty-first century, two centuries after Darwin's birth. The term has been historically recontextualized within twenty–first-century debates concerning secularism and religion in culture.[21] Darwin has been relocated within a cultural context that would have been alien to him, and transfigured into an iconographic figurehead of viewpoints he did not advocate, and for which he probably would have had little sympathy. Today, "Darwinism" has come to designate an ideology for two significant groups in contemporary western culture: those wishing to advocate a biologically grounded atheism, and those opposing it.[22]

Those who now continue to speak specifically of "Darwinism" – as opposed to "evolutionary biology" – generally use the term to designate a worldview,[23] rather than a provisional scientific theory that has been developed and modified down the decades, and will continue to be so in the future. It is a development of questionable credibility, not least in that it leads to the ideological contamination of an essentially *empirical* discipline. Darwinism, as a scientific theory, is open to falsification;[24] Darwinism, as an ideology, lies beyond meaningful scientific investigation, precisely because it is a creedal statement, not a scientific viewpoint.

This important point was anticipated in 1885, when Thomas H. Huxley, the great champion of Charles Darwin's ideas in Victorian England, declared that science "commits suicide when it adopts a creed."[25] Science, when at its best and most authentic, has no creed or ideology, whether religious or anti-religious. Its public standing would be risked if it was contaminated by religious or anti-religious agendas.

Science may not have a creed; nevertheless, as Huxley himself pointed out, however, it has one, and only one, article of faith.[26]

> The one act of faith in the convert to science, is the confession of the universality of order and of the absolute validity in all times and under all circumstances, of the law of causation. This confession is an act of faith, because, by the nature of the case, the truth of such propositions is not susceptible of proof.

While there are those who insist that science makes and requires no judgment of faith, this is clearly not the case. Yet this article of faith is not the foundation of a metaphysically grounded ideology, but a presupposition demanded by the application of the scientific method. Huxley rightly identifies the functional presupposition of the natural sciences, without drawing any ideological conclusions on its basis.

Yet there are other writers, also claiming to stand in Darwin's intellectual lineage, who advocate Darwinism as a worldview – specifically, a worldview from which purpose, design, and transcendence are eliminated. Empirical evolutionary science is here supplemented with a philosophical or religious patina informed by a metaphysical naturalism. For example, the Harvard evolutionary naturalist Richard Lewontin insists upon an absolute commitment to materialism, in advance of scientific investigation. A "willingness to accept scientific claims that are against common sense" is the necessary price for the *a priori* exclusion of the divine. "We cannot allow a Divine Foot in the door."[27] God is thus excluded because of a prior dogmatic commitment to materialism, not on account of a commitment to the investigation of nature, wherever this leads us. Materialism is here regarded as the controlling and foreclosing presupposition, not the warranted empirical outcome, of the scientific method.[28]

However, this dogmatic assertion that Darwinism is an essentially atheistic worldview is not limited to materialist scientists. Writers linked with the creationist and "Intelligent Design" movements in North America vigorously oppose the teaching of evolution in schools, arguing that "Darwinism" is intrinsically atheistic. If "Darwinism" is understood as a scientific theory of evolution, this is clearly not the case; if it is understood as an ideology, in the sense in which it is advocated by Richard Dawkins (born 1941) and Daniel Dennett (born 1942), the criticism is defensible. The only loser in this unhelpful and largely sterile controversy is the public perception of the objectivity of the natural sciences.

In his landmark essay "Darwin Triumphant: Darwinism as a Universal Truth," Richard Dawkins sets out his conviction that Darwin's theory of evolution is more than just a scientific theory, on the same epistemological level as other such provisional theories. Darwinism is to be seen as a world-view, a totalizing account of reality, a "universal and timeless" principle, capable of being applied throughout the universe. In comparison, rival worldviews such as Marxism are to be seen as "parochial and ephemeral,"[29] lacking the grounding in a scientific understanding of reality that is so characteristic of Darwin's theory of natural selection, and the understandings of the world and human nature that emerge from it. Darwinism is not being presented as a representative element of the scientific enterprise, with a legitimate place at the round table of ethical and social debate. It is clearly understood as *the* defining account of reality.

Where most evolutionary biologists would agree that Darwinism offers a *description* of reality, Dawkins goes further, holding that it is to be seen as an *explanation* of things. Darwinism is a worldview, a *grand récit*, a metanarrative[30] – that is to say, a totalizing framework, by which the great questions of life are to be evaluated and answered. Dawkins's advocacy of Darwinism as a "worldview" has provoked a response from postmodern writers, for whom any metanarrative – whether Marxist, Freudian, or Darwinian – is to be resisted as a matter of principle.[31] Although this criticism of Dawkins is often portrayed as postmodern critique of science, it is clearly a critique of a worldview alleged to be based upon science.

Taking a similar approach, Dennett argues that Darwinism is a "universal acid" that erodes outdated, superfluous metaphysical notions, from the idea of God downwards.[32] Darwinism, he asserts, achieves a correlation of "the realm of life, meaning, and purpose with the realm of space and time, cause and effect, mechanism and physical law."[33] The Darwinian world is devoid of purpose and transcendence, in that all can and should be explained by the "standard scientific epistemology and metaphysics." The Darwinian worldview demystifies and unifies our experience of the world, and places it on more secure naturalist foundations.[34] Belief in God can be reductively explained on its basis, allowing Darwinism to be presented as an atheist worldview.

On the other side of the argument, creationists and the "Intelligent Design" movement – who represent quite distinct approaches to the question of biological origins – argue that Darwinism, as an ideology, is "a necessary implication of a philosophical doctrine called scientific naturalism, which is based on the a priori assumption that God was always absent from the realm of nature."[35] Darwinism – again, when understood as a *worldview* – is held to necessarily exclude God as a matter of principle. The non-scientific suggestion that the theory of evolution is anti-theistic has led to widespread rejection of this scientific idea in many religiously active contexts, especially the United States.[36] An important aspect of the debate occasioned by the emergence of the "Intelligent Design" movement concerns whether Darwinism, as taught within the science curriculum of public schools, is to be considered as a scientific theory or as a worldview.[37]

Regarding Darwinism as a worldview or ideology has important consequences,[38] not least of which is its encumbrance with complex and disturbing questions of power. An ideology can be defined as a set of "shared ideas or beliefs which serve to justify the interests of dominant groups."[39] Ideologies are reinforced by social structures, which frequently use power as a means of reinforcing the regnant ideology – for example, in the public school system, in academic culture, and in the media.[40] If Darwinism is presented as a worldview, it ceases to be a matter purely of science, and becomes embroiled in a cultural war, which has the potential to damage both its own scientific credentials, as well as those of the scientific community at large. It is imposed through an act of political and social conformity, rather than discerned through an act of scientific discovery. The specter of "ideologically correct science" haunts any attempt to transmute a scientific theory into a fixed view of reality.[41]

Yet there is another consequence of regarding Darwinism as an ideology: the tendency of both its advocates and critics to use religious language and imagery when referring to it. Every worldview, whether religious or secular, has its orthodoxies and heresies.[42] Although the concepts of "heresy" and "orthodoxy" had their origins within early Christianity, they have been found to be useful by other religious traditions on the one hand, and political and scientific ideologies on the other. The development of Darwinism, for example, has witnessed the rise and fall of ways of thinking and schools of thought, with the terms "heresy" and "orthodoxy" being widely used within the field to identify friends and foes.[43] For example, Motoo Kimura's concept of neutral evolution (by which inconsequential amino acid replacements in proteins may account for the bulk of sequence differences between species) was regarded as heretical by many biologists when it was first introduced in the late 1960s.[44] Today it is a part of Darwinian orthodoxy. The appropriation of religious language to describe such controversies is an indication both of the seriousness with which all sides take their positions, as well as the feeling that certain positions within the Darwinian spectrum are downright dangerous. If evolution can be regarded as a religion, then it has both its orthodoxies and heresies.[45]

Figure 2.3   Daniel C. Dennett, University Professor and Austin B. Fletcher Professor of Philosophy, and Director of the Center for Cognitive Studies at Tufts University, photographed in his office at Tufts, November 28, 2005.

Figure 2.4 British evolutionary biologist, philosopher, and author Richard Dawkins listens to a question during a press conference on the occasion of his being granted an honorary doctorate by the Universitat de València, March 31, 2009.

The exchanges between Dawkins and Dennett and their opponents thus reflect an important cultural and historical debate over the cultural authority and character of Darwinism.[46] Is it a scientific theory, similar to Einstein's theory of general relativity, which, though clearly important in a specific domain, has limited relevance to a broader cultural agenda? Or is it to be compared with Marxism, a way of understanding the world, which, if correct, has major implications for a much broader cultural and social agenda?[47] Is it, as Dawkins asserts, a "universal truth"? Although this debate was initiated by the publication of Darwin's *Origin of Species* itself,[48] it has re-emerged as a significant point of contention following the more recent rise of creationism within conservative Protestant groups in the United States.

The Metaphysical Inflation of Evolutionary Thought

Evolutionary thought is notoriously prone to metaphysical expansion and inflation, whether accidental or intentional. This type of abuse, however, is not limited to evolutionary thought. It is virtually impossible to formulate a scientific theory without making implicit metaphysical assumptions, however cautiously these may be framed. Metaphysical expansion of scientific theorizing sometimes takes the form of identifying the apparent metaphysical presuppositions of a theory; at other times, the apparent metaphysical consequences of the same theory are the focus. In both cases, the process of inference is hazardous, not least on account of the problem of transferability of epistemic authority from the scientific theory itself to the secondary metaphysical claims it is held to endorse.

Perhaps the most obvious discussion within the philosophy of science to illustrate this point is the debate between various forms of realism and instrumentalism. Is a successful scientific theory to be thought of as offering a tightened grip on the deep structures of reality, or as nothing more than a useful instrument for organizing and making sense of observations?[49] Copernicus's heliocentric theory of the solar system explained the observational evidence equally well, whether it was considered as a representation of how things really were, or a useful way of thinking and organizing ideas that did not necessarily imply ontological commitment to its terms – the position famously defended in Andreas Osiander's foreword to *De revolutionibus*.

Newtonian physics offers an excellent example of a successful predictive scientific theory that appeared to rest on metaphysical assumptions of varying degrees of questionability – such as the claims that forces are real, that inertial mass is primitive, and that space is substantival.[50] Each of these three metaphysical assumptions proved controversial, and was subjected to increasingly acute criticism. Yet Newton's theory worked: it proved capable of reliable prediction in the classical world, irrespective of the truth of its alleged metaphysical precommitments.

More recently, a debate has arisen over the metaphysical presuppositions and implications of quantum mechanics.[51] In part, this debate is grounded in the history of the discipline. Quantum theory developed with two quite different formalisms (Werner Heisenberg's matrix mechanics, and Erwin Schrödinger's wavefunctions). Heisenberg initially offered a merely instrumental understanding of his formalism,[52] whereas Schrödinger regarded his theory in essentially realist terms, seeing it as a description of the evolution of continuous matter waves. The formalisms were subsequently shown to be equivalent; their metaphysical implications were, however, radically different.[53]

For historical reasons, the so-called "Copenhagen" interpretation of quantum theory has now become dominant.[54] Its more striking metaphysical assumptions include the belief that all properties of atoms are inherently contextual – that is, irredeemably relative to a specified measuring apparatus; that measurement does not merely "reveal" the measured property, but brings it into being; and that there is a "complementarity" between the dynamic and kinematic aspects of the world. This has led many to make the incautious statement that quantum mechanics is anti-deterministic. Yet other approaches to quantum theory exist, most notably David Bohm's, which is easily interpreted in determinist manners. Quantum mechanics is open to indeterminist and determinist approaches; neither can be said to be "implied" by the theory.[55] Similar ambiguities emerge elsewhere in the field – for example, it is easily shown that quantum mechanics is compatible with two distinct metaphysical viewpoints, one of which treats particles as individuals, and one which does not.[56]

These observations have important implications for recent attempts on the part of some theologians to use quantum mechanics as a conceptual framework for understanding complex theological issues – such as divine action within the world.[57] It is not always clear that such theologians understand that a distinction must be made between the quantum formalism itself, and various possible metaphysical interpretations of this formalism. What is being demonstrated here is not that quantum mechanics itself creates or protects conceptual space for certain theological positions, but that certain ways of *interpreting* quantum mechanics have this outcome.

So what of evolutionary thought? The same difficulty arises here. Darwinism is vulnerable to those wishing to inflate it metaphysically.[58] For example, it is easily interpreted in terms of a metaphysical naturalism, which is held to be a necessary inference from evolutionary thought. Again, Darwinism is widely regarded as entailing the metaphysical elimination of teleology, which is simply not the case. Existing notions of teleology may, as will become clear, require revision in the light of evolutionary thought; they do not, however, require to be abandoned.

To illuminate the problem more clearly, we may consider a passage from Dawkins's early masterpiece of Darwinian popularization, *The Selfish Gene* (1976). This important and influential work supplements overt scientific description with a covert metaphysic, which represents genes as active agents in control of their own destiny and those of their hosts.[59]

> [Genes] swarm in huge colonies, safe inside gigantic lumbering robots, sealed off from the outside world, communicating with it by tortuous indirect routes, manipulating it by remote control. They are in you and me; they created us, body and mind; and their preservation is the ultimate rationale for our existence.

This passage presents a completely defensible scientific statement – "genes are in you and me" – with a series of rather less defensible metaphysical assertions. We are told, for example, that the preservation of our genes "is the ultimate rationale for our existence." This is, however, simply a presentation of a "gene's eye view" – a hypothetical metaphysical way of interpreting scientific observation, which arguably reached its zenith in the early 1980s.[60] This approach conceived the gene as an active controlling agent, which could be regarded as "manipulating" the destiny of biological entities, including humanity. Yet the empirically verified facts in this statement are limited to the brief statement that genes "are in you and me." The rest is speculative. Metaphysical presuppositions have been smuggled in, and portrayed as if they were scientifically verified facts.

This point becomes clearer by reflecting on the same paragraph, as teasingly rewritten by the Oxford systems biologist Denis Noble. Noble retains what is scientifically valid and verifiable in Dawkins's prose. Then, in a masterly piece of ideological subversion, he identifies *and inverts* Dawkins's non-scientific statements. Noble playfully portrays genes as passive, where Dawkins depicts them as active:[61]

> [Genes] are trapped in huge colonies, locked inside highly intelligent beings, moulded by the outside world, communicating with it by complex processes, through which, blindly, as if by magic, function emerges. They are in you and me; we are the system that allows their code to be read; and their preservation is totally dependent on the joy that we experience in reproducing ourselves. We are the ultimate rationale for their existence.

It will be clear that Dawkins and Noble represent the functional status of genes in completely different ways. The same limited scientific information is interpreted in totally different manners: in both cases, however, what is essentially a metaphysical interpretation of the gene is being presented as scientific fact, as if it were on the same level as empirical statements. Dawkins and Noble cannot both be right. Though both base themselves on the same observational statement, they import and impose quite different metaphysical assumptions upon it. Their statements are thus empirically equivalent, having equally good grounding in observation and experimental evidence.

So which is right? How could we decide which is to be preferred on scientific grounds? As Noble observes, "no-one seems to be able to think of an experiment that would detect an empirical difference between them." The question of the metaphysical presuppositions and consequences of evolutionary thought is entirely legitimate, and is of considerable interest. Nevertheless, it is important to be clear that discussion of this issue is often muddied by confusion over the status of the metaphysical dimensions of evolutionary thought. The challenge facing anyone interested in reflecting on the cultural, religious, ethical, and theological implications of biological evolution is to separate the observational evidence from the accumulated detritus of metaphysical speculation.

A careful survey of recent writings on the philosophical dimensions of modern evolutionary thought suggests that at least three distinct and quasi-incommensurable epistemological or metaphysical frameworks have been identified as providing a proper foundation for neo-Darwinism.[62] The writings of leading founders of the neo-Darwinian synthesis – Theodosius Dobzhansky (1900–75), Bernhard Rensch (1900–90), and Ernst Mayr (1904–2005) – reveal specific metaphysical commitments on the part of their authors, which either inform, or arise from, their evolutionary biology. Given the evidential underdetermination of such views, it should not be the cause for surprise that these are divergent, and possibly inconsistent with each other. This highlights the important observation that a fundamental commitment to a theory, which aims to make sense of empirical biological data, is easily expanded to include views about the nature of the universe that are not necessarily entailed by biological observations.

Conclusion to Part I

This opening section has explored some aspects of the notions of "natural theology" and "Darwinism," noting the breadth of interpretations that have come to be associated with them. It would be easy to restrict the scope of this investigation to rigorously defined notions of "natural theology" and "Darwinism," making for a reasonably simple argument. Yet any attempt to engage with the historical discussion – understood as both a debate *about* history and *within* history – must accommodate the diversity of interpretation that has been one of its characteristic features. No attempt is therefore made to limit the interpretation of either notion. While the concluding chapter of this book will offer some reflections on which form of natural theology might be best adapted to deal with the questions raised for religious belief by evolutionary biology, the work as a whole is characterized by a generosity of interpretations, based on historical description and analysis in its second part, and analytical engagement in its third.

So where should we begin such reflections? As the Darwinian controversies were shaped to no small extent by their historical contexts, the most obvious point at which to begin is to consider the various styles of natural theology that developed in England during the period 1690–1850. The opening chapter of the second part of this work thus considers the distinctive approaches to natural theology that emerged during the English cultural renaissance that is often known as the "Augustan age" (1690–1745).

Notes

1   Freud, Sigmund, "One of the Difficulties of Psycho-Analysis." *Journal of Mental Science* 67 (1921): 34–9, especially 36–8.
2   Freud, "One of the Difficulties of Psycho-Analysis," 37.
3   See Bowler, Peter J., *Evolution: The History of an Idea*. 3rd edn. Berkeley, CA: University of California Press, 2003, 1–26.

4 Richards, Robert J., "Evolution." In *Keywords in Evolutionary Biology*, ed. Evelyn Fox Keller and Elizabeth Lloyd, 95–105. Cambridge, MA: Harvard University Press, 1992.

5 Gayon, Jean, "From Darwin to Today in Evolutionary Biology." In *The Cambridge Companion to Darwin*, ed. Jonathan Hodge and Gregory Radick, 240–64. Cambridge: Cambridge University Press, 2003, 241.

6 Note the important concerns expressed in Scott, Eugenie, and Glenn Branch, "Don't Call It Darwinism." *Evolution: Education and Outreach* 2 (2009): 90–4.

7 Saliba, George, *A History of Arabic Astronomy: Planetary Theories during the Golden Age of Islam*. New York: New York University Press, 1993, 85–120.

8 Murray, Carl D., and Stanley F. Dermott, *Solar System Dynamics*. Cambridge: Cambridge University Press, 2001, 3–4.

9 Judson, Olivia, "Let's Get Rid of Darwinism." *New York Times*, July 15, 2008.

10 For an excellent contemporary presentation of the evolutionary synthesis, see Pigliucci, Massimo, and Gerd B. Müller, *Evolution, the Extended Synthesis*. Cambridge, MA: MIT Press, 2010. For the continuous evolution of Darwinism, see Depew, David J., and Bruce H. Weber, *Darwinism Evolving: Systems Dynamics and the Genealogy of Natural Selection*. Cambridge, MA: MIT Press, 1996; Keller, Evelyn Fox, *Making Sense of Life: Explaining Biological Development with Models, Metaphors, and Machines*. Cambridge, MA: Harvard University Press, 2002; Shanahan, Timothy, *The Evolution of Darwinism: Selection, Adaptation, and Progress in Evolutionary Biology*. Cambridge: Cambridge University Press, 2004, 11–36.

11 For an introduction to the core developments, see Everson, Ted, *The Gene: A Historical Perspective*. Westport, CT: Greenwood Press, 2007, 43–94.

12 See, for example, Kutschera, Ulrich, and Karl J. Niklas, "The Modern Theory of Biological Evolution: An Expanded Synthesis." *Naturwissenschaften* 91 (2004): 255–76; Pigliucci, Massimo, "Do We Need an Extended Evolutionary Synthesis?" *Evolution* 61 (2007): 2743–9; Carroll, Sean B., "EvoDevo and an Expanding Evolutionary Synthesis: A Genetic Theory of Morphological Evolution." *Cell* 134 (2008): 25–36.

13 For comment, see Hull, David L., "Darwinism as a Historical Entity: A Historiographic Proposal." In *The Darwinian Heritage*, ed. David Kohn, 773–812. Princeton, NJ: Princeton University Press, 1985.

14 For the question of whether a unifying narrative may be offered of the development of evolutionary theories, see Smocovitis, Vassiliki Betty, *Unifying Biology: The Evolutionary Synthesis and Evolutionary Biology*. Princeton, NJ: Princeton University Press, 1996, 97–188.

15 For the recent debate over the explanatory potential of the idea, see Nanay, Bence, "Can Cumulative Selection Explain Adaptation?" *Philosophy of Science* 72 (2005): 1099–112; Stegmann, Ulrich E., "What Can Natural Selection Explain?" *Studies in History and Philosophy of Biological and Biomedical Sciences* 41 (2010): 61–6.

16   For comment on these difficulties and their possible resolution, see Reid, Robert G. B., *Biological Emergences: Evolution by Natural Experiment*. Cambridge, MA: MIT Press, 2007, 1–22.

17   Note the points made in Challis, Gregory L., and David A. Hopwood, "Synergy and Contingency as Driving Forces for the Evolution of Multiple Secondary Metabolite Production by *Streptomyces* Species." *PNAS* 100 (2003): 14555–61.

18   See, for example, Fodor, Jerry A., and Massimo Piattelli-Palmarini, *What Darwin Got Wrong*. New York: Farrar, Straus and Giroux, 2010, 95–137.

19   Lenoir, Timothy, *The Strategy of Life: Teleology and Mechanics in Nineteenth Century German Biology*. Chicago: University of Chicago Press, 1989; Corsi, Pietro, "Before Darwin: Transformist Concepts in European Natural History." *Journal of the History of Biology* 38 (2005): 67–83. As Lenoir rightly notes (p. 1), Lamarck is to be credited with inventing the term "biology."

20   In this sense, I agree with Stanley L. Jaki's plea to liberate Darwin's ideas from their acquired metaphysical and philosophical accretions: see Jaki, Stanley L., "Non-Darwinian Darwinism." In *L'evoluzione: Crocevia di scienza, filosofia e teologia*, ed. Rafael Pascual, 41–52. Rome: Edizioni Studium, 2005.

21   Richards, Robert J., *The Meaning of Evolution: The Morphological Construction and Ideological Reconstruction of Darwin's Theory*. Chicago: University of Chicago Press, 1992; Klapwojk, Jacob, *Purpose in the Living World: Creation and Emergent Evolution*. Cambridge: Cambridge University Press, 2008, 41–4.

22   See McGrath, Alister E., "The Ideological Uses of Evolutionary Biology in Recent Atheist Apologetics." In *Ideology and Biology: From Descartes to Dawkins*, ed. Ronald Numbers and Denis Alexander, 329–49. Chicago: University of Chicago Press, 2010. For reflections on the deeper issues, see Dixon, Thomas, "Theology, Anti-Theology, and Atheology: From Christian Passions to Secular Emotions." *Modern Theology* 15 (1999): 299–330.

23   For comment on this approach, see Baxter, Brian, *A Darwinian Worldview: Sociobiology, Environmental Ethics and the Work of Edward O. Wilson*. Aldershot: Ashgate, 2007, 1–12.

24   See the analysis in Dongen, Paul A. M. van, and Jo M. H. Vossen, "Can the Theory of Evolution Be Falsified?" *Acta Biotheoretica*, no. 33 (1984).

25   Lecture on "The Darwin Memorial," given on June 9, 1885; Huxley, Thomas H., *Darwiniana: Essays*. London: Macmillan, 1893, 252.

26   Darwin, Francis, ed., *The Life and Letters of Charles Darwin*. 3 vols. London: John Murray, 1887, vol. 2, 200. For scientific atheism as a belief system, see Dixon, Thomas, "Scientific Atheism as a Faith Tradition." *Studies in History and Philosophy of Science C* 33 (2002): 337–59.

27   Lewontin, Richard C., "Billions and Billions of Demons." *New York Review of Books*, January 9, 1997, 31.

28   Keith Ward argues that materialism is itself a metaphysical belief that is neither implied by scientific practice, nor based on scientific evidence: Ward, Keith, *God, Chance and Necessity*. Oxford: Oneworld, 1996, 98–104.

29   Dawkins, Richard, "Darwin Triumphant: Darwinism as a Universal Truth." In *A Devil's Chaplain*, 78–90. London: Weidenfeld & Nicholson, 2003.

30 For the debated legitimacy of this term in this context, see Pedynowski, Dena, "Science(s): Which, When and Whose? Probing the Metanarrative of Scientific Knowledge in the Social Construction of Nature." *Progress in Human Geography* 27 (2003): 735–52.

31 For an illuminating example, see Davidson, Luke, "Fragilities of Scientism: Richard Dawkins and the Paranoid Idealization of Science." *Science as Culture* 9 (2000): 167–99.

32 Dennett, Daniel C., *Darwin's Dangerous Idea: Evolution and the Meaning of Life*. New York: Simon & Schuster, 1995.

33 Dennett, *Darwin's Dangerous Idea*, 21.

34 Dennett, *Darwin's Dangerous Idea*, 82.

35 Johnson, Philip, "What Is Darwinism?" In *Man and Creation: Perspectives on Science and Theology*, ed. Michael Bauman, 177–90. Hillsdale, MI: Hillsdale College Press, 1993, 189. For further statements of such critiques of Darwinism, see Behe, Michael J., *Darwin's Black Box: The Biochemical Challenge to Evolution*. New York: Free Press, 1996; Woodward, Thomas, *Doubts about Darwin: A History of Intelligent Design*. Grand Rapids, MI: Baker Books, 2003.

36 See, for example, Miller, Jon D., Eugenie C. Scott, and Shinji Okamoto, "Public Acceptance of Evolution." *Science* 313 (2006): 765–6.

37 See the 1992 debate at Southern Methodist University between evolutionists and supporters of the "Intelligent Design" movement over whether Darwinism carries with it "an *a priori* commitment to metaphysical naturalism": Buell, John, and Virginia Hearn, eds., *Darwinism: Science or Philosophy?* Richardson, TX: Foundation for Thought and Ethics, 1994, 6–40.

38 For the general issues, see Walker, Mark, "Introduction: Science and Ideology." In *Science and Ideology: A Comparative History*, ed. Mark Walker, 1–16. London: Routledge, 2003.

39 Giddens, Anthony, *Sociology*. 3rd edn. Cambridge: Polity Press, 1997, 583.

40 See, for example, Althusser, Louis, "Ideology and Ideological State Apparatuses." In *Lenin and Philosophy and Other Essays*, 121–76. New York: Monthly Review Press, 1972.

41 For the issues, see Gordin, Michael, Walter Grunden, Mark Walker, and Zuoyue Wang, "'Ideologisch korrekte' Wissenschaft: Französische Revolution, Sowjetunion, Nationalsozialismus, Japan im Zweiten Weltkrieg, McCarthy-Ära, Volksrepublik China." In *Darwinismus und/als Ideologie*, ed. Uwe Hoßfeld and Rainer Brömer, 29–69. Berlin: Verlag für Wissenschaft und Bildung, 2001.

42 McGrath, Alister E., *Heresy*. San Francisco: HarperOne, 2009, 33–40.

43 Lustig, Abigail, Robert J. Richards, and Michael Ruse, eds., *Darwinian Heresies*. Cambridge: Cambridge University Press, 2004, 1–13.

44 Leigh, Egbert G., "Neutral Theory: A Historical Perspective." *Evolutionary Biology* 20 (2007): 2075–91.

45 Midgley, Mary, *Evolution as a Religion: Strange Hopes and Stranger Fears*. 2nd edn. London: Routledge, 2002, 17.

46 There are important anticipations of this development in the writings of John Dewey: see, for example, Dewey, John, *The Influence of Darwin on Philosophy and Other Essays*. New York: H. Holt, 1910, 1–26.

47   This has been a major theme in the writings of John C. Greene: see Greene, John C., *Darwin and the Modern World View*. Baton Rouge, LA: Louisiana State University Press, 1961, 88–127. Note also his reflections on the importance of Darwinism for natural theology: *Darwin and the Modern World View*, 39–87.

48   See, for example, Cassirer, Ernst, "Darwinism as a Dogma and as a Principle of Knowledge." In *The Problem of Knowledge: Philosophy, Science, and History since Hegel*, 160–75. New Haven, CT: Yale University Press, 1950.

49   For the debate, see Psillos, Stathis, *Scientific Realism: How Science Tracks Truth*. London: Routledge, 1999; Kuipers, Theo A. F., *From Instrumentalism to Constructive Realism: On Some Relations between Confirmation, Empirical Progress, and Truth Approximation*. Dordrecht: Kluwer Academic, 2000.

50   Grant, Edward, *Much Ado About Nothing: Theories of Space and Vacuum from the Middle Ages to the Scientific Revolution*. Cambridge: Cambridge University Press, 1981, 240–54; Hesse, Mary B., *Forces and Fields: The Concept of Action at a Distance in the History of Physics*. London: Nelson, 2005.

51   See Jammer, Max, *The Philosophy of Quantum Mechanics*. New York: John Wiley & Sons, Inc., 1974; Krips, Henry, *The Metaphysics of Quantum Theory*. Oxford: Clarendon Press, 1987.

52   The debates are well described in Cassidy, David C., *Uncertainty: The Life and Science of Werner Heisenberg*. New York: W. H. Freeman, 1992.

53   For comment on the general issue, see Ladyman, James, "Does Physics Answer Metaphysical Questions?" In *Philosophy of Science: Royal Institute of Philosophy Supplement 61*, 179–202. Cambridge: Cambridge University Press, 2007. More generally, see Redhead, Michael, *From Physics to Metaphysics*. Cambridge: Cambridge University Press, 1995, 41–62.

54   For the best discussion of this development, see Cushing, James T., *Quantum Mechanics: Historical Contingency and the Copenhagen Hegemony*. Chicago: University of Chicago Press, 1994, particularly the discussion of the reception of Bohm's theory (144–73).

55   Bell, J. S., *Speakable and Unspeakable in Quantum Mechanics*. 2nd edn. Cambridge: Cambridge University Press, 2004, 169–72.

56   Belousek, Darrin S., "Statistics, Symmetry and the Conventionality of Indistinguishability in Quantum Mechanics." *Foundations of Physics* 30 (2000): 1–34.

57   Note especially the work of the important "Divine Action Project," co-sponsored by the Vatican Observatory and the Center for Theology and the Natural Sciences in Berkeley, summarized and criticized by Wildman, Wesley J., "The Divine Action Project, 1988–2003." *Theology and Science* 2 (2004): 31–75. See further the critical analysis of Saunders, Nicholas, *Divine Action and Modern Science*. Cambridge: Cambridge University Press, 2002, 127–206.

58   For some illuminating recent examples, see Lewens, Tim, "Darwinism and Metaphysics." *Metascience* 16 (2007): 61–9.

59   Dawkins, Richard, *The Selfish Gene*. 2nd edn. Oxford: Oxford University Press, 1989, 21. I am indebted to Denis Noble for making this point: see especially Noble, Denis, *The Music of Life: Biology beyond the Genome*. Oxford: Oxford University Press, 2006, 1–22.

60 Okasha, Samir, *Evolution and the Levels of Selection*. Oxford: Oxford University Press, 2006, 143–72.
61 Noble, *Music of Life*, 13.
62 Delisle, Richard G., "The Uncertain Foundation of Neo-Darwinism: Metaphysical and Epistemological Pluralism in the Evolutionary Synthesis." *Studies in History and Philosophy of Biological and Biomedical Sciences* 40 (2009): 119–32.

Part II

Historical Exposition

Darwin and the English natural
theology tradition

3

English Natural Theology of the Augustan Age, 1690–1745

The period 1690–1745 is widely known as the "Augustan age" in English culture, on account of the self-conscious imitation of the original Augustan writers – the Roman poets Virgil and Horace – by many of the writers of this creative and transformative era.[1] Although the term is often used with a notable lack of precision, the phrase "Augustan age" is generally used to refer to the phase in English literary and cultural history following the Glorious Revolution of 1688, and ending with the death of Alexander Pope (1688–1744). Its core canonical works include John Dryden's *Essay of Dramatic Poesy* (1668) and Pope's *Essay on Criticism* (1711), both of which made an appeal to "nature" in discovering authentic approaches to writing. The "nature" in question is not the untamed nature that later came to be associated with the Romantic movement, but the rational and comprehensible realm of intellectual, aesthetic, and moral order in the universe, which is ultimately held to reflect and embody God's providential design. This classical conception of nature emphasizes its stability and reliability, and above all its capacity to be transferred to human modes of thought and action.

It is not difficult to see how this cultural framework led to the Augustan age being a golden era of natural theology in England. A family of natural theologies emerged, often referred to as the "Newtonian synthesis," which were adapted to the agendas and concerns of this age. One the one hand, they established and maintained a close working relationship between the natural sciences and religion; on the other, they set out a vision of a stable universe, mirrored in the social and political norms of England.

It is not clear that this development could have been predicted on the basis of earlier trends in English theology. The Elizabethan age does not appear to have regarded natural theology as being a theological issue of

Darwinism and the Divine: Evolutionary Thought and Natural Theology, First Edition.
Alister E. McGrath.
© 2011 Alister E. McGrath. Published 2011 by Blackwell Publishing Ltd.

pressing importance or interest. It is certainly true that this age generally regarded the created order as manifesting the wisdom, goodness, and glory of God, intimating a deeper order of things. Yet this way of thinking often led to the formulation of a doctrine of natural law, as much as of a natural theology. The poetics of Sir Philip Sidney (1554–86), for example, clearly reflect the notion of "a theory of innate ideas, divinely scripted on the mind as natural law."[2] Richard Hooker's *Laws of Ecclesiastical Polity* (1594–7), widely regarded as the theological masterpiece of the Elizabethan age, also offered a cautious and underdeveloped account of natural law,[3] with the potential for expansion and conceptual development into a natural theology in a less anxious future age.

It was not until the early seventeenth century that serious interest began to develop within England in the notion of "natural theology." An early example of this emerging awareness of the potential importance of the notion can be found in the natural philosophy of Francis Bacon (1561–1626).[4] Others developed the familiar metaphor of the "two books of God"[5] – nature and Scripture – as the basis of a defensible natural theology. Perhaps one of the clearest statements of this approach is found in the writings of Sir Thomas Browne (1605–82), particularly his idiosyncratic and controversial work *Religio Medici* (1643).[6] Browne here set out his understanding of natural theology with an appeal to the wisdom of the ancients:[7]

> Thus there are two Books from whence I collect my Divinity; besides that written one of God, another of His servant Nature, that universal and publick Manuscript, that lies expans'd unto the Eyes of all: those that never saw Him in the one, have discovered Him in the other. This was the Scripture and Theology of the Heathens: the natural motion of the Sun made them more admire Him than its supernatural station did the Children of Israel; the ordinary effects of Nature wrought more admiration in them than in the other all His Miracles. Surely the Heathens knew better how to joyn and read these mystical Letters than we Christians, who cast a more careless Eye on these common Hieroglyphicks, and disdain to suck Divinity from the flowers of Nature.

Where Hooker integrated his natural theology within a strongly political outlook, well adapted to the circumstances of his day,[8] Browne's approach is politically disengaged.[9] The study of nature is seen as intellectually and spiritually illuminating, but without political consequences.

The Emergence of English Natural Theology

The religious and political traumas of the late seventeenth century inevitably led to the rise of various forms of atheism and materialism, partly as a reaction against the perceived deficiencies of religions, and partly on account of a growing demand for certainty in all matters of belief, whether religious or scientific.[10] Was not the most effective way of eliminating the tensions and warfare that so easily arose from religious disputes simply to abandon religion altogether?

Yet others, fearing the radicalism of atheism, favored an approach that tamed religion and diverted its energies to more acceptable ends. Instead of being the basis for social conflict, religion could be reframed and redirected, becoming the foundation of both a stable social order, and a religiously motivated natural philosophy. Eirenic approaches to religion began to emerge within England, reducing the appeal of atheism or materialism, and emphasizing the importance of a divinely ordained stable social order. For many, an appeal to natural theology seemed to open new conceptual possibilities, allowing a synthesis of social and natural order.

Several factors appear to have shaped this new interest in "natural theology" and "natural religion" at this time in England.[11] We may note three.

1   The rise of biblical criticism called into question the reliability or intelligibility of Scripture, and hence generated interest in the revelatory capacities of the natural world.
2   A growing distrust of ecclesiastical authority led some to explore sources of knowledge that were seen to be independent of ecclesiastical control, such as an appeal to reason or to the natural order.
3   A dislike of organized religion and Christian doctrines caused many to search for a simpler "religion of nature," in which nature was valued as a source of revelation.

In some ways, these developments can be seen as confirming anxieties famously expressed by the leading Swiss Protestant theologian Karl Barth (1886–1968), widely regarded as the most significant recent theological critic of natural theology, concerning the eighteenth-century worldview – namely, that it represented an assertion of human autonomy over and against divine self-revelation.[12] "Natural theology," as understood by Barth, embodies the characteristic tendency of sinful humanity to affirm its epistemic and soteriological independence. Humanity could discover and relate to God under terms of its own choosing, rather than those mandated by the Christian proclamation. If knowledge of God can be achieved independently of God's self-revelation in Christ, then it follows that humanity can dictate the terms and conditions, not to mention the substance, of its knowledge of God.[13]

The background to the emergence of this style of natural theology is, however, rather more complex than Barth allows. Barth's linguistic and geographical horizons may have prevented him from fully appreciating the cultural factors that led to the emergence of Augustan natural theologies, particularly as apologetic tools. It is undoubtedly true that the "autonomy" motif was significant for Deists and others in England at this time wishing to promote a certain style of natural theology. Yet it is not difficult to discern another motif – growing anxiety concerning the reliability of the Christian revelation, and especially specific concerns about the authority of the Bible, reflecting changes in the English cultural scene at this time.[14] The primary motivation for undertaking natural theology within English Christianity during the late seventeenth and eighteenth centuries was not *dogmatic*, but *apologetic*. The church itself did not reject revelation; it realized that it needed to relate the gospel to a culture that no longer felt inclined to accept this notion. Natural theology rapidly became an apologetic tool of no small importance. Although some believed it was designed to affirm religion in an increasingly scientific age, it must also be pointed out that it served to affirm the natural sciences in a persistently religious age.[15]

This acceleration of interest in natural theology thus reflected a growing perception within the English church that an apologetic appeal to the regularity of nature would be much more effective and productive in the public arena than reliance on a sacred text or institution that was increasingly regarded with suspicion. Natural theology was thus seen as an especially promising apologetic tool in a cultural situation that had witnessed significant erosion in the esteem in which both the Bible and the church were held.

This can be seen with particular clarity in Walter Charleton's *Darkness of Atheism Dispelled by the Light of Nature* (1652). Writing in the aftermath of the English Civil War, Charleton (1619–1707) argued that the religious tensions of the Civil War and Commonwealth periods had greatly contributed to the development of atheism in England.[16] It was necessary, he argued, to re-establish belief in God. This, however, could not take place by an appeal to the authority of the church, or to the Bible. Both, he argued, were tarnished by their recent associations with political instability and religious violence. The best defense of religion lay in an appeal to human reason and the ordering and beauty of the natural world. God's existence, he argued, was primarily attested by the ordering and government of the natural world. It was a shrewd move. The religious controversies and wars of the age had left many uneasy about any appeal to religious texts or authorities in reaffirming the existence and nature of God. Charleton clearly regarded the ordering of the world as an indication of its divine design, and believed this approach was well adapted to the prevailing cultural conditions of his age.

Yet Charleton did more than lay the ideological foundations for a new appeal to natural theology; he helped shape the vocabulary of this approach. Charleton subtitled his work *A Physico-Theological Treatise*. In one sense, the term "physico-theology" is simply an alternative way of referring to natural (Greek: *physikos*) theology. However, the term began to be associated, not with natural theology in general, but with a specific approach to natural theology that would gain the ascendancy in England during the Augustan age.

With the restoration of Charles II in 1660, natural theology came to play an increasing role in religious apologetics. The order of nature, which was gradually being clarified and elaborated in the natural sciences of the age, was seen as the basis of a defense of the existence of God. Yet it is important to disentangle two different forms of such arguments:[17]

1 "Order implies an orderer" (an argument *from* design);
2 "There is no purpose without a purposer" (an argument *to* design).

Although these two themes are often elided, and sometimes confused, it is essential to maintain a distinction between them. Early English natural theology tended to proceed from the observation of order in nature to the inference of God as the origin and ground of that order. Yet from 1690, the second approach began to achieve dominance. Here, the observation of design or "contrivance" within nature was held to entail a designer.[18] English natural theology increasingly became concerned with finding "evidence of design" rather than "observation of order." "Physico-theology" increasingly became identified with this quest for design, often framed specifically in terms of the notion of "contrivance."

Newtonian Physics and Natural Theology

The new emphasis on the divine ordering of the world, which emerged from the "mechanical philosophy" of Isaac Newton (1643–1727) and his school,[19] was widely seen as offering a form of religion of maximal intellectual plausibility and minimal social divisiveness. God could be thought of as the divine clockmaker, who had constructed a particularly elegant piece of machinery, and made no demands of anyone other than a due recognition of the order and beauty of the creation, and its implications for the stability of the social order. Natural theology thus came to be seen as a potential means of enhancing social cohesiveness in the late seventeenth and early eighteenth centuries, while at the same time being responsive to scientific advance.

The personal role of Isaac Newton in catalyzing this development must be fully acknowledged.[20]

Figure 3.1 Isaac Newton (1642–1727), English physicist and mathematician. Among other things, Newton discovered the ability of a prism to separate white light into its composite colors.

Indeed, such was the religious and scientific esteem in which Newton was held that some pressed for him to be treated as a saint.[21] Having uncovered the laws governing the behavior of the solar system, Newton argued that the regulation and maintenance of "this most beautiful system of the sun, planets, and comets, could only proceed from the counsel and dominion of an intelligent and powerful Being."[22] Newton was clear that indisputable empirical facts about the physical world, which were open to public observation, demonstrated the existence of God beyond reasonable doubt. The physical ordering of the created order was clear evidence of God's "most wise and excellent contrivances of things." The regular motions of the planets, he argued, "could not spring from any natural causes, but were impressed by an intelligent agent."

Underlying Newton's approach is the fundamental belief that the regularity of the mechanisms of nature points to their origination in the mind of God. The astronomer Johannes Kepler (1571–1630) had been an enthusiastic advocate of this notion, which allowed him to affirm the intellectual synergy of the new astronomy and Christian theology.[23] Kepler regarded geometry as the archetype of the cosmos, coeternal with God as its creator, and therefore taking precedence, both conceptually and chronologically, over the act of creation. In his work *Harmonices Mundi* (1619), Kepler argued that, since geometry had its origins in the mind of God, it was only to be expected that the created order would conform to its patterns:[24]

> In that geometry is part of the divine mind from the origins of time, even from before the origins of time (for what is there in God that is not also from God?) has provided God with the patterns for the creation of the world, and has been transferred to humanity with the image of God.

Newton is known to have held this work of Kepler in high regard, and it is possible that Kepler's emphasis upon the origin of mathematics in the mind of God may have been a theological stimulus to Newton's mathematicization of nature.[25]

The forms of natural theology that emerged from within the Newtonian synthesis tended to emphasize the regularity of the natural order. The existence of "laws of nature" were often held in themselves to indicate, possibly even prove, the existence of a lawgiver – easily identified with, or assimilated to, the Christian notion of God.[26] Although teleological notions could be embedded within this conceptual matrix without difficulty, its prime emphasis lay on the ordering and rationality of nature, rather than the purposes for which such ordering and rationality might have been devised. The rationality of belief in God was defended primarily by arguments *from* design, not *to* design (see 53). Yet the growing tendency to think of the universe in mechanical terms made it increasingly plausible to argue from a mechanism to its designer – an approach characteristic of English physico-theology.

A mechanical approach to nature was seen to offer many advantages to Christian theology. Such a model emphasized the regularity and reliability of the universe, allowed a correlation to be established between the wisdom and intentions of a creator or designer and their final outcome, and lent itself easily to the inference of design within the natural world, and hence of a designer. Although English physico-theology of the late seventeenth and early eighteenth centuries appears to have lacked a rigorous understanding of argumentation by analogy,[27] it is clearly assumed that the mechanical attributes of nature lend some unspecified legitimacy to the use of mechanical models of nature – such as the great cathedral clock of Strasbourg, or a pocket watch.

It is, however, important to appreciate that this shift in conceptualization of nature was not without its critics, still less its problems. Mechanical models of nature were opposed by those who preferred older organic models, which emphasized the organizational unity of the natural world, seeing this as an expression of the wisdom of its creator.[28] Cambridge Platonists such as Henry More (1614–87) and Ralph Cudworth (1617–88), for example, emphasized the coherence and harmoniousness of nature, arguing that nature possessed an "outward frame of things," which pointed to its origins in the "eternal mind" and being of God.[29] The argument, however, is primarily based upon the overall coherence of the natural order, and is perhaps more mystical than rational in its approach. More summarizes the two approaches as follows:[30]

> To the rational and religious there is a double pleasure to carry them on in this way of Philosophy: The one from the observation how far in every thing the concatenation of Mechanical causes will reach which will wonderfully gratify their Reason. The other from a distinct deprehension where they must needs break off, as not being able alone to reach the Effect, which necessarily leads them to a more confirmed discovery of the Principle we contend for, namely the *Spirit* of *Nature*, which is the vicarious power of God upon Matter, and the first step to the abstrusest mysteries in Natural Theologie, which must needs highly gratify them in point of Religion.

More does not treat these two approaches as antithetical. Where writers such as John Wilkins and Robert Boyle were realizing the apologetic potential of the lawfulness of nature, as disclosed by developments in the mechanical and experimental natural philosophy of their day, More preferred to behold nature as a whole, a single entity, reflecting on the theological significance of the harmony of its deeper structures.

Yet whatever the intentions of its original advocates might have been, the approach to natural theology based on mechanical models of the natural world ended up eroding the conceptual space traditionally occupied by God. The amalgam of Newtonian natural philosophy and certain forms of Anglican theology proved popular and plausible in England during a period of political instability and uncertainty. Nevertheless, it was an unstable amalgam – more of a convenient, temporary convergence of vested intellectual and social interests, rather than a resilient, integrated, conceptual fusion. It was not long before the "estrangement of celestial mechanics and religion" began to set in.[31] The somewhat problematic enterprise of "celestial mechanics" increasingly seemed to suggest that the world was a self-sustaining mechanism, which had no need for divine governance or sustenance for its day-to-day operation.

The Protestant Assumptions of English Natural Theology

The religious environment within which English natural theology developed in the late seventeenth and early eighteenth centuries was shaped by a number of factors. One such factor was the manner in which evidence was publicly evaluated, assessed, and interpreted, especially in legal contexts – a matter to which we shall return presently (75–6). At this point, however, it is important to appreciate that the Protestant context within which most English natural theology was undertaken had a significant impact upon its outcome.

The great Oxford mathematician Baden Powell (1796–1860) played a major role in exploring the relationship between science and faith in Victorian England. Important though this contribution is in its own right,[32] he merits mention at this point on account of an *aperçu* in his influential *Order of Nature*, published a year before his death. Reflecting on the relation between science and faith, he comments:[33]

> It has been a peculiarly *Protestant* prejudice to be everywhere looking for arguments and proofs in support of faith: and might easily be construed into a confession of its weakness.

Powell's analysis at this point does little to substantiate such a significant conclusion; nevertheless, it must be considered to be a plausible allegation. Might there be some confessional reason underlying the emergence of English natural theology, reflecting its essentially Protestant roots? It is certainly a theme worth exploring in more detail.

England consolidated its identity as a Protestant nation in the late sixteenth century. Following the complex and tumultuous events of the religious upheavals of the sixteenth century, England navigated its way toward a distinctive religious and political compromise. The origins of this emerged during the reign of Elizabeth I. Recognizing the need to secure religious stability in England, Elizabeth set about crafting a "Settlement of Religion" that would bring at least some degree of unity to a deeply divided nation.[34] While Elizabeth's own inclinations were unquestionably Protestant, she had no intention of causing offense to Catholic Spain, which might pose a significant military threat to England. The Church of England would be reformed in its theology, yet catholic in its institutions, especially its episcopacy.

Elizabeth's "Settlement of Religion" was ultimately a political, rather than a theological, statement, aimed at generating consensus and stability, helped along by a little theological vagueness at awkward points. The English Civil War led to a vicious dispute over the regnant form of Protestantism within England, pitting an essentially royalist Anglicanism against a republican Puritanism. The restoration of the monarchy under Charles II initially led to the emergence of a degree of religious stability. This, however, came under serious threat after his death in 1685, as his successor, James II, sought to convert England to Roman Catholicism. Eventually, the situation was resolved through the Glorious Revolution of 1688, which established William and Mary as Protestant monarchs, guaranteeing freedom of speech and elections.

The context within which a distinctively English natural theology emerged during the Augustan age was clearly significantly influenced by Protestantism.[35] But how did this shape such approaches? Three features of English Protestantism of this age merit close attention: the emergence of the attitude toward nature often described as "disenchantment"; the rejection of the idea of miracles within the present order of nature; and the emphasis upon the providential ordering of nature. We shall consider these three points further in what follows.

The "disenchantment" of nature

One of the consequences of the Protestant Reformation was what is now widely referred to as the "desacralization" or "disenchantment" (*Entzauberung*) of nature. This phenomenon has been studied in depth by scholars of the early modern period, who have noted its implications for the emergence of the natural sciences, as well as for the emergence of secularism and atheism.[36] The phrase "disenchantment of the world" was first used by the sociologist Max Weber in 1917 to refer to trends within Protestantism that emphasized the rationality of the natural world, while at the same time denying its mysteriousness.[37] For Weber, Protestantism encouraged the belief that "there are no mysterious incalculable forces" within the natural world.

Peter Berger's analysis of the role of Protestantism in causing secularization should be noted here.[38] For Berger, Protestantism can be thought of as

causing "an immense shrinkage in the scope of the sacred in reality."
Protestants did not see themselves as living in a world that was "ongoingly
penetrated by sacred beings and forces." Instead, they understood that
world to be "polarized between a radically transcendent divinity and a radically 'fallen' humanity" that was devoid of any sacred qualities or connections. Catholicism had contained secularizing forces through its deeply
symbolic understanding of the natural world, and humanity's place within
it. Protestantism permitted, even encouraged, ways of thinking about nature
that emphasized its rationality and predictability.

This process of "desacralization" or "disenchantment" is easily discerned
in the English situation. Landmark studies of pre-Reformation English religious life have emphasized the close ties between religion, the church, the
seasons of the year, the fertility of the land, and natural symbols.[39] Fifteenth-
century English religious life saw a blending of the sacred and natural, so
that their boundaries became porous and fuzzy. The natural world was considered to have profound spiritual and religious significance; its proper
functioning, however, required the ministrations of the church and its clergy.
Protestantism swept away this raft of assumptions, demanding and legiti-
mating "the destruction of a vast and resonant world of symbols."[40] The
divine was now mediated through a sacred text, rather than a natural world,
studded and emblazoned with sacred symbols.

This development has importance for an understanding of natural theology. Two leading features of this "disenchanted" and "rationalized" reading
of nature are of particular relevance here: first, the characteristic belief that
nature is devoid of mystery and is wholly accessible to the human understanding; and second, that nature itself is no longer to be regarded as being
in any sense "sacred," whether this is understood to mean being intrinsically
worthy of awe or dread, or inhabited by divine or demonic beings. Weber's
analysis of the impact of Protestantism on western understandings of nature
points to a growing emphasis upon the rationality, functionality, and intelligibility of the natural world.[41]

Where older approaches to natural theology embraced its affective and
imaginative aspects,[42] the Protestant emphasis upon the rationality of nature
led to natural theology increasingly being restricted to making sense of the
natural world. There have, of course, been important challenges to this kind
of aesthetic and imaginative deficit, most notably from within the Romantic
movement, with its emphasis on the importance of feeling and imagination
in any engagement with nature.[43] There is clearly a need to extend the scope
of natural theology to include the traditional Platonic triad of truth, beauty,
and goodness.[44] Nevertheless, this "desacralized" account of natural theology became normative for many English writers and is deeply embedded in
William Paley's classic statement of the approach, which we shall consider
in the next chapter.

English natural theology thus proceeded on the assumption that the human mind was capable of grasping at least something of the harmony of the universe. The deeper order of things discerned within nature was capable of elaboration at the intellectual, aesthetic, and moral levels. Alexander Pope's famous aphorism on style can be applied as much to natural theology as to the qualities of order, clarity, and stylistic decorum favored by the Augustan age:[45]

> Those rules of old *discover'd*, not *devis'd*,
> Are Nature still, but Nature methodiz'd.

This emphasis upon the religious significance of the ordering of nature had implications for the development of the natural sciences, which were as positive as they were important. For the religious apologists of the day, science and religion were two sides of the same coin. The image of the "two books of God" – the "book of nature" and the "book of Scripture" – accentuated the comprehensibility of the world.[46] Both could be understood, and represented rationally, whether in the theories of science or the creeds of the church. "Religion and science alike were concerned to describe a cosmos, all of whose phenomena made sense, manifested intelligence and design."[47] This vision of the intellectual harmony of the universe was easily integrated with the need for social cohesion and stability, especially in the aftermath of the Glorious Revolution of 1688.[48]

The cessation of miracles in nature

The distinctively English approach to natural theology emphasized the regularity and ordering of nature and was disinclined to consider reports of miraculous events within nature, which could be attributed to divine causality. Although this could be interpreted as evidence of the growing influence of rationalism upon natural theology, it is in fact an outcome of the Protestant theological convictions of this age. English Protestantism was generally hostile toward the notion of miracles within nature. The crystallization of this viewpoint is closely linked with the Church of England's critique of Roman Catholic attempts to convert its members through an appeal to miraculous healings and exorcisms, which was particularly significant in the late sixteenth century.[49]

Faced with a conspicuous lack of impressive miracles of its own, leading apologists of the Church of England responded by declaring the age of miracles to be past.[50] Miracles were only necessary in the first phase of Christian history; they played no role in the contemporary church. These views were well established as part of the English Protestant critique of Catholicism during the reign of Edward VI. In his *Confession of Faith* (1550), Bishop

John Hooper (1495–1555) declared that, Christ's divine authority having been established by his miracles, there was no need for further miracles in the divine ordering of things.[51] What were today termed "miracles" by Catholic apologists were really the work of Satan. True miracles are directed toward unbelievers, not believers, and are intended to confirm doctrine, not excite superstition. A distinct sociological agenda is easily discerned here: miracles are only for the vulgar and uneducated.

This sixteenth-century assertion of the cessation of miracles can thus be argued to be a distinctively English invention, setting the scene for approaches to natural theology that disregarded "signs and wonders" within nature, and focused instead on the regular – rather than the exceptional – patterns of the natural world. Miracles were traditionally defined in terms of disruption of the natural order of things, or a divine violation or suspension of the laws of nature. Most Protestant writers of this period affirmed miracles in the past, most notably in connection with the ministry of Jesus of Nazareth; they declined, however, to see them as a continuing aspect of the life of the contemporary church. It is certainly true that some Deist writers were critical of the category of the miraculous in general;[52] this critique, however, built upon an existing Protestant disinclination to take the category of the miraculous seriously.

The primary results of the seventeenth-century emphasis on the regularity of nature were thus to marginalize the role of the miraculous in academic theology, and to accentuate the apologetic significance of the regularity of the cosmic mechanism.[53] Yet a secondary result must also be noted: a subtle redefinition of the nature of the miraculous, in order that the category could be meaningfully retained within a Newtonian framework.[54] In his "Discourse of Miracles" (1701), for example, John Locke suggested that a miracle was essentially a "sensible operation" that was "above the comprehension of the spectator, and in his opinion contrary to the established course of nature."[55]

Others, however, argued that the entire mechanism of nature was a miracle, and that the regularization of the miraculous simply made human observers familiar with what were still to be considered miracles. Nehemiah Grew (1641–1712), for example, argued that over-familiarity with what was fundamentally miraculous – namely, the complex world of nature – merely persuaded many that it was "natural," rather than a miracle.[56] The distinction between a "miracle" and the "natural" thus lay in human perception, not in a deeper order of things. Newton himself argued that the essence of a "miracle" was not its divine origin, but its infrequency:[57]

> If [miracles] should happen constantly according to certain laws impressed upon the nature of things, they would be no longer wonders or miracles but would be considered in philosophy as part of the phenomena of nature, notwithstanding that the cause of their causes might be unknown to us.

Miracles, as Newton points out, cannot happen regularly; they are then regarded simply as the natural course of things.

The providential guidance of nature

While miracles within nature were regarded with suspicion, English Protestantism strongly embraced the notion of divine providence.[58] The divine guidance of nature and history was regarded as a "given" by Protestants of the early seventeenth century. Was not the rise of an explicitly Protestant England under Elizabeth I to be seen as the work of divine providence?[59] While many saw the mysterious workings of providence lying primarily in the curious twists and turns of history, others saw it in action in the reliability of the natural order. The notion of the "laws of nature," which gained considerable cultural traction in England during the late seventeenth century, was widely interpreted in terms of divine providence superintending the affairs of nature.[60]

This aspect of the "Augustan age" is so well documented that it need not be discussed further. The notion of divine providence was easily integrated within the framework of a harmonious vision of nature, history, and society, affirming a vision of a stable cosmos on the one hand, and a stable society on the other. Taken together, these developments had considerable implications for the notions of natural theology that became dominant during the late seventeenth century, whether as causes, influences, or synergies. The portrait of the universe developed during the Augustan age was that of a harmonious system, whose regularities reflected and expressed God's providence. English natural theology increasingly came to focus on the law-like regularities of nature. Positively, this was seen as an affirmation of the operation of divine providence; negatively, as a critique of exaggerated and emotive accounts of natural wonders, intended to influence the religiously credible. It would be the regularities of nature, not their alleged violations through miraculous intervention, that would be the chief focus of English natural theology.

A Foundation for Consensus: The Doctrine of Creation

The sixteenth-century Reformation unleashed a torrent of debate over many aspects of Christian theology, which continued unabated in early seventeenth-century England. Arminians and Calvinists were bitterly divided over the doctrine of grace; Anglicans, Presbyterians, Congregationalists, and Independents fought over the doctrine of the church, and the theology and practice of the sacraments.[61] These tensions continued into the Puritan Commonwealth, with theological divisions within Puritanism being heightened, rather than resolved, through its new political power.

The Augustan age wanted nothing of this theological fractiousness. A public theology was required with minimal specific creedal demands and maximum shared common ground. It soon became clear that the doctrine of creation offered the foundation of a unifying public theology, capable of forging the theological and social consensus to which this age aspired. This doctrine had not proved to be contentious, functioning as a source of division neither in the Reformation itself,[62] nor in the theological debates of the Jacobean and Caroline eras. Although nuanced in different ways by Deists and theists, the doctrine easily functioned as the "lowest common denominator" unifying an otherwise disparate, and potentially fractious, English Protestantism. The "Newtonian synthesis" rested largely on an emphasis upon this doctrine, judiciously interpreted as implying the divine providential guidance of the created order.

The significance of this development for natural theology during the Augustan age can hardly be overlooked. The realization that the doctrine of creation offered the basis of a consensual public theology was supplemented by a growing appreciation of its importance for the increasingly significant scientific enterprise. The doctrine of creation affirmed a regular, reliable natural order (while suggesting an equal stability within its social counterpart), which was open to empirical investigation.

If any work may be singled out as solidifying and expressing this consensus on the doctrine of creation, it is John Pearson's *Exposition of the Creed* (1659). Pearson (1613–86) was a learned establishment figure of the Restoration era, who was successively Lady Margaret Professor of Divinity at Cambridge; Master of Trinity College, Cambridge; and finally Bishop of Chester. He served as chaplain to Charles II, and was elected a fellow of the Royal Society in 1667. His *Exposition of the Creed* is noted for its comprehensive engagement with patristic writers, and is often cited as a model of classical Anglican divinity.[63] This work exercised a calming influence in a period of theological turbulence, and can be seen as an important constituent element of the religious consensus that emerged within England in the late seventeenth and early eighteenth centuries. Dr Samuel Johnson (1709–84) spoke highly of Pearson's work, and commended it as a model of persuasive, generous orthodoxy.[64] Most Anglican theologians of the late seventeenth and eighteenth centuries seemed content to base much of their theology on Pearson's *Exposition*, which was treated as a benchmark of Anglican orthodoxy.

As we shall note later in this work (218–22), the understandings of creation that became dominant during the Augustan age assumed a static understanding of a recent creation. The idea that the world was created more or less exactly in its present form some six thousand years ago was integral to the Augustan consensus; these assumptions, however unproblematic they may have seemed in 1690, were increasingly seen as a liability by 1850.

The distinctively English approach to natural theology here outlined wove together a number of intellectual and cultural threads, reflecting the complex situation of the Augustan age. The perceived threat of atheism and materialism allowed thinkers drawn from a wide variety of forms of Protestantism to collaborate on the basis of their lowest common intellectual denominator – the belief in a divine creator, and divine providence. This minimalist approach to matters of theology was credally inclusive, and thus able to generate collaborative enterprises from a surprisingly wide range of individuals who might otherwise disagree on questions of Christology, ecclesiology, or eschatology.[65] Furthermore, this alliance of Protestant Christianity and Newtonian natural philosophy ensured that academic study of the natural world took place within a religious environment, rather than being envisaged as an external threat to religious authority or identity. Indeed, one of its most obvious outcomes was that some of the most enthusiastic practitioners of natural philosophy during the eighteenth century were the clergy of the established church.[66]

Physico-theology: The Appeal to Contrivance

One of the most distinctive features of the styles of natural theology to emerge in England during the eighteenth century is the appeal to natural history in Christian apologetics.[67] Although English apologetic writers prior to 1690 made use of traditional theistic apologetic approaches to the natural world, these lacked the distinctive features of "physico-theology" – namely, a form of natural theology that emphasizes adaptive design in nature directed toward the accomplishment of purposeful ends:[68]

[Earlier writers] were more likely to use a priori reasoning and revealed doctrine. They appealed variously to the order, beauty, and hierarchy of the creation; the logical necessity of a creation or a first cause; the universal belief of all men in God; the providential care of the world and punishment of atheists; the adaptation of the creatures (organic and inorganic) to their own appointed ends and to man's use; the mystery of man's body and of his soul; the impossibility of chance having produced the world; the logical absurdity of atheism; and evidences of divine intervention in nature and in history.

Although cumbersome, the term "physico-theology" can usefully be employed to identify the specific approach to natural theology that focuses on appearances of design within the natural world, both physical and biological.[69] Nature is here understood and interpreted as an intelligently contrived adaptation of means to ends. The approach is often characterized by an appeal to the notion of "contrivance," which is held to indicate both

Effigies Reverendi admodum veri Johannis Wilkins nuper Episcopi Cestriensis.

Figure 3.2   John Wilkins (1614–72), English mathematician and founder of the Royal Society, c. 1655, in an engraving of 1708.

being designed for a specific purpose, and being executed in a manner conducive toward this end. Contrivance thus implies both wisdom in design, and ingenuity in construction. Although many writers saw evidence of design in nature as a whole, emphasis came to be placed increasingly upon the biological domain.

John Wilkins (1614–72) can be seen as a representative of an older position, which made a broad appeal to nature in support of belief in God. In his *Principles and Duties of Natural Religion* (published posthumously in 1675), Wilkins set out four broad arguments for the existence of God: "From the universal consent and agreement of Mankind"; "From the Original of the World"; "From the admirable contrivance of Natural Things"; and "From Providence, and the Government of the World." The third of these arguments outlines the approach that would come to dominate English natural theology in the following century. Wilkins sets out the scope of his sixth chapter, dealing with the notion of contrivance, by appealing to:[70]

> ... that excellent Contrivance which there is in all natural things. Both with respect to that elegance and beauty which they have in themselves separately considered, and that regular order and subserviency wherein they stand towards one another; together with the exact fitness and propriety, for the several purposes for which they are designed. From all which it may be inferred, these are the productions of some Wise Agent.

Wilkins notes how technological advance has enabled a greater appreciation of these divine contrivances: the microscope, for example, discloses more fully how nature is "adorned with all imaginable elegance and beauty."[71] For Wilkins, the intelligent observer of nature can only conclude that it has been "contrived by the wisest agent."[72] Yet this appeal to contrivance is only part of Wilkins's cumulative approach to natural theology. It is enmeshed with a wider range of approaches, reflecting older traditions. In some ways, Wilkins can be seen as a figure of transition, opening the door to a new emphasis upon appearances of design as evidence of divine creation.

It is important to note that an essentially static view of nature underlies Wilkins's natural theology. The natural realm, as now observed, is more or less identical with the primordial realm of divine creation. "The most sagacious man is not able to find out any blot or error in this great volume of the world, as if any thing in it had been an imperfect essay at the first, such as afterwards stood in need of mending: But all things continue as they were from the beginning of the Creation."[73] This fundamental principle is often assumed without discussion as self-evidently true, or else held to rest that any form of development within the natural domain would imply imperfection in the past within the created order – a notion that clearly raised theological difficulties for Wilkins.

Robert Boyle (1627–91), inspired by Galen's account of the teleological aspects of the human muscular system,[74] also appealed to the notion of contrivance in his account of natural theology, arguing that the biological domain held greater apologetic potential than its astronomical counterpart. He declared that he saw "more of admirable contrivance in a man's muscles, than in (what we yet know of) the coelestial orbs," and that the eye of a fly was "(at least as far as appears to us) a more curious piece of workmanship than the body of the sun."[75] For Boyle, the exquisite design and workmanship of the great cathedral clock of Strasbourg – one of the great mechanical marvels of the age[76] – was overshadowed by the greater contrivances of the biological world.[77]

> I never saw any inanimate production of nature, or, as they speak, of chance, whose contrivance was comparable to that of the meanest limb of the despicablest animal: and there is incomparably more art expressed in the structure of a dog's foot, than in the famous clock at Strassburg.

The image of the universe as a clock is often regarded as emblematic of the "mechanical philosophy" of this age,[78] and the natural theology that it developed – God as the cosmic watchmaker. For Boyle, the contemplation of nature was inextricably bound with the contemplation and praise of its creator:[79]

> The knowledge of the works of God proportions our admiration of them, they participating and disclosing so much of the inexhausted perfections of their author, that the further we contemplate them, the more footsteps and impressions we discover of the perfections of their Creator, and our utmost science can but give us a juster veneration of his omniscience.

Those forms of natural theology that dominated the English context prior to 1690 sought to demonstrate the existence of God and a divine order through reflection on the regularities of the natural world. Yet after 1690, these were no longer deemed to be sufficient for the challenges faced by both church and society. It was now necessary to produce evidence of design, of purposes and ends within nature itself, which could be shown to point to a God who actively designed and constructed the world. This transition from a more general appeal to the natural world to one that focused on evidence of design can be seen in one of the most important statements of "physico-theology": John Ray's *Wisdom of God Manifested in the Works of the Creation* (1691). According to Ray (1627–1705), the primary cause and preferred consequence of natural theology was the proper human desire to worship the creator through a proper appreciation of the form of his creation. The primary function of natural theology was thus to reveal and encourage the contemplation of the wisdom of God, rather than to demonstrate the divine power or will. It must be understood that Ray stood at an important juncture, marking a growing reluctance in academic circles to appeal to the category of the "miraculous" in defense of Christian truth claims.[80] Miracles were seen as controverting the laws of nature; was there not greater apologetic potential in appealing to those laws, which could be interpreted as evidence of divine design and wisdom? Ray's emphasis on the regularity of nature, including a subtle marginalization of the miraculous in theistic apologetics, became an important feature of the emerging English approach to natural theology.[81]

While an appeal to miracles continued to be important in popular English Christian apologetics until the end of the eighteenth century,[82] it no longer played a critical role in academic natural theology. At a popular level, an appeal to miracles continued to be one of the strongest weapons in the armory of Christian apologists. Yet the growing scientific emphasis upon the regularity of the world caused appeals to the miraculous to be seen as contrived and naive, perhaps even representing a degeneration into the realm of fairy tale and invention. The dominant view within Anglicanism at this time was that miracles had ceased with the closing of the apostolic period, and were no longer encountered in everyday experience.[83]

Nevertheless, the historical question of the nature of Christ's miracles remained important. Some writers attempted to bridge the gap between these two approaches, by setting Christ's miracles within the context of natural philosophy as a whole. In his *History of the Royal Society* (1667), for example, Thomas Sprat (1635–1713), suggested that there might be a relationship between miracles, which demonstrated the truth of Christ's message in the gospel narratives, and the experiments that uncovered the structure and ordering of the natural world.[84] For Sprat, miracles could be seen as an experimental confirmation of Christ's divine authority to teach:[85]

Figure 3.3 A meeting of the Royal Society in Crane Court, Fleet Street, where it had rooms from 1710 to 1782. Isaac Newton is in the President's chair. Artist's reconstruction. Wood engraving c. 1880.

> Had not the appearance of Christ bin strengthen'd by undeniable signs of almighty Power, no age nor place had bin oblig'd to believe his Message. And these Miracles with which he asserted the Truths that he taught (if I might be allow'd this boldness in a matter so sacred) I would even venture to call Divine *Experiments* of his God-head.

Yet this historical question was not seen as posing challenges to the present observation of the regularity and lawfulness of the natural realm, nor to reflections on the theological significance of these observations. For Sprat, miracles were a divine prerogative to be exercised only in situations of exceptional human dullness, when human beings failed to be attentive to the signs of divine presence and wisdom in the natural order.[86]

> God never left himself without witness in the world; and it is observable that, he has commonly chosen the dark and ignorant Ages, wherein to work Miracles; but seldom or never the times when *Natural Knowledge* prevailed. For he knew that there was not so much need to make use of extraordinary signs, when men were diligent in the works of his hands, and attentive on the impressions of his footsteps on his *Creatures*.

The historical specifics of the period of the ministry of Jesus of Nazareth could thus be affirmed, while at the same time declared to be of no continuing importance in other periods of history, particularly when "natural knowledge" – which Sprat clearly understands to refer to "scientific inquiry"[87] – prevails.

English natural theologians of the late seventeenth century had no doubt that they lived in a time when "natural knowledge" flourished, with implications for natural theology as positive as they were significant. For John Ray, nature discloses evidence of design and intentionality, pointing conclusively to an intelligent agent who "contrived" the natural world. While acknowledging the importance of the inorganic world, it is clear that Ray's real interest lies in the biological realm. Following Galen, he appeals to the complex structure of the human body. "The wonderful art and providence of the Contriver and Former of our bodies, appears in the multitude of intentions he must have in the formation of the several parts, or the qualifications they require to fit them for their several uses."[88]

Ray can be seen as providing a definitive formulation of the argument that would dominate British natural theology. The natural world, especially the world of plants and animals, shows evidence of contrivance, from which the existence of an intelligent agent who is capable of both design and construction may be inferred. Ray's statement of his own approach merits close study:[89]

> There is no greater, at least no more palpable and convincing argument of the existence of a Deity, than the admirable art and wisdom that discovers itself in the make and constitution, the order and disposition, the ends and uses of all the parts and members of this stately fabrick of Heaven and Earth: For if in the works of art (as for example) a curious edifice, or machine, council, design, and direction, to an end appearing in the whole frame, and in all the several pieces of it, do necessarily infer the being and operation of some intelligent architect, or engineer; why should not also, in the works of Nature, that grandeur and magnificence, that excellent contrivance for beauty, order, use, &c. which is observable in them, wherein they do as much transcend the effects of human art, as infinite power and wisdom exceeds finite, infer the existence and efficiency of an omnipotent and all-wise Creator?

There is a vigorous, though often merely rhetorical, rejection throughout Ray's work of any idea that nature could somehow generate such complexities out of its own raw material. For example, he notes the atheist objection that the phenomena he catalogues are mistakenly interpreted as "tokens of skill and contrivance," when in reality they are nothing more than "necessary consequences of the present existence of those creatures to which they belong."[90] Ray's dismissal of such a position as "pretence and sophistry" seems a little curt and superficial to modern readers. Ray's comments may be illuminating in disclosing the rhetorical conventions and assumptions of his age; in the light of later developments, however, they seem disturbingly inadequate.

More significantly, Wilkins and other writers of this school of thought regularly treat "design" and "chance" as mutually exclusive notions.[91] The regularity of the universe precludes chance, as does the operation of divine providence. Wilkins does not provide a detailed discussion of the nature of chance, probably assuming that his readers will concede his point without dispute. However, it must be pointed out that the Christian tradition includes alternative accounts of this matter, in which chance is seen as a means by which God's providential government takes place. For example, Thomas Aquinas holds that the presence of chance in the world is something that God intends, in that this is conducive toward a more varied and hierarchical world than one in which every agent necessarily achieved its end.[92]

The profile of natural theology in the early eighteenth century was boosted considerably through the celebrated "Boyle Lectures."[93] Shortly before his death in 1691, Robert Boyle bequeathed a sum of money that was to endow a series of lectures, to be devoted to "proving the Christian Religion against notorious Infidels." The lectures rapidly became the bulwark of the Church of England's campaign against the growing rise of skepticism within society at large. Boyle himself seemed to see natural theology as the outcome, not the foundation, of his faith.[94] Yet he was not unaware of the apologetic implications of such a natural theology, and its relevance to the situation of the Church of England at that time. Where some sought to distance science and religion,[95] others sought to harmonize them within a comprehensive view of God and the world.

The Boyle Lectures, delivered over the forty-year period 1692–1732, are widely regarded as the most significant public demonstration of the "reasonableness" of Christianity in the early modern period, characterized by that era's growing emphasis upon rationalism and its increasing suspicion of ecclesiastical authority.[96] They sought to offer a publicly persuasive "confutation of atheism" – the title of the first series of Boyle Lectures, delivered in 1692 by Richard Bentley.[97]

These lectures may have raised the profile of English natural theology;[98] they did not, however, advance its substance. Bentley's eight lectures reflect the themes that were then becoming characteristic of English natural theology.[99] The first two lectures were refutations of atheism based on the social role of religion and the impossibility of a purely materialist worldview. The next three lectures dealt with evidence of design in the structure of the human body, while the final three dealt with the theme of "the confutation of atheism from the origin and frame of the world." The notion of contrivance plays a significant role in these lectures. "The contemplation of our own bodies, which have all the stamps and characters of excellent contrivances," Bentley argued, "do very easily and proximately guide us to the wise Author of all things."[100]

Newton's inspiration is evident throughout Bentley's lectures. Yet Newton inspired poets, as much as apologetic preachers and writers of scientific prose. In recent years, the importance of Newton's work as a source of poetic inspiration has been explored.[101] The fundamental themes of Newton's physico-theology are reflected in *Creation* (1712), an epic poem in seven parts by Richard Blackmore (1654–1729). In this poem, Blackmore set out to "demonstrate the existence of a Divine Eternal Mind" by developing arguments based on "the various marks of wisdom and artful contrivance," which are evident in both the "material world and the faculties of the human mind."[102] The opening part of the work emphasizes the derivation of the observed ordering of the world from its creator:[103]

> Order from thee, and from thee distinction came,
> And all the beauties of the wond'rous frame;
> Hence stampt on nature we perfection find,
> Fair as th'idea in th'eternal mind.

Blackmore was emphatic that the intellectual virtues of the created order were not restricted to its rationality; the intrinsic beauty of the heavens pointed to their divine origins:[104]

> Nature's high birth, her heavenly beauties show;
> By ev'ry feature we the parent know.

This latter theme would be developed more extensively in a work also published in 1712 – Joseph Addison's "Ode," to which we shall return presently (72–3).

An essentially Newtonian approach, similar to that of Wilkins and Bentley, was adopted by William Derham in his Boyle Lectures of 1711–12, published as *Physico-Theology: Or, a Demonstration of the Being and Attributes of God* (1713). Throughout this work, we find constant emphasis on the contrivances of the natural world. Derham sees evidence of design throughout the natural world. He lauded Newton's discovery of the role of gravitation in ordering and stabilizing the solar system, declaring that this gravity was a "noble contrivance of the Creator."[105] Yet Derham is clearly impatient to move from the physical to the biological domain; his numerous examples of the "excellent contrivances" of God in creating the world include the dispersion of sensory capacities throughout the human body,[106] and the complex structures of the respiratory system.[107] Even humble vegetables disclose the "Creator's contrivance."[108] Derham concludes his panoramic survey of the contrivances of nature with a declaration that such contrivances exceed in number and in excellence anything that human beings have ever designed or constructed.[109] Again, we must note the accentuation of the biological domain as evidence of divine design – a theme of major importance in understanding the impact of Darwinism.

Derham's seeming neglect of the physical realm was redressed to some extent in his *Astro-Theology: Or, a Demonstration of the Being and Attributes of God, from a Survey of the Heavens* (1714). The work is remarkable on several counts, not least that it is partly based on Derham's own astronomical observations using an early refracting telescope (which he refers to as "Mr Huygens' glass"). This relatively short work offers an important defense of accommodated methods of biblical interpretation in support of the Copernican view of the solar system. After a detailed survey of the heavens, Derham concluded that what was known of astronomy confirmed the existence of a "Contriver and Maker,"[110] ridiculing those who ascribed them to natural necessity or chance. Yet the reader of this work cannot help but notice that the precision of analysis and confidence of exposition that characterized Derham's *Physico-Theology* is not present in its astronomical counterpart. By the middle of the eighteenth century, the biological domain was generally recognized as apologetically more fruitful than its physical counterpart.[111]

This importance of this transition merits more detailed discussion in its own right. The new impetus given to English natural theology in the seventeenth century by the work of Isaac Newton originated from the realms of astronomy and physics. Newton spoke of God's "contrivance" of the solar system, noting with approval how its mechanical subtleties pointed toward an intelligent designer. By the middle of the seventeenth century, the notion of "contrivance" and its associated arguments from design had largely been transferred from the physical to the biological realm. While many writers focused on the observable structures of the living world, holding that these could not be explained without recourse to divine contrivance and providence, others appealed to the mechanisms that seemed to underlie them – most notably, the apparently perfect balance between male and female births. This observation attracted the attention of John Arbuthnot (1667–1735), who contributed a learned article in 1710 concerning "the exact balance that is maintained between the numbers of men and women," which he interpreted teleologically.[112] This perfect balance, he declared, was a sure indication of the operation of divine providence, so "that the Species may never fail, nor perish."[113]

This may reflect, in part, the growing popular interest in natural history around this time, which led to increased popular interest in the plant and animal worlds.[114] The complexities and adaptations of the biological sphere proved much easier to describe and analyze than the movements of the planets, which often required to be described mathematically (and hence inaccessibly). William Paley's celebrated *Natural Theology* (1802) – which makes its apologetic appeal largely to the biological world, for reasons we shall consider in the following chapter – is rightly to be seen as marking the popular climax of this tradition of natural theology.

Natural Theology and the Beauty of Nature

The analysis thus far points to the importance of the ordering of nature in English natural theology of the Augustan age. Where some were initially content to take pleasure in the regularity of the natural world, seeing this as a confirmation of its divine origins, the shifting cultural context led to the emergence of what were perceived by its proponents as a stronger statement of natural theology, which argued from observed instances of "contrivance" within nature to their divine designer. Yet both approaches affirmed the harmony of nature, seeing its divine design or origins as reflected in the beauty of the natural world and the patterns it disclosed. Especially during the early eighteenth century, this led to an appeal to the beauty of the natural world as an element of a natural theology.

A writer who develops this approach with particular clarity is Joseph Addison (1672–1719), founder of the *Spectator* magazine. Addison took the view that a certain capacity to discern and take delight in the beauty of creation was, so to speak, "hard-wired" into human nature.[115] In a series of articles published in the *Spectator*, Addison developed arguments for the inference of God from the observation of nature. In some respects, these can be seen as following the standard pattern of argument typical of the age, reflecting in particular the arguments set out by William Derham in his Boyle Lectures of 1711–12, later published as *Physico-Theology* (1713).[116] For example, in August 1712, Addison declared that "the Supreme Being has made the best Arguments for his own Existence, in the Formation of the Heavens and the Earth, and these are Arguments which a Man of Sense cannot forbear attending to."[117]

Yet Addison extends this "argument from design" by drawing attention to the "pleasures" of imagination derived from viewing nature, whether directly or indirectly through forms of art that imitate her. On this approach, nature is to be thought of, not so much as a "contrivance," but as a work of art. Because nature is conceived as *God's* art, the design argument can now be grounded on what is essentially an *aesthetic* analogy: "it is God the orderer, the consummate artist, the pragmatic designer melding form and function, who is manifested in the natural world."[118]

Addison thus finds evidence of divine design in the harmony of the universe, as expressed in his "Ode" (1712):[119]

> The spacious firmament on high,
> With all the blue æthereal sky,
> And spangled heavens, a shining frame,
> Their great Original proclaim:
> Th' unwearied sun from day to day,
> Does his Creator's pow'r display,
> And publishes to every land
> The work of an Almighty hand.

Addison's natural theology, as expressed in this "Ode," is based on the belief that the regularity and harmony of the firmaments proclaim, display, and publish their divine origination. To use a distinction noted earlier, this is an argument *from* design, rather than an argument *to* design. Although the idea of nature as a divine contrivance is implicit within the "Ode," this is not made explicit. In effect, the work is to be seen as an elaboration on the text "The heavens declare the glory of the Lord" (Psalm 19:1), including its implied assumption that nature actively discloses the divine nature.

Yet Addison's natural theology also makes an appeal to the imagination.[120] In his important "Essays on the Pleasures of the Imagination," Addison argues that the poetic observer of nature has "the modelling of Nature in his own Hands, and may give her what Charms he pleases."[121] This naturally raises the question of whether he holds that the beauty of nature is constructed by the human observer, rather than being intrinsic to nature itself. Is a natural theology discerned from, or imposed upon, nature? It is a difficult question to answer, in that Addison clearly holds that it is possible to construct and inhabit imaginary worlds, partly as a means of escape from the grim realities of everyday life. Consider, for example, the following:[122]

> Our Souls are at present delightfully lost and bewildered in a pleasing Delusion, and we walk about like the Enchanted Hero of a Romance, who sees beautiful Castles, Woods and Meadows; and at the same time hears the warbling of Birds, and the purling of Streams; but upon the finishing of some secret Spell, the fantastick Scene breaks up, and the disconsolate Knight finds himself on a barren Heath, or in a solitary Desart.

Are we to understand that the vision of natural beauty and harmony depicted in the "Ode" is a "pleasing delusion" sustained by an act of imagination, rather than a defensible act of rational inference?

In the end, it is impossible to give a conclusive answer. There are points at which Addison seems to waver in his natural theology – as, for example, when he observes how "chance" formations in a stone can appear designed to its observer, thus simulating an "effect of design."[123] Such a simulation of design by chance clearly raises concerns for Addison's argument from design; nevertheless, they are not pursued. Yet there are other points at which Addison clearly indicates that he regards his natural theology to rest upon an act of reason, reflecting upon what is observed – as, for example, in the concluding quatrain of the "Ode":

> In Reason's ear they all rejoice,
> And utter forth a glorious voice,
> For ever singing, as they shine,
> "The Hand that made us is Divine."

The Problem of Development within Nature

Much English natural theology of the late seventeenth and early eighteenth centuries was content to treat the natural world as a fixed entity. Change was certainly observable within the natural world. Yet this was generally interpreted in terms of cyclical patterns operating within an essentially static framework. The life cycles in which individual human beings, plants, and animals were born, developed, and died were not seen as introducing anything new into the natural world; they were simply cyclical components of an essentially static nature. Nothing fundamentally new took place, in that the same life cycles merely repeated themselves. Newly born animals replaced those that had died. The natural world could be treated as a mechanism, whose regular functioning according to a set of determinable principles was in itself seen as evidence of its design by an intelligent Creator.

Early English natural theology thus operated with an essentially fixed or static notion of the natural world, within which the notion of an evolving creation was virtually impossible to locate. Yet not all were satisfied with such an approach. What if the natural world changed over time? Did the Christian faith necessarily entail that God created the world in precisely the shape and form that we now observe? Although these questions were raised during the patristic age, most English theological writers of the Augustan age do not appear to have been aware of such earlier discussions, let alone to have considered them of potential utility for contemporary discussions. The hesitation over exploring these questions probably reflects a degree of anxiety over straying into possibly heterodox theological pathways. Might a theology of creation that allowed the material world to develop over time compromise core aspects of the Christian doctrine of God?[124]

The attribution of agency or causality to the material world seemed tantamount to atheism, in that it removed any necessity for divine action or agency in the governance of the world.[125] Thomas Hobbes, for example, articulated a form of atheism based upon a deterministic world. God might have created the mechanisms of nature, and initiated their actions. Yet thereafter, further divine involvement was unnecessary.[126] A mechanical model of nature seemed to require an equally mechanical model of divine providence, which seemed to demand a revised and reduced notion of both divine identity and causality.[127] Christian theologians of the seventeenth and eighteenth centuries were alert to this difficulty, even if its resolution proved to be more elusive than many had hoped. Isaac Barrow (1630–77) sought to resolve the issue through interpreting God's ongoing involvement with nature in terms of the injection of energy and activity into the world in an ultimately inscrutable manner.[128]

Assessing Evidence: Changing Public Perceptions

One final matter must be discussed before proceeding further. The works of natural theology published between 1650 and 1800 presuppose an audience that has certain expectations and assumptions concerning how evidence is to be assessed. The evidence suggests that seventeenth- and eighteenth-century audiences and readerships gave precedence to the evidence of the senses.[129] Whether debates concerned the evidence in legal cases, scientific argumentation, or even natural theology, emphasis came to be placed on what could be seen directly.[130] This may be interpreted as a reaction against the perceived inadequacies of certain Renaissance philosophies, which accentuated the importance of absolute certainty; this came to be replaced with the notion of "the probable," based on a reading of "appearances."

Some have seen the empirical philosophy of Francis Bacon as lying behind this development, most notably his idea of putting nature on trial, in order that her secrets might be discovered.[131] Nature discloses evidence in her own innate language, unaffected by the inadequacies and peculiarities of human language. This leads to the formulation of preliminary axioms, which in turn lead to the discovery and design of new "trials," thus generating further new axioms, and leading on to successively higher levels of abstraction. Yet whatever its origins, the predominant account of natural history – and hence natural theology – in the early eighteenth century is that of the direct observation of the world of nature, leading to the conclusion that it demonstrates evidence of design. Design is thus understood, not as something that is *inferred* from observation, but as something that is itself *observed* within nature.

This becomes clear from a close reading of leading representatives of "physico-theology," the form of natural theology that focuses on evidence of design. William Derham speaks of "contrivance" – that is, that something has been designed and constructed – as being "shown" or "manifested" within nature, and capable of being discerned directly by the observer. The divine design of nature is something that can be directly read off the appearances of nature. Aspects of human nature, such as respiration, "plainly shew design, reason, and contrivance";[132] the eyelids are a "manifestation of the Creator's contrivance";[133] the muscles of the eye are "manifestly an act of contrivance and design."[134] Derham is particularly impressed by the circulation of blood in the fetus in the human womb, which he declares to be a "prodigious work of nature, and manifest contrivance of the Almighty Creator."[135] Nor does this discernment of contrivance require faith on the part of the observer; for Derham, all peoples of every nation can "with admiration see the great Creator's wonderful art and contrivance in the parts of animals and vegetables."[136]

Yet the weakness of this position could not be overlooked. What if observations were misinterpreted, or misunderstood? To what extent did the observation of nature simply represent the unconscious repetition of socially dominant paradigms of interpretation? In the early nineteenth century, such approaches to evidence came under close scrutiny, leading to significant modification of public perceptions concerning their reliability. As we shall see, these cultural shifts had important implications for natural theology.

Our attention now turns to possibly the most famous popular English work of "physico-theology" – William Paley's *Natural Theology* (1802).

Notes

1   See Doering, Detmar, *Die Wiederkehr der Klugheit: Edmund Burke und das "Augustan Age."* Würzburg: Königshausen & Neumann, 1990, 27–99.

2   Stillman, Robert E., *Philip Sidney and the Poetics of Renaissance Cosmopolitanism*. Aldershot: Ashgate, 2008, 210. A possible source of Sidney's approach to natural law is the German Lutheran theologian Philip Melanchthon (1497–1560), whose ideas Sidney would have encountered through colleagues such as Hubert Languet (1518–81). On Melanchthon on natural law, see Wengert, Timothy J., *Human Freedom, Christian Righteousness: Philip Melanchthon's Exegetical Dispute with Erasmus of Rotterdam*. New York: Oxford University Press, 1998, 139–58.

3   See especially Hooker, Richard, *Laws of Ecclesiastical Polity*, I.ii.3. In *Works of Richard Hooker*. 6 vols. Cambridge, MA: Belknap Press, 1977–93, vol. 1, 59–60. See further Voak, Nigel, *Richard Hooker and Reformed Theology: A Study of Reason, Will, and Grace*. Oxford; New York: Oxford University Press, 2003, 112–18.

4   Peterfreund, Stuart, "Imagination at a Distance: Bacon's Epistemological Double-Bind, Natural Theology, and the Way of Scientific Discourse in the Seventeenth and Eighteenth Centuries." *The Eighteenth Century: Theory and Interpretation* 21 (2000): 110–40.

5   Howell, Kenneth J., *God's Two Books: Copernican Cosmology and Biblical Interpretation in Early Modern Science*. Notre Dame, IN: University of Notre Dame Press, 2002, 109–35.

6   On this unusual and eclectic work, see Preston, Claire, *Thomas Browne and the Writing of Early Modern Science*. Cambridge: Cambridge University Press, 2005, 42–81.

7   Browne, Thomas, *Religio Medici*. London: Pickering, 1845, 39–40.

8   Kirby, W. J. Torrance, *Richard Hooker's Doctrine of the Royal Supremacy*. Leiden: Brill, 1990, 92–122.

9   Berensmeyer, Ingo, "Rhetoric, Religion, and Politics in Sir Thomas Browne's *Religio Medici*." *Studies in English Literature 1500–1900* 46 (2006): 113–32.

10   For the role of science in relation to the quest for certainty, see Van Leeuwen, Henry G., *The Problem of Certainty in English Thought, 1630–1690*. 2nd edn. The Hague: Nijhoff, 1990, 90–120.

11 Westfall, Richard S., "The Scientific Revolution of the Seventeenth Century: A New World View." In *The Concept of Nature*, ed. John Torrance, 63–93. Oxford: Oxford University Press, 1992.

12 For Barth's general assessment of this development, see his important essay on humanity in the eighteenth century: Barth, Karl, *Die Protestantische Theologie im 19. Jahrhundert*. Zurich: Evangelischer Verlag, 1957, 16–59. On the importance of natural theology in relation to the "autonomy" theme, see Gestrich, Christof, *Neuzeitliches Denken und die Spaltung der dialektischen Theologie: Zur Frage der natürlichen Theologie*. Tübingen: Mohr, 1977, 381–93.

13 On this general point, see Prenter, Regin, "Das Problem der natürlichen Theologie bei Karl Barth." *Theologische Literaturzeitung* 77 (1952): 607–11; Torrance, Thomas F., "The Problem of Natural Theology in the Thought of Karl Barth." *Religious Studies* 6 (1970): 121–35.

14 For the best study of this development, see Reventlow, Henning, *Bibelautorität und Geist der Moderne: Die Bedeutung des Bibelverstandnisses für die Geistesgeschichtliche und politische Entwicklung in England von der Reformation bis zur Aufklärung*. Göttingen: Vandenhoeck & Ruprecht, 1980, 161–469.

15 For this complex dynamic, see Gaukroger, Stephen, "Science, Religion and Modernity." *Critical Quarterly* 47, no. 4 (2005): 1–31.

16 See here Lewis, Eric, "Walter Charleton and Early Modern Eclecticism." *Journal of the History of Ideas* 62 (2001): 651–64.

17 For an important early clarification of this point, see Philipp, Wolfgang, "Physicotheology in the Age of Enlightenment: Appearance and History." *Studies on Voltaire and the Eighteenth Century* 57 (1967): 1233–67.

18 See, for example, Cheyne, George, *Philosophical Principles of Religion Natural and Reveal'd*. 2nd edn. London: George Strahan, 1715, 45: "All of nature supposes Design and Contrivance, and consequently is a sign of Production or Creation."

19 See the arguments of Jacob, Margaret C., *The Newtonians and the English Revolution 1689–1720*. Ithaca, NY: Cornell University Press, 1976, especially 162–200.

20 Cornell, John F., "Newton of the Grassblade? Darwin and the Problem of Organic Teleology." *Isis* 77 (1986): 405–21; Gascoigne, John, "From Bentley to the Victorians: The Rise and Fall of British Newtonian Natural Theology." *Science in Context* 2 (1988): 219–56.

21 For this intriguing development, see Iliffe, Robert, " 'Is He Like Other Men?' The Meaning of the *Principia Mathematica* and the Author as Idol." In *Culture and Society in the Stuart Restoration*, ed. Gerald Maclean, 159–76. Cambridge: Cambridge University Press, 1995.

22 Newton, Isaac, "General Scholium." In *Sir Isaac Newton's Mathematical Principles of Natural Philosophy and His System of the World*, 543–7. Berkeley, CA: University of California Press, 1962.

23 Schoot, Albert van der, "Kepler's Search for Form and Proportion." *Renaissance Studies* 15 (2001): 59–78, especially 59–61.

24 Kepler, Johann, *Gesammelte Werke*, ed. Max Caspar. 22 vols. Munich: C. H. Beck, 1937–83, vol. 6, 233. For medieval notions of the world as a machine, see Bartlett, Robert, *The Natural and Supernatural in the Middle Ages*. Cambridge: Cambridge University Press, 2008, 35–70.

25 Other possible sources should be noted, not least the works of Isaac Barrow: see especially Malet, Antoni, "Isaac Barrow on the Mathematization of Nature: Theological Voluntarism and the Rise of Geometrical Optics." *Journal of the History of Ideas* 58 (1997): 265–87.

26 For the development of this idea, see Osler, Margaret J., *Divine Will and the Mechanical Philosophy: Gassendi and Descartes on Contingency and Necessity in the Created World*. Cambridge: Cambridge University Press, 2004, 118–46; Harrison, Peter, "The Development of the Concept of Laws of Nature." In *Creation: Law and Probability*, ed. Fraser Watts, 13–36. Aldershot: Ashgate, 2008.

27 For the issue in Galileo, see Daston, Lorraine, "Galilean Analogies: Imagination at the Bounds of Sense." *Isis* 75 (1985): 302–10.

28 Greene, John C., *The Death of Adam: Evolution and Its Impact on Western Thought*. Ames: Iowa State University Press, 1961, 12–13; Glacken, Clarence J., *Traces on the Rhodian Shore; Nature and Culture in Western Thought from Ancient Times to the End of the Eighteenth Century*. Berkeley, CA: University of California Press, 1973, 377–8.

29 Mandelbrote, Scott, "The Uses of Natural Theology in Seventeenth-Century England." *Science in Context* 20 (2007): 451–80.

30 More, *Immortality of the Soul* (1659); as cited by Mandelbrote, "The Uses of Natural Theology in Seventeenth-Century England," 461.

31 Odom, Herbert H., "The Estrangement of Celestial Mechanics and Religion." *Journal of the History of Ideas* 27 (1966): 533–58; Buckley, Michael J., "The Newtonian Settlement and the Origins of Atheism." In *Physics, Philosophy and Theology: A Common Quest for Understanding*, ed. Robert J. Russell, William R. Stoeger, and George V. Coyne, 81–102. Vatican City: Vatican Observatory, 1988; Force, James E., "The Breakdown of the Newtonian Synthesis of Science and Religion: Hume, Newton and the Royal Society." In *Essays on the Context, Nature and Influence of Isaac Newton's Theology*, ed. R. H. Popkin and J. E. Force, 143–63. Dordrecht: Kluwer Academic, 1990.

32 For an assessment, see especially Corsi, Pietro, *Science and Religion: Baden Powell and the Anglican Debate*. Cambridge: Cambridge University Press, 1988, 143–208.

33 Powell, Baden, *The Order of Nature Considered in Reference to the Claims of Revelation*. London: Longman, 1859, 145.

34 For the process, see Haugaard, William P., *Elizabeth and the English Reformation: The Struggle for a Stable Settlement of Religion*. Cambridge: Cambridge University Press, 1970, 52–78.

35 The importance of the body of French Protestant refugees known as the "Huguenots" to this question must not be overlooked: Baillon, Jean-François, "Early Eighteenth-Century Newtonianism: The Huguenot Contribution." *Studies in the History and Philosophy of Science* 35 (2004): 533–48.

36 Scribner, Robert W., "The Reformation, Popular Magic, and the 'Disenchantment of the World'." *Journal of Interdisciplinary History* 23 (1993): 475–94; Hanegraaff, Wouter J., "How Magic Survived the Disenchantment of the World." *Religion* 33 (2003): 357–80.

37 See especially Schluchter, Wolfgang, *Die Entzauberung der Welt: Sechs Studien zu Max Weber*. Tübingen: Mohr Siebeck, 2009.

38 Berger, Peter, *The Sacred Canopy: Elements of a Sociological Theory of Religion*. Garden City, NY: Doubleday, 1967, 111–13.

39 Duffy, Eamon, *The Stripping of the Altars: Traditional Religion in England c. 1400–c. 1580*. New Haven, CT: Yale University Press, 1992, 37–51; Bartlett, *The Natural and Supernatural in the Middle Ages*, 1–33.

40 Duffy, *Stripping of the Altars*, 591.

41 See Schluchter, Wolfgang, *The Rise of Western Rationalism: Max Weber's Developmental History*. Berkeley, CA: University of California Press, 1981, 139–74.

42 See, for example, Crowther-Heyck, Kathleen, "Wonderful Secrets of Nature: Natural Knowledge and Religious Piety in Reformation Germany." *Isis* 94 (2003): 253–73; Ogilvie, Brian W., *The Science of Describing*. Chicago: University of Chicago Press, 2006, 87–138.

43 Eldridge, Richard, "Kant, Hölderlin, and the Experience of Longing." In *The Persistence of Romanticism: Essays in Philosophy and Literature*, 31–51. Cambridge: Cambridge University Press, 2001.

44 McGrath, Alister E., *The Open Secret: A New Vision for Natural Theology*. Oxford: Blackwell, 2008, 18–20; 219–313.

45 Pope, Alexander, *Essay on Criticism*. London: W. Lewis, 1711, 8.

46 Harrison, Peter, *The Bible, Protestantism, and the Rise of Natural Science*. Cambridge: Cambridge University Press, 1998, 121–56; Howell, *God's Two Books*, 13–38.

47 Levine, George Lewis, *Darwin and the Novelists: Patterns of Science in Victorian Fiction*. Chicago: University of Chicago Press, 1991, 24.

48 For an excellent review of trends in English natural theology around this time, with reflection on its broader cultural aspects, see Brooke, John Hedley, *Science and Religion: Some Historical Perspectives*. Cambridge: Cambridge University Press, 1991, 192–225.

49 Walsham, Alexandra, "Miracles and the Counter Reformation Mission to England." *Historical Journal* 46 (2003): 779–815.

50 Walker, D. P., *Unclean Spirits: Possession and Exorcism in France and England in the Late Sixteenth and Early Seventeenth Centuries*. Philadelphia, PA: University of Pennsylvania Press, 1981; Walker, D. P., "The Cessation of Miracles." In *Hermeticism and the Renaissance: Intellectual History and the Occult in Early Modern Europe*, ed. Ingrid Merkel and Allen G. Debus, 111–24. Washington, DC: Folger Books, 1988.

51 Hooper, *Brief and Clear Confession of the Christian Faith*, article 57; in Hooper, John, *The Later Writings of Bishop Hooper*. Cambridge: Parker Society, 1852, 44–5.

52 Shaw, Jane, *Miracles in Enlightenment England*. New Haven, CT: Yale University Press, 2006, 158–62.

53 Westfall, Richard S., *Science and Religion in Seventeenth-Century England*. Ann Arbor, MI: University of Michigan Press, 1973, 203–4.

54 As pointed out by Harrison, Peter, "Newtonian Science, Miracles, and the Laws of Nature." *Journal of the History of Ideas* 56 (1995): 531–53.

55 Locke, John, *The Works of John Locke*. 12th edn. 10 vols. London: Thomas Tegg, 1823, vol. 9, 256–65; quote at 256.

56 Grew, Nehemiah, *Cosmologia Sacra: Or a Discourse of the Universe as It Is the Creature and Kingdom of God*. London: W. Rogers, 1701, 195. See further Garrett, Brian, "Vitalism and Teleology in the Natural Philosophy of Nehemiah Grew (1641–1712)." *British Journal for the History of Science* 36 (2003): 63–81.

57 Newton, unpublished note, cited in Westfall, *Science and Religion*, 203. For further comment, see Force, James E., "Providence and Newton's Pantokrator: Natural Law, Miracles, and Newtonian Science." In *Newton and Newtonianism: New Essays*, ed. James E. Force and Sarah Hutton, 65–92. Dordrecht: Kluwer, 2004.

58 Belief in divine providence was not a marginal feature of early modern England, but "part of the mainstream," enjoying "near universal acceptance": Walsham, Alexandra, *Providence in Early Modern England*. Oxford: Oxford University Press, 1999, 2.

59 Walsham, Alexandra, "A Very Deborah? The Myth of Elizabeth I as a Providential Monarch." In *The Myth of Elizabeth I*, ed. Thomas S. Freeman and Susan Doran, 143–68. Basingstoke: Palgrave, 2003.

60 Schechner, Sara, *Comets, Popular Culture, and the Birth of Modern Cosmology*. Princeton, NJ: Princeton University Press, 1997, 68–70.

61 See the debates discussed in Wallace, Dewey D., *Puritans and Predestination: Grace in English Protestant Theology 1525–1695*. Chapel Hill, NC: North Carolina University Press, 1982; Tyacke, Nicholas, *Anti-Calvinists: The Rise of English Arminianism c. 1590–1640*. Oxford: Clarendon Press, 1987; White, Peter, *Predestination, Policy and Polemic: Conflict and Consensus in the English Church from the Reformation to the Civil War*. Cambridge: Cambridge University Press, 1992; Spinks, Bryan D., *Two Faces of Elizabethan Anglican Theology: Sacraments and Salvation in the Thought of William Perkins and Richard Hooker*. Lanham, MD: Scarecrow Press, 1999; Lim, Paul Chang-La, *In Pursuit of Purity, Unity and Liberty: Richard Baxter's Puritan Ecclesiology in its Seventeenth-Century Context*. Leiden: Brill, 2004.

62 See, for example, Calvin's doctrine of creation, which maps out a broadly consensual approach, with individual points of distinction: Zachman, Randall C., "The Universe as the Living Image of God: Calvin's Doctrine of Creation Reconsidered." *Concordia Theological Monthly* 61 (1997): 299–312.

63 The work includes approximately 2,000 references to the Bible, and roughly the same number of quotations from ancient authors, both classical philosophers and Christian theologians, usually in their original languages. There is surprisingly little analysis in the learned literature of Pearson's approach to theology, or its impact on his age and beyond. Most attention has focused on his 1672 defense of the authenticity of the letters of Ignatius of Antioch: see, for example, Quantin, Jean-Louis, "The Fathers in Seventeenth Century Anglican Theology." In *The Reception of the Church Fathers in the West: From the Carolingians to the Maurists*, ed. Irena Backus, 987–1008. Leiden: Brill, 2003.

64 For Johnson's relationship to the theology of the Restoration era, including Pearson, see Reddick, Allen H., *The Making of Johnson's Dictionary, 1746–1773*. Cambridge: Cambridge University Press, 1998, 156–60.

65 Jacob, *The Newtonians and the English Revolution 1689–1720*, 162–200.

66 Brooke, *Science and Religion*, 203.

67 Glacken, *Traces on the Rhodian Shore*, 375–428.

68 Gillespie, Neal C., "Natural History, Natural Theology, and Social Order: John Ray and the 'Newtonian Ideology'." *Journal of the History of Biology* 20 (1987): 1–49, especially 9.

69 See further Ogilvie, Brian W., "Natural History, Ethics, and Physico-Theology." In *Historia. Empiricism and Erudition in Early Modern Europe*, ed. Gianna Pomata and Nancy G. Siraisi, 75–103. Cambridge, MA: MIT Press, 2005; Harrison, Peter, "Physico-Theology and the Mixed Sciences: The Role of Theology in Early Modern Natural Philosophy." In *The Science of Nature in the Seventeenth Century*, ed. Peter Anstey and John Schuster, 165–83. Dordrecht: Springer, 2005.

70 Wilkins, John, *Of the Principles and Duties of Natural Religion*. 6th edn. London: Chiswell, 1710, 78.

71 Wilkins, *Of the Principles and Duties of Natural Religion*, 80.

72 Wilkins, *Of the Principles and Duties of Natural Religion*, 83.

73 Wilkins, *Of the Principles and Duties of Natural Religion*, 78.

74 For the impact of Galen's teleological anatomical arguments on this age, see Rivers, Isabel, "'Galen's Muscles': Wilkins, Hume, and the Educational Use of the Argument from Design." *Historical Journal* 36 (1993): 577–97; Siraisi, Nancy G., "Vesalius and the Reading of Galen's Teleology." *Renaissance Quarterly* 50 (1997): 1–37.

75 Boyle, Robert, *The Works of the Honourable Robert Boyle*, ed. Thomas Birch. 2nd edn. 6 vols. London: Rivingtons, 1772, vol. 5, 402–4. See also Fisch, Harold, "The Scientist as Priest: A Note on Robert Boyle's Natural Theology." *Isis* 44 (1953): 252–65.

76 On the role this clock played in the debates of this age, see Shapin, Steven, *The Scientific Revolution*. Chicago, IL: University of Chicago Press, 1996, 34–7.

77 Boyle, *Works*, vol. 5, 404. The term "art" is here to be understood as "skill."

78 For the significance of the analogy of the clock, see McLaughlin, Peter, "Die Welt als Maschine. Zur Genese des neuzeitlichen Naturbegriffs." In *Macrocosmos in Microcosmo. Die Welt in der Stube. Zur Geschichte des Sammelns 1450–1800*, ed. Andreas Grote, 439–51. Opladen: Leske & Budrich, 1994.

79 Boyle, *Works*, vol. 2, 30.

80 The best study is Shaw, *Miracles in Enlightenment England*, especially 21–50. Note her important distinction between *miranda* and *mirabilia* (or *miracula*): Shaw, 5, 31. For the background, see Walker, "The Cessation of Miracles"; Daston, Lorraine, "Marvelous Facts and Miraculous Evidence in Early Modern Europe." *Critical Inquiry* 18 (1991): 93–124.

81 Ray's work, first published in 1691, predates Newton's influential statement of the design argument, set out in the second edition of his *Principia*. The influence and prestige of Newton were such that his endorsement lent the new approaches to argument from design a new academic credibility, which helps explain the explosion of interest in the approach in the early eighteenth century. Although Ray produced the first workable definition of a biological species, he had nothing like the academic reputation of Newton. See Raven, Charles E., *John Ray, Naturalist: His Life and Works*. Cambridge: Cambridge University Press, 1986, 181–201.

82   For example, William Paley's *Evidences of Christianity* (1794) opens with an extended appeal to the miraculous in the apostolic age as confirmation of Christian truth-claims. Paley's *Natural Theology* (1802) also involves a recognition of the importance of the miraculous, and leads Paley to be cautious in his emphasis on the "laws of nature." Miracles, after all, represent an abrogation of such laws.

83   Dear, Peter R., "Miracles, Experiments, and the Ordinary Course of Nature." *Isis* 81 (1990): 663–83.

84   Sprat, Thomas, *History of the Royal Society of London*. London: J. Martyn, 1667, 10–11. See further McGuire, James E., "The Rhetoric of Sprat's Defence of the Royal Society." *Archives internationales d'histoire des sciences* 55 (2005): 203–10.

85   Sprat, *History of the Royal Society of London*, 352.

86   Sprat, *History of the Royal Society of London*, 350.

87   Sprat, *History of the Royal Society of London*, 87, 134.

88   Ray, John, *The Wisdom of God Manifested in the Works of the Creation*. 9th edn. London: Royal Society, 1727, 140. See further Zeitz, Lisa M., "Natural Theology, Rhetoric, and Revolution: John Ray's *Wisdom of God*, 1691–1704." *Eighteenth Century Life* 18 (1994): 120–33.

89   Ray, *Wisdom of God*, 30.

90   Ray, *Wisdom of God*, 357–8.

91   See, for example, Ray, *Wisdom of God*, 36, 119, 128, 207, 318.

92   See, for example, Thomas Aquinas, *Summa contra Gentiles*, III.74, which demonstrates that divine providence does not exclude fortune or chance: "divina providentia non subtrahit a rebus fortunam et casum."

93   Jacob, *The Newtonians and the English Revolution 1689–1720*, 143–61.

94   On which see the excellent study of Wojcik, Jan W., *Robert Boyle and the Limits of Reason*. Cambridge: Cambridge University Press, 1997. Note also the older study of Fisch, "The Scientist as Priest."

95   See Gieryn, Thomas F., "Distancing Science from Religion in Seventeenth-Century England." *Isis* 79 (1988): 582–93.

96   Dahm, John J., "Science and Apologetics in the Early Boyle Lectures." *Church History* 39 (1970): 172–86.

97   Gascoigne, "From Bentley to the Victorians."

98   For comment on their impact, see Dahm, "Science and Apologetics in the Early Boyle Lectures," especially 175 n. 17.

99   Bentley, Richard, *Sermons Preached at Boyle's Lecture*. London: Francis MacPherson, 1838, 1–200.

100 Bentley, *Sermons Preached at Boyle's Lecture*, 52. Newton regarded Bentley's use of the notion of "contrivance" as excessive, and objected to his citing the inclination of the earth's axis of rotation as evidence for the existence of a Deity: Letter dated December 10, 1692, reprinted in *Sermons Preached at Boyle's Lecture*, 207.

101 Fara, Patricia, and David Money, "Isaac Newton and Augustan Anglo-Latin Poetry." *Studies in the History and Philosophy of Science* 35 (2004): 549–71.

102 Blackmore, Richard, *Creation: A Philosophical Poem*. Philadelphia: Robert Johnson, 1806, liii.

103 Blackmore, *Creation*, 56.
104 Blackmore, *Creation*, 56.
105 Derham, William, *Physico-Theology: Or, a Demonstration of the Being and Attributes of God*. 6th edn. London: W. & J. Innys, 1723, 34.
106 Derham, *Physico-Theology*, 143–4.
107 Derham, *Physico-Theology*, 155–6.
108 Derham, *Physico-Theology*, 404–5.
109 Derham, *Physico-Theology*, 356.
110 Derham, William, *Astro-Theology: Or, a Demonstration of the Being and Attributes of God, from a Survey of the Heavens*. 7th edn. London: Innys & Manby, 1738, 214–15.
111 Earlier writers noted the diversity of approaches to natural theology, interpreting the varying emphases placed upon physics and biology as reflecting the particular interests of individual authors: see, for example, Westfall, *Science and Religion*. Nevertheless, Westfall correctly notes that eighteenth-century teleological approaches to natural theology were at their most sophisticated when applied to the biological domain.
112 Arbuthnot, John, "An Argument for Divine Providence, Taken from the Constant Regularity Observ'd in the Births of Both Sexes." *Philosophical Transactions of the Royal Society* 27 (1710): 186–90.
113 For reflections on such probabilistic approaches to arguments from design, see Sober, Elliott, "Sex Ratio Theory, Ancient and Modern: An 18th Century Debate About Intelligent Design and the Development of Models in Evolutionary Biology." In *The Sistine Gap – Essays on the History and Philosophy of Artificial Life*, ed. Jessica Riskin, 131–62. Chicago: University of Chicago Press, 2007.
114 See Allen, David Elliston, *The Naturalist in Britain: A Social History*. Princeton, NJ: Princeton University Press, 1994, 22–44. Allen notes the importance of personal motivations (including natural theology and Romantic philosophy) and technological developments (especially the microscope) in developing this interest from the seventeenth century onwards.
115 Lund, Roger D., "Laughing at Cripples: Ridicule, Deformity and the Argument from Design." *Eighteenth Century Studies* 39 (2005): 91–114.
116 Zeitz, Lisa M., "Addison's 'Imagination' Papers and the Design Argument." *English Studies* 73 (1992): 493–502, especially 494–5.
117 *The Spectator*, no. 465 (August 23, 1712); cited Zeitz, "Addison's 'Imagination' Papers," 494.
118 Zeitz, "Addison's 'Imagination' Papers," 495. For evaluations of the relation of theology and aesthetics at this point in Addison's thought, see Saccamano, Neil, "The Sublime Force of Words in Addison's 'Pleasures'." *English Literary History* 58 (1991): 83–106; Syba, Michelle, "After Design: Joseph Addison Discovers Beauties." *Studies in English Literature* 49 (2009): 615–35.
119 *The Spectator*, no. 465 (August 23, 1712).
120 For a classic study of this issue, see Thorpe, Clarence DeWitt, "Addison's Theory of the Imagination as 'Perceptive Response'." *Papers of the Michigan Academy of Science, Arts, and Letters* 21 (1936): 509–30.

121   On this point, see Walker, William, "Ideology and Addison's Essays on the Pleasures of the Imagination." *Eighteenth Century Life* 24, no. 2 (2000): 65–84, 81.

122   Walker, "Ideology and Addison's Essays," 80.

123   As noted by Syba, "After Design," 634.

124   This was certainly a concern of many around this time, not least on account of suspicion over notions such as "energetic substance" in the writings of the Cambridge Platonists. See especially Henry, John, "Occult Qualities and the Experimental Philosophy: Active Principles in Pre-Newtonian Matter Theory." *History of Science* 24 (1986): 335–81; Henry, John, "Medicine and Pneumatology: Henry More, Richard Baxter, and Francis Glisson's Treatise on the Energetic Nature of Substance." *Medical History* 31 (1987): 15–40.

125   A point emphasized by Hunter, Michael, "Science and Heterodoxy: An Early Modern Problem." In *Reappraisals of the Scientific Revolution*, ed. David C. Lindberg and Robert S. Westman, 437–60. Cambridge: Cambridge University Press, 1990.

126   See Mintz, Samuel I., *The Hunting of Leviathan: Seventeenth-Century Reactions to the Materialism and Moral Philosophy of Thomas Hobbes.* Cambridge: Cambridge University Press, 1970, 69–88; Tuck, Richard, "The 'Christian Atheism' of Thomas Hobbes." In *Atheism from the Reformation to the Enlightenment*, ed. Michael Hunter and David Wootton, 102–20. Oxford: Clarendon Press, 1992.

127   For the cultural implications of this shift, see Taylor, Charles, *A Secular Age.* Cambridge, MA: Harvard University Press, 2007, 221–95.

128   Malet, "Isaac Barrow on the Mathematization of Nature," 272–4.

129   See especially Shapiro, Barbara J., *Probability and Certainty in Seventeenth-Century England: A Study of the Relationships between Natural Science, Religion, History, Law, and Literature.* Princeton, NJ: Princeton University Press, 1983.

130   For the relevance of this to "facts of nature," see Shapiro, Barbara J., *A Culture of Fact: England, 1550–1720.* Ithaca, NY: Cornell University Press, 2003, 105–67.

131   Pesic, Peter, "Wrestling with Proteus; Francis Bacon and the 'Torture' of Nature." *Isis* 90 (1999): 81–94. For Bacon's impact on natural theology in this period, see Peterfreund, "Imagination at a Distance."

132   Derham, *Physico-Theology*, 155.

133   Derham, *Physico-Theology*, 108.

134   Derham, *Physico-Theology*, 96.

135   Derham, *Physico-Theology*, 153.

136   Derham, *Physico-Theology*, 27.

4

A Popular Classic: William Paley's *Natural Theology* (1802)

Natural theology played a major cultural role in Victorian England, offering a conceptual framework that allowed engagement between the Christian faith, the arts, and the natural sciences. Nineteenth-century writings, whether religious or secular, academic or popular, found the ideas traditionally developed by natural theology to be fertile and productive topics of debate and reflection.[1] The notion of the harmonious adaptation of the natural world to its environment made possible the development of a range of theological teleologies throughout the English Renaissance and Enlightenment.[2] One of the works that exercised a formative influence, especially at the popular level, in securing public interest in the topic was William Paley's celebrated work *Natural Theology* (1802). In many ways, Paley's landmark work can be seen as marking the high-water point of English natural theology in general, and "physico-theology" in particular.

In view of the importance of Paley's *Natural Theology* in shaping popular perceptions of God's involvement within, and disclosure by, the natural world, we shall consider this work and its arguments in some detail.

Introducing Paley's *Natural Theology*

William Paley (1743–1805) was educated at Christ's College, Cambridge.[3] In 1763, he achieved the highest score in Cambridge University's final year mathematics examination, which won him the title of "Senior Wrangler." At the time, this was seen as representing one of the greatest intellectual achievements in England, opening doors to future advancement in the academy,

Darwinism and the Divine: Evolutionary Thought and Natural Theology, First Edition.
Alister E. McGrath.
© 2011 Alister E. McGrath. Published 2011 by Blackwell Publishing Ltd.

Figure 4.1 English writer and theologian William Paley (1743–1805), c. 1790.

law, medicine, and church. Paley was elected a fellow of Christ's in 1766, and in 1768 was appointed to a tutorship.

During his time as tutor at Christ's College, Paley lectured on the philosophy of Samuel Clarke, Joseph Butler, and John Locke.[4] He also delivered a systematic course on moral philosophy, which subsequently formed the basis of his treatise *The Principles of Moral and Political Philosophy* (1785). This work, noted for its clarity of presentation rather than its originality of argument, immediately became a set text for moral philosophy at Cambridge University.[5] By this time, Paley had left Cambridge, having initially become rector of Musgrave in Westmorland, and subsequently archdeacon of Carlisle.[6] Increasingly, Paley found himself drawn to the field of apologetics, being troubled by the rise of skeptical approaches to Christianity. His first major work of apologetics was *Horae Paulinae, or the Truth of the Scripture History of St Paul* (1790), followed by *A View of the Evidences of Christianity* (1794). This latter work took the form of a reworking of older works, most notably Nathaniel Lardner's *The Credibility of the Gospel History* (1748) and John Douglas's *Criterion* (1757).

Finally, he published the work of apologetics for which he is best remembered, and which is to be considered in this chapter: *Natural Theology: Or, Evidences of the Existence and Attributes of the Deity Collected from the Appearances of Nature* (1802), based on a series of sermons composed in the 1780s or 1790s. Here, as in earlier works, Paley borrowed extensively from earlier writers, most notably John Ray's *Wisdom of God* (1691) and William Derham's *Physico-Theology* (1713). However, he also drew significantly on Bernard Nieuwentyt's little-known work *The Religious Philosopher* (1718).[7] In view of the importance of this obscure book for the shape of Paley's argument, we shall consider it in more detail later in this chapter.

Paley's *Natural Theology* has every right to be considered a classic work.[8] It remained in print for one hundred years, and is known to have gone through more than fifty editions in Britain alone. A conservative estimate of its sales figures suggests that 80,000 copies of the work were sold, over half of which were published after 1835. It is often stated that Paley's *Natural Theology* was "required reading" at Cambridge University – in other words, that it was a "set text," upon which examination questions might be set. It is certainly true that two of Paley's earlier works achieved this status – namely his *Principles of Moral and Political Philosophy* (1785) and *A View of the Evidences of Christianity* (1794). Yet, as Aileen Fyfe has convincingly demonstrated, *Natural Theology* enjoyed no such official status.[9] It was unquestionably discussed and debated, in that "natural theology" was a topic of no small interest at the time. Yet any suggestion that Cambridge was wedded to Paley's text or ideas needs to be treated with skepticism. Charles Darwin, himself a student at Christ's College, Cambridge (1828–31), unquestionably became familiar with Paley's text, but probably did not study it in any detail until after he had left Cambridge.[10]

Paley's extensive dependence upon apologetic writings of the period 1690–1720 means that his own approach reflects, and is ultimately dependent upon, the approaches and assumptions of earlier generations of British natural theologians, such as Ray and Derham. Though published in the opening of the nineteenth century, Paley's work is essentially a republication of the approaches of the late seventeenth and early eighteenth centuries. The enormous popular success of Paley's *Natural Theology* masks an important weakness: while its ideas may have captivated the imagination of many in early Victorian culture, it generally failed to engage with the more difficult questions many were now beginning to ask. The late eighteenth century had raised some questions unknown to earlier generations of natural theologians, which Paley seemed disinclined to consider, let alone answer.

The intellectual landscape underwent massive changes in the eighteenth century, not least on account of the critiques directed against natural theology by David Hume (1711–76) and Immanuel Kant (1724–1804). While Paley is aware of Hume's significance, he does not engage with his arguments in his *Natural Theology*.[11] As Brooke and Cantor have pointed out, the atheist is an imaginary interlocutor in many natural theologies of the period, including Paley's apologetic work.[12] Yet Paley's imagined atheist often seems to play softball, throwing questions at Paley that are easily answered, at least rhetorically. Hume's critique of natural theology, for example, is not explicitly engaged.

Paley's failure to engage with such critiques is, of course, easily understood. The first edition of his *Natural Theology* would have been bought and read by a generally conservative readership, which would have been unlikely to have been unduly concerned about such issues.[13] Just as Newtonian natural theology offered stability to an English readership unsettled by the dramatic political uncertainties around the time of the "Glorious Revolution," so Paley's natural theology offered reassurance to an equally unsettled conservative readership, troubled by the Napoleonic war on the one hand, and increasing religious skepticism in English culture on the other.[14] Where scientific advance seemed to lead to atheism in France, as the works of Laplace indicated, Paley established a context within which scientific advance was accommodated within the ample girth of a suitably generous natural theology. Paley's vision for natural theology offered a significant degree of religious and political stability at a time when many feared both internal and external insecurity. It pointed to the fixed laws of science having counterparts in fixed laws of society, both of which were grounded in the divine nature.

As noted earlier, Paley's *Natural Theology* can be seen as the late flowering of the form of natural theology, widely known as "physico-theology," which came to dominate English thought from about 1690. This approach often focused on aspects of anatomy, particularly human anatomy, which was held to disclose evidence of purpose and design.[15] This emphasized the notion of "contrivance." Paley's genius was to so organize his material around a controlling analogy that its imaginative power more than adequately compensated for its argumentative weaknesses. In the present chapter, we shall explore Paley's approach in the light of its historical precedents, its substantial proposals, and its significance in setting the scene for the Darwinian controversies.

Paley's Source: Bernard Nieuwentyt's *Religious Philosopher* (1718)

We begin, however, by exploring an often neglected aspect of Paley's work: its extensive borrowing from a relatively unknown work by a Dutch pastor and philosopher – Bernard Nieuwentyt's *The Religious Philosopher* (1718). Nieuwentyt (1654–1718) remains a relatively obscure writer, even in his native Holland,[16] and is noted particularly for his mathematical achievements and his critique of Spinoza. Yet, as we shall suggest in what follows, Nieuwentyt was destined to have a much greater (if ultimately anonymous) impact on British and American thought, due to his championing by one of the most influential religious minds of the early nineteenth century.

Nieuwentyt's work is to be set against a significant native Dutch tradition of interpretation – a way of reading the "Book of Nature,"[17] and developing analogies to aid this process of "reading." A particular tradition of natural theology developed in the Low Countries, based on the close examination of the natural world as a means of deepening an appreciation of the wisdom of God. The invention of the microscope by Christian Huygens enhanced this sense of wonder, by opening up new worlds for human inspection.[18] Nieuwentyt can be seen as a late representative of this Dutch form of natural theology, which is ably represented in his *Religious Philosopher*.

In 1848, a letter appeared in the *Athenaeum*, one of London's many literary magazines. Its author chose to identify himself only as "Verax." His charge was simple: that William Paley, the distinguished author of *Natural Theology*, had plagiarized some of its most significant elements without acknowledgment from an earlier work.[19] Far from offering an original contribution to the debate about whether God could be known in or through nature, Paley had simply produced a "mere running commentary" on an earlier work by Dr Bernard Nieuwentyt. Verax then set out the contents of each work in tabular form, allowing the reader to note the similarities of argument and form between the two works. Verax declared that Paley followed Nieuwentyt "even in matters of detail" – above all, in deploying the central, critical illustration of a watch.

Figure 4.2   Movement view of a gold open-faced, quarter repeating, perpetual pocket watch. No. 3 (or No. 33) by Abraham-Louis Breguet. Paris c. 1790.

At certain points, Paley identifies those upon whom he has drawn – most notably, in his discussion of astronomy, where he explicitly refers to "some obliging communications received (through the hands of the Lord Bishop of Elphin) from the Rev. J. Brinkley, M.A., Andrew's Professor of Astronomy in the University of Dublin."[20] Yet Paley's only acknowledgment of his indebtedness to the Dutch writer is somewhat oblique, noting how Dr Nieuwentyt reckoned that the human body used more than one hundred muscles every time it breathed.[21]

Did Verax have a point? Nieuwentyt invites his readers to imagine finding a watch "in the middle of a sandy down, a desert, or solitary place."[22] Paley invites his to imagine finding a watch on "a heath."[23] Other points of similarity might be noted, as follows.

Nieuwentyt:[24]
So many different wheels, nicely adapted by their teeth to each other ... Those wheels are made of brass, in order to keep them from rust; the spring is steel, no other metal being so proper for that purpose ... Over the hand there is placed a clear glass, in the place of which if there were any other than a transparent substance, he must be at the pains of opening it every time to look upon the hand.

Paley:[25]
A series of wheels, the teeth of which catch in and apply to each other ... The wheels are made of brass, in order to keep them from rust; the spring of steel, no other metal being so elastic ... Over the face of the watch there is placed a glass, a material employed in no other part of the work, but in the room of which if there had been any other than a transparent substance, the hour could not have been seen without opening the case.

The ensuing correspondence in the *Athenaeum* made it clear that there was a widespread acceptance of Paley's dependence upon the early work, but disagreement over its significance. "J.S." noted a second reference on Paley's part to Nieuwentyt and argued that Paley was guilty of little more than failing to give proper acknowledgment to his Dutch predecessor for the use of his argument.[26] The editor of the journal interposed at this point, indicating that he believed the charge of plagiarism against Paley to be justified by the evidence. "B.E.N." concluded the correspondence a week later, surveying the evidence for plagiarism, and concluding that Paley seemed to have a somewhat deficient view of "literary morality."[27]

It was not the first time that Paley had been accused of plagiarism. In February 1792, Paley was accused of having included sections of a spelling textbook entitled *An Introduction to the Study of Polite Literature* without acknowledgment in Paley's 1790 work *The Young Christian Instructed in Reading and in the Principles of Religion.*[28] Paley conceded the fact, but argued that his work was of no commercial significance. It was intended as a resource for the Sunday Schools of Carlisle. By means of compensation, if any were needed, Paley offered Robertson the rights to this work. In fact, the extent of plagiarism was trivial, and Paley's apology went far beyond anything necessary.

Paley may have borrowed the image of the watch from his Dutch colleague without proper acknowledgment; however, the use he makes of it shows a clarity of thought and originality of approach that go far beyond the approach found in *The Religious Philosopher.* Nieuwentyt is clearly not a "physico-theologian." He hardly ever refers to any aspect of nature being "contrived."[29] However, the work is suffused with references to God as creator, and above all the manifestation of the divine wisdom in the created order. The notion of intentional design for certain ends and goals is clearly present.[30] Yet the overall apologetic strategy developed seems closer to that of John Wilkins than to that of William Derham, in that teleological arguments – though present – do not play a dominant role. For example, consider Nieuwentyt's reflections on the analogy between creation and a watch:[31]

> We may apply all that has been said above to demonstrate, that there is such a Wise, Mighty, and Merciful Being as God in case we can make appear with as great (not to say a much greater) Certainty and Conviction, from the Construction of the visible World, and all that passes therein, that there is a God and Great Creator, who in Wisdom has made them all; as we can shew from the Structure of a Watch, and the Uses that result from the same, that it has been made and put together by a judicious and skilful Workman.

While Nieuwentyt clearly assumes that nature has been designed for certain goals, his interest focuses particularly on the intricacy and workmanship of the creation, which he interprets as a manifestation of the wisdom and skill of a creator God.[32] Nieuwentyt echoes the themes of English natural theology prior to 1690, rather than the more teleological versions found thereafter.

Paley's genius lay in his appreciation of the growing plausibility of mechanical analogies for creation in the early nineteenth century. For Robert Boyle and other apologists of the seventeenth century, the only form of machinery that an educated readership could be expected to know at first hand was clockwork. By Paley's day, in the middle of the English Industrial Revolution, machinery was such a familiar element of the cultural landscape that his core argument from a mechanical analogy carried far more appeal and imaginative power than in earlier ages. The argument that nature was "contrived" resonated strongly with his readership. In what follows, we shall consider this critically important notion in greater detail.

The Watch Analogy: The Concept of Contrivance

Paley's argument hinges around a controlling analogy – the biological world is analogous to a watch. The apologetic strategy developed by Paley rests upon establishing this vivid analogy, which possesses sufficient imaginative potential to carry his readers along and subvert the evidential force of objections that might be raised against his approach. Paley's analogy of the watch may be derivative; the use he makes of it shows an ingenuity and creativity that cannot be overlooked.

For Paley, the Newtonian image of the world as a mechanism immediately suggested the metaphor of a clock or watch, raising the question of who constructed the intricate mechanism that was so evidently displayed in the functioning of the world. It is an important argument, which ran counter to the growing perception that the Newtonian concept of a mechanistic universe actually eroded the traditional Christian view of God. Surely, many argued, conceiving the universe as a mechanism led to the view of an absent God, a clockmaker whose clock could function without any further need for divine involvement or superintendence?[33] For some, the mechanistic model of the universe implied a cold, lifeless deity and a satanic metaphysics – a universe empty of meaning.[34]

Paley sought to rehabilitate an appeal to mechanism through the notion of contrivance. "Contrivance, if established, appears to me to prove everything which we wish to prove."[35] The notion of contrivance had become an integral component of English natural theology since the time of Newton. Yet it had gained a new plausibility through the growing popular familiarity with, and interest in, machinery. Where Robert Boyle had to illustrate the notion of contrivance with some obscure references to "pneumatic machines" that were clearly unfamiliar to his readers, Paley could appeal to mechanical devices that his readers encountered and experienced in everyday life. England led the way in the Industrial Revolution between 1750 and 1830, developing new mechanical methods of production that rapidly outstripped its economic rivals in Europe. Paley's appeal to the significance of mechanism as indicative of design carried considerable cultural plausibility. His approach to natural theology was crafted with the new cultural environment of the Industrial Revolution in mind.

Writing against the backdrop of the emerging Industrial Revolution, Paley set out to exploit the apologetic potential of the growing popular interest in machinery – such as watches, telescopes, stocking-mills, and steam engines – on the part of England's ruling class.[36] How, Paley asked, could such complex mechanical technology come into being by purposeless chance? Paley develops this point by his appeal to the analogy of the watch. In setting the context, Paley highlights the disanalogy between a stone and a watch, when both are encountered while crossing a heath.[37]

> In crossing a heath, suppose I pitched my foot against a *stone*, and were asked how the stone came to be there: I might possibly answer, that, for any thing I knew to the contrary, it had lain there for ever; nor would it perhaps be very easy to show the absurdity of this answer. But suppose I had found a *watch* upon the ground, and it should be inquired how the watch happened to be in that place; I should hardly think of the answer which I had before given, – that, for any thing I knew, the watch might have always been there.

What distinguishes the watch from the stone? The nub of Paley's answer can be summed up in the single word *contrivance* – a system of parts arranged to work together for a purpose, manifesting both design and utility. Paley used the term "contrivance" to convey the dual notions of design and fabrication, appealing to the popular interest in machinery characteristic of the new age of industrialization then emerging in England.

Following through his argument, Paley then offers a detailed description of the watch, noting in particular its container, coiled cylindrical spring, many interlocking wheels, and glass face. All show evidence of design for a specific identifiable purpose. Having carried his readers along with this careful analysis, Paley turns to draw his critically important conclusion:[38]

> This mechanism being observed (it requires indeed an examination of the instrument, and perhaps some previous knowledge of the subject, to perceive and understand it; but being once, as we have said, observed and understood), the inference we think is inevitable, that the watch must have had a maker: that there must have existed, at some time and at some place or other, an artificer or artificers who formed it for the purpose which we find it actually to answer, who comprehended its construction and designed its use.

Paley's extended discussion of the watch is intended to establish a framework of interpretation, capable of being transferred to other objects that appear to show evidence of design. Paley's detailed analysis of the watch mechanism is intended to establish that it is a *contrivance*, showing evidence of being initially designed and subsequently constructed for a specific purpose, and thus indicating the existence of a designer. Paley is quite clear that this "designer" might be a group of people, rather than an individual; and that the present existence of a contrivance is no indication that its designer is still alive. These points will be addressed later in his argument; his concern at this early stage is to move on quickly to apply this framework of interpretation to the contrivances of the natural – especially the biological – world. Paley postpones his discussion of astronomy until a later point in the work, anxious not to lose the conceptual momentum he has built up through his detailed reflections on the implications of the mechanism of the watch.

Why? The answer lies in Paley's conviction that complexity is a hallmark of contrivance. "Some degree therefore of *complexity* is necessary to render a subject fit for this species of argument."[39] For Paley, the controlling analogy of God as a watchmaker was thus best applied to the biological domain, which Paley regarded as being more valuable apologetically than that of astronomy. As we noted earlier (64; 65), earlier English physico-theologians had drawn the same conclusion. Although a later chapter of *Natural Theology* is devoted to astronomy,[40] Paley clearly did not consider this to be particularly significant apologetically. Astronomy might well attest to the magnificence and wonder of God to believers; it could not, however, prove that existence in the first place.[41]

> My opinion of Astronomy has always been, that it is *not* the best medium through which to prove the agency of an intelligent Creator; but that, this being proved, it shows, beyond all other sciences, the magnificence of his operations. The mind which is once convinced, it raises to sublimer views of the Deity than any other subject affords; but it is not so well adapted, as some other subjects are, to the purpose of argument.

Paley suggests that observation of the planets and stars points to their "simplicity." "We see nothing, but bright points, luminous circles, or the phases of spheres reflecting the light which falls upon them."[42]

For Paley, the inference of design rests upon the evidence of complexity. "We deduce design from relation, aptitude, and correspondence of *parts*. Some degree therefore of *complexity* is necessary to render a subject fit for this species of argument."[43] While conceding that the planet Saturn gives an indication of complexity, on account of its ring system, Paley stresses that this is the exception, not the rule. When viewed in the framework established by Paley's watch analogy, astronomical phenomena proved to be relatively apologetically sterile. The simplicity of the heavens failed to establish their divine provenance. Nevertheless, echoing themes reflecting pre-1690 approaches to natural theology, Paley insisted that astronomical regularities were nevertheless an important manifestation of the "wisdom of the Deity."[44]

In contrast, Paley was clear that the complexity of biological life on earth was such that it had to be seen as a "contrivance." This important and heavily freighted word implies both the ideas of *design* and *construction* – each of which Paley held to be evident in the biological world. Paley was deeply impressed by Newton's discovery of the regularity of nature, especially in relation to the area usually known as "celestial mechanics." It was clear that the entire universe could be thought of as a complex mechanism, operating according to regular and understandable principles. It was like a watch: something that showed evidence of design and construction. Mechanism presupposes contrivance, implying a creator who possesses both a sense of purpose for a mechanism, and an ability to design and fabricate it.

The human body in particular, and the biological world in general, could be seen as mechanisms that had been designed and constructed, perfectly adapted to their needs and specific situations. This is the critically important point that is established by Paley's use of the analogy of the watch. The same complexity and utility evident in the design and functioning of a watch can also be discerned in the natural world. Each feature of a biological organism, like that of a watch, showed evidence of being designed in such a way as to adapt the organism to survival within its environment. Complexity and utility are observed; the conclusion that they were designed and constructed by God, Paley holds, is as natural as it is correct.

Nature, Paley argued, shows signs of "contrivance" – that is, purposeful design and fabrication. Nature bears witness to a series of biological structures that are "contrived" – that is, constructed with a clear purpose in mind. "Every indication of contrivance, every manifestation of design, which existed in the watch, exists in the works of nature."[45] Indeed, Paley argues, nature shows an even greater degree of contrivance than the watch. He is at his most persuasive when dealing with the immensely complex structures of the human eye and heart, each of which can be described in mechanical terms. Anyone using a telescope, he points out, knows that the instrument was designed and manufactured. Who, he wondered, could possibly look at the complexities of the human eye, and fail to see that it also has a designer?

Paley reinforces this rhetorical point by proposing a further mechanical analogy for the biological realm. The eye, he suggests, is analogous to a telescope.[46]

There is precisely the same proof that the eye was made for vision, as there is that the telescope was made for assisting it. They are made upon the same principles; both being adjusted to the laws by which the transmission and refraction of rays of light are regulated … What could a mathematical-instrument-maker have done more, to show his knowledge of his principle, his application of that knowledge, his suiting of his means to his end … to testify counsel, choice, consideration, purpose?

Having developed this analogy, Paley emphasizes the superiority of the eye over the telescope. The eye is more ingeniously designed than the telescope, and is better adapted to cope with a wide range of circumstances, such as the light levels or the distances of objects to be viewed. For Paley, this demands that both the eye and telescope be considered to be contrivances. And since the eye is more ingenious and functional than the telescope, the creator of this natural contrivance is worthy of greater admiration and praise than the creator of the telescope.[47]

Paley does not develop a philosophy or theology of analogy, and offers no explicit theory of evidence that allows him to argue from the evidence of nature to the probability of theistic belief. His argument is fundamentally analogical: the notion of contrivance, exemplified by a watch or telescope, is deemed to be sufficiently persuasive that it does not require detailed justification. In some respects, Paley's argument can be seen to be a forerunner of the modern "inference to the best explanation," in that Paley proposes that the existence of a wise creator is more persuasive and probable than any other explanation of the complexity found within the biological domain.[48] Paley is aware that other explanations could conceivably be offered for the evidence he gathers; he nevertheless holds that his theistic explanation will resonate, deeply and naturally, with his readers.[49] Yet his insistence that "contrivance proves design"[50] suggests that his predominant line of thought is that, contrivance having been *observed* in nature, it is a matter of logical and rhetorical necessity to infer the existence of a designer.

So much attention is paid to Paley's analogy of the watch that later stages of his argument are often overlooked. As we noted earlier, Paley's analogy could lead to belief in a multiplicity of designers, rather than one. As Hume had pointed out, "a great number of men join in building a house or ship, in rearing a city, in founding a commonwealth: why may not several deities combine in contriving and framing a world?"[51] Nor need the original designer still exist, in that the watch will continue to exist, independent of the fate of its contriver. And what of the moral character of the designer? Though Paley does not mention Hume's critiques of natural theology explicitly,[52] he can hardly have been unaware of Hume's suggestion that this world is "faulty and imperfect." It could, Hume argued, have been the first botched attempt at creation on the part of "some infant deity," or the "production of old age and dotage" of some creator God who had lapsed into an incompetent senility.[53]

Paley deals with these concerns through a long and cumulative argument, the later stages of which are often overlooked by his interpreters. First, he addresses the question of whether there is only one creator. His argument, though complex, reduces to the assertion that there is a consistency of purpose and design within nature, which points to there being only one mind lying behind what is observed. The constancy and universality of the laws of nature, for example, clearly point to a single rationality expressed within the natural world. Furthermore, Paley suggests, to speak of design immediately implies that the designer is a person, rather than an abstract force. But is the designer good and wise?

Paley's argument at this point is based on an argument from perfection, which had been developed by a number of earlier writers.[54] One of the more significant proponents of this view was Charles Darwin's paternal grandfather, Erasmus Darwin (1731–1802), noted for his work *Zoönomia; or the Laws of Organic Life* (1794–96). Paley argues that the character of a designer would be disclosed in that which is designed. Since natural contrivances appear to have come into being for the good of those who bear or exhibit them, it is reasonable to conclude that the creator intends good for the creation – and is therefore himself good.

So what of suffering within the biological realm? What about apparent defects within the natural world? Paley is alert to this difficulty, yet argues that the problem lies at the level of implementation of an objective, not the objective itself.[55]

> Contrivance proves design: and the predominant tendency of the contrivance indicates the disposition of the designer. The world abounds with contrivances: and all the contrivances which we are acquainted with, are directed to beneficial purposes. Evil, no doubt, exists; but is never, that we can perceive, the *object* of contrivance. Teeth are contrived to eat, not to ache; their aching now and then is incidental to the contrivance, perhaps inseparable from it: or even, if you will, let it be called a defect in the contrivance: but it is not the object of it.

Paley's argument is that the purpose for which something is created discloses the character of its creator. There is no reason for supposing that God wills evil for his creatures. The object of these divine contrivances is invariably good, even if their implementation may have painful outcomes.[56]

The notion of "contrivance" had earlier been discussed by Hume, who dismissed it as lacking evidential force when applied to nature. Yet the way in which he frames his argument plays into Paley's hands. Hume's critique of the notion of contrivance rests on the possible lack of intelligence or ingenuity on the part of the one who actually constructs the contrivance.[57]

> But were this world ever so perfect a production, it must still remain uncertain, whether all the excellences of the work can justly be ascribed to the

workman. If we survey a ship, what an exalted idea must we form of the ingenuity of the carpenter, who framed so complicated, useful, and beautiful a
machine? And what surprise must we feel, when we find him a stupid mechanic,
who imitated others, and copied an art, which, through a long succession of
ages, after multiplied trials, mistakes, corrections, deliberations, and controversies, had been gradually improving.

Hume's point here is that the excellent execution of a design proves nothing
about the "ingenuity" of the mechanic, who might simply have imitated
others, in a dull and derivative manner. Yet even if the watchmaker is an
ignorant artisan who is simply following someone else's design, the criticism
concedes the existence of the design in the first place. Hume appears to misunderstand the meaning of "contrivance" in this paragraph, apparently
understanding it simply as a "production." Paley's "watchmaker" is not
simply the one who produces or assembles the watch, but the one who
designed it in the first place.

Paley on Intermediary Causes within Nature

As we have seen, Paley's analysis of the biological world argues that the
observation of contrivance can only be interpreted as evidence, proof, or
testimony of design. Since the character of the contriver is revealed in the
nature and goals of the contrivances, the goodness and wisdom of God can
be said to be disclosed in the works of God found in the natural world. As
we noted earlier, both the biological and astronomical realms revealed the
wisdom of God, although Paley nuances this in significantly different manners. The complexity of biological structures represents proof of God's contrivance of the natural world; the regularity of the astronomical world does
not prove God's existence, but supplements this belief, once developed, by
attesting to God's magnificence.

Underlying Paley's argument is a strong doctrine of divine causality. The
character of God is disclosed in the works of God, which are taken to be
special creations. Yet although Paley has a static concept of creation (in that
the created order does not develop or evolve), he is alert to its activity. The
observer of nature sees movement, energy, and action – as in the forces of
nature. Paley is adamant, not merely that nature is *designed*, but that it is
active. He illustrates this point by returning to his controlling analogy of the
watch. The watch clearly shows evidence of design. But when it is actively
working, it shows evidence of more than this:[58]

When we see the watch *going*, we see proof of another point, *viz.* that there
is a power somewhere, and somehow or other, applied to it; a power in

> action; – that there is more in the subject than the mere wheels of the machine; – that there is a secret spring, or a gravitating plummet; – in a word, that there is force, and energy, as well as mechanism … The watch in motion establishes to the observer two conclusions: One; that thought, contrivance, and design, have been employed in the forming, proportioning, and arranging of its parts … The other; that force or power, distinct from mechanism, is, at this present time, acting upon it.

Paley thus points to the activity of the natural world as evidence of God's power, supplementing that already noted as evidence of God's contrivance.

So does the divine watchmaker cause or contrive everything *directly*? Or can some things within the natural world be attributed to intermediate causes? Paley concedes the existence of what he terms "second causes,"[59] but insists that they are to be regarded as part of the overall mechanism through which God, as creator and governor of the world, regulates the creation.[60]

> There may be many second causes, and many courses of second causes, one behind another, between what we observe of nature, and the Deity: but there must be intelligence somewhere; there must be more in nature than what we see; and, amongst the things unseen, there must be an intelligent, designing author.

Whatever creativity they may possess is to be contextualized and subsumed within the overall framework of God's providential design and fabrication of the natural world. Indeed, the very existence of such "second causes" and the manner of their correlation are themselves additional evidence of the wisdom of God.

The attentive reader will note that Paley is slightly sensitive at this point, alert to the notion that any recognition of any form of causality within the natural world itself would be deemed "atheist" by at least some of his readers. Yet Paley has some well-honed analogies at his disposal to allow him to deal with this point. In view of the importance of his argument, we may set it out in full.[61]

> If it be demanded, whence arose either the contrivance by which the young animal is produced, or the contrivance manifested in the young animal itself, it is not from the reason of the parent that any such account can be drawn. He is the cause of his offspring, in the same sense as that in which a gardener is the cause of the tulip which grows upon his parterre, and in no other. We admire the flower; we examine the plant; we perceive the conduciveness of many of its parts to their end and office: we observe a provision for its nourishment, growth, protection, and fecundity; but we never think of the gardener in all this. We attribute nothing of this to his agency; yet it may still be true, that without the gardener, we should not have had the tulip: just so it is with the succession of animals even of the highest order. For the contrivance discovered in the structure of the thing produced, we want a contriver. The parent is not that contriver.

The most important analogy here is that of parents creating their own children. In doing so, he argues, the parents do not themselves create the design or contrivance evident in their offspring. While parents play an intermediate causal role in this process, it is within the context of "the plan itself, attributed to the ordination and appointment of an intelligent and designing Creator."[62] There is no developed theory of intermediary causality in Paley's natural theology, the logical rigor of which would have been enhanced considerably through the use of, for example, Aquinas's theory of secondary causality.[63]

It remains unclear what the theological consequences might have been if Paley were to have conceded this possibility. Charles Kingsley, for example, saw evolution as a natural extension of Paley's approach, resting on a more developed notion of causality than that explicitly recognized by Paley himself. As Kingsley commented in 1871: "We knew of old that God was so wise that He could make all things: but behold, He is so much wiser than even that, that He can make all things make themselves."[64] Paley does not consider that biological contrivance might *emerge* under God's providential guidance, leaving the field clear for another possibility of its explanation – namely, that contrivance is to be seen as the outcome of prolonged evolutionary selection and symbiosis with its surroundings.

The Vulnerability of Paley's Approach

There is much more that could be said about Paley's approach, particularly the overall trajectory of the complex argument by which he concludes the continuing existence of a single creator God from the complexity of the biological world.[65] Yet our concern here is not merely to understand Paley's argument, but to note how it generated a framework of reference and contextualization that is essential to understanding the theological impact of Darwin's *Origin of Species* (1859). Although the sales of Paley's *Natural Theology* had reached a plateau by this stage, his ideas remained a significant influence within Victorian popular culture. Many readers of the *Origin of Species* would evaluate its ideas within Paley's framework. Many – but not all. As we shall see, English academic culture was well aware of the shortcomings of Paley's approach by this stage.

Yet Darwin himself seems to have anticipated that some of his readers would evaluate him by comparing him with Paley. Echoes of Paley's works are found throughout the *Origin of Species*. Stephen Jay Gould, for example, has pointed out how Darwin's statement of his principle of natural selection is deeply indebted to the language and imagery found in Paley's writings, even though Darwin would later draw some very different conclusions.[66] Paley's detailed descriptions of the adaptations to be found in plants and animals – such as the human eye – had a significant impact upon Darwin. To win over a popular readership, Darwin would need to be able to match Paley's skill at describing nature and developing analogies to explain it – and above all, to provide a superior explanation of what was observed.

So what aspects of Paley's approach are of particular importance in understanding the impact of Darwin on English natural theology? Three points seem to be of especial importance.

First, perhaps the most obvious feature that needs to be highlighted is Paley's essentially static notion of creation. Throughout his argument, Paley assumes that there is a designed, unchanging order to things. This position was becoming difficult to maintain in the early nineteenth century, due to the growing body of geological knowledge that pointed to the extinction of previously living species. The notion that all created species still existed, widespread in the English natural theology literature of the late seventeenth and early eighteenth centuries, was shaken by the discovery of the remains of giant mammoths by George Louis Buffon (1707–1788) and of the quadrupeds of the Paris basin by Georges Cuvier (1768–1832). Geological investigation appeared to suggest that the world had undergone significant change since the divine creation.

Although Paley mentions the existence of fossils,[67] he fails to engage the deeper questions that they raise concerning the permanence of the created order. There is no obvious reflection on the conclusion that seemed to follow inevitably from the fossil evidence: namely, that every creature that God had originally created was still in existence. Paley followed John Ray in believing that the very idea of entire species being lost through extinction was unthinkable: "no such thing, I dare say, hath happened since the first creation."[68] Yet Ray's declaration was made in 1691, long before the discovery of fossils indicating that species had become extinct. Paley's tendency to repeat the ideas and approaches of earlier writers here causes him some difficulty, as he has no inherited arguments to use against more recent scientific developments – such as the discovery of fossil remains.

Following the earlier English physico-theological tradition, Paley seems to assume that the observable world, including its mechanisms, exists in more or less the form in which God originally created it. This rendered Paley's approach vulnerable to any suggestion that the biological realm had changed, or that complexity had evolved – one of the core themes, of course, of Charles Darwin's concept of descent with modification. Yet Kingsley rightly discerned that Paley's natural theology contained within itself the seeds of a response to this development.[69]

> We might accept all that Mr. Darwin, all that Professor Huxley, has so learnedly and so acutely written on physical science, and yet preserve our natural theology on exactly the same basis as that on which Butler and Paley left it.

That we should have to develop it, I do not deny. That we should have to relinquish it, I do.

Second, Paley assumes, following the earlier English tradition, that any notion of a "contrived" world necessarily excludes chance. In part, this rests on Paley's dysteleological definition of chance as "the operation of causes without design." How could such a complex structure as the human eye arise by chance?[70]

> I desire no greater certainty in reasoning, than that by which chance is excluded from the present disposition of the natural world. Universal experience is against it. What does chance ever do for us? In the human body, for instance, chance, i.e. the operation of causes without design, may produce a wen, a wart, a mole, a pimple, but never an eye.

Paley's natural theology proceeds on the assumption that the ordering of nature excludes chance, rather than recognizing that chance might be a means toward an ordered end. There is no suggestion that chance might be a catalyst for the emergence of higher levels of order. Nor is there any willingness to concede that "chance" might mean an absence of a proper understanding of causal sequences that had caused certain things to happen.

Third, Paley's argument rests on the core belief that contrivance is observed within nature, and that divine design may be deduced from this observation. The notion that such contrivances arose by accident is dismissed as unthinkable. Paley similarly rules out any notion that biological utility might follow, rather than precede, the origination of anatomical parts.[71]

> To the marks of contrivance discoverable in animal bodies, and to the argument deduced from them, in proof of design, and of a designing Creator, this turn is sometimes attempted to be given, namely, that the parts were not intended for the use, but that the use arose out of the parts.

The important point here is Paley's constant assumption that contrivance is something that is observed – that it may be "read off" the natural world. Contrivance is observed; design is deduced. "We deduce design from relation, aptitude, and correspondence of *parts*."[72]

As has often been observed, many aspects of Paley's approach to natural theology echo those of two generations before him, particularly the evidence assembled by John Ray, Joseph Addison, and William Derham, writing between 1690 and 1720. Yet Paley's approach is not determined solely by the evidence he advocates, but by the manner in which he interprets it. While Paley concedes the role of inference in reaching his conclusions, this is always treated as something straightforward and unproblematic.[73] For

Paley, examination of a watch leads to an inferential form of reasoning, which leads inexorably to the obvious conclusion: "the inference, we think, is inevitable, that the watch must have had a maker."[74] Paley here follows earlier English writers from the period 1690–1720, during which such assumptions were regarded by many as self-evidently true.

Paley's argument can be read and understood at many levels. A superficial reading of the text indicates his conviction that he has offered "proof" for the existence of a wise and benevolent Creator, especially in the face of challenges from those who argued that nature was capable of generating complexity from within itself. When Paley is read against his social context, we find embedded within his text a series of assumptions concerning the nature of proof and evidence, which locates it in the thought world of the early eighteenth century, suggesting that Paley may have borrowed rather more than some choice illustrations from his predecessors within the English natural theology tradition. The intellectual framework within which natural phenomena are to be interpreted, along with the style of argument deployed in their interpretation, belongs to an earlier age. This allows us to reconstruct something of Paley's intended readership, suggesting that it was popular, rather than academic; conservative, rather than radical.

When Paley speaks of offering a "proof" of the existence of a creator, it is clear that he does not mean a *logical* proof, but rather a rhetorical demonstration according to familiar conventions, similar to that then encountered in a court of law.[75] Yet the evidentiary conventions that Paley assumes to be somehow self-evidently correct turned out to be socially situated in the eighteenth century, and prone to erosion and alteration. English legal convention and practice were about to change. Parliamentary debates between 1821 and 1828, and then again from 1833 to 1837, focused on a series of issues relating to evidence and its interpretation in criminal cases. Central to the debate was this question: to what extent did facts of observation require interpretation and collation if they were to serve as evidence?

Where earlier generations regarded evidence as speaking for itself, the mood was changing. Even in Paley's time, a public debate was developing over the place of evidence and inference, which would seriously weaken Paley's approach. In contrast, Darwin's *Origin of Species* was alert to this shift in approaches to the assessment of evidence, and its implications for the public assessment of theoretical accounts of the origins of the natural world. Paley's assumptions about the nature and interpretation of evidence were about to be called into question. Inevitably, this concern about his use of evidence came to be transferred also to the conclusions that he drew on its basis.

Sadly, these three concerns lead us to draw a conclusion that is as inevitable as it is critical. When taken as a totality, Paley's approach to natural theology has to be seen as an intricate and beautifully constructed house of cards. The removal of any one of a number of cards would cause the whole edifice to collapse. This vulnerability is not of Paley's own making, nor is it due to his failings; it was an integral aspect of the "physico-theology" movement from its beginnings in the late seventeenth century, which only became apparent over an extended period of time, as critical cultural assumptions began to change. Late seventeenth-century assumptions about the natural world and the nature of evidence were beginning to look decidedly shaky in the early nineteenth century. Yet they remained embedded within Paley's approach.

In the end, it was not Darwin who caused this intellectual edifice to disintegrate. As we shall see, during the first half-century after the publication of *Natural Theology*, Paley's approach was systematically deconstructed by Christian theologians, alert to its vulnerabilities on the one hand, and to potentially superior approaches on the other. Darwin may have administered the *coup de grâce* to a mortally wounded form of natural theology; the fatal wounds, however, were administered much earlier. We shall consider these important developments in the following chapter.

Notes

1   There is a huge literature. For some representative examples, see Young, Robert M., "Natural Theology, Victorian Periodicals, and the Fragmentation of a Common Context." In *Darwin's Metaphor: Nature's Place in Victorian Culture*, 126–63. Cambridge: Cambridge University Press, 1985; Fraser, Hilary, *Beauty and Belief: Aesthetics and Religion in Victorian Literature*. Cambridge: Cambridge University Press, 1986; Topham, Jonathan, "Beyond the 'Common Context': The Production and Reading of the Bridgewater Treatises." *Isis* 89 (1998): 233–62; Jager, Colin, "*Mansfield Park* and the End of Natural Theology." *Modern Language Quarterly* 63 (2002): 31–63.

2   For a meticulous treatment of this theme, see Glacken, Clarence J., *Traces on the Rhodian Shore; Nature and Culture in Western Thought from Ancient Times to the End of the Eighteenth Century*. Berkeley, CA: University of California Press, 1973.

3   For biographies, see Barker, Ernest, *Traditions of Civility: Eight Essays*. Cambridge: Cambridge University Press, 1948, 193–262; Clarke, M. L., *Paley: Evidences for the Man*. London: SPCK, 1974; LeMahieu, D. L., *The Mind of William Paley: A Philosopher and His Age*. Lincoln, NE: University of Nebraska Press, 1976.

4   For an assessment of Paley's influence at Cambridge, see Garland, Martha McMackin, *Cambridge before Darwin: The Ideal of a Liberal Education, 1800–1860*. Cambridge: Cambridge University Press, 1980, 52–69.

5   Clarke, *Paley: Evidences for the Man*, 126–7.

6   There is little doubt that Paley's Anglican theological roots are reflected in his apologetic approach: see the fine essay of Hitchin, Neil, "Probability and the Word of God: William Paley's Anglican Method and the Defense of the Scriptures." *Anglican Theological Review* 77 (1995): 302–407. Whether Paley's *Natural*

Theology can be considered a classic work of Anglican thought is very much open to question: see Cole, Graham, "William Paley's *Natural Theology*: An Anglican Classic?" *Journal of Anglican Studies* 5 (2007): 209–25. For comments on the form of Anglicanism adopted by Paley and his circle, see Waterman, A. M. C., "A Cambridge 'Via Media' in Late Georgian Anglicanism." *Journal of Ecclesiastical History* 42 (1991): 419–36.

7   The original title of this work was *Het regt Gebruik der Werelt Beschouwingen* ("The right use of world concepts"), published in Dutch in 1715.

8   I here follow the argument of Fyfe, Aileen, "Publishing and the Classics: Paley's *Natural Theology* and the Nineteenth-Century Scientific Canon." *Studies in the History and Philosophy of Science* 33 (2002): 433–55. Fyfe's analysis suggests that the sales of *Natural Theology* began to slow down significantly from 1850 onwards.

9   Fyfe, Aileen, "The Reception of William Paley's *Natural Theology* in the University of Cambridge." *British Journal for the History of Science* 30 (1997): 321–35.

10   In his autobiography, Darwin indicates familiarity with Paley's ideas while he was a student at Cambridge: Darwin, Francis, ed., *The Life and Letters of Charles Darwin*. 3 vols. London: John Murray, 1887, vol. 1, 47: "I did not at that time trouble myself about Paley's premises; and, taking these on trust, I was charmed and convinced by the long line of argumentation." However, a closer reading of the passage indicates that he was referring primarily to Paley's earlier works, *The Evidences of Christianity* and *Moral Philosophy*. While Darwin mentions Paley's *Natural Theology* here, the context does not imply that Darwin knew this work at this stage.

11   LeMahieu, *The Mind of William Paley*, 30. Paley's strategy appears to be to deal with Humean concerns indirectly, without naming their source, through use of his controlling analogy of the watch. For a critical evaluation of Hume's critique of natural theology, see Sennett, James, "Hume's Stopper and the Natural Theology Project." In *In Defense of Natural Theology: A Post-Humean Assessment*, ed. James F. Sennett and Douglas Groothuis, 82–104. Downers Grove, IL: InterVarsity Press, 2005.

12   Brooke, John Hedley, and Geoffrey Cantor, *Reconstructing Nature: The Engagement of Science and Religion*. New York: Oxford University Press, 2000, 196–8.

13   See especially Eddy, Matthew D., "The Rhetoric and Science of William Paley's *Natural Theology*." *Theology and Literature* 18 (2004): 1–22.

14   This point is explored by Brooke, John Hedley, *Science and Religion: Some Historical Perspectives*. Cambridge: Cambridge University Press, 1991, 210–13.

15   For documentation of this obsession with anatomy and its apologetic and theological implications, see Vidal, Fernando, "Extraordinary Bodies and the Physicotheological Imagination." In *The Face of Nature in Enlightenment Europe*, ed. Lorraine Daston and Gianna Pomata, 61–96. Berlin: Berliner Wissenschafts-Verlag, 2003.

16   He merits a brief mention in Israel, Jonathan I., *Enlightenment Contested: Philosophy, Modernity, and the Emancipation of Man, 1670–1752*. Oxford:

Oxford University Press, 2008, 385–6. Israel notes Nieuwentyt's commitment to an empirical method, and its implications for natural theology.

17 See Jorink, Erik, *Het Boeck der Natuere: Nederlandse Geleerden en de Wonderen van Gods Schepping 1575–1715*. Leiden: Primavera Pers, 2006.

18 Ruestow, Edward G., *The Microscope in the Dutch Republic: The Shaping of Discovery*. Cambridge: Cambridge University Press, 1996, 8–9; 149–73.

19 Verax, "Dr Paley's 'Natural Theology'." *Athenaeum*, no. 1085 (1848): 803.

20 Paley, William, *Natural Theology: Or, Evidences of the Existence and Attributes of the Deity*. 12th edn. London: Faulder, 1809, 378.

21 Paley, *Natural Theology*, 139.

22 Nieuwentyt, Bernard, *The Religious Philosopher; Or, the Right Use of Contemplating the Works of the Creator*. London: Senex & Taylor, 1718, lxv.

23 Paley, *Natural Theology*, 1.

24 Nieuwentyt, *The Religious Philosopher*, xlv.

25 Paley, *Natural Theology*, 2–3.

26 J.S., "Dr Paley's 'Natural Theology'." *Athenaeum*, no. 1089 (1848): 907–8.

27 B.E.N., "Dr Paley's Natural Theology." *Athenaeum*, no. 1090 (1848): 933–4. For further comment, see "The Charges of Plagiarism against Dr Paley." *Methodist Quarterly Review* 31 (1849): 159–61.

28 For the episode, see Ferré, Frederick, "William Paley, 1743–1805." In *Dictionary of Literary Biography: British Philosophers, 1500–1799*, ed. Philip B. Dematteis and Peter S. Fosl, 299–306. Columbia, SC: Bruccoli Clark Layman, 2001.

29 One of the mere two references to the notion of "contrivance" that I noted uses the term to refer to an artificially formulated argument: Nieuwentyt, *The Religious Philosopher*, 4.

30 See, for example, the representative statements at Nieuwentyt, *The Religious Philosopher*, iv; xii; 40; 45; 67; 71; 95; 104; 214; 227; 242; 258; 282.

31 Nieuwentyt, *The Religious Philosopher*, xlvii.

32 See the representative statements at Nieuwentyt, *The Religious Philosopher*, 44; 59; 69; 108; 112; 115; 131; 139; 153; 188; 213; 214; 244; 248; 273. Variants of the phrase "wisdom of the Creator" recur throughout the work.

33 These points are explored in Odom, Herbert H., "The Estrangement of Celestial Mechanics and Religion." *Journal of the History of Ideas* 27 (1966): 533–58.

34 William Blake comes to mind: see, for example, Raine, Kathleen, *Blake and Tradition*. 2 vols. London: Routledge & Kegan Paul, 1969, vol. 2, 165–70.

35 Paley, *Natural Theology*, 408.

36 Gillespie, Neal C., "Divine Design and the Industrial Revolution: William Paley's Abortive Reform of Natural Theology." *Isis* 81 (1990): 214–29.

37 Paley, *Natural Theology*, 1.

38 Paley, *Natural Theology*, 3.

39 Paley, *Natural Theology*, 379. Paley's argument emphasizes highly differentiated structures, adapted for specific purposes. This contrasts with other approaches to natural theology, which emphasized the structural unity of nature – such as that later found in the works of Richard Owen (111–12).

40 This chapter includes material contributed by Paley's friend John Law and the Dublin Astronomer Royal John Brinkley. Paley scrupulously acknowledges the origins of this material.

41   Paley, *Natural Theology*, 378.
42   Paley, *Natural Theology*, 379.
43   Paley, *Natural Theology*, 379.
44   For a good account of Paley's apologetic use of astronomical material, see Barrow, John, and Frank J. Tipler, *The Anthropic Cosmological Principle*. Oxford: Oxford University Press, 1986, 78–83; 261.
45   Paley, *Natural Theology*, 17–18.
46   Paley, *Natural Theology*, 18–19.
47   A point stressed by Nuovo, Victor, "Rethinking Paley." *Synthese* 91 (1992): 29–51, especially 31–2.
48   See the arguments of Sober, Elliott, *The Philosophy of Biology*. Boulder, CO: Westview Press, 1993, 30–6; Gliboff, Sander, "Paley's Design Argument as an Inference to the Best Explanation, or, Dawkins' Dilemma." *Studies in History and Philosophy of Biological and Biomedical Sciences* 31 (2000): 579–97.
49   Sweet, William, "Paley, Whately, and 'Enlightenment Evidentialism'." *International Journal for Philosophy of Religion* 45 (1999): 143–66.
50   Paley, *Natural Theology*, 467.
51   Hume, David, *Dialogues Concerning Natural Religion*. New York: Penguin, 1990, 77.
52   There is a brief reference to Hume's *Dialogues* at a late stage in the argument: Paley, *Natural Theology*, 512.
53   Hume, *Dialogues Concerning Natural Religion*, 79. See further Oppy, Graham, "Hume and the Argument for Biological Design." *Biology and Philosophy* 11 (1996): 519–34.
54   Baldwin, John T., "God and the World: William Paley's Argument from Perfection Tradition – a Continuing Influence." *Harvard Theological Review* 85 (1992): 109–20.
55   Paley, *Natural Theology*, 467.
56   Paley's discussion of the place of pain and suffering in nature is complex, and cannot be engaged with here. The two main points he develops are: first, that "the Deity has superadded *pleasure* to animal sensations, beyond what was necessary for any other purpose"; second, that "in a vast plurality of instances in which contrivance is perceived, the design of the contrivance is *beneficial*." See Paley, *Natural Theology*, 454–5. Other writers around this time were more skeptical: Bowler, Peter J., "Sir Francis Palgrave on Natural Theology." *Journal of the History of Ideas* 35 (1974): 144–7.
57   Hume, *Dialogues Concerning Natural Religion*, 77.
58   Paley, *Natural Theology*, 417.
59   Paley, *Natural Theology*, 418.
60   Paley, *Natural Theology*, 419–20.
61   Paley, *Natural Theology*, 54–5.
62   Paley, *Natural Theology*, 432.
63   See, for example, Maurer, Armand, "Darwin, Thomists, and Secondary Causality." *Review of Metaphysics* 57 (2004): 491–515.
64   Kingsley, Charles, "The Natural Theology of the Future." In *Westminster Sermons*, v–xxxiii. London: Macmillan, 1874.
65   The argument is set out rigorously in Nuovo, "Rethinking Paley."

66   Gould, Stephen Jay, *The Structure of Evolutionary Theory*. Cambridge, MA: Belknap Press, 2002, 118–21.

67   Paley, *Natural Theology*, 62. English awareness of these issues was raised considerably through the publication of Buckland's *Vindiciae Geologicae*. Buckland, William, *Vindiciae Geologicae: Or the Connexion of Geology with Religion Explained*. Oxford: Oxford University Press, 1820.

68   Ray, John, *The Wisdom of God Manifested in the Works of the Creation*. 9th edn. London: Royal Society, 1727, 124. Note also p. 138: "There is not to this day one species lost of such as are mention'd in histories, and consequently and undoubtedly neither of such as were first created." Ray's argument here is that, since all species are endowed with means of ensuring their survival and reproduction, there is no reason why any species should die out.

69   Kingsley, "The Natural Theology of the Future."

70   Paley, *Natural Theology*, 62–3. Note that a "wen" is an abnormal growth or a cyst protruding from a surface, especially the surface of the skin.

71   Paley, *Natural Theology*, 67.

72   Paley, *Natural Theology*, 379.

73   See, for example, Paley, *Natural Theology*, 73; 85; 341–2.

74   Paley, *Natural Theology*, 3.

75   For the importance of the socially constructed notion of "received opinion" in shaping such perceptions, see Patey, Douglas, *Probability and Literary Form: Philosophic Theory and Literary Practice in the Augustan Age*. Cambridge: Cambridge University Press, 1984, 3–13. A settled mode of thought over an extended period of time was easily assumed to rest upon a secure evidential basis, when in fact it represented a social convention, open to challenge and erosion over time. Paley clearly assumes the consensus of an earlier age, which probably persisted among his readership, in his mode of assembling evidence and developing his argument.

5

Beyond Paley: Shifts in English Natural Theology, 1802–52

William Paley's *Natural Theology* (1802) was a landmark in popular English natural theology, setting standards and shaping perceptions for a generation.[1] At one level, it can be seen as articulating a view of the origins and development of the natural world that was diametrically opposed to the approach that would be set out just over half a century later by Darwin in his *Origin of Species* (1859). Darwin's work is often represented as marking the triumph of dynamic and non-teleological accounts of nature over their static and teleological predecessors; of chance and change over design and permanence; and of secularism and naturalism over clericalism and supernaturalism.[2] Yet English approaches to natural theology changed significantly between 1802 and 1859, with the result that there is much less direct continuity between Paley's approach and the styles of English natural theology that commanded support on the eve of the publication of Darwin's *Origin of Species* than many appreciate.[3]

One of the most distinctive features of Paley's work is his evident enthusiasm and awe for the natural world, which reflected his own "intense appreciation of God's creation."[4] Indeed, this enthusiasm is widely credited with the development of a growing popular interest in natural history in the early nineteenth century. Paley's detailed description of natural beauty and intricacy – his book included no illustrations or diagrams[5] – generated a new interest in nature itself, arising from the theological interpretation Paley placed upon it.[6] Yet whatever its popular impact, Paley's approach to natural theology was one of a number being explored by English theological apologists and natural philosophers in the opening decade of the nineteenth century. Paley's argument that the utility of each feature of a complex biological organism was evidence of divine design increasingly became one option among alternatives – such as

Darwinism and the Divine: Evolutionary Thought and Natural Theology, First Edition.
Alister E. McGrath.
© 2011 Alister E. McGrath. Published 2011 by Blackwell Publishing Ltd.

the more idealist notion that the fundamental harmony and unity of nature pointed to its divine origins.[7]

The increasingly important evangelical constituency tended to be hostile toward such approaches to theology, whether derived from Paley or elsewhere, anxious that they seemed to prioritize nature as a source of the knowledge of God over the Bible. The primary concern of evangelical critics of Paley was the apparently autonomous position that he ascribed to natural theology. It was, they argued, presented as a self-sufficient religious system, which made no necessary or substantial connection with the specifics of the Christian faith, and especially the text of the Christian Bible.[8] Natural theology should properly be understood as a confirmation of divine revelation in Scripture, not as the source or basis of an independent knowledge of God. While praising Paley's attacks

Figure 5.1 The Central Court and Arcades of the Oxford University Museum. This engraving shows the interior of Oxford University's Museum of Natural History in 1860. The collection was arranged along the lines suggested by William Paley's *Natural Theology* in 1836 (see note 1).

on atheism, many evangelicals were clearly concerned that his approach represented an unintentional advocation of deism. In fact, William Paley (and subsequently the authors of the Bridgewater Treatises) took the view that the proper role of natural theology was to complement revealed theology, not to displace it. Yet this was not always clear to his readers.

Nevertheless, despite these concerns, it is important to note that evangelical assessments of the relative merits and drawbacks of Paley's approach to natural theology were mixed.[9] Evangelicalism around this time was a complex movement of shifting alliances and approaches, within which no particular approach to natural theology can be said to have achieved dominance, let alone general acceptance. Some evangelicals recognized that Paley's natural theology was an important apologetic resource for the church at a time of increased religious skepticism.

The logical and rhetorical use made by Paley of the central image of *Natural Theology* came under increasingly critical scrutiny in the 1830s. Lingering British suspicion of the revolutionary tendencies of French atheist and Deist writers led to Paley's argument based on the controlling image of a watch being tarnished by its political associations. Had not the French revolutionary writer Voltaire used a similar analogy?[10] More significantly, the internal logic of the analogy was subjected to skeptical challenge. The distinction between the stone and the watch rests upon observational familiarity, not their intrinsic identities.[11] Might not even stones be held to be designed in some kind of way? And, more importantly, it was argued that the argument from design based on Paley's analogy of the watch depended upon prior familiarity with their construction and purpose.[12] The inference of design was culturally conditioned, shaped by prevailing societal beliefs and norms. As time passed, and these became displaced by alternative beliefs, it became clear that this inference was not as "natural" or "rational" as some had naively assumed.[13]

The Impact of Geology upon Paley's Natural Theology

As already hinted, developments were taking place in the scientific field, which threatened to encroach upon the territory of natural theology. The growing public interest in geology led to some significant modifications to Paley's paradigm for natural theology, based upon geological considerations.[14] Paley himself had little interest in such matters, having chosen to focus primarily upon the biological realm. Others, however, had realized the significance of the developing field of geology for natural theology. On his appointment as reader in geology at Oxford University in 1819, William Buckland (1784–1856) delivered an inaugural lecture emphasizing both the importance of geology as a scientific discipline in its own right, and its positive role within a natural theology.[15] The approach developed by Buckland has a superficial similarity to that of Paley, its most obvious difference lying in its extension to the geological domain. The geological records, Buckland argued, bore witness to the wisdom of God. Even seemingly disastrous events had positive outcomes, under God's providential guidance. Natural acts of apparent "wanton destruction or natural decay" – such as the destruction of primeval forests – had good outcomes, in that they provided a supply of coal "to supply the wants and reward the industry of man in these latter ages of the world."[16] From this and other examples, Buckland inferred a general principle:[17]

> In all these and a thousand other examples that might be specified of design and benevolent contrivance, we trace the finger of an Omnipotent Architect

providing for the daily wants of its rational inhabitants, not only at the moment in which he laid the first foundations of the earth, but also through the long series of shocks and destructive convulsions which he has caused subsequently to pass over it.

Yet although a casual reading of Buckland might suggest an obvious affinity with Paley, closer study reveals significant differences, most notably Buckland's careful statement of a notion of historically progressive creation. Buckland suggested in his lecture that natural history had developed over time, having been "superintended" by God in a gradual progress toward ideal and benevolent ends. Where some argued for an essentially static creation, Buckland suggested that the Christian doctrine of divine providence pointed more in the direction of a divinely "superintended" development within the natural order.[18]

> [Many sciences exhibit] the most admirable proofs of design and intelligence originally exerted at the Creation; but many who admit these proofs still doubt the continued superintendence of that intelligence, maintaining that the system of the Universe is carried on by the force of the laws originally impressed on matter, without the necessity of fresh interference or continued supervision on the part of the Creator.

The complex picture of the geological development of the earth disclosed by the geological record, Buckland suggests, can be seen as a confirmation "of an overruling Intelligence continuing to superintend, direct, modify, and control the operation of the agents, which he originally ordained."[19]

Buckland's discussion of the geological record, including the evidence for past catastrophes, moves him significantly beyond Paley, both scientifically and theologically. For Buckland, the geological record demonstrates that the earth has changed, whether this is to be interpreted theologically in terms of direct divine intervention or operation through secondary causes.[20] The geological evidence clearly pointed to a time when the surface of the earth had been both uninhabited and uninhabitable. This being the case, Buckland argued, living beings – including humanity – must have arisen at a later stage.[21] Creation cannot be thought of as an instantaneous action, but must include progressive elements. Latent within Buckland's account of geological history is thus what can only be described as an evolutionary account of the origins of life, even though it lacks any notion of the evolution of *species*, as this would later be understood.[22] Buckland could see that the notion of "laws impressed upon matter" was consistent with a dynamic creation development under divine superintendence, not simply a more traditional static notion of creation.[23]

Mention should also be made of the "homological" approach to natural theology developed in the 1840s by Richard Owen, the distinguished comparative anatomist.[24] Owen defined homology as "the same organ in different animals under every variety of form and function." Adopting what appeared to be a Platonic notion of archetypes, Owen argued that an ideal "archetype" could be argued to be the template for the skeletons of the various classes of vertebrate animals.

Owen argued that there was evidence of homological relationships within nature, in the form of correspondences between organs in different animals. The wing of a sparrow, the flipper of a seal, the paw of a cat, and a human hand each manifested a common plan of structure, with identical or very similar arrangements of bones and muscles. Taking this idea to its conclusion, Owen affirmed that the ideal exemplar for vertebrate animals existed as an idea in the Divine Mind. It will be clear that this approach opened up important conceptual possibilities for natural theology.

Developments such as these led to the development of alternative visions of natural theology more adapted to these trends in the Victorian era, most notably in the Bridgewater Treatises, which we shall consider presently. But first, we must consider a figure who had considerable impact on the development of English natural theology in the nineteenth century, partly on account of his own proposals for how Paley's approach was to be modified, but mostly on account of his influence on the process of changing English opinion on what constituted evidence, and how such evidence was to be interpreted.

Henry Brougham: A Natural Theology of the Mind

Paley's contribution to natural theology was subjected to much criticism in the 1830s and beyond, not least in the light of shifting views within the legal profession in particular, and English educated culture in general, about the nature of evidence and its interpretation. Yet Paley was also criticized on account of his truncated and impoverished view of nature. Why, some of his critics asked, did he limit himself to the material realm of nature? Why not extend his approach to consider the human mind? Such an approach is to be found in the religious works of Henry Lord Brougham (1778–1868), who served as Lord Chancellor in Earl Grey's ministry from 1831 to 1834, overseeing the passing into law of the 1833 Abolition of Slavery Act.

Henry Lord Brougham's *Discourse of Natural Theology* (1835) defined natural theology as discovering "the existence and attributes of a Creator, by investigating the evidences of design in the works of the creation, material as well as spiritual."[25] Following Paley, Brougham appealed to evidence of "design and contrivance" throughout the created order,[26] regarding this as an adequate defense of the existence and attributes of God as creator. Though clearly dependent at many points upon Paley,[27] Brougham expresses misgivings about his approach at several points, most notably his "limited and unexercised powers of abstract discussion." Yet it is clear that Brougham has moved beyond Paley, both in terms of the evidence that he presents, and in the manner of its interpretation.

The most important point at which Brougham diverges from Paley on matters of interpretation concerns the philosophy of induction. While commenting on Paley's famous image of the watch found on a heath, Brougham stresses the importance of an "inductive philosophy" in allowing the observer of such a watch to draw the conclusion that it was constructed, and hence witnesses to its original constructor.[28] Brougham's extensive references to "inductive science," and the manner in which inferences may be drawn from observation,[29] move him significantly beyond Paley's somewhat simplistic attitudes toward "proof."

Yet Brougham moves still further beyond Paley in his reflections on the implications of the inductive process itself. Brougham notes that Paley failed to include any discussion of the workings of the human mind in his account of the realm of nature. Is not the ordered and structured nature of human reasoning itself to be considered as showing evidence of divine design? Surely a robust natural theology must engage with the phenomena of the human mind, not just of material nature?[30]

> The phenomena of mind, at the knowledge of which we arrive by this inductive process, the only legitimate intellectual philosophy, afford as decisive proofs of design as do the phenomena of matter, and they furnish those proofs by the strict method of induction. In other words, we study the nature and operations of the mind, and gather from them evidences of design, by one and the same species of reasoning, the induction of facts.

Brougham's argument here is that the material and spiritual worlds alike demonstrate evidence of contrivance. "The structure of the mind," he insisted, "affords evidence of the most skilful contrivance."[31] This aspect of nature had, he argued, been overlooked by previous natural theologians (such as Ray and Derham), who needlessly neglected the "mind and its operations."[32] William Paley is singled out for particular criticism, in that he never once mentioned the mind or its functions.[33] Brougham declares that Paley may represent a stylistic improvement upon Derham; his arguments, however, are equally inadequate. Is not the human mind part of nature, and hence to be regarded as falling within the scope of natural theology? Why does Paley give matter priority over mind?[34]

> Is there any reason whatever to draw this line; to narrow within these circles the field of Natural Theology; to draw from the constitutions and habits of matter alone the proof that one intelligent Cause creates and supports the universe? Ought we not rather to consider the phenomena of the mind as

more peculiarly adapted to help this inquiry, and as bearing a nearer relation to the Great Intelligence which created and which maintains this system?

The argument here is not especially original.[35] Aspects of this approach can be identified in the earlier tradition of English natural theology. Yet Brougham has woven it into a coherent statement, capable of being grasped and used by his readership.

Brougham does not appear to be informed historically about the provenance of this argument, which is found in both Athanasius of Alexandria and Augustine of Hippo. Both argue that the creation of humanity in the image of God carries with it the capacity to use reason to find its way back to God. Athanasius, for example, emphasizes the epistemological consequences of the divine creation of humanity, noting its implications for the human engagement with the natural world.[36]

> God knew the limitations of humanity; and though the grace of being made in the image of God was sufficient to give them knowledge of the Word, and through Him of the Father, as a safeguard against their neglect of this grace, God also provided the works of creation as a means by which the Maker might be known ... Humanity could thus look up into the immensity of heaven, and by pondering the harmony of creation, come to know its Ruler, the Word of the Father, whose sovereign providence makes the Father known to all.

A similar line of argument is found in the writings of Augustine of Hippo. Brougham's work was, of course, written before the publication of the Anglo-Catholic series "The Library of the Fathers" (1838–85), which considerably raised the profile of patristic theology within certain sections of Anglicanism.[37]

Figure 5.2   Portrait of the British polymath William Whewell (1794–1866).

Brougham is an important witness to the complex process of reception and revision of the older English tradition of natural theology in the 1830s. Where Paley had argued that the enterprise of natural theology, as he understood the notion, was best restricted to the biological realm, others began to challenge this. Brougham, as we have seen, insisted on extending the approach from the adaptations and complexity of plants and animals to the workings of the human mind – a theme that would be developed further in the natural theology of William Whewell (123–6). Others would urge the importance of reconnecting natural theology with the physical sciences, especially astronomy and geology.

Yet Brougham's importance to the development of natural theology in the 1830s and beyond lies only partly in his own contributions to the subject. As Lord Chancellor, Brougham was instrumental in setting out what many regard as the most significant revision of English criminal law of its age. In 1833, Brougham set up a Royal Commission, composed of five practicing lawyers, to undertake a thorough and radical review of English criminal law. In the end, this Commission issued eight reports over the period 1834–45.[38] Their recommendations included reflecting on the nature and interpretation of evidence, and its implications for criminal trials.[39] These changing understandings of the nature and interpretation of evidence that developed in England around this time had major implications for the theory and practice of natural theology, and we shall consider them in the following section.

Evidence, Testimony, and Proof: A Shifting Context

What constitutes evidence? And how is it to be interpreted? These questions were fundamental to many debates in theology, philosophy, and the natural sciences in the late seventeenth and eighteenth centuries. Their relevance to natural theology, especially those emphasizing "evidence of design," will be obvious. What can legitimately be regarded as "evidence" of contrivance or divine artifice? And what publicly acceptable norms of interpretation are deployed in arriving at such conclusions?[40]

A close reading of English writers who developed such approaches to natural theology between 1690 and 1720 suggests that they regarded neither of these questions as worth raising in detail, or as giving rise to any significant difficulties. Writers such as John Ray and William Derham, later to be followed by William Paley, focused their energies on the accumulation of evidence that they believed pointed inexorably to "proof of design, and of a designing Creator" (Paley). Yet there appears at times to be an unstated assumption that the quantity of evidence thus adduced relieves the natural theologian of any obligation to clarify the structure of the argument by which it is interpreted as constituting proof of design.

In England during the period 1650–1850, the intellectual context within which most attention was given to the question of evidence and its public interpretation was that of the law courts. The point at issue here is the distinction between observational and theoretical terms – between what is observed, and how this is interpreted.[41] During the sixteenth and seventeenth centuries, the English legal system took the view that facts were relatively easily established by reliable persons, allowing guilt or innocence to be determined by eyewitness testimony.[42]

> The legal system taught Englishmen that facts, or at least the ephemeral facts of human action, could be established with a high degree of certitude by witness testimony, and that ordinary persons had sufficient ability to evaluate that testimony for credibility.

The attitudes toward evidence characteristic of seventeenth-century England can be seen in the writings of Sir Matthew Hale (1609–76).[43] In his reflections on evidence, Hale argues that when multiple observations and reports "concur and concenter in the evidence of the same thing, their very multiplicity and consent make the evidence the stronger, as the concurrent testimonies of many Witnesses or many Circumstances even by their multiplicity and concurrence make an evidence more concludent."[44]

Such views continued to be expressed in the following century.[45] In a landmark study of the rhetoric and conventions of the eighteenth century, Alexander Welsh pointed out that the predominant theory of criminal trials in England during this period was that of "evidence" as that which is evident, and the related notion of "facts speaking for themselves."[46] No special legal training was required for the observation or interpretation of criminal evidence; the facts in the case were sufficient to speak for themselves. It was an approach summed up in the maxim *da mihi facta dabo tibi ius* ("give me the facts, and I will give you justice").

Assumptions such as these are deeply embedded in the English "physico-theology" tradition of the late seventeenth and early eighteenth centuries. How else are we to account for John Ray's apparent assumption that the mere exhibition of the beauty and complexity of the natural world is sufficient to persuade his readers of the existence and wisdom of a creator God? Ray follows the evidentiary assumptions of his day, and we can hardly criticize him for doing so. Yet it is important to understand the cultural context within which his argument is set, reflecting certain assumptions that Ray assumes to be "common sense,"[47] but are evidently the outcome of a complex process of socialization. What Ray takes for granted as obvious, routine, and uncontroversial reflect the social conventions and convictions of his age. They are socially constructed notions, not ideas that are intrinsic to the evidence under consideration. Sociologically, belief in God was a settled intellectual conviction of the age; the work of Ray and Derham is best seen as reinforcing an existing belief, while lacking the evidentiary and argumentative resources to establish this *de novo*.

The importance of evidence to Paley can be seen from the extended subtitle of his *Natural Theology*, namely: *Evidences of the Existence and Attributes of the Deity*. Although Paley is writing more than a century later than Ray, he follows in this same evidentiary tradition, obviously believing that the clear presentation of an accumulation of evidence is sufficient to make his case. As noted earlier, when Paley speaks of offering a "proof" of the existence of a creator, it is evident that he does not mean a logical proof, but rather a rhetorical demonstration, similar to that then encountered in a court of law. Yet the intellectual context within which his appeal to evidence is mounted is that of a much earlier period in English history. The context was changing, and Paley's approach was already dated.

Where earlier generations regarded evidence as speaking for itself, early nineteenth-century writers were much more alert to the complexities of the assessment and interpretation of evidence, especially in criminal trials. In her careful study of these shifting attitudes to evidence around this time, Jan-Melissa Schramm comments:[48]

> The eighteenth-century idea of "facts speaking for themselves" became increasingly discredited as both lawyers and authors realized that professional representations were required to render "facts" effective as pieces of evidence ... To concede that facts were complex rather than self-evident was to open the way for legal and literary feats of analysis and rhetorical power.

Paley was well aware of the importance of deploying rhetoric to cover up awkward argumentative *lacunae*, and clearly saw the need for a rigorous argumentative structure as a means of solidifying the impact of his accumulation of observations of the natural world. Yet, to an increasingly sophisticated reading public, this approach would increasingly have come to be seen as out of place. The "proofs" that Paley offered might stand up in a seventeenth-century court of law; they would not in the early nineteenth century.

The landmark transition took place on June 9, 1836, on the eve of the Victorian age, when His Majesty's Commissioners on Criminal Law finally laid to rest the notion that a safe conviction or acquittal rested on the assessment of self-evident facts.[49] The concept of evidence was recognized to be a *theoretical*, not an *empirical* notion. It is not something that is observed within or read off from nature. Evidence is shaped by assumptions, by hypotheses that create a framework within which an observation plays a particularly significant role. Evidence is determined by a set of assumptions that generate a field of inquiry, a context for asking questions, in the context of which (and only in the context of which) something can appear as "evidence."[50]

The Commissioners emphasized the importance of trained advocates, who would be able to demonstrate how observations were to be correlated with the prosecution's theory of how the prisoner was guilty, and the defense's theory of the prisoner's innocence. Part of the role of such an advocate was to challenge what might turn out to be inaccurate or false witnesses; yet perhaps the most significant role such an advocate would play was the *interpretation* of ambivalent evidence. Evidence was to be set in a theoretical context. An observation only becomes "evidence" when set within the context of a theory of how a crime was undertaken, and by whom. The same observation might serve as "evidence" for several different outcomes, depending upon the theory of events within which it was located. The Royal Commission of 1836 emphasized the importance of what they termed "giving order and connexion to a mass of facts," and pointed to the need for skilled interpreters of these observations to be able to explain their significance to a jury.[51]

This point was made by the novelist Charles Dickens in June 1836, while acting as a reporter for the *Morning Chronicle*. Dickens was reporting on *Norton versus Melbourne*, a notorious case, which rested on demonstrating that the then prime minister, Lord Melbourne, had committed adultery with Caroline Norton. Since nobody had seen this take place at first hand, the case depended upon the interpretation of circumstantial evidence. Dickens summarizes the crucial evidential point as follows:[52]

> It was perfectly clear that there was no direct evidence of the fact of adultery; it was also perfectly clear that the law did not require direct evidence of the fact, but that it merely required evidence of such circumstances as would lead by fair and just inference to it.

Note the key word: *inference*. If something cannot be proven directly, it may be inferred from observation. If nobody observed the act of adultery, making an eyewitness account impossible, debate turns to the question of whether a theoretical framework predicated upon committing adultery is to be judged the best interpretation of the circumstantial evidence that is available.

What is the significance of this transition for English natural theology of that age? Perhaps it is important to emphasize that the Royal Commission's recommendations of 1836 reflected as much as caused a shift in English understandings of the nature of evidence. Their recommendations consolidated, perhaps even accelerated, the move toward inference-based approaches to the evaluation of evidence. Facts were now deemed to require *interpretation* and *correlation* in order to serve as evidence. It was not sufficient merely to observe, and then to accumulate such observations, hoping it might serve as "proof"; it was necessary to ask which narrative of events offered the best fit to what had been observed. Such judgments inevitably rested upon probability, rather than certainty. Natural theology, if it was to remain a credible enterprise, could no longer hope to argue that alleged "evidence of design" proved the existence of God as its originator. More sophisticated and nuanced engagement with the observation of the natural world was required.

One such approach was developed by the Cambridge philosopher of science William Whewell (1794–1866). In his *Philosophy of the Inductive Sciences*

(1840), Whewell used a highly suggestive visual image to communicate the capacity of a good theory to make sense of, and weave together, observations. "The facts are known but they are insulated and unconnected ... The pearls are there but they will not hang together until some one provides the string."[53] The "pearls" are the observations and the "string" is a theory that *connects* and *unifies* the data. A good theory, Whewell asserted, allows the "colligation of facts," establishing a new system of relations with each other, unifying what might have otherwise been considered to be disconnected and isolated observations. Paley identifies pearls and assumes their significance will be evident to all. Whewell, while appreciating the same pearls, is more concerned to find the best string on which to thread them. Observing individual pearls in isolation discloses little, if anything, of the bigger picture within which they are located. Whewell insists that the significance of individual pearls only emerges when the manner of their colligation – that is to say, their relation to one another – is established. It is necessary to give "order and connexion to a mass of facts" by establishing the best theoretical string on which these pearls may be threaded, and thus enabling them to disclose a meaningful pattern that transcends the contribution of any individual pearl.

As we shall see, the demonstration of the consonance between Christian thought and the observation of the natural world now became an important element in Victorian approaches to natural theology. To explore this further, we shall consider the celebrated Bridgewater Treatises, which included a landmark contribution by Whewell himself.

A New Approach: The Bridgewater Treatises

A remarkable series of eight works of natural theology appeared during the years 1833–6, which are collectively known as the Bridgewater Treatises.[54] These were the result of a munificent bequest made by the eighth Earl of Bridgewater, Francis Henry Egerton (1756–1829), who bequeathed £8,000 to the Royal Society as a payment to the person or persons chosen by its president who would be invited to "write, print and publish, one thousand copies of a work" on natural theology, the specific topics of which were to be:[55]

> The Power, Wisdom and Goodness of God, as manifested in the Creation: illustrating such work by all reasonable arguments – as for instance the variety and formation of God's creatures in the animal, vegetable, and mineral kingdoms; the effect of digestion and thereby of conversion; the construction of the hand of man, and an infinite variety of other arguments; as also by discoveries ancient and modern, in arts, sciences, and the whole extent of literature.

Egerton himself was interested in the field of natural theology, and had written a treatise on the topic (now lost). Although Egerton is known to have been influenced by Paley, his brief for natural theology extends significantly beyond Paley's somewhat narrow and restrictive focus on the biological realm as evidence of divine contrivance.

Under the terms of Egerton's will, the choice of authors lay in the hands of the president of the Royal Society.[56] Egerton's bequest of £8,000 was to be paid to "such person or persons" as the president of the Royal Society should nominate to write "a work" of natural theology. It was, however, not clear what Egerton had in mind: the will suggested a single volume, whether written by a single individual, or a group of authors. Davies Gilbert (1767–1839) was president of the Royal Society at the time of the execution of the will. After confirming that Egerton's family would not contest the terms of the will, Gilbert consulted the Archbishop of Canterbury and Bishop of London to identify potential authors. This process was a highly sensitive matter, as the sum of money being offered for their services was very substantial by the standards of the time. Many aspiring authors wrote to offer their services.

It is not clear how the decision was reached to commission eight works on natural theology, rather than a single work. William Howley (1766–1848), then Archbishop of Canterbury, had suggested that a valuable publication could best be produced by "selecting a certain number of eminent persons" to write on different topics. It is entirely possible that the figure of eight was arrived at by dividing the amount of the bequest in such a way that each author would receive exactly £1,000. The eight authors who were finally commissioned to write treatises, with their respective titles and dates of first publication, were:

1 Thomas Chalmers, *On the Power, Wisdom, and Goodness of God as Manifested in the Adaptation of External Nature to the Moral and Intellectual Constitution of Man* (1833).
2 John Kidd, *On the Adaptation of External Nature to the Physical Condition of Man* (1833).
3 William Whewell, *Astronomy and General Physics Considered with Reference to Natural Theology* (1833).
4 Charles Bell, *The Hand: Its Mechanism and Vital Endowment as Evincing Design* (1833).
5 Peter Mark Roget, *Animal and Vegetable Physiology Considered with Reference to Natural Theology* (1834).
6 William Buckland, *Geology and Mineralogy Considered with Reference to Natural Theology* (1836).
7 William Kirby, *On the History, Habits and Instincts of Animals* (1835).

8 William Prout, *Chemistry, Meteorology, and the Function of Digestion Considered with Reference to Natural Theology* (1834).

In appointing these authors, Gilbert appears to have provided little in the way of specific directions concerning their specific responsibilities.[57] Apart from making sure that the authors were familiar with the Earl of Bridgewater's will and the identity and proposed topics of their fellow authors, Gilbert appears to have left his authors to organize themselves. There was no figure who held overall responsibility for ensuring collaboration and consistency between the authors. The outcome was perhaps inevitable: a diversity of approaches to their topics, linked with quite different expectations concerning their readerships.

Within fifteen years of their publication, more than 60,000 copies of the Bridgewater Treatises were in print,[58] exceeding the cumulative sales of Paley's *Natural Theology*. The eight volumes had a collective force that helped shape something of a "common context" within Victorian intellectual life. Building upon (although at points significantly departing from) the approach of William Paley,[59] the Bridgewater Treatises set out the importance of interpreting Scripture in the light of new scientific findings, while at the same time maintaining that belief in God was implicit in the order of nature, and that something of God's nature and character could be elucidated through sound empirical investigation.[60] Robert Young identifies four fundamental points concerning the emergence of this early Victorian consensus:[61]

1 In the early decades of the nineteenth century, there existed a common intellectual context across intellectual disciplines, such as theology, social theory, and the natural sciences.[62]

2 There was a relatively homogeneous and satisfactory natural theology, set out in William Paley's classic *Natural Theology* (1802) and related works. These works were discussed in detail in the periodical literature in the first four decades of the century. The Bridgewater Treatises (1833–6) can be seen as an attempt to codify this tradition in the light of detailed findings in the several sciences. Though initially reasonably successful, this synthesis began to unravel in subsequent decades.

3 The impact of scientific findings progressively altered this coherent natural theology until it was virtually devoid of content as a discipline in its own right.

4 The common intellectual context fragmented in the 1870s and 1880s, partly through the development of specialist societies and periodicals, and increasing professionalization within the sciences.[63]

While this notion of a "common context" must be treated with caution, it nevertheless offers a helpful framework for appreciating the role played by natural theology in the 1840s and 1850s. On the one hand, it reaffirmed the reliability of a Christian vision of reality, particularly in the light of increasing scientific knowledge; on the other, it lent religious legitimacy to the development of the sciences, implying that their development emphasized the fundamental harmony between science and religion.[64] Where science had once been presented, in the aftermath of the French Revolution (1789), as the ally of skepticism and atheism, it could now be seen as part of an intellectually secure and socially stabilizing synthesis of religion, arts, and science. The fact that so many of the authors of the Bridgewater Treatises were highly regarded "gentlemen of science" did much to ensure that these volumes, individually and collectively, were taken very seriously by the British intelligentsia.[65] The treatises contributed significantly to the stabilization of religious belief on the one hand, and to the popularization of the natural sciences on the other.

So in what ways, and to what extent, can the Bridgewater Treatises be said to have redirected or refocused Paley's vision of natural theology?[66] With the obvious exception of Thomas Chalmers, all the Bridgewater Treatises were written by "gentlemen of science," with little in the way of professional theological expertise or concerns. The predominant approach adopted by the writers was that of setting out contemporary scientific wisdom on their designated topics, and then attempting to establish some *post hoc* connections with a theological framework, often consisting of vague affirmations of the divine origination of the universe, and its continuing providential government. In many ways, these can be seen as amplifications of Paley's approach, offering analyses that are more extended, systematic, and up-to-date than those of Paley, even if the same mode of argument is often used. For example, Peter Mark Roget's account of animal and vegetable physiology is far more detailed and systematic than Paley's; his conclusion, however, is substantially the same: such adaptations offer "the clearest and most palpable proofs of contrivance and design."[67]

Similarly, Sir Charles Bell offers a detailed and richly illustrated examination of the mechanism of the human hand, identifying the many ways in which it is adapted to its functions. The structure of the hand, he argues, "presents the best and last proof of the principle of adaptation, which evinces design in the creation."[68] The observation of adaptation is regarded as clearly consistent with the notion of divine origination or design. Substantially the same principle is set out by William Prout.[69]

> Animals in cold climates have been provided with a covering of fur. Men in such climates cover themselves with that fur ... Now, since the animal did not clothe itself, but must have been clothed by another, it follows that whoever clothed the animal, must have known what the man knows, and must therefore have reasoned like the man ... The man who clothes himself in fur to keep

off the cold performs an act directed towards a certain end; in short, an act of
design. So, whoever, directly or indirectly, caused the animal to be clothed
with fur to keep off the cold must likewise have performed an act of design.

Once more an adaptation to a specific environment is interpreted as an act
of design, rather than a natural development. Although Prout at times concedes that design is something that is to be indirectly inferred, rather than
directly observed,[70] his approach is best regarded as essentially an amplification of Paley's. William Kirby's extended reflections on animal instincts also
argue from adaptation to design: "every thing was adapted by its structure
and organization for the situation in which it was to be placed."[71]

The most philosophically sophisticated of the treatises is that of William
Whewell, whose contributions to the development of the philosophy of science would be significant for the clarification of the scientific method. Two
aspects of Whewell's natural theology are of particular importance to our
study: first, his views of the inductive character of knowledge of the natural
world; and second, his emphasis upon nature being characterized by certain physical laws, which themselves act as indications of the divine origins
and governance of the creation. We shall consider each of these points
separately.

Although Whewell's landmark discussions of the importance of induction
within the scientific method had yet to be published, there are clear traces of
such lines of thought in his Bridgewater Treatise. Paley's somewhat simplistic notions of "evidence" and "proof," echoed at points in most of the treatises of the "gentlemen of science," are discreetly abandoned, in favor of
a more inductive approach to evidence, similar to that set out in a legal
context by the Royal Commission of 1836.

As we noted earlier, Whewell argues that the scientific method cannot be
characterized simply in terms of the accumulation of evidence.[72] For Whewell,
the mind was not simply passive in the act of cognition; rather, it actively
contributed ideas that gave intelligible form to sense-impressions. Generalized
knowledge only occurred when sensations were informed by mental
conceptions, raising the question of which such mental conceptions were to
be deemed the most adequate to accommodate sense-impressions. Whewell
thus argues that the key question concerns the identification of the best
theoretical framework within which empirical observations may be
positioned and accommodated. Whewell is thus an early advocate of what
we would now call the "theory-laden nature of observation." In his
Philosophy of the Inductive Sciences, he remarks that there is "a mask of
theory over the whole face of nature."[73] In other words, we see nature
through theoretical spectacles. It is therefore entirely proper to inquire as to
which such theoretical framework offers the best apprehension of nature. To
use Whewell's figure of speech, the question concerns which theoretical mask

best fits over the face of nature. Which offers the best theoretical fit? Or, to use another of Whewell's images (119), which theoretical string is best suited to link together the observational pearls?

Whewell's divergence from Paley at this point is as clear as it is significant. Paley identifies observational pearls, and assumes their evidentiary significance is a matter of assertion, rather than argument. Whewell holds that such pearls, in isolation, mean little; what gives them their significance is the manner of their colligation – the way in which they relate to one another. To use the language of the 1836 Commission, the issue is finding a theory that is best able to give "order and connexion to a mass of facts."

So how do these ideas find their application in natural theology? In the preface to his Bridgewater Treatise, Whewell speaks of his "prescribed object" being to "lead the friends of religion to look with confidence and pleasure on the progress of the physical sciences, by showing how admirably every advance in our knowledge of the universe harmonizes with the belief of a most wise and good God."[74] Scientific knowledge may serve to "nourish and unfold our idea of a Creator and Governor of the world" – but not, in Whewell's view, to prove the existence of such a God. "The views of the creation, preservation, and government of the universe, which natural science opens to us, harmonize with our belief in a Creator, Governor and Preserver of the world."[75] Where Paley speaks of the natural world proving God's existence and wisdom, Whewell speaks more cautiously of nature providing "indications" of the wisdom and power of God.[76] The Christian understanding of God is seen as a theoretical string on which the pearls of scientific observation may be strung.

This increasing recognition of the inductive character of natural theology distanced these new ways of thinking from the older approaches of the Augustan age. Baden Powell's *Connexion of Natural and Divine Truth* (1838) suggested that the recognition of the inductive character of the natural sciences causes difficulty for traditional approaches to natural theology, forcing it to position itself either as a form of the natural sciences, or as a form of revealed truth.[77] In either case, the capacity of natural theology to bridge the gap between the two disciplines became increasingly difficult to maintain.

The second point that characterizes Whewell's natural theology in his Bridgewater Treatise is his emphasis upon the importance of the laws of nature. Nature operates according to certain fixed and constant laws, which can be established by scientific observation and analysis. "Our knowledge of nature is our knowledge of laws." For Whewell, the observation that "nature acts by general laws" is consistent with "our conception of the Divine Author."[78] Such laws are to be found in the biological realm, as well as that of consciousness. The structure and function of the natural world as a whole are to be accounted for "by the will and power of one supreme being acting by fixed laws."[79]

God is thus to be understood as a "designing Intelligence," whose tools for the creation and preservation of the natural world are the laws of nature.[80] Whewell had already explored this point in an important 1830 review of Lyell's *Principles of Geology*,[81] in which he argued that both the realms of geology and biology disclose such regularities. "The geologist sees … in all the arrangements, whether of the organic or mineral world, the sure marks of a First Cause acting by uniform, invariable laws." Recognition of the existence and importance of these laws is not inconsistent with teleological approaches to natural theology. To recognize a goal within the natural order does not preclude a law-like explanation for the means by which this end is achieved. Where Paley's concept of "contrivance" emphasized the teleological aspects of nature and their potential theological implications, Whewell preferred to focus on the regularities of the natural order. Here, he argued, was to be found a more secure basis for a defensible natural theology. Where Paley's doctrine of special creation presupposed direct divine intervention, Whewell's clear preference is for an indirect conception of divine action, mediated through laws. Charles Darwin would later use Whewell's statement of this principle as an epigram for his *Origin of Species*:[82]

> But with regard to the material world, we can at least go so far as this; we can perceive that events are brought about not by insulated interpositions of Divine power, exerted in each particular case, but by the establishment of general laws.

Although some nineteenth-century writers represent Whewell as adopting an interventionist approach to divine action, especially in relation to the biological realm, there is nothing in Whewell's writings that lends firm support to such a thesis.[83] Whewell's most characteristic thought is that God's creative and providential activity is to be discerned primarily within the regularities of the natural order.

So how is humanity able to discover such laws? Here, we come to an aspect of Whewell's natural theology that is too easily overlooked – namely, his theological understanding of human nature. For Whewell, the capacity of the human mind to make sense of the natural world was itself something that demanded explanation. Why was the human mind so capable of accommodating the deep structure of nature? The fact that the human mind was able to discern the rationality and ordering of nature was itself of theological significance. As one anonymous reviewer of Whewell's Bridgewater Treatise correctly noted:[84]

> Instances of design in the creation of the universe, specially exhibited in individual cases, as in the eye, the foot, &c., have already been seized on, and

explained with a force and felicity which can hardly be surpassed. It remained to see if, when philosophy had pushed her researches to the general physical laws which prevail in the creation, those laws could be made to yield to the popular literature of the country materials for similar proof of the designing mind, and of the attributes of the Ruler of the universe.

Whewell, the reviewer concluded, had been conspicuously successful in this enterprise. The human mind was capable of discovering the regularities of the universe on the one hand, and subsequently inferring its divine origination on the other. "Mr. Whewell gets a glimpse of no law, without a reverent perception of the powers, functions and endowments of the intellect which traces it; and in observing these, he is led constantly upwards to the mightier intellect, which framed man and the universe."[85]

Underlying Whewell's approach is his belief that the human ability to discern the rationality and ordering of nature, and hence the character of God, points to a fundamental harmony between the mind of God, the human mind, and the laws of nature. In one sense, the idea of God is thus not so much the final conclusion of reflection on the natural world, but its presupposition. The idea of God is not "extracted from the phenomena, but assumed in order that the phenomena may become intelligible to the mind."[86] A core theme of Whewell's complex argument is the correspondence between the structures and orders of the natural world with human mental architecture. The human capacity to make sense of the natural world is itself an indication of its divine origins and endowments.[87] Yet the overall consistency of Whewell's approach is nevertheless clear: the Christian conception of God is consistent with what is observed within the natural world, providing an intellectual scaffolding that gives intelligibility to both what is observed and the process of observation itself. Whewell has moved beyond Paley, distancing himself from any notion of nature "proving" God's existence or character, and instead accentuating the capacity of such a God to make sense of reality.

The analysis presented in this chapter thus far suggests that Paley's approach to natural theology was gradually being displaced by alternative approaches by the middle of the nineteenth century, prompted partly by shifting cultural attitudes toward evidence and proof on the one hand, and scientific advances on the other. Yet hostility toward Paley's approach was also developing on another front. Some prominent theologians were expressing increasing anxiety about the merits of "physico-theology" and its potentially negative impact on the public perception of the plausibility and appeal of the Christian faith. In the final section of this chapter, we shall consider the criticisms made of Paley by a writer now widely regarded as the greatest English theologian of the nineteenth century – John Henry Newman (1801–90).

John Henry Newman: The Theological Deficiencies of Paley

Given the status of Newman as a theologian, it is perhaps surprising that relatively little attention has been paid to his developing attitude toward the natural sciences in Victorian England, not least as they relate to natural theology.[88] During his time as vicar of the University Church, Oxford (1828–42), Newman became increasingly aware of early signs of the development of a scientific culture within Oxford University, and its potential implications for both the Christian faith and the study of Christian theology.[89] Newman had no particular criticisms to make of scientific advance; his concern was to clarify the proper relationship between theology and the natural sciences, avoiding confusion and conflation. Part of this process of clarification concerned the proper place and limits of natural theology.

The essential elements of Newman's critique of Paley were in place by 1832. Natural theology, Newman argued, was useful for reinforcing a faith that already existed; it was not sufficient to bring that faith into being in the first place. Furthermore, the essence of religious faith did not consist in an intellectual analysis of reality, but the struggle against sin. In what is clearly a critique of Paley's natural theology, Newman argued that it simply missed the mark, offering a vision of religion that bore little relationship to the actual reality of Christianity itself.[90]

> It is easy to speak eloquently of the order and beauty of the physical world, of the wise contrivance of visible nature, and of the benevolence of the objects proposed in them; but none of those topics throw light upon the subject which it most concerns us to understand, the character of the Moral Governance, under which we live.

These concerns are repeated throughout Newman's later writings, including two lectures delivered in Dublin in 1855 as rector-elect of the new Catholic University of Dublin. In these lectures, which predate the publication of Darwin's *Origin of Species*, Newman set out his vision for an authentically Christian university, capable of engaging with scholarship on the one hand, and retaining its Christian roots on the other.[91] The two lectures in question were entitled "Christianity and Physical Science" and "Christianity and Scientific Investigation." In the first lecture, Newman set out to engage the suspicion that "there is some contrariety between the declarations of religion and the results of physical enquiry."[92]

Although the "warfare" model of the relation of science and religion had yet to emerge, Newman was clearly aware of growing tensions, indicated by his reference to the "antagonism that is popularly supposed to exist between

Figure 5.3 Cardinal John Henry Newman, c. 1870.

Physics and Theology."[93] Newman argues for the essential independence of science and faith, holding that both, when rightly understood, have their own distinct spheres of influence and authority. Theology "contemplates the world not of matter but of mind; the supreme intelligence; souls and their destiny; conscience and duty; the past, present, and future dealings of the Creator and the creature."[94] It therefore follows that, if "Theology be the philosophy of the supernatural world and Science the philosophy of the natural, Theology and Science, whether in their respective ideas, or again in their own actual fields, are incommensurable, incapable of collision, and needing at most to be connected, never to be reconciled."[95]

So what of natural theology? Newman had made his distaste for Paley's "physico-theology" clear during the 1830s, developing two lines of argument against it: first, that it failed to establish a coherent connection between natural world and faith in God; and second, that it failed to connect with the specific emphases of the Christian faith. In his 1855 Dublin lectures, Newman gave them more extensive discussion, while now adding a third argument, reflecting Newman's unease about the emphasis upon the regularity of nature, more associated with the Bridgewater Treatises than with Paley. How, Newman asked, could this be reconciled with the Christian belief in miracles?

Newman's first point is that the arguments from nature can only be inductive, and thus fail to establish the core ideas of faith. While they may be of service to those who already believe in God, offering reinforcement of these beliefs, natural theology lacks the evidential and argumentative rigor to establish such a belief in the first place. Newman famously rejected traditional arguments from design: "I believe in design because I believe in God; not in God because I see design."[96] Paley's natural theology, Newman suggested, was as likely to lead to atheism as to belief in God.

Second, Newman raises concerns about the "God" disclosed by natural theology. If "God" amounted to little more than what the telescope or the microscope disclosed of nature, then "divine truth is not something separate from Nature, but it is Nature with a divine glow upon it."[97] Such a notion of God is limited to a rational principle of interpretation, lacking any sense of transcendence, holiness, or majesty. Physical theology, Newman insisted, taught "exclusively" only three divine attributes: power, wisdom, and goodness; yet it remained silent concerning the real essence of the Christian vision of God – namely, the divine holiness, justice, mercy, and providence.[98]

What, on the contrary, are those special Attributes, which are the immediate correlatives of religious sentiment? Sanctity, omniscience, justice, mercy, faithfulness. What does Physical Theology, what does the Argument from Design, what do fine disquisitions about final causes, teach us, except very indirectly, faintly, enigmatically, of these transcendently important, these essential portions of the idea of Religion. Religion is more than Theology; it is something relative to us; and it includes our relation towards the Object of it. What does Physical Theology tell us of duty and conscience?

Newman thus draws his conclusion: while natural theology may be of some support to faith, it cannot create it. Paley's approach to natural theology may indeed be apologetically useful in demonstrating the capacity of the Christian faith to make sense of the natural order. But, taken on its own, it "cannot tell us anything of Christianity at all."[99]

Newman's third point is perhaps more contestable. An emphasis upon the regularity of nature, he suggests, leads to a frame of mind that is reluctant to concede any violation of the fixed laws of nature through miracles, leading to a tendency to deny the notion of the miraculous altogether.[100]

This so-called science [of natural theology] tends, if it occupies the mind, to dispose it against Christianity. And for this plain reason, because it speaks only of laws; and cannot contemplate their suspension, that is, miracles, which are of the essence of the idea of a Revelation. Thus, the God of Physical Theology may very easily become a mere idol; for He comes to the inductive mind in the medium of fixed appointments, so excellent, so skilful, so beneficent, that, when it has for a long time gazed upon them, it will think them too beautiful to be broken, and will at length so contract its notion of Him as to conclude that He never could have the heart (if I may dare use such a term) to undo or mar His own work; and this conclusion will be the first step towards its degrading its idea of God a second time, and identifying Him with His works.

Elsewhere, Newman defined miracles as events that were "inconsistent with the constitution of nature," or which "cannot be referred to any law, or accounted for by the operation of any principle, in that system."[101] Newman was careful, however, to insist that the notion of a miracle "does not necessarily imply a violation of nature"; rather, he argued, it requires the "interposition of an external cause" that can be traced back to God.[102]

Newman's apprehension here is that natural theology seems to draw its inspiration from a settled, regular, ordered account of nature, which creates a predisposition to reject divine intervention. An emphasis upon the human ability to explain the natural order leads to a loss of any sense of mystery. "A sense of propriety, order, consistency, and completeness gives birth to a rebellious stirring against miracle and mystery."[103] This can be seen as an extension of his concern about the rationalizing tendencies of natural theology, which reduced God to a rational principle, evacuated of transcendence, majesty, and glory.

Newman's concerns are significant, in that they point to disquiet within English theology over the potentially debilitating effects of natural theology. Apologetically, it appeared to offer little in the way of support to faith; theologically, it seemed to commend a vastly reduced conception of God, which was inadequate as an object of worship and adoration. In many ways, Newman can be seen as continuing the High Church tradition of suspicion concerning the theological merits of an appeal to the natural sciences in support of faith.[104]

Robert Browning's "Caliban Upon Setebos": A Literary Critique of Paley

Some aspects of Newman's theological critique of Paley find their literary expression in a poem by Robert Browning (1812–89). "Caliban upon Setebos," published in 1864, is thought to have been drafted during the years 1859–60, and at certain points clearly reflects the intellectual debates arising from Darwin's *Origin of Species*.[105] The imagery of the poem is partly shaped by Shakespeare's *Tempest*, which depicts Caliban as a semi-human inhabitant of Prospero's enchanted island. It is widely thought that one theme of Browning's poem is the idea of Caliban as a Darwinian "missing link" between humanity and the lower primates, raising the question of what theological reflections upon nature such a creature might be capable of developing.[106] The poem is rich in reflection on the animal life of the mysterious island, echoing the imagery of Darwin's account of his voyage of discovery on the *Beagle*, published in 1845. At times, it seems as if Browning wishes us to imagine Caliban's island as one of those making up the Galápagos archipelago.

The subtitle of the poem – "Natural Theology in the Island" – signals its relevance to our theme. While it is clear that Browning is here referring to the discipline of "natural theology" in general, rather than Paley's specific work *Natural Theology*, there can be little doubt that Paley is a concealed intertextual presence within the poem.[107] What can be known of God from nature? In the narrative of *The Tempest*, Caliban was taught by his dead mother, Sycorax, to worship the god Setebos.

Figure 5.4   Lithographed portrait of Robert Browning, c. 1880.

So how can this belief be reinforced, or given additional substance, through reflection on the island's natural habitat?

Browning makes it clear that knowledge of God must be derived from reflection on nature. God, he intimates, does not speak; he is "The Quiet." Caliban is thus dependent on his own reflections for further information. He does not argue for the existence of a god, but rather presumes the existence of this god, and he proceeds to amplify and clarify the characteristics of that god from the world around him. It soon becomes clear that Caliban's capacity to confirm and substantiate his belief in the god Setebos from observation of the natural habitat of his island raises some serious difficulties. The moral ambiguity of nature is such that Caliban is unable to discern whether Setebos is equally ambivalent.

For example, weakness is observed in nature. Since Setebos made all things, does it not follow that he intended to create weakness? That he designed it? And why would Setebos want to create weakness? Caliban explores the idea that his deity wanted to irritate his creatures for his personal amusement. Where Paley interpreted the moral ambivalence of nature in the light of his Christian presuppositions, Caliban is under no obligation to do so. He extrapolates directly from entities within nature to the one who created them, and whose moral qualities are demonstrated in the created order. If there is weakness in nature, he concludes, it is because weakness was *meant* to be there.

After noting the moral ambivalence of the natural world, Caliban finds himself at something of a loss to know how to extrapolate from the natural world to the god he has been taught lies behind it. In the end, he seems reduced to reassertion of beliefs, rather than analysis of his observations.[108]

> Such shows nor right nor wrong in Him,
> Nor kind, nor cruel: He is strong and Lord.

Furthermore, what if Setebos was a Platonic demiurge – a creator who was subordinate to some greater god?[109]

> What knows, – the something over Setebos
> That made Him, or He, may be, found and fought,
> Worsted, drove off and did to nothing, perchance.
> There may be something quiet o'er His head,
> Out of His reach, that feels nor joy nor grief.

Caliban's attempts to determine the moral and personal characteristics of Setebos thus fail, frustrated by a lack of clarity about the status and limits of the controlling analogies he must use to argue from nature to God.[110] Is Caliban discerning the character of Setebos from a critical analysis of the natural world? Or is he creating Setebos in his own image, and selectively observing nature in order to reinforce this belief?

This brings us to the novel element in Browning's reflections, which became an increasingly significant influence in the critical evaluation of Paley's approach to natural theology after 1850. In 1854, the novelist George Eliot published an English translation of the second edition of Ludwig Feuerbach's *Essence of Christianity*,[111] introducing Feuerbach's anti-theistic ideas into Victorian culture.[112] Feuerbach's most distinctive idea is that the notion of God is essentially a human construction, resulting from the "projection" or "objectification" of human feelings and longings. God is constructed by the human mind, based on our experiences, including both inner subjective feelings and our experience of the world around us.[113] The supposedly supernatural and superhuman divinities of human religion are actually involuntary projections of the essential attributes of human nature. As Eliot translated him, Feuerbach declares that "Theology is Anthropology ... there is no distinction between the predicates of the divine and human nature, and, consequently, no distinction between the divine and human subject."[114] Far from representing an authentic knowledge of God, religion is "man's earliest and also indirect form of self-knowledge."[115] Humanity constructs the divine from the natural, extrapolating from the natural world to an imagined and mentally constructed divinity.

The implications of the Feuerbachian critique of religion for natural theology will be obvious, and they are explored in Browning's "Caliban upon Setebos." Throughout the poem, Caliban constructs the identity and characteristics of Setebos by identifying and extrapolating his own qualities. Caliban's theological musings regularly begin by identifying his own characteristics, and then ascribing them to Setebos. Paley holds that there is an analogy between God and the natural world, which is grounded in a doctrine of creation yet modulated by the Christian vision of God. The observation of defects within creation is thus not understood to imply that such defects are to be mapped onto the moral character of God. Caliban, lacking any such theological framework, can only interpret nature in terms of what he actually sees. There are no theological filters upon which he can draw to nuance his observations, or his consequent conclusions.

In his perceptive study of Browning, Clyde de L. Ryals suggests that "Caliban upon Setebos" deals with both "the Higher Critics' thesis that God is created in the image of man, and with the natural theologians' claim that the character of God can be derived from the evidences of nature."[116] The question that Feuerbach raises, which is noted though not fully developed by Browning, is whether natural theology simply represents the projection of human longings onto the domain of nature. The human mind determines, for reasons it does not fully understand or control, that it would be good if there were a god; and then proceeds to construct and defend such a notion through a highly selective and theoretically filtered engagement with the natural world. Where traditional Christian theology held that God created the world in a manner that reflected the divine being, Feuerbach argued that humanity created God in a manner that reflected human longings and aspirations, as much as any valid engagement with the natural world.

English Natural Theology on the Eve of the Darwinian Revolution

The half-century following the publication of *Natural Theology* witnessed further significant developments in the field, partly as a reaction against Paley, and partly in response to cultural and intellectual trends within English culture as a whole. During the decade before the publication of Darwin's *Origin of Species*, evolutionary ideas increasingly became common currency in advanced and intellectual circles. These ideas had yet to filter down to the popular level; yet their widespread tacit acceptance within the Victorian educational and cultural elite did much to ease the passage of Darwin's notion of "natural selection" on its publication.

In considering the impact of Darwinism upon religious thought, it is vitally important to make a distinction between the understandings of such ideas as creation and providence that were encountered within popular religion on the one hand, and those of a Christian intelligentsia on the other. The latter, even before Darwin published his *Origins*, had come to appreciate the many different literary genres to be found in the Bible. Darwin's proposed mechanism of evolutionary development certainly appeared startling to some; the notion of at least some form of evolutionary development within nature was, however, gaining increasing acceptance within the intelligentsia by this time.[117]

Alongside this gradual shift toward evolutionary ways of thinking, Victorian intellectuals were becoming disenchanted with the natural theology of the early nineteenth century. These shifting attitudes of the Victorian age reflect a disenchantment with the excessive rationalism and evidentiary failings of "physico-theology." One incident will serve to illustrate the growing reaction against this once dominant approach to Christian apologetics. In March 1860, a collection of seven independently written theological essays appeared, entitled *Essays and Reviews*.[118] It sparked a ferocious reaction on the part of many more conservative church leaders, partly on account of its progressive approach to revelation. One of its more perceptive chapters explored the shaping of English religious thought. While the account of this matter offered by Hugh Pattison (1813–84) might today seem a little simplistic, his argument reflected anxieties about the apologetic approaches of an earlier age, and their detrimental impact upon Victorian Anglicanism.

Pattison argued that the publication of John Locke's *Reasonableness of Christianity* (1695) ushered in a period of barren rationalism in English religious thought, which needlessly imprisoned it within a mindset dedicated to proving that Christianity was true.[119]

> It was not merely that Rationalism then obtruded itself as a heresy, or obtained a footing of toleration within the Church, but the rationalizing method possessed itself absolutely of the whole field of theology. With some trifling exceptions, the whole of religious literature was drawn into the endeavour to "prove the truth" of Christianity.

Pattison chose to review his topic between the dates 1688 and 1750, which would initially seem to suggest that Pattison was not dealing with the present state of Victorian theology. However, as commentators have rightly pointed out,[120] his argument in this essay was based on his belief that nineteenth-century High Church theology was decrepit precisely because it was really an eighteenth-century theology, locked into a bygone worldview.[121] Instead of confronting modern problems and concerns, many sections within Anglicanism were merely repeating the solutions of a much earlier age, compounding rather than resolving the difficulties faced by Christian apologetics in the 1860s. Yet these problems were obvious a generation earlier.

An important debate over the scope, methods, and outcomes of natural theology was thus under way within English Christianity before the publication of Darwin's *Origin of Species*. Darwin's ideas unquestionably contributed to that debate, significantly eroding the appeal of Paley's approach to natural theology. Yet the debate about the merits of Paley's natural theology had begun long before Darwin. Nor did Darwin's theory of natural selection lead to the abandonment of natural theology as a whole, even if it may have made a family of approaches based on Paley's *Natural Theology* increasingly problematic.[122] Given the importance of Darwin to our narrative and analysis, we must now turn to consider his concept of "natural selection" in considerably more detail.

Notes

1   For example, Oxford University's natural history collection was arranged along lines suggested by the chapters of Paley's *Natural Theology* in 1836. The idea was to "familiarize the eye to those relations of all natural objects which form the basis of the argument in Dr Paley's *Natural Theology*; to induce a mental habit of associating natural phenomena with the conviction that they are the media of Divine manifestation; and by such association to give proper dignity to every branch of natural science." See Vernon, Horace M., and K. Dorothea E. Vernon, *A History of the Oxford Museum*. Oxford: Clarendon Press, 1909, 36.

2　A trend noted and criticized some time ago by Greene, John C., "Reflections on the Progress of Darwin Studies." *Journal of the History of Biology* 8 (1975): 243–73, especially 250.

3　See, for example, Brooke, John Hedley, "Natural Theology and the Plurality of Worlds: Observations on the Brewster–Whewell Debate." *Annals of Science* 34 (1977): 221–86.

4　LeMahieu, D. L., *The Mind of William Paley: A Philosopher and His Age.* Lincoln, NE: University of Nebraska Press, 1976, 79.

5　Some later editions of *Natural Theology* included illustrations added by their editors.

6　This trend was accentuated by the Bridgewater Treatises (1833–6): see Topham, Jonathan, "Science and Popular Education in the 1830s: The Role of the Bridgewater Treatises." *British Journal for the History of Science* 25 (1992): 397–430.

7　This point is emphasized by Bowler, Peter J., "Darwinism and the Argument from Design: Suggestions for a Reevaluation." *Journal of the History of Biology* 10 (1977): 29–43.

8　See, for example, the anonymous reviews of Paley's *Natural Theology* in *Christian Observer* 2 (1803): 162–6, 240–4, 369–74; and *Evangelical Magazine* 11 (1803): 494–5.

9　See Topham, Jonathan, "Science, Natural Theology, and Evangelicalism in the Early Nineteenth Century: Thomas Chalmers and the Evidence Controversy." In *Evangelicals and Science in Historical Perspective*, ed. D. N. Livingstone, D. G. Hart, and M. A. Noll, 142–74. Oxford: Oxford University Press, 1999.

10　Irons, William J., *On the Whole Doctrine of Final Causes.* London: Rivingtons, 1836, 122. Voltaire argued it was impossible to speak of the natural world as a clock, without proposing a clockmaker: "J'ai toujours regardé l'atheisme comme le plus grand égarement de la raison, parce qu'il est aussi ridicule de dire que l'arrangement du monde ne prouve pas un artisan suprème, qu'il serait impertinent de dire qu'une horloge ne prouve pas un horloger." For comment on Voltaire's statement, see Ages, Arnold, "Voltaire and the Problem of Atheism: The Testimony of the Correspondence." *Neophilologus* 68 (1984): 504–12, especially 509.

11　Irons, *On the Whole Doctrine of Final Causes*, 123–5.

12　Irons, *On the Whole Doctrine of Final Causes*, 124–7.

13　John Henry Newman, writing in 1870, recognized that the case for design now had to be proved, rather than merely assumed. For comment, see Roberts, Noel K., "Newman on the Argument from Design." *New Blackfriars* 88 (2007): 56–66, especially 57–8.

14　On this growing interest, see Klaver, J. M. I., *Geology and Religious Sentiment: The Effect of Geological Discourse on British Society and Literature between 1829 and 1859.* Leiden: Brill, 1997, 15–84. While Klaver's analysis relates to a slightly later period, Buckland's work fits within the earlier part of the narrative identified by Klaver (87–101). For its theological dimensions, see Brooke, John Hedley, "The Natural Theology of the Geologists: Some Theological Strata." In *Images of the Earth: Essays in the History of the Environmental Sciences,* ed. L. J. Jordanova and Roy Porter, 53–74. Chalfont St Giles: British Society for the History of Science, 1997.

15 Buckland, William, *Vindiciae Geologicae: Or the Connexion of Geology with Religion Explained*. Oxford: Oxford University Press, 1820, 10–22. See Greene, Mott T., "Genesis and Geology Revisited: The Order of Nature and the Nature of Order in Nineteenth-Century Britain." In *When Science and Christianity Meet*, ed. Ronald L. Numbers and James C. Livingstone, 139–60. Chicago: University of Chicago Press, 2003.

16 Buckland, *Vindiciae Geologicae*, 12.

17 Buckland, *Vindiciae Geologicae*, 12.

18 Buckland, *Vindiciae Geologicae*, 18. For comment on this notion, see Bowler, Peter J., *Fossils and Progress: Paleontology and the Idea of Progressive Evolution in the Nineteenth Century*. New York: Science History, 1976; Lyons, Sherrie L., "Thomas Huxley: Fossils, Persistence, and the Argument from Design." *Journal of the History of Biology* 26 (1993): 545–69.

19 Buckland, *Vindiciae Geologicae*, 19. For detailed comment, see Rupke, Nicolaas A., *The Great Chain of History: William Buckland and the English School of Geology (1814–1849)*. Oxford: Clarendon Press, 1983.

20 Buckland, *Vindiciae Geologicae*, 18–19.

21 Buckland, *Vindiciae Geologicae*, 21. For the question of the age of the earth in such discussions, see Roberts, Michael B., "Genesis Chapter 1 and Geological Time from Hugo Grotius and Marin Mersenne to William Conybeare and Thomas Chalmers (1620–1825)." In *Myth and Geology*, ed. L. Piccardi and W. B. Masse, 39–49. London: Geological Society, 2007.

22 Buckland is careful to leave open the idea that the origins of humanity, though situated in a specific geological context, may rightly be seen as arising from "the will and fiat of an intelligent and all-wise Creator": see Buckland, *Vindiciae Geologicae*, 21.

23 Buckland, *Vindiciae Geologicae*, 18.

24 For the approach, see Camardi, Giovanni, "Richard Owen, Morphology and Evolution." *Journal of the History of Biology* 34 (2001): 481–515. For the historical context, see Rupke, Nicolaas A., "Richard Owen's Vertebrate Archetype." *Isis* 84 (1993): 231–51; Gardiner, Brian G., "Edward Forbes, Richard Owen, and the Red Lions." *Archives of Natural History* 201 (1993): 349–72. Although Owen's homological classification could easily be accommodated within Darwin's theory of natural selection, Owen refused to countenance such a possibility.

25 Brougham, Henry, *A Discourse of Natural Theology*. 4th edn. London: Charles Knight, 1835, 11–12. For a significant contemporary response to Brougham's work, see Turton, Thomas, *Natural Theology Considered with Reference to Lord Brougham's Discourse on That Subject*. London: Parker, 1836.

26 See Brougham, *A Discourse of Natural Theology*, 24, 28, 40, 45, 95, 114, 118.

27 Brougham, *A Discourse of Natural Theology*, 37, 38, 55, 123–5. Brougham served as an editor of the 1836 edition of Paley's *Natural Theology*, which included his own supplementary comments on the text: Brougham, *A Discourse of Natural Theology*, vi.

28 Brougham, *A Discourse of Natural Theology*, 31–6.

29 See, for example, Brougham, *A Discourse of Natural Theology*, 10, 25, 31, 33, 40, 55, 79, 95, 105.

30 Brougham, *A Discourse of Natural Theology*, 40.

31 Brougham, *A Discourse of Natural Theology*, 40.

32 Brougham, *A Discourse of Natural Theology*, 36–7.

33 Brougham, *A Discourse of Natural Theology*, 37.

34 Brougham, *A Discourse of Natural Theology*, 37–8. Thomas Turton criticizes Brougham at this point for failing to develop a natural theology of the imagination, noting the importance of this faculty for poetry and literature: Turton, *Natural Theology*, 80–3.

35 As pointed out, with extensive documentation, by Turton, *Natural Theology*, 134–49.

36 Athanasius, *De incarnatione Verbi*, 3.

37 Pfaff, Richard W., "The Library of the Fathers: The Tractarians as Patristic Translators." *Studies in Philology* 70 (1973): 329–44. For the attitude of Tractarians to the natural sciences, especially geology, around this time, see Corsi, Pietro, *Science and Religion: Baden Powell and the Anglican Debate*. Cambridge: Cambridge University Press, 1988, 106–40; Rupke, *Great Chain of History*, 267–74.

38 For details, see Farmer, Lindsay, "Reconstructing the English Codification Debate: The Criminal Law Commissioners, 1833–45." *Law and History Review* 18 (2000): 397–425.

39 See further Lobban, Michael, *The Common Law and English Jurisprudence, 1760–1850*. Oxford: Clarendon Press, 1991; Hostettler, John, *The Politics of Criminal Law: Reform in the Nineteenth Century*. Chichester: Barry Rose, 1992; Wiener, Martin, *Reconstructing the Criminal: Culture, Law and Policy in England, 1830–1914*. Cambridge: Cambridge University Press, 1990. For religious aspects of the reforms, see Follett, Richard R., *Evangelicalism, Penal Theory, and the Politics of Criminal Law Reform in England, 1808–30*. New York: Palgrave, 2001, 90–108.

40 For an excellent study of this question in the later nineteenth century, see Schramm, Jan-Melissa, *Testimony and Advocacy in Victorian Law, Literature, and Theology*. Cambridge: Cambridge University Press, 2000, especially 1–23.

41 For a rigorous exploration of this point, see Morawski, Lech, "Law, Fact and Legal Language." *Law and Philosophy* 18 (1999): 461–73.

42 See Shapiro, Barbara J., "The Concept 'Fact': Legal Origins and Cultural Diffusion." *Albion* 26 (1994): 227–52, quote at 233. For a fuller statement of this approach, see Shapiro, Barbara J., *A Culture of Fact: England, 1550–1720*. Ithaca, NY: Cornell University Press, 2003.

43 See Cromartie, Alan, *Sir Matthew Hale, 1609–1676: Law, Religion, and Natural Philosophy*. Cambridge: Cambridge University Press, 1995.

44 Cited by Shapiro, "Concept 'Fact'," 232.

45 See Shapiro, Barbara J., *Probability and Certainty in Seventeenth-Century England: A Study of the Relationships between Natural Science, Religion, History, Law, and Literature*. Princeton, NJ: Princeton University Press, 1983; Patey, Douglas, *Probability and Literary Form: Philosophic Theory and*

Literary Practice in the Augustan Age. Cambridge: Cambridge University Press, 1984.

46   Welsh, Alexander, *Strong Representations: Narrative and Circumstantial Evidence in England*. Baltimore, MD: Johns Hopkins University Press, 1992; Shapiro, Barbara J., "Circumstantial Evidence: Of Law, Literature, and Culture." *Yale Journal of Law and the Humanities* 5 (1993): 219–41.

47   As the anthropologist Clifford Geertz emphasizes, the notion of "common sense" must be recognized to be socially constructed and negotiated: see Geertz, Clifford, "Common Sense as a Cultural System." In *Local Knowledge: Further Essays in Interpretative Anthropology*, ed. Clifford Geertz, 73–93. New York: Basic Books, 1983.

48   Schramm, *Testimony and Advocacy*, 20–1.

49   For a full discussion of the issues, see Cairns, David J. A., *Advocacy and the Making of the Adversarial Criminal Trial, 1800–1865*. Oxford: Clarendon Press, 1998, 37–53; 67–96.

50   See further Morawski, "Law, Fact and Legal Language."

51   The *Second Report from His Majesty's Commissioners on Civil Law* (1836), 10. Published in *Parliamentary Papers*, vol. 36. London, 1836.

52   Cited in Schramm, *Testimony and Advocacy*, 112. Schramm's entire discussion of "Dickens and the Bar" (109–23) repays study.

53   Whewell, William, *Philosophy of the Inductive Sciences*. 2 vols. London: John W. Parker, 1847, vol. 2, 36.

54   More fully, as the Bridgewater Treatises on the Power, Wisdom and Goodness of God as Manifested in the Creation. The treatises were published individually; there was no collected edition.

55   The terms of the will were printed in the prefatory material to each published treatise: see, for example, Chalmers, Thomas, *On the Power, Wisdom, and Goodness of God as Manifested in the Adaptation of External Nature to the Moral and Intellectual Constitution of Man*. 2 vols. London: Pickering, 1839, vol. 1, 9.

56   For what is known of this process of selection, see Brock, W. H., "The Selection of the Authors of the Bridgewater Treatises." *Notes and Records of the Royal Society of London* 21 (1966): 162–79.

57   See the analysis in Topham, Jonathan, "Beyond the 'Common Context': The Production and Reading of the Bridgewater Treatises." *Isis* 89 (1998): 233–62. Topham notes (p. 238) that Peter Mark Roget acted as an "unofficial secretary" for the group, but had no authority to impose a common approach upon the authors as a whole.

58   Topham, "Beyond the 'Common Context'," 241–2.

59   Note, for example, suggestions that Paley's influential work lacked scientific rigor at points, particularly in relation to its organization of material: see Roget, Peter Mark, *Animal and Vegetable Physiology Considered with Reference to Natural Theology*. 2 vols. London: Pickering, 1834, ix–x.

60   For this notion of a "common context," see especially Young, Robert M., "Natural Theology, Victorian Periodicals, and the Fragmentation of a Common Context." In *Darwin's Metaphor: Nature's Place in Victorian Culture*, 126–63. Cambridge: Cambridge University Press, 1985. For more recent reflections, see Moore,

Charles, "Wallace's Malthusian Moment: The Common Context Revisited." In *Victorian Science in Context*, ed. Bernard Lightman, 290–311. Chicago: University of Chicago Press, 1997; Topham, "Beyond the 'Common Context'."

61 Young, "Natural Theology, Victorian Periodicals, and the Fragmentation of a Common Context," 128–9.

62 On which see Young, Robert M., "Malthus and the Evolutionists: The Common Context of Biological and Social Theory." *Past and Present* 43 (1969): 109–45. For further exploration of such issues, see Snyder, Laura J., *Reforming Philosophy. A Victorian Debate on Science and Society*. Chicago: University of Chicago Press, 2006, 7–32.

63 For the importance of professionalization for the academic community, especially at Oxford, see Engel, Arthur J., *From Clergyman to Don. The Rise of the Academic Profession in Nineteenth-Century Oxford*. Oxford: Clarendon Press, 1983.

64 See, for example, Thackray, Arnold, *Gentlemen of Science: Early Years of the British Association for the Advancement of Science*. Oxford: Clarendon Press, 1981, 224–45.

65 For Buckland's status as a scientific celebrity around this time, see Rupke, *Great Chain of History*, 64–74. On the more general issue of the importance of celebrity authors and cultural authorities in encouraging the rise of popular science, see Topham, Jonathan, "Scientific Publishing and the Reading of Science in Nineteenth-Century Britain: A Historiographical Survey and Guide to Sources." *Studies in History and Philosophy of Science A* 31 (2000): 559–612.

66 For useful comments, see Topham, Jonathan, "Biology in the Service of Natural Theology: Darwin, Paley, and the Bridgewater Treatises." In *Biology and Ideology: From Descartes to Dawkins*, ed. Denis R. Alexander and Ronald Numbers, 88–113. Chicago: University of Chicago Press, 2010.

67 Roget, *Animal and Vegetable Physiology*, 38. See also the comments at ix, 3, 82, 95, 176, 200, 341, 372.

68 Bell, Charles, *The Hand: Its Mechanism and Vital Endowment as Evincing Design*. London: Pickering, 1833, 40.

69 Prout, William, *Chemistry, Meteorology, and the Function of Digestion Considered with Reference to Natural Theology*. London: Pickering, 1834, 23.

70 Prout, *Chemistry, Meteorology, and the Function of Digestion*, 24. Prout's reflections on the fitness of chemistry for life are capable of extension: see Barrow, John, "Chemistry and Sensitivity." In *Fitness of the Cosmos for Life: Biochemistry and Fine-Tuning*, ed. John D. Barrow, Simon Conway Morris, Stephen J. Freeland, and Charles L. Harper, 132–50. Cambridge: Cambridge University Press, 2007.

71 Kirby, William, *On the History, Habits and Instincts of Animals*. London: Pickering, 1835, 468.

72 On which see Brooke, John Hedley, "Indications of a Creator: Whewell as Apologist and Priest." In *William Whewell: A Composite Portrait*, ed. Menachem Fisch and Simon Schaffer, 149–73. Oxford: Clarendon Press, 1991; Yeo, Richard R., "William Whewell, Natural Theology and the Philosophy of Science in Mid-Nineteenth Century Britain." *Annals of Science* 36 (1979): 493–516.

73 Whewell, *Philosophy of the Inductive Sciences*, vol. 1, 1.

74 Whewell, William, *Astronomy and General Physics Considered with Reference to Natural Theology*. London: Pickering, 1833, vi.

75 Whewell, *Astronomy and General Physics*, 2.

76 Whewell, *Astronomy and General Physics*, 126–7. See also 128.

77 See, for example, Powell, Baden, *The Connexion of Natural and Divine Truth*. London: Parker, 1838, 1–5. For a close discussion of Powell's developing (and often complex) views on the relation of science and faith, see Corsi, *Science and Religion*; Curtis, R. C., "Baden Powell and the Whewell Legend." *Annals of Science* 47 (1990): 301–12.

78 Whewell, *Astronomy and General Physics*, 3.

79 Whewell, *Astronomy and General Physics*, 320.

80 See further Ruse, Michael, "William Whewell and the Argument from Design." *Monist* 60 (1977): 244–68. Note especially the comments concerning Whewell's concept of teleology.

81 Whewell, William, "Lyell's Principles of Geology." *Quarterly Review* 43 (1830): 411–69.

82 Whewell, *Astronomy and General Physics*, 307.

83 The origins of this misunderstanding seem to lie with Baden Powell. See especially Curtis, "Baden Powell and the Whewell Legend."

84 "Astronomy and General Physics Considered with Reference to Natural Theology," 587.

85 "Astronomy and General Physics," 589.

86 Whewell, *Philosophy of the Inductive Sciences*, vol. 1, 705–6.

87 Although Whewell himself did not develop this approach with the rigor one might anticipate, it received further elaboration and development in the Bridgewater Treatise by Thomas Chalmers. See Rice, Daniel F., "Natural Theology and the Scottish Philosophy in the Thought of Thomas Chalmers." *Scottish Journal of Theology* 24 (1971): 23–46; Smith, Crosbie, "From Design to Dissolution: Thomas Chalmers' Debt to John Robison." *British Journal for the History of Science* 12 (1979): 59–70; and especially Topham, "Science, Natural Theology, and Evangelicalism in the Early Nineteenth Century."

88 For a useful overview, see Hodgson, Peter E., "Newman and Science." *Sapientia* 54 (1999): 395–408.

89 See especially the important study of Turner, Frank M., "John Henry Newman and the Challenge of a Culture of Science." *The European Legacy* 1 (1996): 1694–704.

90 Newman, John Henry, *Fifteen Sermons Preached before the University of Oxford*. London: Rivingtons, 1880, 114–15.

91 These were published in 1852 as *The Idea of a University Defined and Illustrated*. Later editions of this work included subsequent lectures, including the two noted above.

92 Newman, John Henry, *The Idea of a University*. 7th edn. London: Longmans, Green, 1887, 429.

93 Newman, *The Idea of a University*, 429.

94 Newman, *The Idea of a University*, 434.

95 Newman, *The Idea of a University*, 432.

96   Newman, letter to William Robert Brownlow, April 13, 1870; in Newman, John Henry, *The Letters and Diaries of John Henry Newman*, ed. Charles Stephen Dessain and Thomas Gornall. 31 vols. Oxford: Clarendon Press, 1963–2006, vol. 25, 97. For further comment on Newman and arguments from design, see Roberts, "Newman on the Argument from Design"; Mongrain, Kevin, "The Eyes of Faith: Newman's Critique of Arguments from Design." *Newman Studies Journal* 6 (2009): 68–86.

97   Newman, *The Idea of a University*, 39.

98   Newman, *The Idea of a University*, 453.

99   Newman, *The Idea of a University*, 454.

100   Newman, *The Idea of a University*, 454.

101   Newman, John Henry, *Two Essays on Scripture Miracles*. 2nd edn. London: Pickering, 1870, 4.

102   Newman, *Two Essays on Scripture Miracles*, 4.

103   Newman, *The Idea of a University*, 217–18.

104   See especially Olson, Richard G., "Tory-High Church Opposition to Science and Scientism in the Eighteenth Century: The Works of John Arbuthnot, Jonathan Swift, and Samuel Johnson." In *The Uses of Science in the Age of Newton*, ed. John G. Burke, 171–204. Berkeley, CA: University of California Press, 1983.

105   See Loesberg, Jonathan, "Darwin, Natural Theology, and Slavery: A Justification of Browning's *Caliban*." *ELH* 75 (2008): 871–97.

106   For an early evaluation of this possibility, see Howard, John, "Caliban's Mind." *Victorian Poetry* 1 (1963): 249–57.

107   See here Karr, Jeff, "Caliban and Paley: Two Natural Theologians." *Studies in Browning and His Circle* 13 (1985): 38–9. It is also possible that Browning engages with Robert Chambers's much-discussed *Vestiges of the Natural History of Creation*. On this influential work, see Secord, James A., *Victorian Sensation: The Extraordinary Publication, Reception, and Secret Authorship of Vestiges of the Natural History of Creation*. Chicago: University of Chicago Press, 2000.

108   Robert Browning, "Caliban upon Setebos," lines 98–9.

109   Robert Browning, "Caliban upon Setebos," lines 129–33.

110   A point emphasized by Armstrong, Isobel, "Browning's 'Caliban' and Primitive Language." In *Robert Browning in Contexts*, ed. John Woolford, 76–85. Winfield, KS: Wedgestone Press, 1998.

111   For reflections on how Eliot's philosophical convictions shaped her novels, see Gatens, Moira, "The Art and Philosophy of George Eliot." *Philosophy and Literature* 33 (2009): 73–90.

112   Hill, Susan E., "Translating Feuerbach, Constructing Morality: The Theological and Literary Significance of Translation for George Eliot." *Journal of the American Academy of Religion* 65 (1997): 635–53. For the impact of Feuerbach in New England around this time, see Hurth, Elisabeth, "When 'Man Makes God': Feuerbachian Atheism in New England." *ESQ: A Journal of the American Renaissance* 42, no. 4 (1996): 254–89.

113   For further discussion, see Hüsser, Heinz, *Natur ohne Gott: Aspekte und Probleme von Ludwig Feuerbachs Naturverständnis*. Würzburg: Königshausen

& Neumann, 1993; Harvey, Van A., *Feuerbach and the Interpretation of Religion*. Cambridge: Cambridge University Press, 1995. As Harvey correctly notes, Feuerbach's later writings offer a more complex account of the origins of religion. These were generally not picked up in Victorian England.

114   Feuerbach, Ludwig, *The Essence of Christianity*. Translated by George Eliot. New York: Harper & Row, 1957, xxxvii.

115   Feuerbach, *The Essence of Christianity*, 13.

116   Ryals, Clyde de L., *The Life of Robert Browning: A Critical Biography*. Oxford: Blackwell, 1993, 151.

117   For the background to this development, see Desmond, Adrian, *The Politics of Evolution: Morphology, Medicine, and Reform in Radical London*. Chicago: University of Chicago Press, 1992, 1–24; Corsi, Pietro, *Evolution before Darwin*. Oxford: Oxford University Press, 2010.

118   See Shea, Victor, and William Whitla, eds., *Essays and Reviews: The 1860 Text and Its Reading*. Charlottesville, VA: University Press of Virginia, 2000. Benjamin Jowett's important essay "On the Interpretation of Scripture" was especially controversial, appearing only months after Darwin's *Origin of Species*.

119   Pattison, Mark, "Tendencies of English Religious Thought, 1688–1750." In *Essays and Reviews*, 254–99. London: Parker, 1860, quote at 259. For further details of Pattison, see Jones, H. S., *Intellect and Character in Victorian England: Mark Pattison and the Invention of the Don*. Cambridge: Cambridge University Press, 2007.

120   For example, see Francis, Mark, "The Origins of *Essays and Reviews*: An Interpretation of Mark Pattison in the 1850s." *Historical Journal* 17 (1974): 797–811, especially 807.

121   Pattison, "Tendencies of English Religious Thought, 1688–1750," 255. Pattison suggested that a real Anglican would "omit that period from the history of the Church altogether." The historical basis of this argument is questionable; that, however, is not the point at issue here.

122   See, for example, England, Richard, "Natural Selection, Teleology, and the Logos: From Darwin to the Oxford Neo-Darwinists, 1859–1909." *Osiris* 16 (2001): 270–87. England argues that some Oxford neo-Darwinists saw Darwin's revision of Paley's teleology as emphasizing aspects of adaptation that confirmed their Christian belief, thus reinforcing rather than undermining their scientific commitment to the theory of natural selection.

6

Charles Darwin, Natural Selection, and Natural Theology

On January 22, 1950, Dorothy L. Sayers wrote to Sir Richard Gregory, a former editor of the leading British scientific journal *Nature*, thanking him for a recent gift of a book. By this time, Sayers had become an authority on the writings and intellectual context of the great Florentine poet Dante Alighieri (c. 1265–1321),[1] including how that age interpreted the Bible and thought about such issues as creation and cosmology. She ventured an opinion on scientific matters to Gregory, based on her immersion in this most fascinating of eras:[2]

> If Galileo, not to say Darwin, could have done their stuff in the 14th century, instead of after the Reformation and the Council of Trent, they would have had very much less trouble with the Church. It would have taken more than a few apes to flummox men like Albertus Magnus and Aquinas, and a heliocentric universe would have suited Dante down to the ground.

Sayers does not elaborate on the reasons for this flamboyant judgment. Nevertheless, there are good reasons for thinking that it might possibly be sound on both counts. The rise of religious controversy during the sixteenth century led to retrenchment within the Catholic church, anxious to defend itself against what it regarded as the dangerous Protestant innovations of the age.[3] A tactic designed to preserve Catholicism from what was seen as recent Protestant distortions had the unintended consequence of locking Catholicism into earlier patterns of biblical interpretation. Traditionalist readings of the Bible were enforced defensively, leading to the petrification of a pre-scientific worldview in the theological dogma of the church. Far from being a critic of the Bible on scientific grounds, Galileo may be seen as preparing the ground

Darwinism and the Divine: Evolutionary Thought and Natural Theology, First Edition.
Alister E. McGrath.
© 2011 Alister E. McGrath. Published 2011 by Blackwell Publishing Ltd.

Figure 6.1   Engraving of HMS *Beagle*, the ship that carried Charles Darwin during the voyage that inspired his theory of evolution.

for the creative reappropriation of older Catholic methods of biblical interpretation, which were surprisingly well adapted to cope with the shifting cosmological consensus.[4] But what of Sayers's judgment about Darwin?

The publication of Charles Darwin's *Origin of Species* (1859) is rightly regarded as a landmark in nineteenth-century science; it is also no less significant a landmark in the history of natural theology. On December 27, 1831, HMS *Beagle* set out from the southern English port of Plymouth on a voyage that lasted almost five years. Its mission was to complete a survey of the southern coasts of South America, and afterwards to circumnavigate the globe. The small ship's self-financing gentleman naturalist was Charles Darwin (1809–82). During the long voyage, Darwin noted some aspects of the plant and animal life of South America, particularly the Galápagos Islands and Tierra del Fuego, which seemed to him to require explanation, yet which were not satisfactorily accounted for by existing theories, including transformist theories of evolution, and Paley's notion of "special creation." The opening words of the first edition of the *Origin of Species* set out the riddle that Darwin was determined to solve:[5]

When on board H.M.S. Beagle as naturalist, I was much struck with certain facts in the distribution of the organic beings inhabiting South America, and in the geological relations of the present to the past inhabitants of that continent. These facts seemed to throw some light on the origin of species – that mystery of mysteries, as it has been called by one of our greatest philosophers.

The historical account of how Darwin's views emerged, came to be published, and were received remains clouded by past controversies, present prejudices, and the tendency of scholars to repeat the views of their predecessors without rigorously confirming them. The Darwin anniversary year of 2009 saw much attention to Darwin in the media, as well as the appearance of a plethora of new works, aiming to cast new light on Darwin's times, his ideas, and their broader impact. It has to be said that some more popular accounts of Darwin have been disappointing intellectually, with old stereotypes being dusted off, dressed up, and given a new lease of life.

For example, the myth of the Galápagos finches still seems to be taken seriously in some quarters. Darwin, according to this still influential, but historically discredited narrative, is supposed to have discovered evolution while on the Galápagos Islands in a "eureka moment" when he observed the beaks of the finches. This idea appears to date back to the publication of ornithologist David Lack's book *Darwin's Finches* (1947).[6] In fact, it was Darwin's subsequent reflections on his observations, after his return to England, that gradually moved him toward a theory of natural selection.[7] As his recent biographers correctly note, Darwin was "confused by the Galápagos finches" at the time of his visit to the islands, and was "unaware of the importance of their different beaks." At this stage, he "had no sense of a single, closely related group becoming specialized and adapted to different environmental niches."[8] Darwin did not fully appreciate the significance of his finches until he had returned to England and a leading ornithologist – John Gould of the Zoological Society of London – pointed out to him that, despite many superficial resemblances, the species were all distinctly different.[9]

Furthermore, Darwin's insights were not those of the lone explorer and genius, experiencing a moment of breakthrough in splendid isolation. In recent years, scholarship has placed increasing emphasis upon the importance of understanding Darwin's cultural environment, which included many resources and individuals who would catalyze his scientific development.[10] Darwin is increasingly being seen as an intellectual explorer who drew upon the intellectual resources of his day in a collaborative and collegial manner, even if he would ultimately challenge and change the consensus of his generation.[11]

Yet by far the most contentious assertions concern both Darwin's religious views, and the impact of his evolutionary views upon Victorian England and today's religious debates. Some assert that Darwin personally caused the "Victorian crisis of faith," thus overlooking the impact of biblical criticism and geology upon contemporary religious convictions.[12] On this view, the Victorian age of faith was plunged into profound religious crisis by the publication of the *Origin of Species*, which inaugurated yet another great battle in the endless war between science and religion. Others have asserted that Darwin's theory faced implacable opposition from the Church of England. The reality may be somewhat more nuanced and complex, but it is much more interesting and intellectually satisfying. The nineteenth-century Anglican theologian Aubrey Moore (1848–90) famously argued that, under the guise of a foe, Darwin had done Christianity the work of a friend. How? By liberating it from a defective vision of God.[13]

Our concern in this chapter is not to document the fine detail of the development of Darwin's theory of natural selection,[14] or the historical details of its publication and reception.[15] It is to identify the core elements of Darwin's ideas, as these were published in the *Origin of Species* (1859),[16] and assess their importance for the forms of natural theology that were regnant in England around this time. We begin by considering the core elements of Darwin's theory.

The Development of Darwin's Views on Natural Selection

Darwin's own account of how he developed his theory of natural selection makes it clear that it was later reflection on observations that brought about his insights. When he boarded the *Beagle* in 1831, he tells us, he was inclined to the view that the flora and fauna of a given region would be determined by their physical environment. His observations gradually caused him to question this belief, and to search for alternative explanations – one of which gradually came to dominate his thinking.[17]

> During the voyage of the *Beagle* I had been deeply impressed by discovering in the Pampean formation great fossil animals covered with armor like that on the existing Armadillos; secondly, by the manner in which closely allied animals replace one another in proceeding southwards over the Continent; and thirdly, by the South American character of most of the productions of the Galápagos archipelago, and more especially by the manner in which they differ slightly on each island of the group; none of these islands appearing to be very ancient in the geological sense. It was evident that facts such as these, as well as many others, could be explained on the supposition that species gradually become modified; and the subject haunted me.

What prompted Darwin to develop his new theory? There is no reason to suggest that Darwin's notion of "natural selection" came about in a moment of inspiration, on the Galápagos or anywhere else. His theory began taking shape in 1837 and 1838.

We must pause here, and reflect on the important distinction between a "logic of discovery" and a "logic of confirmation." To simplify what is rather a complex discussion, a "logic of discovery" concerns how someone arrives at a scientific hypothesis, whereas a "logic of confirmation" concerns how that hypothesis is subsequently shown to be reliable and realistic.[18] Sometimes hypotheses arise from a long period of reflection on observation; sometimes they come about in a flash of inspiration. Yet if the "logic of discovery" can often be more inspirational than rational, the same is clearly not true of the "logic of justification." Here, any hypothesis – however it is derived – is rigorously and thoroughly checked against what may be observed, in order to determine the degree of "empirical fit" between theory and observation. In Darwin's case, the logics of discovery and justification both seem to have been based primarily on extensive reflection on often puzzling observations.[19] So what were these puzzling observations, and how did he manage to solve their relationship?

As Darwin later reflected on his own observations, and supplemented them with those of other naturalists, a number of points emerged as being of particular significance. For Darwin, four broad features of the natural world seemed to require close attention, in the light of problems and short-comings with existing explanations, such as "transformism," or the concept of "special creation" offered by religious apologists such as William Paley.[20] While this latter theory offered explanations of these observations, they seemed increasingly cumbersome and forced. A better explanation, Darwin believed, had to lie to hand.

1   Many creatures possess "rudimentary structures," which have no apparent or predictable function – such as the nipples of male mammals, the rudiments of a pelvis and hind limbs in snakes, and wings on many flightless birds. In some cases, organs that serve dual purposes may be functional in one respect, and rudimentary in the other.[21] How might these be explained on the basis of Paley's theory, which stressed the importance of the individual design of species? Why should God design redundancies? Darwin's theory accounted for these with ease and elegance.

2   Some species were known to have died out altogether. The phenomenon of extinction had been recognized before Darwin, and was often explained on the basis of "catastrophe" theories, such as a "universal flood," as suggested by the biblical account of Noah. Darwin did not deny that such catastrophic extinctions had occurred. Yet the fossil records, Darwin argued, suggested that they were relatively rare.[22] The norm appeared to be gradual extinction, which was part of the process of "descent with modification," in which parental species are continu- ously replaced by modified descendants over extended periods of time.

Once more, Darwin's theory offered a neater account of the observable evidence. Paley's approach might indeed be able to deal with a catastrophic extinction event; it could only deal with the more common phenomenon of gradual extinction with some difficulty.

3   Darwin's research voyage on the *Beagle* had persuaded him of the uneven geographical distribution of life forms throughout the world.[23] In particular, Darwin was impressed by the peculiarities of oceanic island populations, such as the finches of the Galápagos Islands. Darwin noted that in these contexts, the total number of species was often small compared to an equal area of continental land, and that the proportion of endemic species is very high. In the case of oceanic islands, entire classes were often conspicuous by their absence. Furthermore, species found on oceanic islands were often similar to, but not identical with, those of neighboring mainlands.[24] Once more, the doctrine of special creation could account for this, yet in a manner that seemed forced and unpersuasive. Darwin's theory offered a much more plausible account of the emergence of these specific populations.

4   Various forms of certain living creatures seemed to be adapted to their specific needs. Darwin held that these could best be explained by their emergence and selection in response to evolutionary pressures. The notion of "adaptation" is based on the idea that populations of organisms change over time as a result of natural selection. Adaptive evolution is driven by increased survival rates or increased reproductive rates, reflecting how well an organism is adapted to its environment. Darwin's concept of natural selection provided the mechanism that explained how organisms change over time; evolutionary adaptation explains why they do. Paley's theory of special creation proposed that these creatures were individually designed by God with those specific environmental needs in mind. Darwin proposed that they developed over time in response to local environmental pressures. He noted that similar environments can contain entirely different species groups, suggesting that evolution took place locally, rather than universally. Where Paley saw adaptation as a static situation, Darwin saw it as a dynamic, ongoing development.[25]

Many more examples could be given to illustrate the phenomena that needed explanation. It is clear that a number of explanations could be offered for what was actually observed in nature. None of the observations noted above could conceivably be regarded as "proofs" of natural selection; nevertheless, they possessed a cumulative force in suggesting it was the best explanation of what was actually observed, when compared with the two most prominent alternatives at the time – transformism and special creation. The debate concerned which of these explanations was the best.

The elusive and significant word "best" is, of course, somewhat difficult to define. Does it designate the simplest theory? The most elegant? The most natural? As we noted in the previous chapter, the great English natural philosopher William Whewell used a rich visual image to communicate the capacity of a good theory to make sense of, and weave together, observations. "The facts are known but they are insulated and unconnected ... The pearls are there but they will not hang together until some one provides the string."[26] The "pearls" are the observations and the "string" is a grand vision of reality, a worldview, which *connects* and *unifies* the data. A grand theory, Whewell maintained, allows the "colligation of facts," which links together and unifies what might otherwise be considered to be random observations. Continuing this analogy, we might say that the "pearls" were the observations that Darwin had accumulated; but what was the best string on which to thread them?

Darwin's task was to make sense of a series of observations about the natural world. Indeed, he had even contributed to these himself, through his voyage on the *Beagle*. Yet Darwin's voyage on the *Beagle* was more productive in terms of the ideas it ultimately generated in Darwin's mind than the biological specimens he brought home with him, even though these two are interconnected. The challenge was to find a theoretical framework that could accommodate these observations as simply, elegantly, and persuasively as possible. Darwin's method is a textbook case of the method of "inference to the best explanation," which is now widely regarded as lying at the core of the scientific method.[27]

Darwin was quite clear that his theory of natural selection was not the only explanation of the biological data that could be adduced. He did, however, believe that it possessed greater explanatory power than its rivals, such as the "transformist" theories of the French naturalists Georges-Louis Leclerc, Comte de Buffon (1707–88) and Jean-Baptiste Lamarck (1744–1829),[28] or the doctrine of independent acts of special creation, as set out in the writings of William Paley. This led Darwin to draw his famous conclusion: "Light has been shown on several facts, which on the belief of independent acts of creation are utterly obscure."[29] Darwin's language at this point must be noted carefully. He is not speaking about "proof" of his theory; he is asserting its explanatory capacity, and assuming that this is correlated with its truth. A comment added to the sixth edition of the *Origin of Species* makes this point clear.[30]

> It can hardly be supposed that a false theory would explain, in so satisfactory a manner as does the theory of natural selection, the several large classes of facts above specified. It has recently been objected that this is an unsafe method of arguing; but it is a method used in judging the common events of life, and has often been used by the greatest natural philosophers.

While some writers have unwisely made prediction a cornerstone of the scientific method, Darwin himself was quite clear that his theory of natural selection did not predict, and could not predict. That was just the nature of things.[31] In a letter praising the perspicuity of the biologist F. W. Hutton (1836–1905), Darwin singled out this point for special comment.[32]

> He is one of the very few who see that the change of species cannot be directly proved, and that the doctrine must sink or swim according as it groups and explains phenomena. It is really curious how few judge it in this way, which is clearly the right way.

The statement that "the doctrine must sink or swim according as it groups and explains phenomena" is of critical importance. The nature of the scientific phenomena was such that prediction was not possible for Darwin. This point, of course, led some philosophers of science, most notably Karl Popper, to suggest that Darwinism was not really scientific.[33] Yet this judgment is now widely held to rest on a somewhat attenuated understanding of the scientific method. Happily it was subsequently corrected by Popper himself.

Problems, Prediction, and Proof: The Challenge of Natural Selection

The *Origin* went through six editions, and Darwin worked constantly to improve his text, adding new material, amending existing material, and, above all, responding to criticisms in what can only be described as a remarkably open manner. Of the 4,000 sentences in the first edition, Darwin had rewritten three in four by the time of the final sixth edition of 1872. Interestingly, some 60 percent of these modifications took place in the last two editions, which introduced some "improvements" that now seem unwise – for example, his imprudent incorporation of Herbert Spencer's potentially misleading phrase "the survival of the fittest."[34]

The contents of these successive editions of the *Origin of Species* make it clear that Darwin's new theory faced considerable opposition on many fronts. There is no doubt – for the historical evidence is clear – that some traditional Christian thinkers saw it as a threat to the way in which they had interpreted their faith. Yet there can also be no doubt – for the historical evidence is equally clear – that other Christians saw Darwin's theory as offering new ways of understanding and parsing traditional Christian ideas. More importantly, however, Darwin's theory provoked scientific controversy, with many scientists of his day raising concerns about the scientific foundations of "natural selection."

If the successive editions of the *Origin* are anything to go by, Darwin's theory was assaulted by many scientists of the day, who deemed it to have significant defects. Most of the revisions represent responses to specifically scientific criticisms of his work. Yet as historians of science have pointed out, this is the norm, not the exception, in scientific advance. Criticism of a theory is the means by which – to use a Darwinian way of speaking – we discover whether it has survival potential. The reception of a scientific theory is a communal affair, in which a "tipping point" is gradually reached through a process of debate and reflection, often linked with additional research programs. Darwin's theory appears to have met more sustained opposition from the scientific community than from its religious counterpart, especially on account of its failure to offer a convincing account of how innovations were transmitted to future generations.

A good example of such scientific criticism is found in Fleeming Jenkin's concerns about "blending inheritance."[35] Jenkin (1833–85) was an engineer, heavily involved in the business of developing underwater telephone cables, who was appointed as professor of engineering at University College, London, in 1866, before taking up a chair in engineering at Edinburgh in 1868.[36] In an anonymous review of Darwin's work,[37] Jenkin asserted that the evidential base of Darwin's theory was deficient; he based "large conclusions" on "small facts." Jenkin identified several problems with his approach, including what Darwin clearly already believed to be a potentially fatal flaw in his theory. While Jenkin's article arguably did little more than convince Darwin of the correctness of conclusions that he had already reached on his own, the force of Jenkin's argument is known to have caused him some discomfort. Jenkin published his review in a popular journal that was well known for asserting its independence from religious and ecclesiastical influence. For Jenkin, the issue was the scientific vulnerability, not the religious consequences, of Darwin's theory.

In addition to querying whether what was known of geological history provided sufficient time for Darwin's evolutionary developments to take place, Jenkin pointed out that, on the basis of existing understandings of hereditary transmission, any novelties would be diluted in subsequent generations. Yet Darwin's theory depended on the transmission, not dilution, of such characteristics. In other words, Darwin's theory lacked a viable understanding of genetics. Darwin responded to Jenkin in the fifth edition of the *Origin*, in effect accommodating Jenkin's concerns within an existing understanding of the mechanics of transmission.[38] It was a good holding move, but it did not solve the problem.

Darwin's own theory of genetics is known as "pangenesis," based on hypothetical "gemmules" – minute particles that somehow determine all characteristics of the organism.[39] These "gemmules" had never been observed; nevertheless, Darwin argued that it was necessary to propose their existence to make sense of the observational data at his disposal. Each cell of an organism, and even every part of each cell, was understood to produce gemmules of a specific type corresponding to the cell or cell part. These were able to circulate throughout the body and enter the reproductive system. Every sperm and egg contained these hypothetical gemmules, and they were thus transmitted to the next generation. Yet this theory simply could not account for the hypothetical difficulty raised by Jenkin.

The answer, of course, lay in the writings of the Austrian monk Gregor Mendel (1822–84), whose research into the genetic transmission of certain characteristics of peas demonstrated how certain traits could indeed be passed down, without dilution, to later generations.[40] Yet while Mendel knew about Darwin, it seems that Darwin did not know about Mendel.[41] There is no evidence for the assertion, commonly encountered in the popular literature, that unread copies of Mendel's paper were found among Charles Darwin's effects after his death.[42] Mendel possessed a copy of the German translation of the third edition of Darwin's *Origin of Species*, and marked the following passage with double lines in the margin. It was clearly of considerable importance to him. In Darwin's original English, this reads:[43]

> The slight degree of variability in hybrids from the first cross or in the first generation, in contrast with their extreme variability in the succeeding generations, is a curious fact and deserves attention.

This curiosity would not remain mysterious for much longer, and Mendel might well have taken some pleasure from the thought that his theory was able to explain this "curious" fact.[44] Yet the confluence of Mendel's theory of genetics and Darwin's theory of natural selection still lay some years in the future.[45] Jenkin's objection simply could not be answered at the time.

Yet even though Darwin did not believe that he had adequately dealt with all the problems that required resolution, he was confident that his explanation was the best available. While recognizing that it lacked rigorous proof, Darwin clearly believed that his theory could be defended on the basis of criteria of acceptance and justification that were already widely used within the natural sciences, and that its explanatory capacity was itself a reliable guide to its truth. As Darwin noted, there were indeed those who argued that his was an "unsafe method of arguing" – but Darwin correctly pointed out that such forms of reasoning were widely used in everyday situations, and found to be acceptable and reliable. We often find ourselves trusting a way of thinking, believing it to be true, but not being able to offer the decisive proof that some insist is essential for an opinion to be held with integrity.

Darwin believed firmly that his new theory could coexist with anomalies and apparent contradictions, and that it would ultimately prove to be correct. In bringing his argument to its conclusion in the *Origin of Species*, Darwin asserted that his theory would still be shown to be correct, despite the contradictions, anomalies, and difficulties that it faced.[46]

> A crowd of difficulties will have occurred to the reader. Some of them are so grave that to this day I can never reflect on them without being staggered; but, to the best of my judgement, the greater number are only apparent, and those that are real are not, I think, fatal to my theory.

Darwin here anticipates some themes in today's philosophy of science, most notably the capacity of a valid scientific theory to coexist with apparent anomalies and disconfirmations, without predicting novel observations. Where experience seems to contradict a scientific theory, the most likely outcome is an internal readjustment of the system, rather than its rejection.[47] The failure of a theory to correlate with observation may rest upon one of its subsidiary hypotheses, rather than the core idea of the theory itself.[48]

More recent studies, especially in the philosophy of biology, have raised interesting questions about whether prediction really is essential to the scientific method, while offering assessments of the interplay of prediction and accommodation in scientific explanation.[49] This issue emerged as important in the nineteenth-century debate between William Whewell and John Stuart Mill over the role of induction as a scientific method.[50] Whewell emphasized the importance of predictive novelty as a core element of the scientific method; Mill argued that the difference between prediction of novel observations and theoretical accommodation of existing observations was purely psychological, and had no ultimate epistemological significance.

The debate, of course, continues. In their recent discussion of the issue,[51] leading philosophers of biology Christopher Hitchcock and Elliott Sober argue that while prediction can occasionally be superior to accommodation, this is not always the case. Situations can easily be envisaged where accommodation is superior to prediction. Prediction is neither intrinsically nor invariably to be preferred to accommodation. The relevance of this point to the scientific character of Darwin's approach will be obvious. Yet it also raises some significant doubts about the reliability of popular accounts of the scientific method – above all, the relentless insistence that science proves its theories, leaving nothing to faith.[52]

These themes are developed in a somewhat pointed manner in William K. Clifford's influential essay *The Ethics of Belief* (1877). Clifford here argued that "it is wrong always, everywhere, and for anyone, to believe anything upon insufficient evidence."[53] This was, he argued, not simply an intellectual responsibility; it was a fundamentally *moral* duty. Nobody should be allowed to believe something that was argumentatively or evidentially underdetermined. Most would, of course, agree with Clifford, at least in principle, although Clifford's use of the phrase "insufficient evidence" is more than a little vague, not least when he comes to deal with that cornerstone of the scientific explanation – the question of justified inference. Happily, Clifford – who was a mathematician – knew enough about the more empirical sciences to be aware that the scientific method relies upon inference. Yet, even so, his account of the scientific method is clearly deeply problematic. It seems quite incapable, for example, of dealing with the troublesome issue of the "underdetermination of theory by evidence,"[54] one of the persistent difficulties that cloud the horizons of those who prefer to keep their science simple and untroubled by philosophical and historical inconveniences. If Clifford's unrealistic account of the scientific method were to be applied to Darwin's *Origin of Species*, we should have to reject either Darwin's work as unscientific and even unethical, or Clifford's account of the place of belief in science. Happily, this matter is easily resolved, and it is Clifford who is to be judged as unsatisfactory.

The inadequacies of Clifford's approach are the subject of the famous essay "The Will to Believe" (1897), in which the psychologist William James (1842–1910) argued that human beings find themselves in a position where they have to choose between intellectual options that are, in James's words, "forced, living, and momentous."[55] We all, James argues, need what he terms "working hypotheses" to make sense of our experience of the world. These "working hypotheses" often lie beyond total proof, yet are accepted and acted upon because they are found to offer reliable and satisfying standpoints from which to engage the real world. For James, faith is a particular form of belief, which is pervasive in everyday life. James defined faith as follows: "Faith means belief in something concerning which doubt is still theoretically possible." This leads James to declare that "faith is synonymous with working hypothesis."

James's emphasis on the importance of such "working hypotheses" finds ample exemplification in the *Origin of Species*. Darwin's theory had many weaknesses and loose ends. Nevertheless, he was convinced that these were difficulties that could be tolerated on account of the clear explanatory superiority of his approach. His "working hypothesis," he believed, was sufficiently robust to resist the many difficulties that it faced.

There is much more that could be said about the origins, development, and statement of Darwin's theory of natural selection. As our concern is primarily to identify Darwin's impact on natural theology, particularly that set out by William Paley, we shall not pursue these historical questions further, except where they have a direct bearing on the specific issues of concern to this study.

Natural Selection and Natural Theology:
An Assessment of Darwin's Impact

It is widely agreed that Darwin's theory of natural selection was of critical importance to late Victorian reflections on natural theology. Although the nature of that influence is often portrayed in consistently negative terms, it is clear that many saw Darwin as opening up new possibilities for natural theology, either by forcing necessary modifications to older approaches, or by reinforcing the concept of "laws impressed upon nature."[56] Darwin himself was concerned to promote natural selection, rather than to criticize natural theology. In what follows, we shall consider four main points concerning Darwin's impact upon natural theology, beginning with his relation to Paley's approach.

Darwin's relation to Paley

It is impossible to understand the young Darwin without seeing his ideas through a refracting lens, shaped by the writings of William Paley and others influenced by him, such as John Bird Sumner (1780–1862), later to become Archbishop of Canterbury.[57] There is a physical and intellectual continuity between the young Darwin and Paley. A college tradition holds that Darwin occupied the same room as Paley had before him at Christ's College, Cambridge. Furthermore, Darwin refers with warmth to Paley's classic *Natural Theology* (1802), which in many ways defines one of the positions that he eventually believed he had to reject. It is, however, unlikely that Darwin was required to read Paley's *Natural Theology* while at Cambridge. As Aileen Fyfe has demonstrated, various Cambridge colleges identified two of Paley's works as "set texts," on which examination questions might legitimately be set: his *View of the Evidences of Christianity* (1794) and *Principles of Moral and Political Philosophy* (1785).[58] There is no indication that Paley's *Natural Theology* was a set text prior to 1833. Darwin's own memories of his Cambridge years confirm that he read both Paley's *Evidences* and *Principles* while at Cambridge. Although Darwin refers to *Natural Theology*, he does not specifically state that he read it during his Cambridge years.[59]

> In order to pass the BA examination, it was, also, necessary to get up Paley's *Evidences of Christianity*, and his *Moral Philosophy*. This was done in a thorough manner, and I am convinced that I could have written out the whole of the Evidences with perfect correctness, but not of course in the clear language of Paley. The logic of this book and, as I may add, of his *Natural Theology* gave me as much delight as did Euclid. The careful study of these works, without attempting to learn any part by rote, was the only part of the

Academical Course which, as I then felt and as I still believe, was of the least use to me in the education of my mind. I did not at that time trouble myself about Paley's premises; and taking these on trust, I was charmed and convinced by the long line of argumentation.

Whenever Darwin may have read Paley's *Natural Theology*, he was delighted by the detailed descriptions of the adaptations to be found in plants and animals – such as the human eye. These seem to have become normative for Darwin, determining an intellectual and iconic context within which he would frame and defend his own views. Darwin may have exaggerated slightly in stating that he had committed Paley to memory; nevertheless, echoes of Paley's works are found throughout the *Origin of Species*. Stephen Jay Gould, for example, has pointed out how Darwin's statement of his principle of natural selection is deeply indebted to the language and imagery found in Paley's writings, even though Darwin would later draw some very different conclusions.[60] Among several points of similarity, Gould notes the following:

1 Both Paley and Darwin develop analogical forms of argument, moving from an analogy drawn from human existence to the natural world itself. Paley argues from the design of a watch to presumed design in nature; Darwin argues from artificial selection in farming and stockbreeding to a presumed analogical process within nature.[61]
2 Both Paley and Darwin cite the same examples from nature, including the human eye; the former to demonstrate their divine "contrivance," the latter to demonstrate how an evolutionary process might arrive at such an outcome.

Yet other parallels might easily be noted. For example, both writers assume that natural processes work toward God, and can be seen as adopting essentially teleological outlooks[62] – even though they have very different understandings of what this entails. Paley bases this assumption upon the assumed benevolence of God, which he holds to be confirmed by an inspection of nature; Darwin upon his observations that natural selection aims at the improvement of individual beings to better their prospects of surviving and reproducing. For Paley, adaptation within nature takes place "for the effectuating of a purpose beneficial to the species."[63] Where multiple possibilities might have arisen within nature, "the law that actually prevails is the most beneficial."[64] Or, as Paley concludes at the end of *Natural Theology*, having surveyed the natural world, "in a vast plurality of instances in which contrivance is perceived, the design of the contrivance is *beneficial*."[65] For Darwin, "natural selection works solely by and for the good of each being."[66] Or, to put this another way:[67]

Every one who believes, as I do, that all the corporeal and mental organs (excepting those which are neither advantageous nor disadvantageous to the possessor) of all beings have been developed through natural selection, or the survival of the fittest, together with use or habit, will admit that these organs have been formed so that their possessors may compete successfully with other beings, and thus increase in number.

As we saw earlier, Paley's view is essentially that God created the world in a manner that displays the divine wisdom in both design and execution – a notion that Paley expresses using the word "contrivance." The famous image of God as the divine watchmaker expressed both these ideas of design and skillful fabrication. Darwin rejects this model, arguing that natural selection offers a more plausible account of things. It is highly significant that Darwin himself chose to adopt Paley's heavily loaded term "contrivance" in one of his own works, dealing with the methods of fertilization of orchids.[68] Darwin's *On the Various Contrivances by which British and Foreign Orchids are Fertilised by Insects* appeared in 1862, shortly after the appearance of the *Origin of Species*. Although it was not a commercial success, it had the potential to make a significant contribution to the debate about the implications of Darwin's theory for natural theology. Asa Gray is reported as declaring that "if the Orchid-book (with a few trifling omissions) had appeared before the 'Origin,' the author would have been canonised rather than anathematised by the natural theologians."[69] Indeed, a review in the *Literary Churchman* had only one criticism to make of this work – namely, that Darwin's expression of admiration at the "contrivances" found in orchids amounted to an unnecessarily indirect manner of saying, "O Lord, how manifold are Thy works."[70]

Darwin's familiarity with the arguments and controlling analogies of Paley's *Natural Theology* is evident at many points throughout his works. His fundamental strategy appears to have been to demonstrate that images and observations popularized by Paley and his successors in support of belief in special creation could better be explained by his theory of natural selection. Darwin, it must be emphasized, had no quarrel with the idea of God, nor even with the notion of God as creator. His dispute was specifically with the doctrine of special creation – namely, that God created individual species adapted to specific environments within an essentially static natural order.

Darwin on religion

This naturally leads us to reflect on Darwin's attitudes toward religion. Did his theory of evolution turn him into an atheist crusader against religious belief, as some seem to suggest? Sadly, Darwin's authority and example are

Figure 6.2 Daguerreotype of Anne Elizabeth Darwin (Annie), 1849.

continually invoked to justify metaphysical and theological claims that go far beyond anything that he himself expressed in, or associated with, his evolutionary biology. Happily, the fundamentally *historical* question of Darwin's religious views is relatively easy to answer, thanks to the intensive scholarly study of Darwin and his Victorian context in the last few decades.[71]

The view that Darwin was indeed an atheist on account of his evolutionary doctrine was vigorously advocated in freethinking publications in England, especially in the later years of the nineteenth century – such as Edward Aveling's pamphlet *The Religious Views of Charles Darwin* (1883).[72] Aveling's statements were subsequently repeated in publications issued by secularist organizations and writers, such as George William Foote (1850–1915), a leading secularist, founder of the journal *The Freethinker*, and president of the National Secular Society from 1890 until 1915.[73]

There are several important passages in Darwin's writings that can be interpreted to mean that Darwin ceased to believe in an orthodox Christian conception of God on account of his views on evolution. The problem is that there are other passages that variously point to Darwin maintaining a religious belief, or to his losing an orthodox Christian faith – which, it must be emphasized, is not the same as ceasing to believe in God – for reasons quite other than evolutionary concerns. The tragic death of Darwin's daughter Annie in 1851 at the age of ten, for example, seems to have eroded whatever little lingering belief he may have had in a benevolent divine providence.[74] However, a note of caution must be injected: on the basis of the published evidence at our disposal, it is clear that Darwin himself was far from consistent in the matter of his religious views. It would therefore be extremely unwise to draw any confident conclusions on these issues.

It seems that Darwin abandoned what we might call "conventional Christian beliefs" at some point in the 1840s, although the dating of this must probably remain elusive. Yet there is a substantial theoretical gap between "abandoning an orthodox Christian faith" and "becoming an atheist." Christianity involves a highly specific conception of God; it is perfectly possible to believe in a god other than that of Christianity, or to believe in God and reject certain other aspects of the Christian faith. Indeed, the "Victorian crisis of faith" – within which Darwin was both spectator and participant – can be understood as a shift away from the specifics of Christianity toward a more generic concept of God, largely determined by the ethical values of the day. Darwin, like many others, appears to have moved toward what might reasonably be described as a "deist" conception of God, rather than the more specific divinity of the Christian faith.[75] It is not difficult to discern a more or less continuous trajectory from the Christian orthodoxy of his Cambridge years to a non-biblical deism at the time of the publication of the *Origin of Species*, and subsequently to a more thoroughly agnostic position in later life. Indeed, many would argue that, as a matter of historical fact, many scientists have held religious views that were heterodox, at least to some degree.[76]

While Darwin's religious beliefs unquestionably veered away from what we might loosely call "Christian orthodoxy," they are not replaced with anything even remotely resembling the aggressive and ridiculing form of atheism we unfortunately find in some of those who have presented themselves as his champions in more recent times. There is little in Darwin's writings to point to any such conclusion. In 1879, while working on his autobiography, Darwin commented on his personal religious confusion: "My judgement *often fluctuates* ... In my most extreme fluctuations I have never been an Atheist in the sense of denying God. I think that generally (and more and more as I grow older), *but not always*, that an Agnostic would be the more correct description of my state of mind."[77]

Many have praised the prescience and cool neutrality of Darwin's *Origin of Species*, noting its Olympian social and political detachment and scrupulous religious neutrality. It is to Darwin's letters that we must turn for illumination of both the fluctuations of his religious beliefs over time, as well as his reluctance to comment on religious matters, including his own personal beliefs. Yet when the context demanded it, Darwin seems to have been willing not merely to go on record concerning, but to emphasize, the consilience of religious faith and the theory of natural selection.

It would be tedious to illustrate this in detail. A representative example lies to hand in his reference to "laws impressed on matter by the Creator," which is given a higher profile in the second edition of the *Origin* than in the first.[78] Darwin's emphasis upon the role of natural laws in governing evolutionary processes prompted some to suggest that Darwin had achieved for biology what Newton had achieved for physics. Ernst Haeckel, for example, wrote of Darwin as the "new Newton," who had uncovered the natural laws governing the biological domain.[79] Darwin's theory of natural selection was comparable to Newton's law of gravity. Taken together, they offered a unitary vision of the natural world.[80] As Newtonian physics had led to the emergence of a new style of natural theology, might not Darwinian biology have a similar outcome? Newton had uncovered the laws of physics; Darwin those of biology.

Such lines of reflection might well end up leading to a deistic conception of God, rather than a Trinitarian God. But there is not even the whiff of a personal atheism here. While some might argue that Darwin may have made it possible to be an intellectually fulfilled atheist, Darwin did not himself draw that conclusion. It is difficult to believe that his references to a Creator in the *Origin of Species* were simply contrived to mollify his audience, representing crude deceptions aimed at masking a private atheism that Darwin feared might discredit his theory in the eyes of the religious public. As Darwin himself commented to Asa Gray in May 1860, concerning his *Origin of Species*, he had no intention of writing "atheistically," and did not believe that his views on natural selection entailed atheism:[81]

> I can see no reason, why a man, or other animal, may not have been aboriginally produced by other laws; and that all these laws may have been expressly designed by an omniscient Creator, who foresaw every future event and consequence. But the more I think the more bewildered I become.

Darwin seems to have regarded religious beliefs as a private matter and was reluctant to talk about his own religious commitments. Yet the needs of the situation regularly obliged him to say something on this matter. The evidence points to reluctant, painful, and diplomatic self-disclosure of Darwin's beliefs, not the fabrication or manipulation of those beliefs for tactical purposes. Darwin's enemy was not God, nor even the Church of England, but a specific view of God that limited the act of creation to a series of specific past divine actions, leading to a fixed, static biological realm.

Perhaps the most important point to be noted is that, if Darwin did indeed develop heterodox religious views, these are not necessarily to be attributed to his doctrine of natural selection. Darwin did not see this doctrine as entailing difficulties for religious belief, let alone as entailing atheism. Thomas Huxley, who was inclined to emphasize the anti-religious aspects of Darwin's thought, was quite clear that "the doctrine of Evolution is neither Anti-theistic nor Theistic."[82] Darwin's theory denied any direct divine creation of biological organisms. The question that remained open was whether it also denied indirect involvement, such as action through secondary causes.

This naturally leads us to consider how Darwin's views on teleology impacted on natural theology.

Design and purpose: The question of teleology

By far the most significant question raised for existing approaches to natural theology by Darwin's theory of natural selection was its revisionist account of teleology. How could one meaningfully speak of the divine "design" of the natural order, when that appeared to have emerged over an extended period of time by essentially natural processes? In turning to consider this question, it is important to appreciate that discussion of Darwin's theory of natural selection for natural theology often focuses on those specific conceptions of natural theology predominant in England at the time – most notably, William Paley's "physico-theology." As we have emphasized, this specific form of natural theology – which emphasizes "evidence of design" – represents a late seventeenth-century development, in some ways peculiar to England. Other approaches to natural theology were in circulation, most notably those that appealed to the order of nature, or the natural laws apparently embedded within its structures.[83] The impact of Darwinism upon natural theology cannot be discussed as if Paley is the sole or normative representative of this tradition.

In April 1860, Thomas H. Huxley commented that what impressed him most forcibly on his first reading of Darwin's *Origin of Species* was the "conviction that teleology, as commonly understood, had received its death-blow at Mr Darwin's hands."[84] Paley's natural theology, as noted earlier, is resolutely teleological, holding that living organisms possess adaptations to their environments that must be considered to be designed with specific goals in mind. Paley's notion of a "contrivance" entails design with a definite objective in mind. Darwin's theory of natural selection, in marked contrast, eliminates any notion of divine design. This point was stated clearly by Darwin in his *Autobiography*:[85]

> The old argument from design in Nature, as given by Paley, which formerly seemed to me so conclusive, fails, now that the law of natural selection has been discovered. We can no longer argue that, for instance, the beautiful hinge of a bivalve shell must have been made by an intelligent being, like the hinge of a door by man. There seems to be no more design in the variability of organic beings, and in the action of natural selection, than in the course which the wind blows.

Darwin's critique here is directed specifically against arguments for the existence of God that argue from "contrivance" to a designer. The example Darwin provides – the "beautiful hinge of a bivalve shell," noted and admired by Paley[86] – should not be seen as directly "designed" by a divine intelligence.

It is often asserted that Darwin destroyed the notion of teleology in biology; in fact, he redirected the notion. The problem faced by both Darwin's supporters and critics was that Darwin's selection-based teleology did not conform to any familiar model of teleological explanation. Darwin's contemporaries were divided both as to whether he was a supporter or critic of teleology, and also as to whether this was to be praised or blamed.[87] Asa Gray and Albert von Kölliker both held that Darwin was teleological in his thinking, the former regarding this as a virtue and the latter as a vice; Hermann von Helmholtz and Karl Ernst von Baer both regarded Darwin as a critic of teleology, the first seeing this as a positive development, and the second as a cause for concern.[88]

Those arguing that Darwin rejected teleology make two fundamental assumptions:[89]

1   The only "non-trivial" teleological explanations are those that appeal either to divine design or to some kind of internal vital force;
2   Darwinian selection explanations appeal to neither of these explanations.

The first of these assumptions is clearly false; once this is appreciated and conceded, the intrinsically teleological nature of Darwin's view of natural selection can be understood, and his own distinct notion of teleology explored. We do Darwin no service by forcing other people's notions of teleology upon him; we must clarify his own views and assess their significance.

Both the terminology and conceptualities of teleology are deeply embedded in Darwin's evolutionary thought.[90] Darwin's explanations based on natural selection are intrinsically teleological, in the sense that an "advantage" (Darwin's preferred term) conferred upon an organism by a trait is held to explain its increase, or presence, in a population. Traits are differentially selected due to their consequences.[91]

> It may be said that natural selection is daily and hourly scrutinising, throughout the world, every variation, even the slightest; rejecting that which is bad, preserving and adding up all that is good; silently and insensibly working, whenever and wherever opportunity offers, at the improvement of each organic being in relation to its organic and inorganic conditions of life.

Even allowing for a degree of poetic license on Darwin's part here, it is clear that he envisages the process of "natural selection" as being anything but random. As one of his recent interpreters has noted, Darwin views natural selection as a fundamentally "non-random process that promotes adaptations by selecting combinations that 'make sense' – that is, are useful to the organisms."[92] As Darwin himself wrote in 1860: "I am inclined to look at everything as resulting from designed laws, with the details, whether good or bad, left to the working out of what we may call chance."[93] Natural selection is clearly teleological in some sense of the term. The real question concerns how Darwin's idiosyncratic notion of teleology related to those with which his contemporaries were familiar.

It seems clear that Darwin and Huxley initially understood the term "teleology" in significantly different ways. Huxley appears to have appreciated this. Having declared, after his first reading of the *Origin of Species*, that Darwin seemed to have eliminated traditional notions of design and purpose, he found himself, after a closer reading of Darwin, coming to a more cautious view in 1869. Certain *types* of teleology – but not all – were challenged by Darwin.[94]

The doctrine of Evolution is the most formidable opponent of all the commoner and coarser forms of Teleology. But perhaps the most remarkable service to the philosophy of Biology rendered by Mr. Darwin is the reconciliation of Teleology and Morphology, and the explanation of the facts of both, which his views offer. The teleology which supposes that the eye, such as we see it in man, or one of the higher vertebrata, was made with the precise structure it exhibits, for the purpose of enabling the animal which possesses it to see, has undoubtedly received its death-blow. Nevertheless, it is necessary to remember that there is a wider teleology which is not touched by the doctrine of Evolution, but is actually based upon the fundamental proposition of Evolution.

Figure 6.3 Asa Gray (1810–88), American botanist. Photograph, 1880s.

As Huxley rightly noted, the evolutionary process itself embodied a distinctive concept of teleology. Progressive trends in a creative evolutionary process could form the basis of a viable revised natural theology. Darwin did not think there were reasons for supposing that any aspect of the evolutionary process – including the origins of variations – was divinely guided. Yet that does not amount to the rejection of teleology as such.

Others were more upbeat about correlating Darwin's notion of teleology with its more traditional counterparts. In an article published in *Nature* in 1874, Asa Gray took a more explicitly teleological approach to Darwin's theory of natural selection. He spoke warmly of "Darwin's great service to Natural Science in bringing back to it Teleology: so that instead of Morphology *versus* Teleology, we shall have Morphology wedded to Teleology."[95] Gray clearly saw Darwin's explanation of adaptation as *restoring* notions of function and purpose to biology. Darwin professed himself delighted at the tone of Gray's positive account of his achievements. Yet he singled out for special comment Gray's observations on his approach to teleology:[96]

> What you say about Teleology pleases me especially, and I do not think any one else has ever noticed the point. I have always said you were the man to hit the nail on the head.

Nevertheless, although Darwin retained the notion of teleology in his notion of natural selection, it was far from the traditional concept of teleology that Gray accepted. Gray took the view that Darwin's hypothesis "would leave the doctrines of Final Causes, utility, and special design, just where they were before."[97] It is very difficult to see how this could be the case. Gray appears to have assumed that, because Darwin saw evolution in teleological terms, he therefore saw it in *traditional* teleological terms. This is clearly not correct.[98]

So how does this relate to Paley's vision of natural theology? It is often assumed that Darwin discredited and destroyed Paley's vision for natural theology, along with any such natural theologies that were implicitly or explicitly teleological in character. In fact, this is not the case. This point was recognized by Huxley in 1869, who rightly noted that the "teleological and the mechanical views of nature are not, necessarily, mutually exclusive." Huxley took the view that Paley's approach was capable of extension or modification to cope with the theory of natural selection, retaining a revised notion of teleology.[99]

> The acute champion of Teleology, Paley, saw no difficulty in admitting that the "production of things" may be the result of trains of mechanical dispositions fixed beforehand by intelligent appointment and kept in action by a power at the centre, that is to say, he proleptically accepted the modern doctrine of Evolution; and his successors might do well to follow their leader, or at any rate to attend to his weighty reasonings, before rushing into an antagonism which has no reasonable foundation.

It should not be the cause for surprise that many natural theologians of the 1860s and 1870s took the view that Darwin actually rescued Paley's approach to natural theology, by placing it on a firmer intellectual foundation through rectifying a faulty and ultimately fatal premise. Charles Kingsley (1819–75), then a canon of Westminster Abbey, was certainly one to take this viewpoint. In his 1871 lecture "On the Natural Theology of the Future," Kingsley singled out Darwin's work on orchids as "a most valuable addition to natural theology."[100] Insisting that the word "creation" implies process as much as event, Kingsley went on to argue that Darwin's theory clarified the mechanism of creation. God did not merely make things; he made them with the capacity to make themselves, thus opening up new possibilities within creation.[101] Similarly, Frederick Temple (1821–1902) – later to become Archbishop of Canterbury – gave this approach added ecclesiastical acceptability in his 1884 Bampton Lectures at Oxford University, when he declared that God "did not make the things, we may say; no, but He made them make themselves."[102]

Where Paley thought of a static creation, within which God seemed to play only a figurehead role, Kingsley argued that Darwin made it possible to see creation as a dynamic, fundamentally teleological process, directed by divine providence. Deism, for Kingsley, offered only a "chilling dream of a dead universe ungoverned by an absent God"; Darwinism, when rightly interpreted, offered a vision of a living universe constantly improving under the wise direction of its benevolent creator. "Of old it was said by

Him without whom nothing is made: 'My Father worketh hitherto, and I work.' Shall we quarrel with Science if she should show how those words are true?" The "conflict" between science and religion was thus "a storm in a Victorian teapot."[103] The teleological mechanism proposed by Darwin for this ongoing divine involvement with nature might not be quite what Paley had envisaged; for Kingsley, the new mechanism could nevertheless be accommodated within the framework of the Christian doctrines of creation and providence. For Paley, the teleology lay in the outcomes; for Darwin, as interpreted by Kingsley, it lay within the process itself.

Paley's specific conception of teleology may have been severely eroded by Darwin's theory of natural selection. In part, this reflects Paley's deliberate decision to focus on the biological realm on account of its intrinsic complexity, which Paley regarded as essential to the assertion of contrivance, and hence the inference of divine design. "Some degree therefore of *complexity* is necessary to render a subject fit for this species of argument."[104] Darwin offered a rival account of how this complexity arose, which, in the end, seemed to many to be superior as an explanation.

Yet perhaps Paley's decision to steer clear of the cosmological and physical realms of nature on account of their "simplicity" may have been a tactical misjudgment. What if the ultimate grounds of biological complexity lay in the deeper physical structure of things? Huxley's 1869 remarks about a "wider teleology" deserve closer attention. What, he muses, if there is some form of teleology that is woven into the deeper structure of things? What if the elemental structure of the universe is such that it will give rise to such processes?[105]

> Nevertheless, it is necessary to remember that there is a wider teleology which is not touched by the doctrine of Evolution, but is actually based upon the fundamental proposition of Evolution. This proposition is that the whole world, living and not living, is the result of the mutual interaction, according to definite laws, of the forces possessed by the molecules of which the primitive nebulosity of the universe was composed. If this be true, it is no less certain that the existing world lay potentially in the cosmic vapour, and that a sufficient intelligence could, from a knowledge of the properties of the molecules of that vapour, have predicted, say the state of the fauna of Britain in 1869, with as much certainty as one can say what will happen to the vapour of the breath on a cold winter's day.

It is clear that the state of scientific knowledge of the 1860s was simply inadequate to sustain Huxley's speculative judgment. Nevertheless, with the passing of time, the insight of his comments has become increasingly clear. Might the key to the potentiality and directionality of biological evolution lie in the fixed physical and chemical properties of the elements of the universe, as these emerged from the "big bang"? The discussion that Huxley perhaps hoped to catalyze is now well and truly under way, and we shall return to consider its implications in Chapter 8.

The benevolence of God: Providence and animal pain

As we noted earlier, Paley's approach to nature is optimistic, positive, and, to its critics, uncritically simplistic. Paley holds that nature exudes evidence of divine wisdom at every point, with every creature of the living world expressing its delight in its existence in its own distinctive manner.[106]

> It is a happy world after all. The air, the earth, the water, teem with delighted existence. In a spring noon, or a summer evening, on whatever side I turn my eyes, myriads of happy beings crowd upon my view.

Paley's enthusiastic exploration of the intrinsic happiness of the creation reflects the world of a hunting parson of the Regency age: "Happiness is found with the purring cat, no less than with the playful kitten; in the arm-chair of dozing age, as well as in either the sprightliness of the dance, or the animation of the chase."[107] If there are any blemishes within nature, these reflect nothing more than an imperfect actualization of God's benevolent purposes for creation.

Paley's somewhat blithe and Panglossian reflections on nature overlook more than can be permitted. Where Wordsworth and other Romantics saw nature as a moral educator, others were beginning to suspect that the only ethic evident within nature was that of the struggle for survival. This insight was popularized in Alfred Lord Tennyson's poem *In Memoriam* (1849), widely regarded as one of the most important English poems of the nineteenth century. Written in response to the death of a close friend, Arthur Henry Hallam (1811–33), Tennyson's poem explores a wide range of issues, including the status of religious faith and its warrants in nature.[108]

It is often suggested that Tennyson's poem includes reflection on some themes from Robert Chambers's *Vestiges of the Natural History of Creation* (1844), although there is no direct evidence that the evolutionary sections of the poem were written after the publication of this work.[109] *The Vestiges of the Natural History of Creation*, published anonymously, is widely regarded as having secured a degree of acceptance for evolutionary perspectives,[110] even though these perspectives are quite distinct from those later developed by Darwin. Although its evidential analysis was flawed in many respects, the *Vestiges* popularized the notion of the progressive transmutation of species through a developmental process governed by God-given laws.

In Memoriam represents a powerful critique of natural theology in general, whether in the forms defended by Paley, or as reflected in the authors of the Bridgewater Treatises. Nature is presented as profoundly ambiguous; it does not point clearly toward God. While nature may indeed resonate with religious faith at points, it is more often perceived to be in conflict with faith. The real foundation of faith lies not in the observation of nature, but in the inner experience of individuals.[111]

> God is love, transcendent, all-pervading! We do not get this faith from Nature or the world. If we look at Nature alone, full of perfection and imperfection, she tells us that God is disease, murder and rapine. We get this faith from ourselves, from what is highest within us.

Tennyson lists some of the favorite evidence of the natural theologians – the wings of birds, and the complex structure of the eye – and declares them to be flawed and faulty pointers to God.[112]

> I found Him not in world or sun
> Or eagle's wing, or insect's eye;
> Nor thro' the questions men may try,
> The petty cobwebs we have spun.

For Tennyson, nature was not the wise, good, and beautiful moral educator advocated by some Romantic poets, nor by Paley. Nature is characterized by violence, competition, death, and destruction. This idea is expressed in one of the best-known sections of the poem, which sets out the central vulnerability of Paley's natural theology. Nature has brought man into being, but gives him no firm reason to suppose there is anything beyond the realm of the natural.[113]

> Man, her last work, who seem'd so fair,
> Such splendid purpose in his eyes,
> Who roll'd the psalm to wintry skies,
> Who built him fanes of fruitless prayer,
>
> Who trusted God was love indeed
> And love Creation's final law—
> Tho' Nature, red in tooth and claw
> With ravine, shriek'd against his creed.

Tennyson's point was simple: those who spoke naively and sentimentally of God's love being expressed in nature had to offer a convincing explanation of its vicious cycles of violence, pain, and suffering. What Paley termed "happy beings" have to eat in order to survive; and they generally end up by eating other "happy beings," who one imagines are not too happy about this state of affairs. This point was not lost on Darwin himself, who wrote of the "struggle for existence" within nature:[114]

> We behold the face of nature bright with gladness, we often see superabundance of food; we do not see, or we forget, that the birds which are idly singing round us mostly live on insects or seeds, and are thus constantly destroying life; or we forget how largely these songsters, or their eggs, or their nestlings, are destroyed by birds or beasts of prey; we do not always bear in mind, that though food may be now superabundant, it is not so at all seasons of each recurring year.

The force of Darwin's point can hardly be overlooked. Interestingly, this specific concern is not to be seen as a direct outcome of his theory of natural selection. Darwin's misgiving here is based simply on the observation of the natural world as we know it. Nor was Darwin's unease limited to the fact that survival requires killing and eating. He was particularly disturbed by the behavior of parasites, who kept their host alive as long as possible in order to ensure their own survival.[115]

> I cannot see as plainly as others do, and as I should wish to do, evidence of design and beneficence on all sides of us. There seems to me too much misery in the world. I cannot persuade myself that a beneficent and omnipotent God would have designedly created the Ichneumonidae [parasitic wasps] with the express intention of their feeding within the living bodies of caterpillars or that a cat should play with mice.

Even before Darwin developed his distinctive account of the origins of the biological world that we know, he had identified the fundamental difficulty that Paley's vision of a "contrived" world faced.

Natural history was thus a titanic, extended "struggle for existence." Darwin's awareness of the importance of competition within nature was crystallized by his reading of Thomas Malthus's *Essay on the Principle of Population*, first published anonymously in 1798.[116] The ideas he found there played no small part in helping Darwin formulate the principles that he believed to underlie the process of natural selection.[117] Although Malthus was mainly concerned about the social consequences of unchecked population growth, Darwin noted the implications for the biological realm, particularly in relation to the phenomenon of the extinction of species. Given that resources are not infinite, offspring must compete with each other if they are to survive and reproduce.[118]

> In October 1838, that is, fifteen months after I had begun my systematic enquiry, I happened to read for amusement "Malthus on Population," and

being well prepared to appreciate the struggle for existence which everywhere goes on from long-continued observation of the habits of animals and plants, it at once struck me that under these circumstances favourable variations would tend to be preserved, and unfavourable ones to be destroyed. The result of this would be the formation of new species. Here then I had at last got a theory by which to work.

In a competitive environment, offspring with environmental advantages will fare better than those without, and thus shape the characteristics of later generations. Competition, occasionally leading to extinction, can thus be said to be built into the Darwinian paradigm.[119] It was not an idea that was easy to reconcile with the notion of divine providence.

Yet this does not appear to have concerned Darwin unduly. His belief in divine providence had been eroded long before his evolutionary theory began to emerge. Some suggest that Darwin's theory of descent with modification by natural selection led him to abandon the doctrine of special providence, along with miracles and other notions of direct divine intervention in nature. Yet Darwin appears to have abandoned such beliefs by the late 1830s, and not as a consequence of his evolutionary thought. Darwin's travels on the *Beagle* led him to witness events that called into question his early belief in divine providence. For example, while in South America, Darwin witnessed at first hand the terrible struggle for existence faced by the natives of the Tierra del Fuego; he saw the devastating effects of an earthquake; and he began to grasp the magnitude of the staggering numbers of species that had become extinct – each of which, according to Paley, was providentially created and valued by God. We can see here the beginnings of the wearing away of any belief in divine providence, which would become characteristic of the later Darwin. If a crisis point was reached, it may have been precipitated by the death of Darwin's daughter Annie in 1851, at the age of ten, which – as noted earlier (158) – some see as marking a watershed in Darwin's religious convictions. Yet this loss of faith in providence dates from much earlier in his career.

In one sense, Darwin's theory did not raise any new difficulties for natural theology. The question of how apparent evil and suffering in nature can be reconciled with a good creator God was a regular topic of debate within all schools of natural theology, and is a major topic in the later parts of Paley's *Natural Theology*.[120] Paley is aware of at least some of the issues noted by Darwin, and discusses, for example, why various insects use poison to subdue or kill their prey, and why animals eat each other.[121] He argues that these cannot really be considered to be evil; in one sense, they are just natural. The question of animal suffering was not, however, high on the cultural agenda. Suffering was primarily seen as an issue affecting human beings.

Figure 6.4   Queen Victoria's favorite pets. Sir Edwin Landseer (1803–73): *Hector, Nero and Dash with the parrot, Lory*, 1838, oil on canvas, 120.2 × 150.3 cm. Commissioned by Queen Victoria.

Yet by the 1850s, the cultural mood had changed. A heightened awareness of the problem of suffering within the animal kingdom had developed.[122] "At the beginning of the nineteenth century the English would have been surprised to hear themselves praised for special kindness to animals ... [By] as early as the 1830s, despite the circumambient evidence to the contrary, the English humane movement had begun to claim kindness to animals as a native trait and to associate cruelty to animals with foreigners."[123] The Society for the Prevention of Cruelty to Animals was founded in London in 1824. In 1847, the Vegetarian Society of Great Britain was founded, reflecting growing public unease about cruelty to animals. In the same year, Dr Marshall Hall published a controversial series of articles on the questionable ethics of animal experimentation in the medical journal *The Lancet*. Animals came increasingly to be portrayed in literature as possessing sentient natures, and quasi-human characteristics. Anna Sewell's *Black Beauty* (1877) is the best-known work of this kind;[124] it was not, however, the first.[125] "To be a literate middle-class Englishperson by mid-century was to develop one's sensibility and sympathy through the vicarious experience of reading narratives of animal suffering."[126]

The problems raised for Christian theology by the presence of suffering in the world had been known long before Darwin's theory of natural selection emerged. Yet there is no doubt that Darwinism has added further layers of complexity to this long-standing question. Darwin's *Origin of Species* may be said to have made the problem of suffering within the animal kingdom more significant and intense for Christian apologists, for two main reasons.

First, Darwin's theory made the maintenance of an absolute ontological distinction between humanity and the animal kingdom problematic. Ontological boundaries were destabilized, and shown to be porous. The inevitable outcome of Darwin's views was to highlight the evolutionary links between humanity and the animal kingdom, thus making the human appear more animal, and the animal appear more human. Although this general principle is clearly assumed (though understated for tactical reasons) throughout the *Origin of Species*, Darwin made it explicit in his later work *The Descent of Man* (1871). Darwin himself explicitly affirmed the capacity of animals to experience feelings in his *Expression of the Emotions in Man and Animals* (1872).[127]

Second, Darwin's understanding of the evolutionary process envisages the emergence of the animal kingdom as taking place over an extended period of time, entailing suffering and apparent wastage of hitherto unimaginable proportions. Darwin did not discover the problem of suffering; he magnified it, and raised fundamental questions about its purpose and utility.[128] What purpose had been served by species that are now extinct? Was their suffering in vain? Darwin himself was acutely aware of this point: "What a book a devil's chaplain might write on the clumsy, wasteful, blundering law, and horribly cruel works of nature!"[129] An old problem was given a new urgency and intensity. If Darwin did not create a new theological problem at this point, he certainly brought an old one into sharp focus, emphasizing the chronological extension of the suffering of the natural world, and the relatively limited positive outcomes of this suffering.

Conclusion to Part II

There is much more that needs to be said about Darwin's importance for Christian theology. Any comprehensive account of the religious impact of Darwin in Victorian England would have to include discussion of his impact on the interpretation of the Genesis creation narratives, and the distinct identity of humanity and its place in the cosmos. These are important issues, and are to be seen as part of the overall impact of evolutionary thought on religion. We shall return to some of these topics in later chapters.

There is a sense in which the Darwinian controversies over science and religion were shaped by a distinctively English intellectual and cultural environment, not least in terms of the specific forms of "physico-theology" that emerged during the Augustan age and continued to shape attitudes in the early Victorian age. Many English writers of that age, lacking a detailed knowledge of the Christian theological tradition, assumed that this local form of natural theology was universal, and drew what can now be seen to be somewhat extravagant conclusions on the basis of this assumption. Had Darwin developed his ideas in Paris, Rome, or Berlin, the religious debates of the age might well have taken a very different form. William Paley's approach to natural theology is not "typical" or "representative" of the Christian tradition; it is a late popular manifestation of an approach whose intellectual roots are to be traced back to the aftermath of the "Glorious Revolution" of the late seventeenth century. The English political climate of the day was such that natural theology seemed to some to offer a degree of social, intellectual, and religious harmony in the aftermath of a period of bitter division.[130]

It will be clear from the brief analysis of Darwin's theory, set against its cultural context, that its perceived religious implications were shaped to no small extent by prevailing approaches to natural theology. Paley's approach, which probably had its greatest influence at a more popular level and appears to have been in decline by 1850, presupposed an essentially static theology of creation, and argued specifically from the perception of contrivance within the biological realm to the notion of divine design. At every level, this approach was called into question by Darwin's *Origin of Species*.

Yet Paley's was not the only approach to natural theology. A rival set of English approaches to natural theology, developed in the Bridgewater Treatises, made their appeal to the more intellectually sophisticated sections of Victorian society,[131] who were often more predisposed to accept evolutionary thinking, and open to the suggestion that this could be reconciled with the Christian faith. It is therefore important to emphasize once more the significance of Darwin's citation of a passage from Whewell's Bridgewater Treatise, with its emphasis upon law-like behavior within the natural world. Natural theology did not die with the appearance of Darwin's *Origin of Species*; it simply took new directions. As we noted earlier, both Charles Kingsley and Thomas H. Huxley believed that Paley's approach could be corrected and given a new lease of life in the new intellectual climate. Dorothy Sayers's brief comment, noted at the beginning of this chapter, may express more wisdom than is usually appreciated.

Up to now, our approach has been rigorously historical. Our concern has been to explore something of the origins of English natural theology, in order that the impact of Darwin's thought upon its development might be understood more thoroughly. In the remainder of this work, our approach will be contemporary and international, focusing on the twenty-first century's assessment of some of the debates that emerged during the Victorian age.

Notes

1   For the story of this development, see Reynolds, Barbara, *The Passionate Intellect: Dorothy L. Sayers' Encounter with Dante*. Kent, OH: Kent State University Press, 1989.

2   Sayers, Dorothy L., *The Letters of Dorothy L. Sayers: 1944–1950*, ed. Barbara Reynolds. Swavesey: Dorothy L. Sayers Society, 1998, 482.

3   On which see McGrath, Alister E., *Christianity's Dangerous Idea: The Protestant Revolution*. San Francisco: HarperOne, 2007, 17–36.

4   For detailed discussion of the theological and historical questions, see Carroll, William E., "Galileo and the Interpretation of the Bible." *Science & Education* 8 (1998): 151–87.

5 Darwin, Charles, *On the Origin of the Species by Means of Natural Selection*. London: John Murray, 1859, 1. All references are to the first edition of the *Origin* (1859) unless otherwise specified. On the importance of the *Beagle* voyage for Darwin's development, see Sulloway, Frank J., "Darwin's Conversion: The Beagle Voyage and Its Aftermath." *Journal of the History of Biology* 15 (1982): 325–96.

6 Lack, David, *Darwin's Finches*. Cambridge: Cambridge University Press, 1947. This book is based partly on the research presented in Lack, David, "The Galapagos Finches (*Geospizinae*): A Study in Variation." *Occasional Papers of the California Academy of Sciences* 21 (1945): 1–152. For comment, see Steinheimer, Frank D., "Charles Darwin's Bird Collection and Ornithological Knowledge During the Voyage of H.M.S. Beagle, 1831–1836." *Journal of Ornithology* 145 (2004): 300–20.

7 Sulloway, Frank J., "Darwin and His Finches: The Evolution of a Legend." *Journal of the History of Biology* 15 (1982): 1–53; Sulloway, Frank J., "Darwin and the Galápagos: Three Myths." *Oceanus* 30 (1987): 79–85.

8 Desmond, Adrian, and James Moore, *Darwin*. London: Michael Joseph, 1991, 209.

9 Sulloway, "Darwin and His Finches," 57–8.

10 See especially Manier, Edward, *The Young Darwin and His Cultural Circle: A Study of Influences Which Helped Shape the Language and Logic of the First Drafts of the Theory of Natural Selection*. Dordrecht: Reidel, 1978.

11 The idea that Darwin hesitated to publish his theories for more than twenty years, anxious about a potentially negative reception within the scientific or religious communities, is still repeated, even though there is no compelling historical evidence in its support: see Wyhe, John van, "Mind the Gap: Did Darwin Avoid Publishing His Theory for Many Years?" *Notes and Records of the Royal Society* 61 (2007): 177–205.

12 The notion of a Victorian "crisis of faith" has been subjected to critical analysis in recent years, and appears to need significant modification. See, for example, the recent revisionist account of Larsen, Timothy, *Crisis of Doubt: Honest Faith in Nineteenth-Century England*. Oxford: Oxford University Press, 2006. For a nuanced version of the received view, see the variety of opinions in Helmstadter, Richard J., and Bernard V. Lightman, eds., *Victorian Faith in Crisis: Essays on Continuity and Change in Nineteenth-Century Religious Belief*. Stanford, CA: Stanford University Press, 1990.

13 For further discussion, see England, Richard, "Natural Selection, Teleology, and the Logos: From Darwin to the Oxford Neo-Darwinists, 1859–1909." *Osiris* 16 (2001): 270–87. England argues that some Oxford neo-Darwinists saw Darwin's revision of Paley's teleology emphasizing aspects of adaptation that confirmed their Christian belief, thus reinforcing rather than undermining their scientific commitment to the theory of natural selection.

14 The analogical basis of the concept of "natural selection" is of particular interest: see Young, Robert M., "Darwin's Metaphor and the Philosophy of Science." *Science as Culture* 16 (1993): 375–403. Darwin's use of metaphorical language merits closer study: see, for example, the suggestive approach of Beer, Gillian, "'The Face of Nature': Anthropomorphic Elements in the Language of *The*

Origin of Species." In *Languages of Nature: Critical Essays on Science and Literature*, ed. Ludmilla J. Jordanova, 207–43. New Brunswick, NJ: Rutgers University Press, 1986.

15   There are many excellent accounts of these developments, including Janet Browne's outstanding volumes: Browne, Janet, *Charles Darwin: Voyaging*. Princeton, NJ: Princeton University Press, 1996; and Browne, Janet, *Charles Darwin: The Power of Place*. Princeton, NJ: Princeton University Press, 2003. On the complex process of the reception of Darwin's ideas, see especially Glick, Thomas F., *The Comparative Reception of Darwinism*. Austin: University of Texas Press, 1972; Hull, David L., *Darwin and His Critics: The Reception of Darwin's Theory of Evolution by the Scientific Community*. Cambridge, MA: Harvard University Press, 1973; Ellegård, Alvar, *Darwin and the General Reader: The Reception of Darwin's Theory of Evolution in the British Periodical Press, 1859–1872*. Chicago: University of Chicago Press, 1990; Numbers, Ronald L., *Darwinism Comes to America*. Cambridge, MA: Harvard University Press, 1998. For some factors affecting the religious reception of Darwin's ideas, see Livingstone, David N., "Darwinism and Calvinism: The Belfast-Princeton Connection." *Isis* 83 (1992): 408–28.

16   As is often noted, the title of Darwin's book is slightly misleading. It is not really about the "origin of species," in that it deals with evolutionary changes in general and the factors that control them.

17   Darwin, Francis, ed., *The Life and Letters of Charles Darwin*. 3 vols. London: John Murray, 1887, vol. 1, 82.

18   For a good account of the distinction, see Chauviré, Christiane, "Peirce, Popper, Abduction, and the Idea of Logic of Discovery." *Semiotica* 153 (2005): 209–21.

19   See the reflections of Kleiner, Scott A., "The Logic of Discovery and Darwin's Pre-Malthusian Researches." *Biology and Philosophy* 3 (1988): 293–315.

20   Kleiner, Scott A., "Problem Solving and Discovery in the Growth of Darwin's Theories of Evolution." *Synthese* 62 (1981): 119–62, especially 127–9. Note that substantially the same issues can be discerned in Johann Kepler's explanation of the solar system: Kleiner, Scott A., "A New Look at Kepler and Abductive Argument." *Studies in History and Philosophy of Science* 14 (1983): 279–313.

21   Such as flowers, which serve the dual purpose of producing gametes and attracting pollinators, such as bees or moths.

22   For Huxley's assessment of the fossil record, see Lyons, Sherrie L., "Thomas Huxley: Fossils, Persistence, and the Argument from Design." *Journal of the History of Biology* 26 (1993): 545–69; Lyons, Sherrie L., "The Origins of T. H. Huxley's Saltationism: History in Darwin's Shadow." *Journal of the History of Biology* 28 (1993): 463–94.

23   Bowler, Peter J., "Geographical Distribution in the *Origin of Species*." In *The Cambridge Companion to the "Origin of Species,"* ed. Michael Ruse and Robert J. Richards, 153–72. Cambridge: Cambridge University Press, 2009.

24   See further Kottler, Malcolm J., "Charles Darwin's Biological Species Concept and Theory of Geographic Speciation: The Transmutation Notebooks." *Annals of Science* 35 (1978): 275–97.

25   After Darwin, adaptation "could no longer be considered a static condition, a product of a creative past, and became instead a continuing dynamic process." Mayr, Ernst, *The Growth of Biological Thought*. Cambridge, MA: Belknap Press, 1982, 483.

26   Whewell, William, *Philosophy of the Inductive Sciences*. 2 vols. London: John W. Parker, 1847, vol. 2, 36. For a detailed assessment, see Snyder, Laura J., *Reforming Philosophy. A Victorian Debate on Science and Society*. Chicago: University of Chicago Press, 2006, 33–94. The influence of Whewell's approach to induction on the development of Darwin's theory is disputed: see, for example, Ruse, Michael, "Darwin's Debt to Philosophy: An Examination of the Influence of the Philosophical Ideas of John F. Herschel and William Whewell on the Development of Charles Darwin's Theory of Evolution." *Studies in the History and Philosophy of Science* 6 (1975): 159–81.

27   For the best general statement of this method, see Lipton, Peter, *Inference to the Best Explanation*. 2nd edn. London: Routledge, 2004.

28   On which see Corsi, Pietro, "Before Darwin: Transformist Concepts in European Natural History." *Journal of the History of Biology* 38 (2005): 67–83. On Darwin's concerns with this approach, see Sloan, Phillip R., "Darwin, Vital Matter, and the Transformism of Species." *Journal of the History of Biology* 19 (1986): 369–445.

29   Darwin, Charles, *On the Origin of the Species by Means of Natural Selection*. 6th edn. London: John Murray, 1872, 164.

30   Darwin, *Origin of Species*. 6th edn., 444. This comment is not present in earlier editions of the work.

31   See especially the detailed study of Lloyd, Elisabeth Anne, "The Nature of Darwin's Support for the Theory of Natural Selection." In *Science, Politics, and Evolution*, 1–19. Cambridge: Cambridge University Press, 2008.

32   *Life and Letters of Charles Darwin*, vol. 2, 155. Hutton deserves much greater attention as a perceptive interpreter of Darwin: see, for example, Stenhouse, John, "Darwin's Captain: F. W. Hutton and the Nineteenth-Century Darwinian Debates." *Journal of the History of Biology* 23 (1990): 411–42.

33   Popper, Karl R., "Natural Selection and the Emergence of Mind." *Dialectica* 32 (1978): 339–55. For a careful evaluation of Popper's statements on this question, see Watkins, John, "Popper and Darwinism." In *Karl Popper: Philosophy and Problems*, ed. Anthony O'Hear, 191–206. Cambridge: Cambridge University Press, 1996.

34   Spencer used the phrase in his *Principles of Biology* (1864); Darwin incorporated it into the fifth edition of the *Origin*: "This preservation of favourable variations, and the destruction of injurious variations, I call Natural Selection, or the Survival of the Fittest." Darwin, Charles, *On the Origin of the Species by Means of Natural Selection*. 5th edn. London: John Murray, 1869, 91–2.

35   On which see Morris, Susan W., "Fleeming Jenkin and *The Origin of Species*: A Reassessment." *British Journal for the History of Science* 27 (1994): 313–43; Bulmer, Michael, "Did Jenkin's Swamping Argument Invalidate Darwin's Theory of Natural Selection?" *British Journal for the History of Science* 37 (2004): 281–97.

36   For an excellent biography, see Cookson, Gillian, and Colin Hempstead, *A Victorian Scientist and Engineer: Fleeming Jenkin and the Birth of Electrical Engineering*. Aldershot: Ashgate, 2000.
37   Jenkin, Fleeming, "Darwin and the Origin of Species." In *Papers Literary, Scientific, Etc.*, ed. Sidney Colvin and J. A. Ewing, 215–63. London: Longmans, 1887. The review was originally published as "The Origin of Species" in the June 1867 number of the *North British Review*.
38   For a summary and analysis of Darwin's response, see Bulmer, "Did Jenkin's Swamping Argument Invalidate Darwin's Theory of Natural Selection?", 287–92.
39   The theory is set out in his 1868 work, Darwin, Charles, *The Variation of Animals and Plants under Domestication*. 2 vols. London: John Murray, 1868. See further Geison, Gerald L., "Darwin and Heredity: The Evolution of His Hypothesis of Pangenesis." *Journal of the History of Medicine* 24 (1969): 375–411; Stanford, P. Kyle, "Darwin's Pangenesis and the Problem of Unconceived Alternatives." *British Journal for Philosophy of Science* 57 (2006): 121–44.
40   For an excellent account of these developments, see Orel, Vítezslav, *Gregor Mendel: The First Geneticist*. Oxford: Oxford University Press, 1996. For Mendel's own somewhat critical view of Darwin's theory, see Callender, L. A., "Gregor Mendel: An Opponent of Descent with Modification." *History of Science* 26 (1988): 41–75; Bishop, B. E., "Mendel's Opposition to Evolution and to Darwin." *The Journal of Heredity* 87 (1996): 205–13.
41   For a good summary of the discussion, see Sclater, Andrew, "The Extent of Charles Darwin's Knowledge of Mendel." *Journal of Biosciences* 31 (2006): 191–3.
42   Rose, Michael R., *Darwin's Spectre: Evolutionary Biology in the Modern World*. Princeton, NJ: Princeton University Press, 1998, 33.
43   Darwin, Charles, *On the Origin of the Species by Means of Natural Selection*. 3rd edn. London: John Murray, 1861, 296.
44   Orel, *Gregor Mendel*, 193.
45   It should also be noted that the inheritance of acquired characteristics was accepted almost universally in Darwin's time. August Weismann's argument against the inheritance of acquired characteristics was not set out until 1904: see Weismann, August, *On Evolution*. London: Edward Arnold, 1904. Strictly speaking, Darwin did not have adequate evidential grounds to reject the Lamarckian possibility of the inheritance of acquired characteristics in the evolution of biological species. Weismann states that multicellular organisms consist of two different type of cells: "germ cells," which contain heritable information, and "somatic cells," which carry out ordinary bodily functions. The "germ cells" are not influenced by environmental influences or morphological changes that take place during the lifetime of an organism. As a result of this "Weismann barrier," acquired traits are lost after each generation, in that they cannot be transmitted. For comment, see Saunders, S. R., "Can Revisionism in Evolutionary Biology Help in Formulating Hypotheses about Hominid Evolution?" *Human Evolution* 7, no. 2 (1992): 25–35.
46   Darwin, *Origin of Species*, 171. For examples of such "difficulties," see Lustig, Abigail J., "Darwin's Difficulties." In *The Cambridge Companion to the*

"*Origin of Species*," ed. Michael Ruse and Robert J. Richards, 109–28. Cambridge: Cambridge University Press, 2009.

47 See Quine, W. V. O., *The Web of Belief*. New York: Random House, 1970; Lakatos, Imre, "Falsification and the Methodology of Scientific Research Programmes." In *Criticism and the Growth of Knowledge*, ed. Imre Lakatos and Alan Musgrave, 91–195. Cambridge: Cambridge University Press, 1970.

48 Greenwood, J. D., "Two Dogmas of Neo-Empiricism: The 'Theory-Informity' of Observation and the Duhem-Quine Thesis." *Philosophy of Science* 57 (1990): 553–74.

49 Lange, Marc, "The Apparent Superiority of Prediction to Accommodation as a Side Effect." *British Journal for Philosophy of Science* 52 (2001): 575–88.

50 Snyder, Laura J., "The Mill-Whewell Debate: Much Ado About Induction." *Perspectives on Science* 5 (1997): 159–98. Snyder elsewhere argues that Whewell's views on induction have been misunderstood, and merit closer attention as a distinctive approach: Snyder, Laura J., "Discoverers' Induction." *Philosophy of Science* 64 (1997): 580–604.

51 Hitchcock, Christopher, and Elliott Sober, "Prediction vs. Accommodation and the Risk of Overfitting." *British Journal for Philosophy of Science* 55 (2004): 1–34. The "weak predictivism" defended by Hitchcock and Sober has parallels elsewhere: see, for example, the careful assessment of approaches in Lange, "The Apparent Superiority of Prediction to Accommodation as a Side Effect"; Harker, David, "Accommodation and Prediction: The Case of the Persistent Head." *British Journal for Philosophy of Science* 57 (2006): 309–21.

52 See Blachowicz, James, "How Science Textbooks Treat Scientific Method: A Philosopher's Perspective." *British Journal for Philosophy of Science* 60 (2009): 303–44.

53 Clifford, William K., *The Ethics of Belief and Other Essays*. Amherst, NY: Prometheus Books, 1999, 70–96.

54 See, for example, Calhoun, Laurie, "The Underdetermination of Theory by Data, 'Inference to the Best Explanation,' and the Impotence of Argumentation." *Philosophical Forum* 27 (1996): 146–60.

55 James, William, "The Will to Believe." In *The Will to Believe and Other Essays in Popular Philosophy*, 1–31. New York: Longmans, Green, 1897.

56 On which see Kohn, David, "Darwin's Ambiguity: The Secularization of Biological Meaning." *British Journal for the History of Science* 22 (1989): 215–39, especially 238; England, "Natural Selection, Teleology, and the Logos," especially 273–5.

57 For the importance of Darwin's essentially theistic notion of natural laws in relation to the development of his idea of natural selection, see Cornell, John F., "God's Magnificent Law: The Bad Influence of Theistic Metaphysics on Darwin's Estimation of Natural Selection." *Journal of the History of Biology* 20 (1987): 381–412.

58 Fyfe, Aileen, "The Reception of William Paley's *Natural Theology* in the University of Cambridge." *British Journal for the History of Science* 30 (1997): 321–35, especially 324–5. As Fyfe notes, Paley's *Natural Theology* was subtitled "Evidences of the Existence and Attributes of the Deity," which may have led to confusion with *Evidences of Christianity* (324).

59   *Life and Letters of Charles Darwin*, vol. 1, 47.

60   Gould, Stephen Jay, *The Structure of Evolutionary Theory*. Cambridge, MA: Belknap Press, 2002, 118–21.

61   Evans, L. T., "Darwin's Use of the Analogy between Artificial and Natural Selection." *Journal of the History of Biology* 17 (1984): 113–40; Largent, Mark A., "Darwin's Analogy between Artificial and Natural Selection in the *Origin of Species*." In *The Cambridge Companion to the "Origin of Species*," ed. Michael Ruse and Robert J. Richards, 12–29. Cambridge: Cambridge University Press, 2009. For reflections on the use of functional analogies in biology, see Wimsatt, William C., "Functional Organization, Analogy, and Inference." In *Functions: New Essays in the Philosophy of Psychology and Biology*, ed. A. Ariew, R. Cummins, and M. Perlman, 173–221. Oxford: Oxford University Press, 2002.

62   On Darwin in this respect, see Lennox, James G., "Darwin *Was* a Teleologist." *Biology and Philosophy* 8 (1993): 409–21.

63   Paley, William, *Natural Theology: Or, Evidences of the Existence and Attributes of the Deity*. 12th edn. London: Faulder, 1809, 315.

64   Paley, *Natural Theology*, 390.

65   Paley, *Natural Theology*, 454.

66   Darwin, *Origin of Species*, 489.

67   *Life and Letters of Charles Darwin*, vol. 1, 310.

68   Michael Ghiselin argues that this book should be interpreted as some kind of "metaphysical satire," being in reality "a deliberate, planned attack" on the natural theology of its day: Ghiselin, Michael T., *The Triumph of the Darwinian Method*. Chicago: University of Chicago Press, 1984, 135. There is little evidence in the text itself, nor in Darwin's other writings, to justify such a conclusion. For further reflections, see Campbell, John Angus, "Of Orchids, Insects, and Natural Theology: Timing, Tactics, and Cultural Critique in Darwin's Post-'Origin' Strategy." *Argumentation* 8 (1994): 63–80.

69   These comments are noted in a letter to Asa Gray, dated July 28, 1862: see *Life and Letters of Charles Darwin*, vol. 3, 272–4. For Gray's own views on the matter, see his essay "Natural Selection not Inconsistent with Natural Theology": Gray, Asa, *Darwiniana: Essays and Reviews Pertaining to Darwinism*. New York: Appleton, 1888, 87–177. This composite piece consists of three essays, originally published in the *Atlantic Monthly* in July, August, and October 1861.

70   *Life and Letters of Charles Darwin*, vol. 3, 274.

71   See, for example, Brooke, John Hedley, "The Relations between Darwin's Science and His Religion." In *Darwinism and Divinity*, ed. John Durant, 40–75. Oxford: Blackwell, 1985; Brown, Frank Burch, *The Evolution of Darwin's Religious Views*. Macon, GA: Mercer University Press, 1986; Spencer, Nick, *Darwin and God*. London: SPCK, 2009.

72   Aveling, Edward, *The Religious Views of Charles Darwin*. London: Freethought, 1883.

73   Foote, George William, *Darwin on God*. London: Progressive Publishing, 1889, 27–9.

74   For a thoughtful account of the religious impact of this tragedy, see Keynes, Randal, *Annie's Box: Charles Darwin, His Daughter and Human Evolution*. New York: Riverhead Books, 2002, especially 266–81.

75 See the idea of "generic divinity" found in the writings of Benjamin Franklin: Morgan, David T., "Benjamin Franklin: Champion of Generic Religion." *Historian* 62 (2000): 723–9. While having difficulties with the Christian idea of God, Franklin was no atheist.

76 See the important studies gathered together in Brooke, John Hedley, and Ian Maclean, eds., *Heterodoxy in Early Modern Science and Religion.* Oxford: Oxford University Press, 2005.

77 *Life and Letters of Charles Darwin*, vol. 1, 304.

78 See the analysis in Brooke, John Hedley, " 'Laws Impressed on Matter by the Creator'? The *Origins* and the Question of Religion." In *The Cambridge Companion to the "Origin of Species,"* ed. Michael Ruse and Robert J. Richards, 256–74. Cambridge: Cambridge University Press, 2009.

79 Cornell, John F., "Newton of the Grassblade? Darwin and the Problem of Organic Teleology." *Isis* 77 (1986): 405–21.

80 Kleeberg, Bernard, "God-Nature Progressing: Natural Theology in German Monism." *Science in Context* 20 (2007): 537–69.

81 *Life and Letters of Charles Darwin*, vol. 2, 312.

82 *Life and Letters of Charles Darwin*, vol. 2, 202.

83 A point emphasized by Bowler, Peter J., "Darwinism and the Argument from Design: Suggestions for a Reevaluation." *Journal of the History of Biology* 10 (1977): 29–43.

84 Huxley, Thomas H., *Lay Sermons, Addresses, and Reviews.* London: Macmillan, 1870, 301.

85 *Life and Letters of Charles Darwin*, vol. 1, 309.

86 See Paley, *Natural Theology*, 341.

87 For what follows, see Beatty, John, "Teleology and the Relationship between Biology and the Physical Sciences in the Nineteenth and Twentieth Centuries." In *Some Truer Method: Reflections on the Heritage of Newton*, ed. Frank Durham and Robert D. Purrington, 113–44. New York: Columbia University Press, 1990.

88 Albert von Kölliker (1817–1905) was Professor of Physiology at the University of Würzburg from 1847; Hermann von Helmholtz (1821–94) was Professor of Anatomy and Physiology at the University of Heidelberg from 1858; Karl Ernst von Baer (1792–1876), a leading embryologist, was based at the St Petersburg Academy of Sciences, in Russia.

89 I here follow the analysis of Lennox, "Darwin *Was* a Teleologist."

90 For the argument that Darwin's language is teleological, but his conceptualities are not, see Ghiselin, Michael T., "Darwin's Language May Seem Teleological, but His Thinking Is Another Matter." *Biology and Philosophy* 9 (1994): 489–92. For a refutation, see Lennox, James G., "Teleology by Another Name: A Reply to Ghiselin." *Biology and Philosophy* 9 (1994): 493–5.

91 Darwin, *Origin of Species*, 84. Note that, from the second edition onwards, Darwin modified the opening of this statement to read "It may *metaphorically* be said …" (my emphasis).

92 Ayala, Francisco J., "Design without Designer: Darwin's Greatest Discovery." In *Debating Design: From Darwin to DNA*, ed. William A. Dembski and Michael Ruse, 55–80. Cambridge: Cambridge University Press, 2004, 60.

93   *Life and Letters of Charles Darwin*, vol. 2, 312.
94   *Life and Letters of Charles Darwin*, vol. 2, 201. This paper was originally published in 1869.
95   Gray, Asa, "Scientific Worthies: Charles Robert Darwin." *Nature* 10, no. 240 (1874): 79–81, 81. See also the fuller exploration of this point in Gray, *Darwiniana*, 288. To understand the importance of this correlation of teleology and morphology, it is necessary to understand the earlier debate over such issues between Geoffroy St Hilaire and George Cuvier: see especially Appel, Toby A., *The Cuvier-Geoffroy Debate: French Biology in the Decades before Darwin*. Oxford: Oxford University Press, 1987.
96   Darwin to Asa Gray, dated June 5, 1874: *Life and Letters of Charles Darwin*, vol. 3, 189.
97   Gray, *Darwiniana*, 145. Ernst Mayr argues that Gray misunderstood Darwin at this point. However, Darwin's endorsement makes this difficult to accept. See Mayr, Ernst, *Toward a New Philosophy of Biology: Observations of an Evolutionist*. Cambridge, MA: Belknap Press, 1988, 240–1.
98   For further discussion of this point, see Gray's 1876 essay "Evolutionary Teleology," in which he argues that design need not be interpreted as referring to specific outcomes, but can instead be seen as the result of universal principles. Darwin does not argue for or against a deity. Gray, *Darwiniana*, 356–90.
99   *Life and Letters of Charles Darwin*, vol. 2, 202.
100 Kingsley, Charles, "The Natural Theology of the Future." In *Westminster Sermons*, v–xxxiii. London: Macmillan, 1874, xxiii. For Kingsley's assessment of Darwinism, see Levy, David M., and Sandra J. Peart, "Charles Kingsley and the Theological Interpretation of Natural Selection." *Journal of Bioeconomics* 8 (2006): 197–218; Hall, Amy Laura, "Charles Kingsley's Christian Darwinism." In *Theology after Darwin*, ed. Michael S. Northcott and R. J. Berry, 41–56. Carlisle: Paternoster, 2009.
101 Kingsley, "The Natural Theology of the Future," xxv. Note Kingsley's emphasis on divine providence in directing the evolutionary process (xxiv–xxv).
102 Temple, Frederick, *The Relations between Religion and Science*. London: Macmillan, 1885, 115. Temple suggested that this approach "rather adds than withdraws force" from the argument for divine involvement in nature. For a contemporary critical reflection on this, see Moore, Aubrey, *Science and the Faith: Essays on Apologetic Subjects*. London: Kegan, Paul, Trench, Trubner, 1889, 56–106. On Temple's historical significance in shaping Victorian Anglican attitudes toward evolution, see Hinchliff, Peter B., *Frederick Temple, Archbishop of Canterbury: A Life*. Oxford: Clarendon Press, 1998, 166–93.
103 Raven, Charles E., *Science, Religion, and the Future*. Cambridge: Cambridge University Press, 1943, 33–50.
104 Paley, *Natural Theology*, 379. See further the earlier discussion at 85–103.
105 *Life and Letters of Charles Darwin*, vol. 2, 201.
106 Paley, *Natural Theology*, 456.
107 Paley, *Natural Theology*, 457–8. For Charles Kingsley's reflections on how suffering could be accommodated within Paley's system, see Kingsley, "The Natural Theology of the Future," xiii–xiv.

108   See here the neglected study of Hough, Graham, "The Natural Theology of *In Memoriam.*" *Review of English Studies* 91 (1947): 244–56.

109   Hough, "The Natural Theology of *In Memoriam,*" 245.

110   For an excellent account of this work and its cultural impact, see Secord, James A., *Victorian Sensation: The Extraordinary Publication, Reception, and Secret Authorship of Vestiges of the Natural History of Creation.* Chicago: University of Chicago Press, 2000.

111   Words of Tennyson spoken in the summer of 1892, as recalled by Tennyson's son, Hallam: see Tennyson, Hallam, *Alfred Lord Tennyson: A Memoir by His Son.* 2 vols. London: Macmillan, 1898, vol. 1, 314.

112   Alfred Lord Tennyson, *In Memoriam,* stanza 124.

113   Alfred Lord Tennyson, *In Memoriam,* stanza 56.

114   Darwin, *Origin of Species,* 62.

115   *Life and Letters of Charles Darwin,* vol. 2, 312.

116   For background and analysis, see Elwell, Frank W., *A Commentary on Malthus' 1798 Essay on Population as Social Theory.* Lewiston, NY: Edwin Mellen Press, 2001. Paley makes no explicit reference to Malthus, although he refers to him indirectly and a little dismissively ("a late treatise upon population"): Paley, *Natural Theology,* 505.

117   For Darwin's earlier explanations of the phenomenon of extinction, see Ospovat, Dov, *The Development of Darwin's Theory: Natural History, Natural Theology, and Natural Selection, 1838–1859.* Cambridge: Cambridge University Press, 1995, 39–59. See also Todes, Daniel P., *Darwin without Malthus: The Struggle for Existence in Russian Evolutionary Thought.* Oxford: Oxford University Press, 1989, 13–19.

118   *Life and Letters of Charles Darwin,* vol. 1, 83. See further Bowler, Peter J., *Charles Darwin: The Man and His Influence.* Cambridge: Cambridge University Press, 1996, 79–86.

119   Darwin, *Origin of Species,* 102: "If any one species does not become modified and improved in a corresponding degree with its competitors, it will soon be exterminated."

120   See Paley's extended discussion (constituting 15 percent of the text of *Natural Theology*) of the "goodness of the Deity": Paley, *Natural Theology,* 454–535.

121   Paley, *Natural Theology,* 468–76.

122   For discussion, see Ritvo, Harriet, *The Animal Estate: The English and Other Creatures in the Victorian Age.* Cambridge, MA: Harvard University Press, 1987; Turner, James, *Reckoning with the Beast: Animals, Pain, and Humanity in the Victorian Mind.* Baltimore, MD: Johns Hopkins University Press, 2001; Kenyon-Jones, Christine, *Kindred Brutes: Animals in Romantic-Period Writing.* Aldershot: Ashgate, 2001.

123   Ritvo, *Animal Estate,* 125–7.

124   For the importance of this work, see Bending, Lucy, *The Representation of Bodily Pain in Late Nineteenth-Century English Culture.* Oxford: Oxford University Press, 2000, 161.

125   See the important analysis in Kreilkamp, Ivan, " 'Petted Things': Wuthering Heights and the Animal." *Yale Journal of Criticism* 18 (2005): 87–110.

126 Kreilkamp, "'Petted Things'," 92.

127 Black, John, "Darwin in the World of Emotions." *Journal of the Royal Society of Medicine* 95 (2002): 311–13. Darwin's attitude to animal experimentation ought also to be noted here: Feller, David Allan, "Dog Fight: Darwin as Animal Advocate in the Antivivisection Controversy of 1875." *Studies in History and Philosophy of Biological and Biomedical Sciences* 40 (2009): 265–71.

128 Kitcher, Philip, *Living with Darwin: Evolution, Design, and the Future of Faith*. Oxford: Oxford University Press, 2009, 123–31.

129 Darwin, letter to J. D. Hooker, July 13, 1856: Darwin, Francis, and A. C. Seward, eds., *More Letters of Charles Darwin*. 2 vols. London: John Murray, 1903, vol. 1, 94. The context suggests that Darwin's comment about wastefulness at this point refers not to the evolutionary process itself, but to the overproduction of spermatozoa or pollen in order to secure fertilization.

130 See the arguments of Jacob, Margaret C., *The Newtonians and the English Revolution 1689–1720*. Ithaca, NY: Cornell University Press, 1976, 162–200. Note also Jacob's analysis of the opponents of this social and intellectual consensus (201–70).

131 George Eliot portrays one of her more literary characters as engrossed in reading Buckland's Bridgewater Treatise: Eliot, George, *The Mill on the Floss*. Harmondsworth: Penguin Classics, 2003, 395–6. See further Shuttleworth, Sally, *George Eliot and Nineteenth-Century Science: The Make-Believe of a Beginning*. Cambridge: Cambridge University Press, 1984, 60–2.

Part III
Contemporary Discussion
Darwinism and natural theology

7

A Wider Teleology: Design, Evolution, and Natural Theology

The present study focuses specifically on the relation between natural theology and evolutionary thought.[1] The second part of this work was concerned with considering some historical aspects of the complex and shifting relationship between evolutionary thought and natural theology, culminating in the publication of Darwin's *Origin of Species* in 1859. The century following the publication of Darwin's work generated substantial debate on these and related questions, which is itself worthy of careful study.[2] It is impossible to discuss more recent debates on this topic without being drawn into their history, especially when it is recalled that "natural theology" designates a spectrum of possibilities. The debates of the nineteenth century may help identify certain positions within that spectrum as now being untenable; nevertheless, a gratifyingly wide range of options remains open today.

In the third part of this study, our concern is primarily with the present-day discussion of the implications of the evolutionary synthesis for natural theology. Historical questions, however, remain important, not least because of the need to challenge regnant assumptions concerning aspects of Christian theology, such as the doctrine of creation. At several points of importance to our themes, relatively recent theological developments have been assumed to represent the Christian consensus down the ages. The retrieval or restatement of older approaches is an important strategy in deepening the quality of the engagement between Christian theology and the natural sciences, and has particular importance for the themes of this work.

In our analysis of Darwin's relationship to the natural theologies of his day, we noted particularly the impact of his theories on two leading themes of natural theology: the concept of teleology, and the problem of

Darwinism and the Divine: Evolutionary Thought and Natural Theology, First Edition.
Alister E. McGrath.
© 2011 Alister E. McGrath. Published 2011 by Blackwell Publishing Ltd.

Figure 7.1 Engraving of the English biologist Thomas Henry Huxley (1825–95), in 1874.

suffering. Although the significance of evolutionary thought for natural theology is now agreed to extend beyond these two traditional themes, it seems entirely appropriate to begin our analysis of the current state of discussion by considering them.

So does Darwinism eliminate any notion of design? Does it destroy the notion of teleology? These questions remain debated intensely within the philosophy of biology,[3] and are clearly of wider significance. As we noted earlier, what impressed Thomas H. Huxley most forcibly on his first reading of Darwin's *Origin of Species* was his "conviction that teleology, as commonly understood, had received its deathblow at Mr Darwin's hands."[4] This has sometimes been misunderstood to imply that it was the notion of teleology in general, rather than a specific form of teleology, which Huxley held to have been discredited by Darwin. This is clearly not the case. Huxley's comments refer to teleology "as commonly understood," a veiled reference to the specific form found in the writings of Paley. This is made clear in his 1887 lecture "On the Reception of the *Origin of Species*," in which Huxley rebutted three common criticisms of Darwin's theory of natural selection, each of which he held to be based on a misrepresentation of Darwin's views.[5]

1   "It is said that [Darwin] supposes variations to come about 'by chance,' and that the fittest survive the 'chances' of the struggle for existence, and thus 'chance' is substituted for providential design."[6] Huxley argues that Darwin has been grossly misunderstood at this point. Darwin was declaring that he did not know what had caused certain things to happen, while locating such events firmly within the context of the laws of causality.

2   "A second very common objection to Mr. Darwin's views was (and is), that they abolish Teleology, and eviscerate the argument from design."[7] This view, of course, is widely repeated in the twenty-first century, and it is important to note Huxley's assessment of its merits. Huxley is quite clear that traditional approaches to teleology – such as that adopted by William Paley[8] – face a severe challenge from Darwin's account of evolution. Yet the theory of evolution, he argues, bears witness to a "wider teleology,"[9] rooted in the deeper structure of the universe.

The teleological and the mechanical views of nature are not, necessarily, mutually exclusive. On the contrary, the more purely a mechanist the speculator is, the more firmly does he assume a primordial molecular arrangement of which all the phenomena of the universe are the consequences, and the more completely is he thereby at the mercy of the teleologist, who can always defy him to disprove that this primordial molecular arrangement was not intended to evolve the phenomena of the universe.

3   Finally, Huxley addresses the question of whether Darwin's theory is anti-theistic. "Having got rid of the belief in chance and the disbelief in design" as integral aspects of Darwin's theory of evolution, Huxley argues, it is obvious that "the doctrine of Evolution is neither Anti-theistic nor Theistic."[10] Huxley suggests that Darwinism can be argued not to have raised new problems for theism, as the problems of relating God to action in the world were already well known. "In respect of the great problems of Philosophy, the post-Darwinian generation is, in one sense, exactly where the præ-Darwinian generations were."[11]

It is difficult to be sure quite what Huxley had in mind when speaking of the "wider teleology" disclosed by the evolutionary process, which he held to be grounded in the "primordial molecular arrangement" of the universe that governed its subsequent development. Nevertheless, such a suggestive way of speaking certainly resonates strongly with the increasingly influential view that the fundamental constants and laws of the universe were such as to make Darwinian evolution possible.[12] In other words, the actuality of biological evolution is ultimately dependent upon the fundamental properties of certain elements of the universe, and those properties were established at the beginning of time.[13] We shall consider this point in more detail shortly (194–7).

The present chapter considers the question of teleology in evolutionary biology, and its potential implications for a Christian natural theology. We begin by considering the question of whether there can be said to be "directionality" within the evolutionary process. The question has been deliberately framed to be one of observation, rather than interpretation. If indeed there appears to be some kind of immanent directionality within nature, we may then proceed to consider how this might be mapped onto various teleological schemes. But our first concern is whether any such directionality may indeed be observed.

Directionality within the Natural World

The standard cosmological model offers a narrative of increasing complexification from the origins of the universe to the present day, which clearly constitutes directionality. The evidence for this is overwhelming, has been widely reviewed in the research literature, and need only be summa-rized very briefly here.[14] The process of evolution at the physical, chemical, and biological levels shows a marked and essentially irreversible trend toward complexity.

The initial cosmic "big bang" created a rapidly expanding universe consist-ing primarily of hydrogen, helium, and small quantities of lithium. These three elements are incapable, individually or in any known combination, of sup-porting or leading to life. After the initial period of rapid expansion, clumps of cosmic material began to aggregate, creating the dense regions of very high pressure and temperature that we call "stars." These conditions led to the emergence of stellar nucleosynthesis, in which nuclear fusion led to the gradual formation of heavier elements, such as carbon, nitrogen, and oxygen – all of which are essential to life. Chemical complexity thus developed over time.[15]

The formation of comets, asteroids, planets, and cool gas clouds brought about a further development. The life-friendly conditions found in some such environments allowed increasingly complex organic molecules to develop over extended periods of time. The mechanisms for this process remain poorly understood. Nevertheless, the directionality of the process is clear. Complex organic chemicals began to appear in the natural environment, cre-ating the possibility for metabolic mechanisms. At some point – again, by processes that are not properly understood – life may be said to have begun.

It is now widely conceded that natural selection does not account for how biological forms and phenotypes arise in the first place. The Darwinian narrative of evolution does not concern the origin of life, but its subsequent development. The process of biological evolution itself led to increased com-plexification of life forms and increasing competition for resources and ecological niches.[16] A strong directional element can be discerned within the evolutionary process, enhanced by the possibilities of evolutionary novelty. Evolution leads to organisms generally becoming larger, more complex, more taxonomically diverse, and more energetically intensive.[17] For exam-ple, brain size increases over time in both primates and hominins.[18]

The directionality of the evolution of the cosmos in general, and the biologi-cal domain on earth, is well established. But what does it mean? Can we move from the descriptive observation of increased complexity in the universe over time to a metaphysical or theological theory of a cosmic purpose? Is direction-ality functionally equivalent to a teleology – a theory of purpose or goal? In part, the answer given to this question depends on how teleology is defined.

Teleology: Introducing an Idea

The term "teleology," already used in the present study, is widely under-stood to designate the perception of purposeful behavior, direction, or goals. It must be made clear immediately that while the concept of teleology can be interpreted in a theistic manner, it is equally open to non-theistic interpretations. For example, "teleology" can be a neutral term, more phenomenological than theoretical, designating simply the observation that certain behaviors or functions appear to be goal-directed; it can also be used in a more developed sense, articulating the idea of processes being directed or driven toward a goal by internal or external forces or agencies. Teleology in this latter sense, when supplemented by certain critical deistic or theistic presuppositions, informs the arguments from design found in English "physico-theology."

The idea of teleology (though not the term itself)[19] originated in the classical era. In his discussion of natural generation, Aristotle argues that explanatory priority must be given to what lies at the end of the process – to its "goal (*telos*)."[20] This is not interpreted in terms of "purpose." Aristotle defends the analogy between artistic production and natural generation. Consider, he argues, the manner in which a house is built. Every aspect of the process is explained by the end product. The same argument can be extended to any act of artistic production. Aristotle holds that the same is also true in the case of natural generation. The only persuasive way to explain the generation of an organism such as an animal, or the formation of its parts, is by reference to the product that lies at the end of the process – that is to say, the *goal* of the process.[21]

While this approach is clearly open to Christian theological interpretation – as seen, for example, in Thomas Aquinas – Aristotle himself did not develop his ideas in a theistic direction. For Aristotle, *telos* designated an apparent internalized goal, not the purpose of an external agent.[22] Teleology must be distinguished from design, despite their frequent conflation in popular writings. Design is to be understood as conscious intent and artifice applied externally to the order of nature, in order to achieve some end or external goal; teleology can be interpreted simply as evidence of function or purpose within nature, as an expression of natural laws and natural order.

In earlier chapters (63–71), we explored notions of teleology that emerged within English natural theology and natural history from the seventeenth to the nineteenth century, noting how arguments from or to design became embedded within English scientific culture.[23] Although teleological arguments were initially linked with physical phenomena, they came to be extended to the biological realm, with William Paley arguing forcibly that the greater complexity of biological organisms was an indication of their "contrivance." Yet this approach to teleology appears to have been specific to the English context. In Germany, for example, the pre-Darwinian period was characterized by a very different understanding of teleology.[24] Whereas English writers tended to think of teleology primarily in terms of the utility of forms imposed on organisms by an external creator, the German tradition conceived teleology as dealing with internal powers of organization in organisms.

Immanuel Kant (1724–1804), for example, understood teleology as a way of interpreting the interrelation of structures and processes in organisms, rather than as an explanation of how organisms originated[25] – irrespective of whether this origination involved theistic intervention or natural processes. For Kant, every aspect of an organism is interrelated. Explanation of the processes and structures observed in living organisms demands reference to the "goal" or "end" that is achieved through them – namely, the origination of the whole organism, which is produced, reproduced, or maintained by these structures or processes. Biological explanation thus has an ineradicably teleological dimension, even though Kant interprets this in terms of the goals of the production, reproduction, or maintenance of the biological organism, rather than the imposition of the "will" of an external agent, such as God.

Although some have argued that rejection of any form of teleology is integral to the evolutionary synthesis, it is clear that this judgment is unreliable, ultimately resting upon preconceptions about precisely what a "teleology" implies. The real (and entirely valid) concern on the part of many natural scientists is that a teleology that ultimately rests upon philosophical or theological presuppositions (whether religious or atheist) will be forcibly imposed upon biological processes. As Ernst Mayr rightly noted, biological resistance to teleological statements or explanations partly reflects an anxiety that they attempt to smuggle unverifiable theological or metaphysical doctrines into supposedly objective scientific accounts of reality.[26] Yet what if some kind of teleology is discerned within, not imposed upon, the biological process? What if an evolutionary teleology is an *a posteriori*, rather than an *a priori*, concept?

In a series of important interventions in this discussion, biologist Francisco J. Ayala has insisted upon the legitimacy and importance of the use of teleological language in biological explanation.[27] The adaptations of organisms can be considered to be explained teleologically when their existence can be accounted for in terms of their contribution to the reproductive fitness of the population. Such adaptations – such as organs, homeostatic mechanisms, or patterns of behavior – are observed to have had a beneficial impact on the survival or reproductive capacities of organisms, which can be considered as the phenomenological "goal" toward which they tend.

Some notion of teleology is thus invoked as an explanation of the familiar functional roles played by parts of living organisms, and to describe the goal of reproductive fitness that plays such a central role in accounts of natural selection.[28]

A teleological explanation implies that the system under consideration is directively organized. For that reason, teleological explanations are appropriate in biology ... Moreover, and most importantly, teleological explanations imply that the end result is the explanatory reason for the *existence* of the object or process which serves or leads to it. A teleological account of the gills of fish implies that gills came to existence precisely because they serve for respiration. If the above reasoning is correct, the use of teleological explanations in biology is not only acceptable but indeed indispensable.

Ernst Mayr also developed much the same point, noting that examples of goal-directed behavior are widespread in the natural world. Indeed, "the occurrence of goal-directed processes is perhaps the most characteristic feature of the world of living systems."[29]

Natural selection itself, the ultimate source of explanation in biology, should be considered to be a teleological process, in that it is directed to the goal of increasing reproductive efficiency and generates the goal-directed organs and processes required for this. Teleological mechanisms in living organisms are thus biological adaptations, which have arisen as a result of the process of natural selection. Such teleological explanations can be considered to be both appropriate and inevitable in biology, yet remain fully compatible with causal accounts. They cannot be reduced to non-teleological explanations without loss of their explanatory content.[30]

Chance, Contingency, and Evolutionary Goals

Eighteenth-century natural theology found the notion of chance disturbing, in that it appeared to undercut notions of divine design and causality. The notion of "contrivance," deployed so frequently by English physico-theologians, emphasized the continuity between design and construction: the same God who conceived the world also executed its creation directly, without intermediates. William Paley, for example, defines chance as "the operation of causes without design," and concludes that a structure as complex as the human eye simply could not arise in this manner.[31] Yet Paley's conclusion is driven by the undefended controlling presupposition that chance and design are mutually exclusive at every level.[32] A more appropriate response is that if something can be said to happen by chance this means "no more than that we do not know enough about its antecedents to predict its outcome with certainty."[33]

One of the more disturbing aspects of English Protestant theology in general, and natural theology in particular, is its manifest lack of familiarity with the theological legacy of Thomas Aquinas. At point after point, Aquinas offers illumination on central themes of natural theology, which appears to have been unknown to writers such as Paley. The doctrine of providence is a case in point. In the thirteenth century, Aquinas provided an intellectual framework that allowed design or teleology to be affirmed, while recognizing the role of chance in bringing about its intended outcomes. Aquinas is emphatic that the notion of divine providence does *not* exclude luck (*fortuna*) or chance (*accidens*).[34] A given process may involve chance to achieve its intended ends. Some recent discussions of the notion of providence assume that, in order to preserve natural causality and human responsibility, it is necessary to deny or exclude the traditional attributes of God.[35] Aquinas's approach lays a robust conceptual foundation for affirming the providence of God without entailing the compromise of the integrity and characteristics of the natural order. Furthermore, it is not difficult to argue, on the basis of statistical methods and by appealing to stochastic processes or chaos theory, that chance is not inherently anti-teleological.[36]

Darwinian evolution is regularly described as a "random" process, which gives contingency and historical accidents the upper hand in determining genetic outcomes. This view is vigorously affirmed by some recent writers. The French atheist biologist Jacques Monod (1910–76) declares that the evolutionary process is governed and directed by "pure chance, absolutely free but blind."[37] Stephen Jay Gould (1941–2002) insisted that "almost every interesting event of life's history falls into the realm of contingency."[38] It is pointless to talk about purpose, historical inevitability, or direction. From its beginning to its end, the evolutionary process is governed by contingencies. "We are the accidental result of an unplanned process ... the fragile result of an enormous concatenation of improbabilities, not the predictable product of any definite process."[39]

Yet this can be viewed in a quite different light. For a theistic evolutionist, such as Arthur Peacocke, chance is not to be seen as a destructive irrationality. The "full gamut of the potentialities of living matter could be explored only through the agency of the rapid and frequent randomization which is possible at the molecular level of the DNA."[40] If there were no genetic mutations, then species would be unalterably fixed and incapable of development into new forms of life. If mutations were too frequent, no species could become established for a sufficient period of time, during which the filtering process of natural selection could act. Chance is essential for the evolutionary process to wend its way, exploring possibilities within biological space. To use Darwin's phrase, "natural selection is daily and hourly scrutinizing, throughout the world, every variation, even the slightest; rejecting that which is bad, preserving and adding up all that is good."[41] Those variations are caused by chance. Yet natural selection is most emphatically not a random process.

While chance might be the engine of evolutionary development, it does not determine its outcomes. Chance powers the search engine; it does not, however, dictate what is found. This point was made with particular force by the Cambridge paleobiologist Simon Conway Morris, who argued that the evolutionary process possessed a propensity to navigate its way to certain apparently predetermined solutions. For Conway Morris the phenomenon of "convergent evolution" – which can be defined as "the recurrent tendency of biological organization to arrive at the same solution to a particular need"[42] – points to the tendency of the evolutionary process to converge on a relatively small number of possible outcomes. "The evolutionary routes are many, but the destinations are limited."[43]

Conway Morris thus invites us to envisage the many theoretically possible pathways to evolutionary outcomes, and reflect on the fact that many of these were not taken. The question of why certain theoretically possible routes were not taken is a question of considerable importance in its own right.[44] However, Conway Morris's emphasis falls upon the relatively small number of outcomes on which the evolutionary process seems to focus. "Life has a peculiar propensity to 'navigate' to rather precise solutions in response to adaptive challenges."[45] "Islands of stability" exist in the midst of an essentially inhospitable ocean of maladaptivity;[46] the evolutionary search engine finds its way to these islands, not on account of its purposeful questing, but because of the inevitability of the points of termination.[47]

Conway Morris uses the image of evolution as a search engine, randomly searching biological space for stable outcomes, and hence allowing "islands of stability" to be identified. The search process may be random, but the destinations are predetermined:[48]

> The view that evolution is open-ended, without predictabilities and indeterminate in terms of outcomes is negated by the ubiquity of evolutionary convergence, [which] ... points to a deeper structure to life, a metaphorical landscape across which evolution must necessarily navigate.

Conway Morris's work strongly suggests that the evolutionary process is more open to teleological interpretation than some of its earlier exponents allowed. In some ways, Conway Morris can be seen as endorsing the earlier conclusion of the Cambridge biochemist Joseph Needham (1900–95), as set out in his 1935 Terry Lectures at Yale University:[49]

> The evolutionary process was shown to not be a matter of chance, but inevitable, granting the general principle of biological organisation and the properties of the chemical elements – a conclusion at least as acceptable to dialectical materialism as to orthodox theology. Vitalism was thus dissolved in universal teleology.

Evolution is not an open-ended process; it is constrained by both internal and external factors. Internal constraints of importance include phylogenetic and developmental factors.[50] Yet there are external constraints that also play an important role in evolutionary development, including the laws of physics, basic geometry, and the fundamental properties of the chemical elements.[51] The importance of these external constraints in developing the teleological aspects of natural theology has not been given due attention;[52] in what follows, we shall consider them further.

The "Wider Teleology" of Evolution

When speaking of the "wider teleology" suggested by the evolutionary process, Huxley referred to the "primordial molecular arrangement," which so clearly played a major role in directing that process. Others came to similar conclusions. The Harvard chemist Josiah Parsons Cooke (1827–94) was convinced that the chemistry of the universe was of critical importance in shaping its development. "There is abundant evidence of design in the properties of the chemical elements alone, and hence that the great argument of Natural Theology rests upon a basis which no theories of organic development can shake."[53] For Cooke, a defensible natural theology must take into account the fundamental properties of the chemical elements, and the biological constraints and possibilities that they provide.[54]

> Before the first organic cell could exist, and before Mr. Darwin's principle of natural selection could begin that work of unnumbered ages which was to end in developing a perfect man, nay, even before the solid globe itself could be condensed from Laplace's nebula, the chemical elements must have been created, and endowed with those properties by which alone the existence of that cell is rendered possible.

Similar conclusions were later expressed by Lawrence J. Henderson (1878–1942), Professor of Biological Chemistry at Harvard University, who argued that "the whole evolutionary process, both cosmic and organic, is one, and the biologist may now rightly regard the universe in its very essence as biocentric."[55] For Henderson, the unique properties of the elements of carbon, nitrogen, and oxygen, as well as certain compounds such as water, were the chemical preconditions for biological development. "This collation of properties," Henderson argued, had to be understood as "a preparation for the processes of planetary evolution."[56] For this reason, "the properties of the elements must for the present be regarded as possessing a teleological character."

More recent discussion of these points has focused on the critical role played by certain fundamental chemical elements, which are in turn determined by their quantum mechanical properties, fixed at the origins of the universe. All living organisms on earth are made up of the same fundamental chemical building blocks consisting chiefly of amino acids, fatty acids, sugars, and nitrogenous bases. The core elements of these core biochemical compounds are hydrogen, carbon, nitrogen, and oxygen.[57] So where did these come from? And what would have happened if they had not been available? And what of the transition metals that are now understood to play a critically important role in a series of essential biochemical processes?[58]

The fundamental properties of the chemical elements, which are exploited *but not created* by biological processes, must be such that metabolic pathways and means of transmission of genetic information are possible. Otherwise, life could not emerge.[59] For Darwinian evolution to take place, the necessary components for that evolutionary process must be in place. If the properties of the elements of the universe, the characteristics of the laws of nature, or the fixed values of the constants of nature had been different, this process would never have taken place.

A brief review of the history of the universe will make this important point clearer. Hydrogen was the first element to be synthesized. Atomic hydrogen began to form about one hundred seconds after the "Big Bang," followed rapidly by the emergence of heavier nuclei, such as deuterium and helium. Yet by then, the very high temperatures required for the nucleosynthesis of heavier elements no longer existed. The universe was in the process of cooling. Only one of the essential building blocks of life – hydrogen – was thus present. Yet the entire evolutionary process depends upon the unusual chemistry of carbon, which allows it to bond to itself, as well as other elements, creating highly complex molecules that are stable over prevailing terrestrial temperatures, and are capable of conveying genetic information (especially DNA). No carbon, no life.[60]

As the universe expanded and cooled, structure formation emerged out of gravitational growth of small primeval departures from homogeneity. Matter started to form clumps, including stars. The formation of stars was essential to the origins of life. The high pressures and temperatures of stellar interiors allowed the process of nucleosynthesis to take place, leading to the chemical enrichment of the interstellar medium.[61]

Yet the formation of stars is critically dependent upon the fundamental constants of the universe.[62] For example, cosmic antigravity is now known to play a critical role in controlling the expansion of the universe, and in particular has increasing importance as our universe becomes ever darker and emptier.[63] "Fortunately for us (and very surprisingly to theorists), λ is very small. Otherwise its effect would have stopped galaxies and stars from forming, and cosmic evolution would have been stifled before it could even begin."[64] Similarly, the strong nuclear force, which defines how firmly atomic nuclei bind together, is of critical importance in determining how stars transmute hydrogen into the heavier atoms of the periodic table – which, as we noted earlier, are essential to life. A small variation in the value of this constant would have prevented such nucleosynthesis of biologically essential elements such as carbon from taking place.[65]

> For carbon to be created in quantity inside stars the *nuclear strong force* must be within perhaps as little as 1 per cent neither stronger nor weaker than it is. Increasing its strength by maybe 2 per cent would block the formation of protons – so that there could be no atoms – or else bind them into diprotons so that stars would burn some billion billion times faster than our sun. On the other hand decreasing it by roughly 5 per cent would unbind deuteron, making stellar burning impossible.

Evolutionary biologists often treat the molecular basis of evolution as being unproblematic, failing to appreciate, in the first place, that the process depends critically upon the chemical properties of certain core elements; and in the second, that the origins of these elements depend upon the apparent fine-tuning of the constants of nature. For example, consider the nucleosynthesis of carbon and oxygen. We have already noted the importance of the constants of nature in permitting stars to form; it turns out, however, that the physics of this process is critically dependent on predetermined resonance levels of atomic nuclei.

The nucleosynthesis of carbon, nitrogen, and oxygen requires the fusion of helium nuclei (or alpha-particles) to yield heavier nuclei. In the case of carbon, the process involves the fusion of three helium nuclei (^{4}He), with beryllium as an intermediate.

$$^4\text{He} + {}^4\text{He} \rightarrow {}^8\text{Be}$$
$$^8\text{Be} + {}^4\text{He} \rightarrow {}^{12}\text{C}$$

Oxygen is formed from the fusion of a carbon nucleus with a further helium nucleus:

$$^{12}\text{C} + {}^4\text{He} \rightarrow {}^{16}\text{O}$$

Yet this process could easily lead to carbon being transmuted totally to oxygen, so that not enough carbon would be produced to allow for the emergence of life. In reality, they exist in about equal amounts. As John Leslie comments: "God would need to be careful which physics he chose."[66]

During the 1950s, the cosmologist Fred Hoyle argued that there had to be a yet undiscovered aspect of the nuclear chemistry of carbon that would allow the production of carbon and oxygen in comparable quantities. It subsequently turned out that the energy levels of certain excited states of these nuclei were fixed at a level permitting both carbon and oxygen to be produced in this way. Hoyle had no doubt that there were significant teleological implications to this observation.[67]

> If you wanted to produce carbon and oxygen in roughly equal quantities by stellar nucleosynthesis, these are the two levels you would have to fix, and your fixing would have to be just where these levels are actually found to be. Another put-up job? Following the above argument, I am inclined to think so. A common sense interpretation of the facts suggests that a superintellect has monkeyed with physics, as well as with chemistry and biology, and that there are no blind forces worth speaking about in nature.

A fuller analysis of this "wider teleology" would detail the critical properties of elements (especially transition metal ions) and compounds (such as water) in relation to the origins and development of life. Such an analysis lies beyond the scope of this work. Our concern is simply to emphasize that the evolutionary process depends upon fundamental elemental properties and possibilities that are now known to have been fixed at the origins of the universe. This sets the Darwinian mechanism in a wider context, and makes it entirely proper to speak of a "wider" or "deeper" teleology. But does it make it possible to speak of "design"?

The Inference of Design and Natural Theology

Design is something inferred, not something observed. English physico-theology often assumed that the observation of "apparent design" led naturally and directly to the conclusion that a Designer existed. For Paley, "contrivance proves design."[68] Contrivance is something that is observed; design is something that is deduced from this observation. This trajectory of argument, evident at several points in William Paley's landmark *Natural Theology* (1802), was called into question by the rise of reflective empirical philosophy, such as that developed by William Whewell (1794–1866). For Whewell, nature did not prove or disclose the Christian vision of God as "Creator, Governor and Preserver of the world";[69] nevertheless, the "views of the creation, preservation, and government of the universe, which natural science opens to us, harmonize with our belief" in such a God. That God is the designer of the world may be inferred from the observation of the world, and may be shown to be harmonious with what is known of the world. Yet nature is not *observed* to be designed. This point was fully appreciated by John Henry Newman, who (as we have seen earlier, 128) declared: "I believe in design because I believe in God; not in God because I see design."[70] For Newman, natural theology was a framework for observational accommodation, not for pseudo-scientific proof.

The inference of design does not require knowledge of the precise goal for which an object is allegedly designed. Returning to Paley's famous example, in order to infer the existence of a watchmaker from the existence of a watch, it is not necessary to know precisely what purpose the watchmaker had in mind in constructing it, nor what precise function the watch serves. The point is simply that its structure suggests design, whereas that of a stone does not. While archeologists regularly dig up lithic artifacts whose function is unknown, they nevertheless draw the entirely reasonable inference that they are some kind of tools because they give every indication of having been designed for some purpose, even if that specific purpose cannot be securely determined from the artifact itself.[71]

The real issue, therefore, is not whether any aspect of the natural order – including mechanisms for biological development – can be said to "prove" God's existence. Most Christian theologians ceased to adopt the approach favored by "physico-theology" by about 1850, moving instead to the apologetic analysis of correspondence, resonance, or consonance between the theoretical framework provided by the Christian faith and our experience of the world around us. The debate now tends to center primarily on the explanatory capaciousness of the Christian faith to accommodate observations of the world.

One of the most important nineteenth-century discussions of the relation between empirical observation and scientific theory is due to the American philosopher and scientist Charles S. Peirce (1839–1914). Peirce spent some thirty years as an active scientist, studying the effects of gravitation with the US Coast and Geodetic Survey. He sought to explore the philosophical implications of scientific approaches to theory development in two important works: *The Fixation of Belief* (1877) and *How to Make Our Ideas Clear* (1878).[72] The distinctive approach to the interpretation of observation that Peirce developed is widely known as "abduction,"[73] and merits close study by any concerned with theological engagement with the natural world.[74]

Peirce's approach can be set out in terms of the following sequence of observation and reflection:[75]

1   The surprising fact, C, is observed;
2   But if A were true, C would be a matter of course.
3   Hence, there is reason to suspect that A is true.

The critical point is "the process of forming explanatory hypotheses,"[76] implicit in the transition from the observation of C to the postulation of A. For Peirce, A is not *deduced*; it is *abducted*. Abduction is the "only kind of argument which starts a new idea."[77] What "logic of discovery" is appropriate to bring about the generation of an explanatory hypothesis, when this often transcends the observational data?

Abduction is thus a process which, though not irrational, transcends the limits of reason. It is, in effect, an *imaginative* approach, which initially requires the generation of imaginative scenarios and subsequently the investigation of whether these illuminate actual observations. Abduction can be likened to an "act of insight" that "comes to us like a flash."[78] Peirce develops a series of images and concepts to articulate what he means by abduction – such as *pattern recognition*, in which a confused tangle of things is made intelligible; the *interrogation* of a system in order to disclose its structures; and developing an *instinct* for the best explanation of phenomena.[79] Peirce's approach is thus grounded in the realm of the observable, yet possesses a capacity to transcend it, reaching beyond its limits to posit an explanatory framework that exceeds what is observed, while at the same time possessing the ability to make sense of the empirical.

This approach was consolidated by developments within the philosophy of science in the 1970s. During this period, the method generally known as "inference to the best explanation" became recognized as the regnant philosophy of the natural sciences, displacing older approaches.[80] Although the terminology is recent, the approach is not. It can be found in the writings of both William Whewell and Charles Darwin. Indeed, it is possible to argue that even William Paley's *Natural Theology* contains a recognizable variant of the approach.[81] The theistic hypothesis is offered by a number of leading thinkers as the simplest, the most complete, and the most plausible explanation of human experience, including the scientific observation of nature.[82]

The core features of this approach can be summarized as follows. This method holds that a hypothesis should be accepted because, if it were true, it would explain the phenomena better than any other. In other words, it is not necessary to prove that it is right; merely that it is better than its rivals, as determined by criteria of epistemic virtue. This point is emphasized by Gilbert Harman, whose seminal article is widely credited with bringing about the renewal of scholarly interest in this approach:[83]

> In making this inference, one infers from the fact that a certain hypothesis would explain the evidence, to the truth of that hypothesis. In general, there will be several hypotheses which might explain the evidence, so one must be able to reject all such alternative hypotheses before one is warranted in making the inference. Thus one infers, from the premise that a given hypothesis would provide a *better* explanation for the evidence than would any other hypothesis, to the conclusion that the given hypothesis is true.

So how is the best explanation determined? Harman himself suggested that a number of criteria might be used to determine which of an ensemble of theoretical possibilities was to be privileged – such as simplicity, plausibility, explanatory comprehensiveness, and the lack of an "ad hoc" character.[84]

Although there are clear difficulties in determining the precise weighting to be attributed to each of a range of possible epistemic virtues, the notion of determining the best "empirical fit" between theory and observation has achieved widespread acceptance.[85] It represents a decisive move away from an older positivist understanding of the scientific method, which holds that science is able to – and therefore ought to – offer evidentially and inferentially infallible evidence for its theories.

It is also important to note that "inference to the best explanation" does not require that such an explanation be *causal*. It is indeed possible to argue that to demonstrate that A causes B amounts to showing that A explains B.[86] But explanation can be framed in quite different terms. It can be thought of as showing how a given event or entity is located within a greater scheme of things, uncovering a deeper rationality that allows those events or entities to be theoretically positioned. Explanatory power is here understood to lie not primarily in causality, but in *ontology* – an understanding of the way things are, of the fundamental order of things. It is by discovering the "big picture" that its individual elements are able to be both known and understood. Pierre Duhem (1861–1916) argued that to explain something "is to strip the reality of the appearances covering it like a veil, in order to see the bare reality itself."[87]

This theme has become of major importance in recent unificationist understandings of scientific explanation, which argue that explanation takes the form of developing a "big picture" that allows new correlations of observations and theories to take place within its framework.[88] Isaac Newton's demonstration that the orbits of the planets and the behavior of terrestrial objects falling freely close to the surface of the earth are due to the same gravitational force represents a classic example of such a "unificationist" approach. Newton was able to demonstrate that, as a result of discerning a "bigger picture" of reality, phenomena that were previously seen as unrelated are shown to be the result of a common set of mechanisms or causal relationships.[89]

The implications of this for natural theology are considerable. Although some philosophers and theologians remain wedded to the notion of natural theology offering a deductive proof of the existence of God,[90] there is every indication of a movement away from such versions of natural theology, which are increasingly recognized to have been culturally conditioned by the agenda of the Enlightenment,[91] including its positivist notion of evidence. Natural theology can be framed in terms of regarding the Christian vision of reality as offering the "best explanation" for what is observed in the empirical world.

Earlier, we noted William Whewell's statement that "a mask of theory covers the face of nature."[92] So which theoretical mask seems to fit the face of nature best? Natural theology is thus not framed in terms of the idea that the observation of nature can *prove* the existence of God through necessary inference; rather, it is argued that the vision of nature that is made possible and legitimate by the Christian faith is found to offer satisfactory intellectual resonance with what is actually observed.[93] Christian theology offers, from its own distinctive point of view, a map of reality or "mask of theory," which, though not exhaustive, is found to correspond to the observed features of nature. It makes possible a way of seeing things that is capable of accommodating the totality of human experience, and rendering it intelligible through its conceptual schemes. There is a clear need for a natural theology to possess adequate conceptual symmetry with what is actually observed, a notion that can be argued to be theologically safeguarded through the doctrine of humanity bearing the *imago Dei*.

The importance of this point in a religious context was emphasized by the French philosopher and social activist Simone Weil, who discovered that faith in God illuminates reality in a far better way than its secular alternatives.[94]

> If I light an electric torch at night out of doors I don't judge its power by looking at the bulb, but by seeing how many objects it lights up. The brightness of a source of light is appreciated by the illumination it projects upon non-luminous objects. The value of a religious or, more generally, a spiritual way of life is appreciated by the amount of illumination thrown upon the things of this world.

Natural theology can be seen as the process of "seeing" nature from the perspective of a Trinitarian ontology, and affirming the degree of conceptual fit of the Kantian net thrown over observation, or the adequacy of the Christian theological map to represent the observed and experienced landscape of reality.

It is therefore neither apologetically necessary nor philosophically possible to "prove" the divine design of the natural world. Design is not something that is, or can be, observed. It is something that is inferred – or, to use Peirce's term, abducted – from observation. Theistic writers regularly affirm that the hypothesis that God designed the universe possesses an explanatory superiority to its atheist alternatives.[95] The recent restatement of traditional teleological arguments in terms of "inference to the best explanation" has given a new injection of intellectual energy into a debate that had been faltering for some years.[96] The evolutionary synthesis can be incorporated into such a general approach, which locates evidence of design in the values of the fundamental constants of nature, the laws of nature, and the creative role of "chance" in bringing about novelty and development – all of which are subsumed under a generalized doctrine of divine providence.[97]

Yet problems remain – perhaps the most obvious of which concerns the problem of suffering and pain within the extended time frame envisaged by the evolutionary process. How, many wonder, could this be accommodated within a Christian theological framework? We shall consider this point in what follows.

Suffering, Evolution, and Natural Theology

In his assessment of the implications of Darwinism for Christian theology (187), Thomas H. Huxley suggested that it did not raise any fundamentally new problems. In one sense, Huxley is right. The questions of how God may act in the world, or why a good God might allow suffering to exist in the world, were debated long before Darwin. Yet in each case, Darwinism may be said to have given a new direction to the debate, however inconclusive it may turn out to be.[98] We shall consider the question of how God might be said to act in the natural world in the next chapter. In the present section, we must consider the issues raised by evolutionary theory for the problem of suffering.

It is important to avoid one sterile line of discussion, which concerns "natural evil." The judgment that any natural process is "evil" is unsustainable, from an evolutionary point of view. Such a moral evaluation is not based on natural criteria, but on the imposition of a human moral framework. We may consider that the shifting of a tectonic plate is "evil," in the light of our perception of its implications. Yet the shifting of tectonic plates is just natural. The additional judgment that it is, or leads to, evil cannot be defended from a scientific perspective.[99] The notion of "evil" is not empirical. It is only because we observe nature through a set of moral and intellectual spectacles that we can draw such conclusions. We can, however, speak of observing or experiencing suffering and pain in nature, and rightly ask why they are there at all.

The problems raised by suffering for classical natural theology are well known,[100] as are their rebuttals. Yet Darwin's approach moves traditional approaches to theodicy into new territory, primarily for two reasons.

1 The contraction of the ontological distance between human beings and other animals, which is a corollary of Darwin's theory of evolution, means that the problem of pain and suffering in the animal kingdom comes to be increasingly significant apologetically.
2 Darwin's model of evolution envisages the emergence of the animal kingdom as taking place over a vastly extended period of time, involving suffering and apparent wastage that go far beyond the concerns of traditional theodicy.

In both cases, Darwinism can be argued to intensify existing concerns with the problem of suffering, most of which were already attracting theological attention. So what theological approaches might be deployed in engaging such questions, seen in a Darwinian perspective? And how are we to evaluate them?

Paley himself argued that the existence of suffering and pain could be accommodated within the notion of the divine "contrivance" of the world. Pain within the natural world might be held to represent "a defect in the contrivance: but it is not the object of it."[101] Creation is thus held to exhibit God's benevolent purposes, even where these are imperfectly executed.[102] Yet the fundamental moral (and aesthetic) ambivalence of nature, many would suggest, is such that Paley's approach, if applied rigorously, could lead to the inference of a morally ambivalent God, if not two gods, one good and the other evil.[103] Gnosticism, after all, had its own form of natural theology.[104]

One approach is, of course, to argue that there is no other way. On this view, God chose the best of all possible worlds. It is very easy to complain about the present state of things, arguing that it seems wasteful, cruel, and pointless. While it may seem natural to wonder whether God could have created a better world than this, we are not in a position to demonstrate that the universe could be otherwise. Perhaps this is the best of all possible worlds after all.

An excellent example of such a Panglossian approach is found in Guy Murchie's *Seven Mysteries of Life* (1978), which offers a highly eclectic view of the great questions of life. Murchie (1907–97), a reporter with the *Chicago Tribune*, offered a grand vision of the universe, which emphasized the interconnectedness of all things, including the evolutionary process. The emergence of life, he argues, demands a universe just like that which we know. In making this point, he undertakes a thought experiment, as follows:[105]

> Honestly now, if you were God, could you possibly dream up any more educational, contrasty, thrilling, beautiful, tantalizing world than Earth to develop spirit in? If you think you could, do you imagine you would be outdoing Earth if you designed a world free of germs, diseases, poisons, pains, malice, explosives and conflicts so its people could relax and enjoy it? Would you, in other words, try to make the world nice and safe – or would you let it be provocative, dangerous, and exciting? In actual fact, if it ever came to that, I'm sure you would find it impossible to make a better world than God has already created.

Even death is not necessarily such a bad thing, Murchie argued. Death within the evolutionary process confers evolutionary advantage,[106] being both a prerequisite and a tool for positive change and progress. Immortal beings that did not change would be slow to respond to environmental changes, if they could respond at all. Death allows for regeneration and for creation of new species, better adapted to new environments and situations.

There is a sense in which Murchie's approach is irrefutable. We cannot produce another universe against which to evaluate the one we know; we can only assert that we believe that a better universe is possible.[107] We are not in a position to demonstrate that there is, or could be, a superior way of constructing this world, or bringing life in general, and humanity in particular, into being. We may complain about the existence of pain and suffering. But that hardly amounts to a disconfirmation of the goodness of the world.

A recent essay on pain by Clifford Woolf, Professor of Anesthesia Research at Harvard Medical School, highlights the importance of this point.[108] Woolf reflects on how human beings would cope with life if they did not experience pain, focusing on the rare inherited neurological condition known as "congenital analgesia." This arises from a random genetic development, which means that sensory neurons acting as the first relay station in the "pain pathway" fail to develop. As a result, the sensory apparatus for the detection of pain is absent. The affected individual cannot feel pain.

As Woolf points out, this could be seen by some as a wonderful development. No pain is experienced in childbirth. Or at the dentist. William Paley's charming reflections on the theological significance of toothache would become unnecessary and irrelevant. Yet, as Woolf points out, the absence of pain "is not a boon; it is a disaster."[109]

> The tips of the fingers of the affected individuals are typically lost through repeated trauma; their tongues and lips are usually mutilated by chewing, and their life spans are significantly shortened … They cannot tell the difference between warmth and scalding hot, and therefore are at constant risk of being scalded. We need pain to survive.

Woolf makes it clear that what he terms "pathological pain" cannot be accommodated in this way. Here, pain is the disease. It has no adaptive function, and its management is an issue of considerable importance. However, his overall argument is emphatic: pain is part of the price of living. That's just the way things are. Could things have been otherwise? Woolf wisely declines to speculate.

Yet Christian natural theology believes that there is a problem here, even if it is one of its own making. The Christian affirmation of the goodness of God seems to be called into question by the existence of pain and suffering within a supposedly good creation. As Thomas F. Torrance rightly remarks:[110]

> If we did not believe that God is good and that the temporal order of things he has conferred upon the universe serves this good will, we would have no problem with decay, decomposition, and death, or with entropy, nor would we find affliction and suffering intolerable, for they would be treated merely as part of the natural process of things.

The problem may be evaded in various ways – for example, by reconceptualizing God in such a manner that divine activity and influence are restricted to within the "process."[111] Yet for many, this dissolves the issue by redefinition, threatening to disconnect language about the nature of God from its grounding in the Christian tradition.

In recent years, there has been a rediscovery of the stability and potential theological fecundity of a Trinitarian framework for dealing with a series of fundamental importance, especially in relation to Christianity's relationship with culture and the natural order.[112] The new interest evident in the apologetic potential of panentheism already has a Trinitarian basis,[113] which could, if further developed, bring intellectual enrichment to questions of evolutionary theodicy. The recent writings of John Haught on evolutionary theodicy also exploit the apologetic potential of some rich Trinitarian motifs.[114]

One of the most important recent discussions of the problem of suffering in evolutionary perspectives is due to Christopher Southgate. In his *Groaning of Creation* (2008), Southgate sets out to offer a theologically rigorous engagement with the problem of suffering in evolution. Rightly recognizing the severe limitations of non-Trinitarian approaches to the question, such as process thought,[115] Southgate develops an approach based on the Pauline motif of the "groaning of creation" (Romans 8). Southgate's concern to remain faithful to core themes of the Christian tradition also leads him to reject the approach of Pierre Teilhard de Chardin, who held that God used "evolutionary centration" to bring about a convergence upon a glorious, God-centered, final culmination of evolution.[116] For Southgate, the biblical theme of "the mighty redeeming act of God inaugurated in the Cross of Christ" seems to offer a much more theologically secure foundation for such reflections.[117]

The problem of evolutionary suffering is thus seen through a theological lens shaped by most of the leading themes of a Trinitarian view of reality – such as the notion of creation *ex nihilo*, and the final consummation, yet specifically excluding the notion of a historical Fall, as traditionally interpreted.[118] Southgate's Trinitarian theology of creation extends to include the notion that God's self-emptying love is expressed in incarnational *kenosis*. His approach weaves together the following themes.[119]

1 Pain, suffering, death, and extinction are inevitable outcomes for a creation that is evolving according to Darwinian principles.
2 An evolving creation is the only means by which God could give rise to all the beauty, diversity, sentience, and sophistication we observe around us in the biosphere.
3 God suffers along with every sentient being in creation. The cross of Christ is interpreted as a historic moment of manifestation and embodiment of divine compassion, in which God assumes ultimate responsibility for the suffering and pain of the "groaning"-created order.

4   The cross and resurrection inaugurate the transformation of the crea-
    tion, which culminates in the final ending of the groaning of creation in
    the eschatological renewal.
5   God regards no creature as a mere evolutionary expedient, but provides
    an eschatological fulfillment for each creature. The non-human creation
    will be represented in heaven.

Southgate's approach is rich in insights – such as the dialectic between disvalue and value within the evolutionary process, which pits the disvalue of
the suffering of individual animals on the one hand against the value of the
survival of their species that this suffering helps to make possible on the
other.[120] It is a point familiar to readers of the environmental ethicist Holmes
Rolston,[121] who argues that processes which are intrinsic to the evolutionary
process can indeed give rise to pain and suffering, but can also be instrumental in enhancing values, by giving rise to new forms of existence. "Although
intrinsic pain is a bad thing, whether in humans or in sheep, pain in ecosys-
tems is instrumental pain, through which the sheep are naturally selected for
a more satisfactory adaptive fit."[122] Rolston expresses this general point
using an often-quoted aphorism: "The cougar's fang sharpens the deer's
sight, the deer's fleet-footedness shapes a more supple lioness."[123]

    In general, three distinct themes have emerged as characteristic of recent
Christian reflections on the apologetic concerns arising from evolutionary
suffering, whether woven together into a coherent tapestry, or asserted individually as significant in their own right.

1   God suffers within the created order, experiencing the pain of creation.
    This theme became significant in Christian theology during the 1970s,
    partly as a result of the influence of Jürgen Moltmann's *Crucified God*
    (1974).[124] The theme of God's suffering within the evolutionary process,
    hitherto confined to the realm of process thought,[125] now became an
    option for mainline theology. God "suffers in, with, and under the creative
    processes of the world, with their costly unfolding in time."[126] In the sym-
    bol of the cross of Christ, Christian theology affirms "a God who partici-
    pates fully in the world's struggle and pain."[127]
2   In order for the world to generate the rich diversity of life that we cur-
    rently know, including human beings, there has to be pain, suffering, and
    death. There is no other way to biological diversity other than through
    processes of development and competition, in which some species die
    out, to be replaced by others. "As the ultimate source of novelty in evo-
    lution, God must also be the cause of instability and disorder, conditions
    essential to life."[128] This claim can be developed in a number of ways,
    whether framed as the "best way" or the "only way" to biological
    fulfillment;[129] the core theme is that we are not in a position to declare

that the pain, suffering, and "disvalues" associated with the evolutionary process are not worth the values they create.

3   The universe must be seen in an eschatological perspective, looking
toward its final consummation and transformation. The importance of
eschatology in relation to the problem of suffering and evil has long been
recognized. We are, many argue, enabled to cope with suffering through
the hope of its final transformation in the New Jerusalem.[130] It has
proved natural to apply such a framework to the question of suffering in
the evolutionary process. This is a major theme of Southgate's approach,[131]
which holds that the animal world will be part of the outcome of cosmic
renewal that is traditionally referred to as "heaven."

These three elements are easily integrated into a rigorously Trinitarian ontology, grounded in the fundamental themes of the Christian faith. Where some
earlier writers tended to develop a theodicy based on a generic notion of
divinity, there has been a fundamental shift in mood in recent years, reflecting the growing confidence within Christian theology, noted earlier (19),
concerning the historical and conceptual foundations of its Trinitarian logic
and its intellectual fertility in interdisciplinary dialogues.

It will, however, be clear that the notion of creation plays a particularly
significant role in any reflections concerning the impact of evolutionary
thought upon natural theology. In the following chapter, we shall consider
this in much greater detail.

Notes

1   The focus of this work, coupled with limits on space, means that it is not possible
to consider the interaction of evolutionary thought with many aspects of religious
life and thought that otherwise might be of interest, such as the interaction between
Darwinism and ethics. For discussions of these issues, see Clayton, Philip, and
Jeffrey Schloss, *Evolution and Ethics: Human Morality in Biological and Religious
Perspective*. Grand Rapids, MI: Eerdmans, 2004; Boniolo, Giovanni, and Gabriele
De Anna, *Evolutionary Ethics and Contemporary Biology*. Cambridge: Cambridge
University Press, 2006; Lemos, John, *Commonsense Darwinism: Evolution,
Morality, and the Human Condition*. Chicago: Open Court, 2008.

2   For some works that explore this development, see Moore, James R., *The Post-
Darwinian Controversies: A Study of the Protestant Struggle to Come to Terms
with Darwin in Great Britain and America, 1870–1900*. Cambridge: Cambridge
University Press, 1979; Bowler, Peter J., *The Eclipse of Darwinism: Anti-
Darwinian Evolution Theories in the Decades around 1900*. Baltimore, MD:
John Hopkins University Press, 1983; Hodgson, Geoffrey M., "Generalizing
Darwinism to Social Evolution: Some Early Attempts." *Journal of Economic
Issues* 39 (2005): 899–914.

3   See, for example, Ruse, Michael, "Teleology: Yesterday, Today, and Tomorrow?" *Studies in History and Philosophy of Biological and Biomedical Sciences* 31 (2000): 213–32.
4   Huxley, Thomas H., *Lay Sermons, Addresses, and Reviews*. London: Macmillan, 1870, 301. Huxley's complex (and not always consistent) attitude toward religion is explored in Gilley, Sheridan, and Ann Loades, "Thomas Henry Huxley: The War between Science and Religion." *Journal of Religion* 61 (1981): 285–308.
5   The most convenient source for the lecture is Darwin, Francis, ed., *The Life and Letters of Charles Darwin*. 3 vols. London: John Murray, 1887, vol. 2, 179–204.
6   *Life and Letters of Charles Darwin*, vol. 2, 199.
7   *Life and Letters of Charles Darwin*, vol. 2, 201.
8   On Paley and others on this point, see Passmore, John, "Darwin's Impact on British Metaphysics." *Victorian Studies* 3 (1959): 41–54.
9   *Life and Letters of Charles Darwin*, vol. 2, 201. Huxley had made these points in an earlier publication, and noted that they had yet to be refuted.
10 *Life and Letters of Charles Darwin*, vol. 2, 202.
11 *Life and Letters of Charles Darwin*, vol. 2, 203–4.
12 McGrath, Alister E., *A Fine-Tuned Universe: The Quest for God in Science and Theology*. Louisville, KY: Westminster John Knox Press, 2009, 127–81.
13 This view appears to be expressed in Frederick Temple's landmark account of science and religion, which argued that God created the elements and properties of the universe in such a manner that it might develop as its creator had intended: Temple, Frederick, *The Relations between Religion and Science*. London: Macmillan, 1885, 115–16.
14 See Stoeger, William R., "The Immanent Directionality of the Evolutionary Process, and Its Relationship to Teleology." In *Evolutionary and Molecular Biology: Scientific Perspectives on Divine Action*, ed. Robert J. Russell, William R. Stoeger, and Francisco Ayala, 163–90. Rome: Vatican Observatory, 1999.
15 McGrath, *Fine-Tuned Universe*, 127–42.
16 Pross, Addy, "On the Emergence of Biological Complexity: Life as a Kinetic State of Matter." *Origins of Life and Evolution of Biospheres* 35 (2005): 151–66.
17 As noted by Bonner, John T., *The Evolution of Complexity by Means of Natural Selection*. Princeton, NJ: Princeton University Press, 1988, 26–96. For the impact of the environment on such developments, see Pacini, Alessandra, Stefano Mazzoleni, Corrado Battisti, and Carlo Ricotta, "More Rich Means More Diverse: Extending the Environmental Heterogeneity Hypothesis to Taxonomic Diversity." *Ecological Indicators* 9 (2009): 1271–4.
18 Sherwood, Chet C., Francys Subiaul, and Tadeusz W. Zawidzki, "A Natural History of the Human Mind: Tracing Evolutionary Changes in Brain and Cognition." *Journal of Anatomy* 212 (2008): 426–54.
19 The English term "teleology" appears to date from 1740, representing a translation of the Latin term *teleologia*, coined in 1728 by the German philosopher Christian von Wolff (1679–1754).
20 See Johnson, Monte Ransome, *Aristotle on Teleology*. Oxford: Clarendon Press, 2005, 159–286; Leunissen, Mariska, *Explanation and Teleology in Aristotle's Science of Nature*. Cambridge: Cambridge University Press, 2010.

21 Cooper, John M., "Aristotle on Natural Teleology." In *Nature and the Good: Essays on Ancient Philosophy*, 107–29. Princeton: NJ: Princeton University Press, 2004.

22 This point was emphasized some decades ago by Grene, Marjorie, "Aristotle and Modern Biology." *Journal of the History of Ideas* 33 (1972): 395–424.

23 For notions of biological teleology prevalent in the seventeenth and eighteenth centuries, see Bates, Don, "Machine *ex Deo*: William Harvey and the Meaning of Instrument." *Journal of the History of Ideas* 61 (2001): 577–93; Garrett, Brian, "Vitalism and Teleology in the Natural Philosophy of Nehemiah Grew (1641–1712)." *British Journal for the History of Science* 36 (2003): 63–81.

24 See Lenoir, Timothy, *The Strategy of Life: Teleology and Mechanics in Nineteenth Century German Biology*. Chicago: University of Chicago Press, 1989, 112–94. Note also his important earlier study: Lenoir, Timothy, "The Göttingen School and the Development of Transcendental *Naturphilosophie* in the Romantic Era." *Studies in the History of Biology* 5 (1981): 111–205. For the possible influence of such a *Naturphilosophie* on Darwin, see Sloan, Phillip R., "'The Sense of Sublimity': Darwin on Nature and Divinity." *Osiris* 16 (2001): 251–69, especially 252–6; Richards, Robert J., *The Romantic Conception of Life: Science and Philosophy in the Age of Goethe*. Chicago: University of Chicago Press, 2002, 514–54.

25 Kolb, Daniel, "Kant, Teleology, and Evolution." *Synthese* 91 (1992): 9–28; Steigerwald, Joan, "Kant's Concept of Natural Purpose and the Reflecting Power of Judgement." *Studies in History and Philosophy of Science C* 37 (2006): 712–34.

26 Mayr, Ernst, *Toward a New Philosophy of Biology: Observations of an Evolutionist*. Cambridge, MA: Belknap Press, 1988, 38–66, especially 39–41; Mayr, Ernst, *What Makes Biology Unique? Considerations on the Autonomy of a Scientific Discipline*. Cambridge: Cambridge University Press, 2004, 39–66, especially 46–7.

27 Ayala, Francisco J., "Teleological Explanations in Evolutionary Biology." *Philosophy of Science* 37 (1970): 1–15; Ayala, Francisco J., "Teleological Explanations vs. Teleology." *History and Philosophy of the Life Sciences* 20 (1998): 41–50.

28 Ayala, "Teleological Explanations in Evolutionary Biology," 12. See also Ayala, Francisco J., "Intelligent Design: The Original Version." *Theology and Science* 1 (2003): 9–32.

29 Mayr, *Toward a New Philosophy of Biology*, 44–5. Note also his view that (p. 59) "the use of so-called 'teleological' language by biologists is legitimate; it neither implies a rejection of physicochemical explanation nor does it imply noncausal explanation."

30 Ayala, "Teleological Explanations in Evolutionary Biology," 8.

31 Paley, William, *Natural Theology: Or, Evidences of the Existence and Attributes of the Deity*. 12th edn. London: Faulder, 1809, 62–3.

32 It is helpful to consider Paley against his intellectual context to appreciate how this confusion might occur: see especially Osler, Margaret J., "Whose Ends? Teleology in Early Modern Natural Philosophy." *Osiris* 16 (2001): 151–68; Osler, Margaret J., *Divine Will and the Mechanical Philosophy: Gassendi and*

Descartes on Contingency and Necessity in the Created World. Cambridge: Cambridge University Press, 2004, 80–101; 118–52; 222–36.

33 Bartholomew, David J., *God, Chance and Purpose*. Cambridge: Cambridge University Press, 2008, 18.

34 See the definitive discussion in Thomas Aquinas, *Summa contra Gentiles*, III.74. For further analysis, see Johnson, Elizabeth A., "Does God Play Dice? Divine Providence and Chance." *Theological Studies* 57 (1996): 3–18; Hoonhout, Michael A., "Grounding Providence in the Theology of the Creator: The Exemplarity of Thomas Aquinas." *Heythrop Journal* 43 (2002): 1–19.

35 An approach taken, for example, in Sanders, John, *The God Who Risks: A Theology of Providence*. Downers Grove, IL: InterVarsity Press, 1998. Sanders's brief and superficial discussion of Aquinas (152–3) seems to miss the point completely.

36 See, for example, the discussion in Peacocke, Arthur R., "Chance and the Life Game." *Zygon* 14 (1979): 301–22; Bartholomew, D. J., "Probability, Statistics and Theology." *Journal of the Royal Statistical Society* A 151 (1988): 137–78.

37 Monod, Jacques, *Chance and Necessity: An Essay on the Natural Philosophy of Modern Biology*. New York: Alfred A. Knopf, 1971, 112–13.

38 Gould, Stephen Jay, *Wonderful Life: The Burgess Shale and the Nature of History*. New York: Norton, 1989, 290.

39 Gould, *Wonderful Life*, 101–2. Similar points were made previously by George Gaylord Simpson: see Simpson, George Gaylord, *The Meaning of Evolution: A Study of the History of Life and of Its Significance for Man*. New Haven, CT: Yale University Press, 1949.

40 Peacocke, Arthur, *Creation and the World of Science*. Oxford: Oxford University Press, 1979, 94.

41 Darwin, Charles, *On the Origin of the Species by Means of Natural Selection*. London: John Murray, 1859, 84.

42 Conway Morris, Simon, *Life's Solution: Inevitable Humans in a Lonely Universe*. Cambridge: Cambridge University Press, 2003, xii.

43 Conway Morris, *Life's Solution*, 24: "Despite the almost crass simplicity of life's building blocks, perhaps we can discern inherent within this framework the inevitable and pre-ordained trajectories of evolution?"

44 See McGhee, George R., "Exploring the Spectrum of Existent, Nonexistent and Impossible Biological Form." *Trends in Ecology and Evolution* 16 (2001): 172–3. For the notion of the "adaptive landscape," see McGhee, George R., *The Geometry of Evolution: Adaptive Landscape and Theoretical Morphospaces*. Cambridge: Cambridge University Press, 2007, 1–30.

45 Conway Morris, *Life's Solution*, 225.

46 Conway Morris, *Life's Solution*, 127.

47 Conway Morris compares this process to the "sophisticated search techniques" of Polynesian navigators, which led to the discovery of the very isolated Easter Island: Conway Morris, *Life's Solution*, 19–21.

48 Conway Morris, Simon, "Darwin's Compass: How Evolution Discovers the Song of Creation." *Science and Christian Belief* 18 (2006): 5–22.

49 Needham, Joseph, *Order and Life*. New Haven, CT: Yale University Press, 1936, 15.

50 McGhee, The Geometry of Evolution, 108–51. See also McGhee, George R., *Theoretical Morphology: The Concept and Its Application.* New York: Columbia University Press, 1999.

51 See the important study of Williams, R. J. P., and J. J. R. Fraústo da Silva, "Evolution Was Chemically Constrained." *Journal of Theoretical Biology* 220 (2003): 323–43.

52 McGrath, *Fine-Tuned Universe*, 155–65.

53 Cooke, Josiah P., *Religion and Chemistry: A Re-Statement of an Old Argument.* New York: Scribner, 1864, vii–viii.

54 Cooke, *Religion and Chemistry*, 265.

55 Henderson, Lawrence J., *The Fitness of the Environment: An Inquiry into the Biological Significance of the Properties of Matter.* Boston: Beacon Press, 1913, 312. On Henderson's approach, see Fry, Iris, "On the Biological Significance of the Properties of Matter: L. J. Henderson's Theory of the Fitness of the Environment." *Journal of the History of Biology* 29 (1996): 155–96.

56 Henderson, Lawrence J., *The Order of Nature: An Essay.* Cambridge, MA: Harvard University Press, 1917, 192.

57 On oxygen, see Catling, D. C., C. R. Glein, K. J. Zahnle, and C. P. McKay, "Why O_2 Is Required by Complex Life on Habitable Planets and the Concept of Planetary 'Oxygenation Time'." *Astrobiology* 5 (2005): 415–38.

58 Williams, R. J. P., and J. J. R. Fraústo da Silva, *The Natural Selection of the Chemical Elements: The Environment and Life's Chemistry.* Oxford: Clarendon Press, 1996.

59 Most scientific definitions of life include the capacity for Darwinian evolution as a core element: see Cleland, Carol E., and Christopher F. Chyba, "Defining 'Life'." *Origins of Life and Evolution of the Biosphere* 32 (2002): 387–93.

60 Similar comments could be made about phosphorus: see Westheimer, Frank H., "Why Nature Chose Phosphates." *Science* 235 (1987): 1173–8.

61 Woosley, Stanford E., Alex Heger, and Thomas A. Weaver, "The Evolution and Explosion of Massive Stars." *Reviews of Modern Physics* 74 (2002): 1015–71.

62 For a good account of the issues, see Rees, Martin J., *Just Six Numbers: The Deep Forces That Shape the Universe.* London: Phoenix, 2000, 2–4. See also the older study of Barrow, John, and Frank J. Tipler, *The Anthropic Cosmological Principle.* Oxford: Oxford University Press, 1986, 367–457.

63 Filippenko, Alexei V., "Einstein's Biggest Blunder? High-Redshift Supernovae and the Accelerating Universe." *Publications of the Astronomical Society of the Pacific* 113 (2001): 1441–8.

64 Rees, *Just Six Numbers*, 3.

65 Leslie, John, *Universes.* London: Routledge, 1989, 4.

66 Leslie, *Universes*, 63.

67 Hoyle, Fred, "The Universe: Past and Present Reflections." *Annual Review of Astronomy and Astrophysics* 20 (1982): 1–35, 16.

68 Paley, *Natural Theology*, 467.

69 Whewell, William, *Astronomy and General Physics Considered with Reference to Natural Theology.* London: Pickering, 1833, 2.

70   For reflections on the inference of design, see Dembski, William A., *The Design Inference: Eliminating Chance through Small Probabilities*. Cambridge: Cambridge University Press, 1998, 47–55.

71   For the problems in determining the function and manner of production of such artifacts, see Andrefsky, William, *Lithics: Macroscopic Approaches to Analysis*. 2nd edn. Cambridge: Cambridge University Press, 2005, 143–99.

72   Originally published in *Popular Science Monthly* 12 (November 1877), 1–15; 286–302.

73   For what follows, see Fann, K. T., *Peirce's Theory of Abduction*. The Hague: Nijhoff, 1970; Anderson, Douglas R., "The Evolution of Peirce's Concept of Abduction." *Transactions of the Charles S. Peirce Society* 22 (1986): 145–64; Brogaard, Berit, "Peirce on Abduction and Rational Control." *Transactions of the Charles S. Peirce Society* 35 (1999): 129–55; Paavola, Sami, "Peircean Abduction: Instinct, or Inference?" *Semiotica* 153 (2005): 131–54.

74   For its application to natural theology, see McGrath, *Fine-Tuned Universe*, 43–8; 83–93.

75   Peirce, Charles S., *Collected Papers of Charles Sanders Peirce*, ed. Charles Hartshorne and Paul Weiss. 8 vols. Cambridge, MA: Harvard University Press, 1960, vol. 5, 189.

76   Peirce, *Collected Papers*, vol. 5, 171.

77   Peirce, *Collected Papers*, vol. 2, 96.

78   Peirce, *Collected Papers*, vol. 5, 181.

79   See the analysis in Hookway, Christopher, "Interrogatives and Uncontrollable Abductions." *Semiotica* 153 (2005): 101–15; Paavola, Sami, "Abduction as a Logic of Discovery: The Importance of Strategies." *Foundations of Science* 9 (2005): 267–83.

80   See the classic statement of this approach in Harman, Gilbert, "The Inference to the Best Explanation." *Philosophical Review* 74 (1965): 88–95. For the best recent statement of this approach, see Lipton, Peter, *Inference to the Best Explanation*. 2nd edn. London: Routledge, 2004. Alternative versions of the approach should be noted, particularly an older approach developed by Hanson, N. R., "Is There a Logic of Scientific Discovery?" *Australasian Journal of Philosophy* 38 (1961): 91–106. See further Paavola, Sami, "Hansonian and Harmanian Abduction as Models of Discovery." *International Studies in the Philosophy of Science* 20 (2006): 93–108.

81   Sober, Elliott, *The Philosophy of Biology*. Boulder, CO: Westview Press, 1993, 30–6.

82   For example, see Swinburne, Richard, *The Existence of God*. 2nd edn. Oxford: Clarendon Press, 2004; Haldane, John, "Philosophy, the Restless Heart, and the Meaning of Theism." *Ratio* 19 (2006): 421–40; Polkinghorne, John, "Physics and Metaphysics in a Trinitarian Perspective." *Theology and Science* 1 (2003): 33–49.

83   Harman, "Inference to the Best Explanation," 89. For further discussion, see McMullin, Ernan, *The Inference that Makes Science*. Milwaukee: Marquette University Press, 1992, 81–95.

84   Harman, "Inference to the Best Explanation," 89. See further Thagard, Paul, "The Best Explanation: Criteria for Theory Choice." *Journal of Philosophy* 75

(1978): 76–92; McMullin, Ernan, "Epistemic Virtue and Theory Appraisal." In *Realism in the Sciences*, ed. Igor Douven and Leon Horsten, 13–34. Leuven: Leuven University Press, 1996; Glass, David H., "Coherence Measures and Inference to the Best Explanation." *Synthese* 157 (2007): 275–96; Psillos, Stathis, "The Fine Structure of Inference to the Best Explanation." *Philosophy and Phenomenological Research* 74 (2007): 441–8.

85   Newton-Smith, W. H., *The Rationality of Science*. London: Routledge & Kegan Paul, 1981, 224: "The ultimate test of the superiority of one theory over another is observational success." For the biological dimensions of the issue, see Kleiner, Scott A., "Explanatory Coherence and Empirical Adequacy: The Problem of Abduction, and the Justification of Evolutionary Models." *Biology and Philosophy* 18 (2003): 513–27. The notion of "empirical fit" was developed in a theological context by the Oxford philosopher of religion Ian T. Ramsey (1915–72) – for example, see Ramsey, Ian T., *Models and Mystery*. London: Oxford University Press, 1964, 17. For a critical analysis, see Tilley, Terrence W., "Ian Ramsey and Empirical Fit." *Journal of the American Academy of Religion* 45 (1977): G963–88.

86   Swinburne, *Existence of God*, 23.

87   Duhem, Pierre, *The Aim and Structure of Physical Theory*. Princeton, NJ: Princeton University Press, 1954, 7.

88   See Morrison, Margaret, *Unifying Scientific Theories: Physical Concepts and Mathematical Structures*. Cambridge: Cambridge University Press, 2000, 35–59. For recent debates over this approach, see Halonen, Ilpo, and Jaakko Hintikka, "Unification – It's Magnificent but Is It Explanation?" *Synthese* 120 (1999): 27–47; Schweder, Rebecca, "A Defense of a Unificationist Theory of Explanation." *Foundations of Science* 10 (2005): 421–35.

89   Forster, Malcolm R., "Unification, Explanation, and the Composition of Causes in Newtonian Mechanics." *Studies in History and Philosophy of Science* 19 (1988): 55–101.

90   See, for example, Craig, William Lane, "The Existence of God and the Beginning of the Universe." *Truth: A Journal of Modern Thought* 3 (1991): 85–96.

91   McGrath, Alister E., *The Open Secret: A New Vision for Natural Theology*. Oxford: Blackwell, 2008, 140–70.

92   Whewell, William, *Philosophy of the Inductive Sciences*. 2 vols. London: John W. Parker, 1847, vol. 1, 1.

93   This is the position that I articulate and defend in recent writings: see especially McGrath, *The Open Secret*; McGrath, *Fine-Tuned Universe*. For other approaches, some of which emphasize natural theology as an attempt to prove God's existence from reason or nature, see Fergusson, David, "Types of Natural Theology." In *The Evolution of Rationality: Interdisciplinary Essays in Honor of J. Wentzel Van Huyssteen*, ed. F. Le Ron Shults, 380–93. Grand Rapids, MI: Eerdmans, 2006.

94   Weil, Simone, *First and Last Notebooks*. London: Oxford University Press, 1970, 147. See also Hort, F. J. A., *The Way, the Truth, the Life: The Hulsean Lectures for 1871*. 2nd edn. London: Macmillan, 1894, 11–12. For Hort, the intellectual case for the Christian faith "is to be found in the light which it brings, far more than in any light which it receives."

95   For example, see Swinburne, *Existence of God*, 110–32; Ward, Keith, *God, Chance and Necessity*. Oxford: Oneworld, 1996, 96–104.

96   See the important analysis in Johnson, Jeffery L., "Inference to the Best Explanation and the New Teleological Argument." *Southern Journal of Philosophy* 31 (1991): 193–203.

97   Schönborn, Christoph von, *Chance or Purpose?: Creation, Evolution, and a Rational Faith*. San Francisco: Ignatius Press, 2007, 69–86. The role of providence is particularly significant for Reformed writers: see, for example, the important discussion of this point by B. B. Warfield Livingstone, David N., and Mark A. Noll, "B. B. Warfield (1851–1921): A Biblical Inerrantist as Evolutionist." *Isis* 91 (2000): 283–304, especially 290–304.

98   For examples of the problems in reaching any meaningful solutions, see Draper, Paul, "Cosmic Fine-Tuning and Terrestrial Suffering: Parallel Problems for Naturalism and Theism." *American Philosophical Quarterly* 41 (2004): 311–21. Draper achieves only a modest degree of resolution of the issues by underplaying and occasionally misunderstanding theistic positions.

99   Here I am completely in agreement with Richard Dawkins, who insists that science offers no basis for determining whether something is good or evil: Dawkins, Richard, *A Devil's Chaplain: Selected Writings*. London: Weidenfeld & Nicholson, 2003, 34. For the debate, see the somewhat mixed collection of essays in Drees, Willem B., ed., *Is Nature Ever Evil? Religion, Science and Value*. London: Routledge, 2003.

100 For example, see Draper, Paul, "Pain and Pleasure: An Evidential Problem for Theists." *Nous* 23 (1989): 331–50.

101 Paley, *Natural Theology*, 467.

102 Paley, *Natural Theology*, 454–5.

103 John Ruskin's vigorous criticism of Paley and his followers at this point merits close consideration: see the account in McGrath, *Fine-Tuned Universe*, 77–82, especially 81–2.

104 For this theme in Robert Browning's poem "Caliban upon Setebos," discussed earlier (130–3), see Youngquist, Paul, "Browning, Gnosis, and the Dilemma of the Demiurge." *Victorian Institute Journal* 17 (1989): 157–68.

105 Murchie, Guy, *The Seven Mysteries of Life: An Exploration in Science and Philosophy*. Boston: Houghton Mifflin, 1978, 622.

106 Murchie, *Seven Mysteries of Life*, 520–38.

107 For some considerations, see Adams, Robert Merrihew, "Must God Create the Best?" *Philosophical Review* 81 (1972): 317–22; Wielenberg, Erik J., "A Morally Unsurpassable God Must Create the Best." *Religious Studies* 40 (2004): 43–62.

108 Woolf, Clifford J., "Deconstructing Pain: A Deterministic Dissection of the Molecular Basis of Pain." In *Pain and Its Transformations: The Interface of Biology and Culture*, ed. Sarah Coakley and Kay Kaufman Shelemay, 27–35. Cambridge, MA: Harvard University Press, 2007.

109 Woolf, "Deconstructing Pain," 28–9.

110 Torrance, Thomas Forsyth, *Divine and Contingent Order*. Oxford: Oxford University Press, 1981, 120. For Torrance's own views on natural theology, see

McGrath, Alister E., *Thomas F. Torrance: An Intellectual Biography*. Edinburgh: T. & T. Clark, 1999, 175–94; Holder, Rodney D., "Thomas Torrance: 'Retreat to Commitment' or a New Place for Natural Theology?" *Theology and Science* 7 (2009): 275–96.

111 See, for example, Griffin, David Ray, *God, Power, and Evil: A Process Theodicy*. Louisville, KY: Westminster John Knox Press, 2004, 275–310.

112 See Levering, Matthew, *Scripture and Metaphysics: Aquinas and the Renewal of Trinitarian Theology*. Oxford: Blackwell, 2004, 197–235; Leupp, Roderick T., *The Renewal of Trinitarian Theology: Themes, Patterns, & Explorations*. Downers Grove, IL: InterVarsity Press, 2008, 19–49. For examples of this approach, see Volf, Miroslav, *After Our Likeness: The Church as the Image of the Trinity*. Grand Rapids, MI: Eerdmans, 1998; Polkinghorne, "Physics and Metaphysics in a Trinitarian Perspective"; Kärkkäinen, Veli-Matti, *Trinity and Religious Pluralism: The Doctrine of the Trinity in Christian Theology of Religions*. Aldershot: Ashgate, 2004, 1–10; McGrath, *Fine-Tuned Universe*, 61–82.

113 Schaab, Gloria L., "A Procreative Paradigm of the Creative Suffering of the Triune God: Implications of Arthur Peacocke's Evolutionary Theology." *Theological Studies* 67 (2006): 542–66. Note the frequent appeal to the Trinitarian theology of the Greek patristic writer Maximus the Confessor in Clayton, Philip, and A. R. Peacocke, eds., *In Whom We Live and Move and Have Our Being: Panentheistic Reflections on God's Presence in a Scientific World*. Grand Rapids, MI: Eerdmans, 2004. The theological potential of the Russian theologian Sergei Bulgakov (1871–1944) does not yet seem to have been appreciated: see, for example, the analysis in O'Donnell, John, "The Trinitarian Panentheism of Sergej Bulgakov." *Gregorianum* 76 (1995): 31–45.

114 Haught, John F., *God after Darwin: A Theology of Evolution*. 2nd edn. Boulder, CO: Westview Press, 2008, 53–4.

115 Southgate, Christopher, *The Groaning of Creation: God, Evolution, and the Problem of Evil*. Louisville, KY: Westminster John Knox Press, 2008, 18–39.

116 For an exploration of this approach, see Grumett, David, "Teilhard De Chardin's Evolutionary Natural Theology." *Zygon* 42 (2007): 519–34.

117 In many ways, Southgate's approach is very similar to the style of natural theology I have defended in this work and elsewhere. Southgate and I differ, however, in our attitude to the theological notion of the Fall, which I continue to regard as an integral, defensible, and constructive element of the "economy of salvation." See McGrath, *A Fine-Tuned Universe*, 77–82.

118 Southgate, *Groaning of Creation*, 5; 28–35.

119 Southgate, *Groaning of Creation*, 16.

120 For the exploration of this point, see Wynn, Mark, "Natural Theology in an Ecological Mode." *Faith and Philosophy* 16 (1999): 27–42; Attfield, Robin, *Creation, Evolution, and Meaning*. Aldershot: Ashgate, 2006, 105–50.

121 For an introduction, see Palmer, Joy A., ed., *Fifty Key Environmental Thinkers*. London: Routledge, 2001, 260–8.

122 Rolston, Holmes, "Environmental Ethics: Values in and Duties to the Natural World." In *Ecology, Economics, Ethics: The Broken Circle*, ed. F. Herbert

Bormann and Stephen R. Kellert, 73–96. New Haven, CT: Yale University Press, 1991, 77.

123   Rolston, Holmes, "Perpetual Perishing, Perpetual Renewal." *Northern Review*, no. 28 (2008): 111–23, 111.

124   For comment and exploration, see Fretheim, Terence E., *The Suffering of God: An Old Testament Perspective*. Philadelphia: Fortress Press, 1984; Fiddes, Paul, *The Creative Suffering of God*. Oxford: Clarendon Press, 1988; Hallman, Joseph M., *The Descent of God: Divine Suffering in History and Theology*. Minneapolis, MN: Fortress Press, 1991; Bouma-Prediger, Steven, "Creation as the Home of God: The Doctrine of Creation in the Theology of Jürgen Moltmann." *Calvin Theological Journal* 32 (1997): 72–90. For a critique of such approaches, see Weinandy, Thomas G., *Does God Suffer?* Notre Dame, IN: University of Notre Dame, 2000.

125   For a critical assessment of this approach, see Frankenberry, Nancy, "Some Problems in Process Theodicy." *Religious Studies* 17 (1981): 179–97.

126   Peacocke, Arthur R., *Paths from Science Towards God: The End of All Our Exploring*. Oxford: Oneworld, 2001, 37.

127   Haught, *God after Darwin*, 50.

128   Haught, *God after Darwin*, 46.

129   See Southgate, *Groaning of Creation*, 40–50.

130   See here Kane, G. Stanley, "Soul-Making Theodicy and Eschatology." *Sophia* 14 (1975): 24–31. There is also some useful material in the survey article of Mostert, Christiaan, "Theodicy and Eschatology." In *Theodicy and Eschatology*, ed. Bruce Barber and David Neville, 97–120. Hindmarsh, South Australia: Australian Theological Forum, 2005.

131   Southgate, *Groaning of Creation*, 78–91.

8

The Concept of Creation: Reflections and Reconsiderations

One of the frustrations accompanying any attempt to explore the relationship between Christian theology and evolutionary thought is that the debate is often deeply polarized, betraying a fundamental disinclination to engage in critical reflection and serious listening. The first casualty of polemics is any willingness to understand the other side of the argument. Sadly, this is one of the most conspicuous and distressing features of the "New Atheist" adoption of Darwin as a secular and secularizing mascot. Recent forms of atheism linked with Darwinism – those of Richard Dawkins and Daniel Dennett come to mind immediately – take their stand on a series of dichotomizations that are as absolute as they are unnecessary. Either creation or evolution. Either chance or design. Either natural processes or divine intervention. Either cranes or sky-hooks.[1] Sadly, this lack of willingness to engage seriously with the questions is also characteristic of religious fundamentalisms, which often adopt eighteenth-century doctrinal norms characteristic of certain relatively small religious groupings and treat these as permanently characteristic of, and normative for, everyone else.

It is therefore of importance to consider the range of viewpoints concerning the doctrine of creation that have emerged within the Christian tradition, particularly where these were not forced or catalyzed by scientific developments that might be held to lead to coerced accommodation between scientific theory and Christian theology. This is especially the case with approaches to the concept of "creation," which requires much more careful exploration than some allow. Earlier Christian views of this concept, especially those of the patristic age, are often marginalized in such discussions, despite their antiquity and authenticity. In the present chapter, we shall seek to redress this situation. First, however, we must explore the theological

Darwinism and the Divine: Evolutionary Thought and Natural Theology, First Edition.
Alister E. McGrath.
© 2011 Alister E. McGrath. Published 2011 by Blackwell Publishing Ltd.

framework of the Augustan age, which did so much to frame Victorian debates over the implications of Darwinism for religious faith.

The Seventeenth Century: The Regnant Theology of Creation

Earlier in this work, we considered the development of English natural theology from the late seventeenth century, noting how its distinctive themes and emphases generated a framework of understanding that caused Charles Darwin's theory of descent with modification through natural selection to be seen as constituting a challenge to the Christian faith. It is, of course, impossible to reverse history, somehow replacing the actual historical realities with their imagined alternatives.[2] Nevertheless, the enterprise is worth undertaking, as it indicates the historical particularity and contingency of some of the responses to Darwin. It also allows us to consider how Darwin's theory relates to older Christian understandings of creation, apparently unknown to leading English theologians of the nineteenth century.

As noted earlier (61–2), Augustan natural theology was deeply influenced by the consensual approach to theology set out in John Pearson's *Exposition of the Creed* (1659). Pearson's influential exposition of the Christian doctrine of creation both reflected and consolidated the theological consensus of the Augustan age, and was of major importance in shaping the conceptual foundations of English natural theology of this age and beyond. So what are the core elements of his approach to the concept of creation?[3] Pearson's careful analysis suggests that the following four themes are seen as being of particular importance.

First, to say that the world is "created" is to recognize the ontological dependence of the world upon God, and its ontological distinction from God. The world does not derive its existence or characteristics from itself, but from God, as its creator. Its existence and characteristics are contingent, not necessary.[4]

> This, then, is the unquestionable doctrine of the Christian Faith, that the vast capacious frame of the world, and every thing any way contained and existing in it, hath not its essence from or of itself, nor is of existence absolutely necessary ... That being which it hath was made, framed, and constituted by another.

This brief statement, extensively amplified by Pearson in his accompanying analysis, lays a significant conceptual foundation for natural theology. Since the created order is contingent, not necessary, it is able to bear at least something of the imprint and characteristics of its creator.

Second, patterns of growth and development observed in the created order today cannot be extrapolated to the primordial act of creation.[5]

> We see the plants grow from a seed; that is their ordinary way of generation: but the first place could not be so generated, because all seed in the same course of nature is from the preexisting plant.

Pearson's point is that the concept of creation necessarily entails the origination of all things out of nothing; it is therefore not possible to conceive that the first plant had its origins from seeds. More importantly, Pearson clearly assumes that all living things, plants and animals, are essentially and unchangeably derived from those originally created. The plants and animals then created are continuous with those we encounter today. "All things were created by the hand of God in the same manner, and at the same time."[6] It is not that the notion of the evolution of species is considered and rejected; the possibility was simply not known to Pearson and his contemporaries in the seventeenth century.

Third, Pearson distinguishes between *direct* and *mediate* creation. Some elements of the natural world were created directly by God; others were "created out of something formerly created out of nothing."[7] Pearson is therefore prepared to recognize a conceptually sequential understanding of creation, in which the earth brought forth plants, and humanity was created out of dust. There is an obvious and unresolved tension here with Pearson's earlier statement, noted above, that "all things were created by the hand of God in the same manner, and at the same time." Pearson thus affirmed his belief that "both heaven and earth and all things contained in them have not their being of themselves, but were made in the beginning; that the manner in which all things were made was by mediate or immediate creation."[8] God thus uses created entities to create further entities, in effect using secondary causes within the created order to advance the work of creation.

Although Pearson does not develop the notion, it will be clear that his idea of "mediate creation" is capable of conceptual expansion to embrace at least the fundamental elements, if not the precise details, of an evolutionary perspective. The line of thought may be expressed as follows:

> God creates A;
> God subsequently creates B from A;
> God therefore creates both A and B; A is created directly, and B through a created intermediary, A.

A variant of this approach was later developed by the conservative Reformed theologian Benjamin B. Warfield (1851–1921), who used it to demonstrate the consistency of a Christian doctrine of creation with some aspects of

Darwinian evolutionary theory.[9] Warfield argued that the term "creation" refers to God's primal act of bringing everything into being from nothing (*ex nihilo*). It thus describes God's initial creation of the universe, yet with the potential for further development under God's sovereign providential guidance. To express this developmental aspect of the matter, Warfield introduces the notion of "mediate creation," by which he meant the direct action of God on material entities, in which God brings about novelty – that is, something that was not originally present in the primary act of creation itself. Warfield does not hold that "naturalistic evolution" and "divine creation" are identical; he does, however, insist that they are consistent with each other, provided both are interpreted correctly.

Fourth, the world is of recent origin. Although Pearson briefly considers theories that suggest that the world might be millions of years old, he takes a firm position that it is a much more recent creation. While later editions of the work state that the creation of the world is to be dated "most certainly within not more than six, or at farthest seven, thousand years,"[10] the first edition of Pearson's *Exposition* states that the creation of the world is to be dated "most certainly within much less than six thousand years." Furthermore, Pearson refutes those philosophers and biblical scholars who suggest that there have been catastrophic destructions of the world by floods and fires in the past.

Such views were commonplace in the seventeenth century, and Pearson is to be seen as reflecting the consensus of the age. In his *City of God*, written during the period 413–27, Augustine of Hippo argued that the world was probably between five and six thousand years old.[11] This view appears to have gained wide cultural acceptance in England by the year 1600. For example, Rosalind, a character in Shakespeare's drama *As You Like It* (believed to have been written in 1599 or early 1600), declares that "the poor world is almost six thousand years old."[12] John Lightfoot (1602–75), Vice-Chancellor of the University of Cambridge, took the view that the world was created on Sunday, September 12, 3928 BC and that man was created five days later, at 9.00 a.m. on Friday, September 17.[13] James Ussher (1581–1656) famously dated creation to 4004 BC, on the basis of his somewhat problematic analysis of biblical chronologies.[14] Pearson here followed the wisdom of his age, having no particular reason to doubt it, and every reason to affirm it. Part of his agenda, it must be remembered, was to create a settled theological consensus in an age of political and religious instability.

The cultural influence of Pearson's work was substantial, and there can be little doubt that its theological framework was regarded as an exemplary embodiment of religious orthodoxy in the late seventeenth century. There being no substantial reason, scientific or theological, to accept any revision to his position, it became crystallized as normative within English Christian, especially

Anglican, circles.[15] The scientific revolution of the sixteenth and seventeenth centuries, which was primarily concerned with the physical sciences, did not call into question the age of the earth, or propose an evolutionary account of human origins. Indeed, the development of "mechanical" approaches to the universe could be argued to presuppose a "stable, uniquely created world maintained by general laws."[16] The idea of biological evolution did not fit into this mechanical worldview. It was not that the possibility of biological evolution was proposed and rejected; the prevailing model of the universe simply made the idea unthinkable.

The Polish sociologist Zygmunt Bauman has noted a general trend relating to any given "prevailing ideological fashion of the day," in which its "commonality is taken for the proof of its sense."[17] The evidence strongly suggests that English theologians of the seventeenth and eighteenth centuries simply assumed that the virtual ubiquity of this belief concerning the age of the earth was an indicator of its veracity. Having no scientific reasons to believe that it was anything else, they repeated past viewpoints.

The geological observations that would point to a much older date were gradually accumulating. The existence of fossils had been known since the classical era; Aristotle, for example, described them, and interpreted them as the remains of life forms. John Ray (1628–1705) noted that some fossils did not seem to correspond to any known living creatures, but argued that this reflected an incomplete contemporary knowledge of the earth's living species. Nicolaus Steno (1638–86) developed the theory of stratification to account for fossils being embedded in rocks,[18] but does not appear to have regarded his interpretation of the fossil record as requiring an extension of traditional biblical chronology.

The realization that the geological record pointed to substantially greater time frames for the history of the earth dates from the late eighteenth century. James Hutton (1726–97) explored the notion of "deep time" in the 1780s,[19] developing the idea that existing rock formations required substantially longer periods of time for their emergence than the biblical chronology permitted. It was not until the 1830s that the possibility that geology demanded considerably greater time than had previously been appreciated began to gain popular and scientific assent.[20] The work of Charles Lyell (1797–1885) was of considerable importance in highlighting the importance of geological issues in determining the age of the earth. William Buckland's Bridgewater Treatise proved particularly important in moving popular opinion away from biblical chronology. Noting the impact of geological discoveries of the last half-century, he argued that traditional biblical chronology was called into question by the "disclosures made by geology, respecting the lapse of very long periods of time, before the creation of man."[21] By 1850, the received consensus concerning the age of the earth was in flux. The traditional biblical chronology, which had crystallized over an extended period of time, was increasingly seen to be at variance with evidence pointing to a much older earth.

English natural theology of the Augustan age (1690–1745) represents a series of significant apologetic moves, constructed on the basis of a cultural consensus – one of the elements of which was that the world was created about six thousand years ago, in more or less its present form. Although many works of theology of this formative age undertook some modest engagement with the theological landmarks of the Christian tradition, this does not appear to have included a detailed or critical engagement with the patristic or medieval Christian understandings of the doctrine of creation. Indeed, there appears to be an implicit assumption that early Christian writers took views that were more or less identical with those of the seventeenth century.

Inevitably, such assumptions became part of a "sacred tradition" of natural theology, leading to the crystallization of the view that the Christian faith was defined by, and limited to, an essentially static view of creation. It is not difficult to see how Darwin's evolutionary views created serious difficulties for such a concept of creation. The erosion of the plausibility of such notions can be argued to have begun in the late eighteenth century, with Darwin's theory representing the climax of an increasingly important critique of traditional views of creation. It is therefore important to consider alternative perspectives within the Christian theological tradition on this matter – such as the views of Augustine of Hippo (354–430).

Creation as Event and Process: Augustine of Hippo

Perhaps the most important early Christian account of the doctrine of creation was developed by Augustine of Hippo in the early fifth century, in response to his reflections on the first three chapters of Genesis. Although Augustine wrote four commentaries on the creation narratives of Genesis,[22] the most significant and influential of these is entitled *De Genesi ad litteram* ("On the Literal Meaning of Genesis"), written between 401 and 415.[23] As the title makes clear, Augustine intended this to be a "literal" commentary on the text, in contrast to the then popular "allegorical" mode of interpretation, which saw the Old Testament as prefiguring the New.

One of the most important ideas developed in this commentary is that God's instantaneous action of creation *ex nihilo* is not to be understood as being limited to the primordial act of origination, but embraces both the origination of the world and the direction of the subsequent unfolding and development of "seminal reasons" (*rationes seminales* or *rationes causales*) embedded within the created order in God's act of creation. Augustine's basic argument is that God created the world complete with a series of dormant multiple potencies, which were actualized in the future through divine providence. Where some might think of creation in terms of God's insertion of new kinds of plants and animals ready-made, as it were, into an already existing world, Augustine rejects this as inconsistent with the overall witness of Scripture. Rather, God must be thought of as creating in that very first moment the potencies for all the kinds of living things that would come later, including humanity. Augustine illustrates this by considering how one might speak of the creation of a tree.[24]

> In the seed then, there was present invisibly everything that would develop in time into a tree. And we must visualize the world in the same way, when God made all things together, as having all things that were made in it and with it ... [This] includes also the beings which earth produced potentially and causally (*potentialiter atque causaliter*) before they emerged in the course of time.

Augustine's notion of "seminal reasons" is of critical importance, and needs careful consideration.[25] In elaborating his idea of instantaneous creation, Augustine argued that certain principles of order were embedded within the creation, which developed as appropriate at later stages. The idea was not original to Augustine, in that earlier Christian writers had noted how the first Genesis creation narrative spoke of the earth and the waters "bringing forth" living creatures, and had drawn the conclusion that this pointed to God endowing the natural order with a capacity to generate living things.[26] Augustine's contribution to the further development of this notion was the use of a powerful metaphor, almost certainly borrowed from Stoic writers, as an organizing principle. Augustine argued that *rationes seminales* were to be conceived as seed-like principles that are present from the cosmic beginning, in each of which is contained the potential for the later development of a specific living kind.[27] Augustine appeals to this notion in his interpretation of Genesis 1:12, which he holds to mean that the earth has received from God the power or capacity to produce things by itself:[28]

> Scripture has stated that the earth brought forth the crops and the trees causally (*causaliter*), in the sense that it received the power of bringing them forth. God created what was to be in times to come in the earth from the beginning, in what I might call the "roots of time."

The image of a seed provided Augustine with a suitable analogy on which he could draw to support his more general thesis about the role of potentially existing entities within the earth prior to their appearance in mature form when the conditions were right: "There is, indeed, in seeds some likeness to what I am describing because of the future developments stored up in them."[29] This also allowed him to maintain his emphasis on the simultaneous creation of all things, while additionally insisting that God, through his providence, was able to direct the subsequent actualization of the potentialities thus created.[30] What some might attribute to chance, the believer attributes to providence.[31] Yet Augustine was emphatic that these *rationes seminales* are not "seeds" in the normal sense of the term. Augustine appears to have conceived the *rationes seminales* as dormant "virtual" entities, enabling the natural world to emerge in its own way and in its own time.[32] The notion of the seed is heuristic, providing an inexact, though helpful, means of visualization for the theologically difficult yet important notion of God continuing to act within nature to actualize the potentialities embedded within the created order at the moment of its creation.[33] The image of the "seed" implies that the original creation contained within it the potentialities for all the living kinds that would subsequently emerge.

Augustine regularly cited John 5:17 (in which Jesus of Nazareth is reported as saying "My Father works until now, and so do I").[34] For Augustine, this text points to the fundamental coordination of the notions of creation and providence, so that the term "creation" has the extended meaning of an *original action* and a *continuing process*. Augustine envisages this in terms of the embedding or implanting of *rationes seminales* within the primordial created order, followed by their actualization at appropriate moments by divine agency. Though Augustine holds that the event and process are notionally distinct, the trajectory of divine agency is seen as continuous.

There are thus two "moments" in creation, corresponding to a primary act of origination, and a continuing process of providential guidance.[35] While conceding that there is a natural tendency to think of creation as a past event, he insists that God must be recognized to be working even now, in the present, sustaining and directing the unfolding of the "generations that he laid up in creation when it was first established."[36]

Augustine insists that this does not mean that God created the world incomplete or imperfect, in that "what God originally established in causes, he subsequently fulfilled in effects."[37] The world was created with an inbuilt potentiality to become what God intended it to be over time, which was bestowed in the primordial act of origination.[38]

> These were made by God in the beginning, when he made the world, and simultaneously created all things, which were to be unfolded in the ages to come. They are perfected, in that in their proper natures, by which they achieve their role in time, they possess nothing that was not already present in them causally. They have, however, just begun, since in them are the seeds, as it were, of the future perfections that would arise from their hidden state, and which would be manifested at the appropriate time.

This process of development, Augustine declares, is governed by fundamental laws, which reflect the will of their creator: "God has established fixed laws governing the production of kinds and qualities of beings, and bringing them out of concealment into full view, so that God's will might be over all."[39]

We see here an explicit affirmation of the role of divine providence in guiding the emergence of the natural world by "fixed laws (*certas leges*)." This notion would play an important role in guiding later thinking on the "laws of nature" or "scientific laws."[40] For our purposes, however, it is important to note Augustine's use of the idea of a providentially directed process of emergence to express a twofold notion of creation, both as primordial event with embedded possibilities, and the subsequence actualization of those possibilities over time.

Augustine's approach allowed him to interpret the first Genesis creation narrative as describing the instantaneous bringing into existence of primal matter, which already contained within it the causal resources for further development. The second Genesis creation narrative can then be interpreted as setting out the subsequent history of the chronological actualization of these causal possibilities from the earth.[41] His use of the notion of *rationes seminales* allowed Augustine both to declare that God made all things simultaneously, and also to state that the various sorts or kinds of living things made their appearance only gradually over unspecified (and presumably extended) periods of time.[42] Furthermore, this approach allowed Augustine to formulate a distinctive account of cosmic origins, based on the analogy of seeds and their dormant potentiality, which envisaged the natural realm as having a God-given capacity to develop.

Augustine's notion of the *rationes seminales* emerges from his biblical exegesis, shaped to some extent by philosophical categories with a history of use within the Christian tradition. His understanding of how these "seeds" develop is, however, shaped by the natural science of his day. Augustine clearly states the principle of "fixity of species," observing that "a bean does not emerge from a grain of wheat, nor does wheat emerge from a bean, or human beings from cattle, or cattle from human beings."[43] Yet on closer examination, Augustine appears to be making a *phenomenological*, rather than a more rigorously scientific, statement.

Elements of this doctrine of creation are found elsewhere in Augustine's writings, although they are not woven into a coherent theological vision. For example, the notion of God's operation through embedded causalities within nature is found in *De Trinitate*, one of Augustine's most widely read works.[44]

It is one thing to create and govern the creation internally, from the zenith of the causal nexus; only God, the creator, can do this. It is another thing to apply some operation externally, in proportion to the strength and capacities assigned to each creature by God, so that what is created may come forth at this or at that time, in this or that way. For in terms of their origins and beginning, all these things have already been created in some form of texture of the elements (*quadam textura elementorum*), and are awaiting the opportunity to come forth.

Having stated this general principle, Augustine then argues that God, having fashioned the world in such a manner that permits the subsequent execution and fulfillment of God's creative intentions, acts within the natural world to bring about the actualization of such potentialities.[45]

> Such an external application of generative causes, which are not natural yet operate according to nature (*non sunt naturales tamen secundum naturam*), takes place in order that those things which are contained in secret within nature may break forth and be externally created in some manner by the unfolding of the appropriate measures, numbers and weights which they have been given in secret (*in occulto*) by the one who "has ordered all things in measure and number and weight" (Wisdom 9:20).

Although Augustine does not develop his idea of God operating within the creation by means that are "not natural yet operate according to nature," this highly fertile notion is clearly capable of further elaboration. We shall explore these ideas further at a later point in this chapter.

Augustine thus interprets God's work of creation as including both an act and a process. The world is held to possess both a temporal beginning and an ontological origin, grounded in the effective will of a God. Yet the affirmation of neither the chronological origins nor the ontological foundations of creation necessarily implies that creation is to be interpreted as a *single complete action*. Rather, the notion of creation is argued to embrace both a primary act of bringing into existence, followed by a secondary act of development and enrichment. This notion, which was grounded in the biblical witness, was provided with theological elaboration from within the Platonic tradition, particularly the idea of "principles" (Greek: *logoi*; Latin: *rationes*) embedded within the creation by its creator.[46] It remains unclear whether the actualization of these embedded potentialities is to be envisaged as an extension of the primordial act of creation, or a fresh act of creation altogether. In both cases, however, it is clearly understood that the term "creation" embraces both a primordial action and subsequent developments.[47]

Even from this brief account of Augustine's theology of creation, it will be clear that it offers a helpful framework within which to develop a Christian account of biological evolution. Implicit within Augustine's account of creation is the notion that creation entails the origination of a potentially multi-leveled reality, whose properties *emerge* under certain conditions that either did not exist, or were not considered appropriate for development, at the origins of the universe. Augustine argues that the universe was brought into being with the intrinsic capacities to develop into its full form, subject to

God's guidance. Augustine was not alone in developing such approaches, which can be found in leading writers of the eastern Christian tradition, such as Maximus the Confessor[48] and Gregory Palamas.[49]

Augustine's ideas were taken up and developed during the Middle Ages. For example, Peter Lombard used Augustine's notion of *rationes seminales* to develop his doctrine of creation, as well as his understanding of the nature of divine causality within the natural order.[50] While certain types of causality were "beyond nature," Peter argued, others were delegated by God to the created order itself. The idea was given a more rigorous statement by Thomas Aquinas in the thirteenth century, and offers a positive framework within which to discuss the relation of Christian understandings of creation and divine causality to evolutionary thought.[51]

Yet these ideas play no role in the natural theology of the Augustan age, or its later statements in the writings of William Paley, who took the view that any assumption that nature is possessed of vital powers or inherent forces sufficient to create its own order was tantamount to atheism.[52] Paley's doctrine of creation was shot through with assumptions of the early modern period, which his generation was neither sufficiently theologically astute nor well enough informed to identify, let alone correct. Earlier, we noted Charles Kingsley's celebrated remark, arising from his reflections on Darwin's *Origin of Species*: "We knew of old that God was so wise that he could make all things; but, behold, he is so much wiser than even that, that he can make all things make themselves."[53] Why, it may reasonably be asked, did Kingsley not develop this idea from his reading of Augustine, rather than of Darwin?[54] Why was he not able to bring this theological framework to his reading of Darwin, and realize its potential resonance with what he found in the *Origin of Species*?

There is a serious historical issue here, in that Christian theologians of the mid-nineteenth century often read Darwin through the theological spectacles of classic Anglican writers such as Joseph Pearson, rather than of Augustine of Hippo. This, however, appears to be a historically conditioned practice, arising from a lack of knowledge of Augustine's characteristic ideas, as set out in *De Genesi ad litteram*.[55] The English Catholic biologist St George Mivart (1827–1900) is one of the few writers of this age to show knowledge of Augustine's approach in this significant treatise and to appreciate the importance of the framework it offered for accommodation of evolutionary perspectives. "St Augustine insists in a very remarkable manner on the merely derivative sense in which God's creation of organic forms is to be understood; that is, that God created them by conferring on the material world the power to evolve them under suitable conditions."[56]

Yet perhaps more significantly, Aubrey Moore (1848–90), widely regarded as one of the Anglican theologians capable of grasping the *real* theological significance of Darwin's theory,[57] explicitly cites Augustine's *De*

Genesi ad litteram in arguing that Augustine adopts an approach to creation "which, without any violence to language, we may call a theory of evolution."[58] Showing a familiarity with both patristic and scholastic theology that was ahead of his time, Moore proceeded to argue that Thomas Aquinas developed a similar approach in his *Summa Theologiae*. Moore's basic argument is that Christianity is *not* committed to a doctrine of the individual special creation of species, and that Augustine offers a framework of theological and apologetic importance in the dialogue with Darwinism. Moore's argument does not appear to have been heeded by late Victorian Christianity; there is no good reason why it should not be taken seriously now. Scientific advance since then has been paralleled by a deeper knowledge and understanding of early Christianity, allowing some of the misjudgments of the past to be corrected.

So what would have happened if Augustine's theology of creation, as set out in *De Genesi ad litteram*, had been widely known and accepted in Victorian England? Sadly, we can only speculate. Although the work was generally known during the Middle Ages (when it was known as the *Hexameron*), it was not widely read thereafter.[59] Despite its theological significance, no English translation of this work appeared until 1982.[60] Nevertheless, it is entirely reasonable to suggest that the progressive notion of creation that Augustine developed in this work could have accommodated the fundamental features of Darwin's approach. While history cannot be rewritten, it is surely proper to insist that this, and other such approaches to creation, are given due weight in contemporary debates about Darwinism and creation.[61] They may not have been known to Victorian theologians; their lack of familiarity with them is historically interesting, but must not be allowed to determine more informed theological engagements with Darwinism.

So what are the implications of Augustine's approach, particularly in relation to the notion of evolution? It must be noted immediately that Augustine is not offering a "scientific" account of creation; indeed, he goes to some trouble to emphasize that his concern is to set out an account of creation that clarifies the relationship between the creation and creator, while remaining agnostic and open about the final details. Augustine's concern is to affirm the divine origination of all reality *ex nihilo*, and its continuing dependence upon God, who guides and directs it toward its intended outcomes. Such theological principles are open to various scientific interpretations, not least concerning the chronology of creation. Perhaps Augustine's concerns are best expressed by suggesting that he is concerned to weave a controlling and illuminating theological strand into a scientific account of the natural order.

Augustine does not attempt any form of systematic translation of his doctrine of creation, particularly as this relates to the *rationes seminales*, to any scientific account of the origins and development of the natural world.[62] In part, this reflects his concern that biblical interpretation or dogmatic formulation might become trapped within the matrix of a specific historical or cultural situation.[63] Augustine argued for exegetical openness, rather than precommitment to existing interpretations of Scripture or doctrine, which might turn out, with the passage of time, to be wrong.[64] The wisdom of this approach can be appreciated from the perspective of the Copernican controversies, in which the church appeared to become needlessly locked into a pre-scientific mode of biblical interpretation,[65] erroneously assuming that a specific, historically located, way of interpreting the biblical text was to be equated with truth.

This point could be extended. Augustine and his contemporaries brought to their reading of Scripture a set of assumptions, inherited from numerous sources – such as their experience of the world, the culture of their day, and their reading of theologians. It is clear that Augustine, though a critical and creative thinker, absorbed a set of "minimally counterintuitive concepts" (Pascal Boyer) from his environment. One of them was that species do not undergo development over the lifespan of a human being. This assumption is clearly open to revision.

Yet although Augustine does not set out anything claiming to be a "scientific" account of reality, he nevertheless offers a theological framework that is well adapted for the accommodation of scientific observation and theoretical reflection. His theory of creation *ex nihilo* provides a schema, a mental map, or a set of theological spectacles allowing us to illuminate a scientific account of things, and bring it into sharp focus. Augustine's approach can function as the basis of a "big picture" approach to reality, emphasizing the capacity of faith to offer an interpretative framework, a conceptual standpoint from which the patterns of the world might be explored. This, it must be emphasized, stands at some considerable conceptual distance from the discredited notion of the "God of the gaps," which seeks God in the shadowy explanatory interstices of the universe.[66]

The doctrine of creation *ex nihilo*, which Augustine rightly discerned as a cornerstone of his belief in the ultimate and total dependency of the created order upon God, maps well onto the prevailing "standard cosmological model," which holds that the universe came into existence in a primordial moment of massive expansion, popularly known as the "Big Bang." The universe cannot be said to have caused its own existence, leaving wide open the question of the processes that led to its origination. The theological net that Augustine's doctrine of creation casts over this primordial event accommodates its uniqueness, while at the same time emphasizing its ultimate dependency upon God.

As we saw earlier (194–7), the universe can be considered to have come into existence with certain fundamental constants and laws embedded within it, governing its future development. The universe came into being already possessing the laws that would govern its subsequent development. That development is shaped by the laws and fundamental constants of nature, which turn out to be "fine-tuned" to values conducive to the emergence of life.[67] This fine-tuning does not really represent a proof of Christian belief in God; nevertheless, it is consonant with the Christian vision of God, which is believed to be true on other grounds, in that it offers a significant degree of intellectual resonance at points of importance. The theological matrix developed by Augustine allows us to "see" fine-tuning as consistent with Christian belief in a creator God, thus affirming conceptual resonance with, but not providing a deductive proof of, the Christian vision of God. Perhaps just as importantly, objections to religious belief based on Darwinism, whatever their merit might be, only come into play *once the biological evolutionary process has begun.* The "wider teleology" observed in the constants and laws of nature, themselves of deep significance for natural theology, remains of apologetic significance; indeed, without it, the evolutionary process itself could not have begun. Paradoxically, the evolutionary paradigm accentuates, rather than diminishes, the apologetic significance of the apparent fine-tuning of the universe.

We may now turn to explore one theme that emerges as significant within the theological matrix of creation, which is implicit in Augustine's doctrine of the *rationes seminales* – namely, that God causes creation to *emerge* over time, rather than creating it instantaneously in its final form.

Evolution and an Emergent Creation

The theological framework developed by Augustine has important implications for the theological accommodation of both contemporary cosmology and evolutionary biology on the one hand, and natural theology on the other. In particular, it is clear that Augustine's notion of creation implies potentialities that were not actualized in the first phase of the history of the universe, but were actualized, or enabled to emerge, once suitable conditions arose.

This approach is easily adapted to the growing interest in emergent approaches to creation. The term *emergence* is now widely used to refer to the development of novel, unpredictable properties and behaviors at increasing levels of complexity within the natural world.[68] Although the concept of "emergence" remains somewhat fluid, the notion is generally agreed to be characterized by four general features.[69]

1 Everything that exists in the world of space and time is held to be ultimately composed of the basic fundamental particles recognized by

physics. However, physics proves inadequate to explain how this material comes to be structured.

2 When ensembles or aggregates of material particles attain an appropriate level of organizational complexity, genuinely novel properties begin to emerge.

3 These emergent properties cannot be reduced to, or predicted from, the lower-level phenomena from which they emerge.

4 Higher-level entities exercise a causal influence on their lower-level constituents.

The overall picture is that of the emergence of complexity from simpler previous physical structures, leading to the creation of higher levels with properties not possessed by lower levels. A simple example of this phenomenon is provided by the behavior of gold metal, noted for its malleability, which allows it to be beaten into gold leaf, typically ten millionths of a centimeter thick. This property of metallic gold, however, only emerges when gold atoms aggregate; they cannot be predicted from the behavior of individual gold atoms.[70] The collective, macroscopic properties of gold cannot be deduced from the quantum mechanical description of gold atoms. An understanding of the behavior of individual gold atoms does not allow us to predict the way in which large assemblies of such atoms will behave. The macroscopic properties of gold are to be considered as emergent. They are already inbuilt into the nature of gold; they exist as potentialities, however, and hence cannot be observed until certain conditions are achieved – in this case, when aggregates of gold emerge.

The general principle here is that of properties of atoms that emerge at higher levels of complexity, yet cannot be predicted from a knowledge of lower levels. The behavior of gold atoms does not allow us to predict their macroscopic properties. The properties of water, many of which are of decisive importance for life,[71] cannot be predicted from knowledge of its two components, elemental hydrogen and oxygen. Similarly, the behavior of individual animals does not necessarily allow us to predict their behavior in groups. The observation of individual chimpanzees, for example, is of little help in predicting their social behavior in groups.[72] Colonies of ants, swarms of bees, and flocks of birds all demonstrate emergent properties of one form or another.[73]

Emergence becomes of particular significance in relation to complex biological structures, such as cells. In the case of such cells, complex signaling pathways emerge, demonstrating emergent properties such as integration of signals across multiple timescales, generation of distinct outputs depending on input strength and duration, and self-sustaining feedback loops.[74] Biological systems, by their very nature, are greater than the sum of their individual components; properties emerge that transcend those of their constituent parts.[75] These properties of biological systems cannot be predicted from a prior knowledge of their physical components.

This does not require the invocation of "new" or "unknown" forces; it can simply mean that collective properties arise from known mechanisms, but the manner in which these are actualized at higher levels cannot be predicted from a knowledge of their behavior at lower levels.[76] Once known, a retrodiction of this behavior may be offered; this, however, is not to be confused with prediction. Furthermore, it is important to avoid the error of believing that there is some temporal, causal process taking place that can be said to "create" a higher level out of the lower one.[77]

The basic idea is that of potential properties intrinsic to a given entity, which only become actualized or operationalized at a certain level of complexity. Such properties, although already present in a latent manner, are not enacted until a suitable context is established for their actualization. It will be clear that Augustine's theory of *rationes seminales*, though developed with a quite different concern in mind, nevertheless possesses a superfluity of interpretative potential, which makes it an appropriate theological framework for engagement with the phenomenon of emergence. Augustine's model of creation is essentially that of the evolution or emergence of more complex entities over time, as primordial possibilities are actualized by their creator. The potentialities already exist; their actualization requires an appropriate context, whether this is understood chronologically or contextually.

While it is clearly unwise to link Augustine's approach to any specific emergentist proposal, it is nevertheless interesting to set it alongside the taxonomy of emergence proposed by Harold Morowitz.[78] The first seven of Morowitz's twenty-eight stages of cosmic emergence concern the domain of the physical sciences. Large-scale cosmic structuring leads to the formation of the stars, rich in hydrogen and helium, which in turn leads to nucleosynthesis and the creation of heavier elements. This in turn leads to the formation of solar systems and the evolution of planets with geospheres. The eighth proposed step is transitional – the emergence of a biosphere. This results in the formation of self-replicating protocells and hence competition for resources. As a result, Morowitz argues, the world becomes Darwinian.

Morowitz's next twelve steps are biological, leading through prokaryotes and eukaryotes to multicellular organisms, and hence to the evolution of mammals. The twenty-first step marks a transition, with the appearance of our primate ancestors. This is followed by a series of cultural developments, such as the emergence of societies of hominids, and the evolution of language, philosophy, and spirituality.

Morowitz's analysis is open to challenge. Yet our concern is not with his specific proposal, but rather with the general principles that lie behind it. Each stage of advancing complexity makes possible still further advances, which could not have taken place at earlier stages. The spontaneous self-organization of cosmological structures leads to the formation of planets; molecular and chemical evolution leads to living cells and life in general; and a Darwinian process of natural selection leads to the emergence of high-level functionality, including the emergence of mind with its capacity to reflect on the natural world.[79] This is clearly capable of being accommodated within the context of the "wider teleology" (Thomas H. Huxley) that we considered in Chapters 6 and 7.

Augustine's approach clearly offers a conceptual framework capable of being extended and adapted to the modern discussion of the issues. An excellent example of this is provided by a recent proposal from the Danish theologian Niels Gregerson, who argues that nature is endowed with God-given propensities to navigate toward a God-determined goal.[80] Gregerson uses the biological term "autopoietic processes" as a conceptual framework to develop leading themes of a doctrine of creation.[81] While going beyond Augustine's specific notion of creation, Gregerson articulates some core themes that can be mapped directly onto Augustine's approach. For example, consider his important reflections on divine causality within nature, which make use of the idea of God as a "triggering cause" within the natural process, bringing about the actualization of potentialities:[82]

> God does not do anything that replaces the ordinary operations of nature. The workings of nature would still be the only triggering causes (like the Thomist concept of secondary causes). God is rather the underlying causality that enables the creatures to trigger themselves forth in their given setting.

Gregerson's model raises a further question. Our analysis thus far has largely focused on Augustine's notion of *rationes seminales* embedded within the created order. How are we to understand the associated idea that God acts within the created order – for example, to actualize the potential of these *rationes seminales*? How can we speak of God acting within nature or the evolutionary process – for example, as a "triggering cause"? We shall consider this in more detail in what follows.

God's Action within the Evolutionary Process

The Christian tradition has insisted upon the involvement of God within the natural world and its processes. One of the most contested areas in contemporary theological reflection concerns the nature of God's interaction within nature.[83] How can the agency of creative action be transferred from God to the created order itself, without implying the conceptual redundancy of God?[84] Those committed to ontological naturalism will dismiss this question, holding that the autonomy of natural processes is liable to be compromised through such theological speculation; others, however, regard it as of determinative importance if a meaningful engagement between evolutionary thought and the Christian faith is to take place.

The language of divine action is integral to both Old and New Testaments. The God of Israel is regularly and definitively depicted and described as a God who acts in history.[85] God's identity and character are made visible in the sphere of human action and reflection.[86] This, it must be emphasized, does not exhaust the depiction of Israel's God, who is represented as substantially more than a thoroughly masculine warrior God, exhibiting divine power in the control and manipulation of nature or in the defeat of Israel's enemies.[87] It is widely agreed that an excessive concentration on God's actions in nature and history can lead to the neglect of important themes (such as the more subtle unobtrusive forms of divine activity in everyday experience), as well as creating an essentially impersonal notion of God.[88] Yet despite these important qualifications, Israel understood and represented God as one who acted in nature and in history.[89] The New Testament maintains this tradition, and focuses it on the life, death, and resurrection of Jesus of Nazareth.[90]

The challenge is thus to integrate – or at least to correlate – this complex matrix of linguistic conventions and theological beliefs with contemporary scientific reflections. Three broad means of understanding divine action within the natural order have emerged in recent years:[91]

1   God is understood to act *directly* as the primary cause, or absolute ontological ground, of every entity or event. This approach classically focuses on God's action of creating and process of sustaining all finite things *ex nihilo*, although the notion of *creatio continua* redefines these notions significantly.
2   God is understood to act *indirectly* through the operation of created or secondary causes, governed by the laws of nature, which were themselves established by God's primary creative action. This can be understood as supplementing, not contradicting, direct divine action.[92]
3   God is understood to act by affecting the nexus of created causes to produce outcomes that would otherwise not have taken place. Chaos theory and quantum theory have increasingly been invoked to provide scientific legitimation for the notion of a space in which God can act, without disrupting the order of nature.

While most theologians affirm the first such approach, the explanatory emphasis since Darwin's time has clearly shifted toward the second and third of these possibilities.

An important distinction is generally drawn between "general divine action" and "special divine action."[93] General divine action designates the creation and sustaining of all reality in so far as this does not necessarily presume any specific providential divine intentions or purposes; special divine action designates specific providential acts, which are envisaged, intended, and executed by God in the natural world. The former is easily interpreted, for example, in terms of the establishment of the laws of nature. The latter, however, raises the question of whether God can be thought of as violating or transcending such laws in acting within the world. Having created the laws of nature, must not God act within them? While these questions are debated throughout the theological community, there are good reasons for thinking that those theologians involved in dialogue with the natural sciences tend to emphasize God's actions within the created structures of nature – in other words, what might be called "non-interventionist" modes of action.

The notion of indirect divine operation within nature by secondary causes governed by the "laws of nature" has played an important role in theological reflection throughout the scientific revolution.[94] Perhaps it was thus unsurprising that early Christian responses to Darwin's evolutionary theory picked up on its emphasis on the "laws impressed on matter by the Creator," a notion that was given a significantly higher profile in the second edition of the *Origin of Species* than in the first.[95] Darwin's approach at this point led to him being compared to Newton; just as Newton had uncovered the laws governing the worlds of astronomy and physics, so Darwin had uncovered those governing the biological world.[96]

This approach was developed by a number of Christian writers in the period immediately following the publication of Darwin's *Origin*, who suggested that God established a framework of laws that guided evolution to its intended outcomes. God acted indirectly upon nature, through the laws that governed its development, established at creation.[97] Aubrey Moore (1848–1890), for example, declared that the scientific laws of nature could be seen as one way of expressing the theological notion of providence. God's action was disclosed in natural laws, which were not to be understood in terms of the quasi-deism of Paley's natural theology, but in terms of an immanentist theology of nature, which Moore held to be much more compatible with Trinitarian Christian doctrine.[98]

> Science had pushed the deist's God further and further away, and at the moment when it seemed as if He would be thrust out altogether, Darwinism appeared, and, under the guise of a foe, did the work of a friend. It has conferred upon philosophy and religion an inestimable benefit, by showing us that we must choose between two alternatives. Either God is everywhere present in nature, or He is nowhere. He cannot delegate his power to demigods called "second causes." In nature everything must be his work, or nothing.

Although Moore's views on secondary causality seem misguided (Aquinas, for example, does not treat such causes as "demigods"), his analysis makes important points.

Yet some argued that an appeal to the laws of nature was a covert admission of the explanatory failure of theism. If events were governed by such laws, those laws were themselves a self-sufficient explanation of the realities of nature. God was, by definition, excluded and hence redundant. This position was discussed at an 1889 symposium on divine design in nature, organized by the Aristotelian Society. George Romanes (1848–1894), one of the more significant theological interpreters of Darwinism, objected to a colleague's interpretation of natural laws as excluding divine action.[99]

> It is tacitly assumed that when any phenomenon has received a proximate explanation at the hands of natural science, it has thereby been proved no longer susceptible of any more ultimate explanation at the hands of what may be termed supernatural theory; it is taken for granted that proof of physical causation is necessarily exclusive of any hypothesis of hyper-physical design.

This, Romanes argued, was clearly incorrect. The laws of nature, he argued, were to be seen as an expression of, not a substitute for, the creative action of a Trinitarian God within the world. Debate on this point has continued subsequently, with attention often focusing on the nature of the biological "laws" discerned within the natural world.[100]

This way of conceiving the manner of God's involvement within the natural process remains a live option for contemporary theology. Aubrey Moore's dismissal of the idea of God acting through "second causes" as being tantamount to deism seems to rest upon a misunderstanding of Thomist notions of causality, possibly arising from reading Aquinas in the light of David Hume's notion of causality.[101] It is important to appreciate that "causation" is ultimately an analogous notion when applied to God. A failure to appreciate the analogical status of the language being used in such discussions leads to God being portrayed as assuming roles that are played by material agents and causes. God is thus conceived as another cause or agent, alongside other causes or agents we are familiar with in the natural order of things.

Since about 1990, however, there has been growing interest in exploring the third option, appealing to quantum theory or chaos theory as offering a conceptual framework for divine action within nature. It is widely argued that the Newtonian worldview entailed a causally closed universe, leaving no room for God's special action in the natural realm. If God acted at all in nature, this would necessarily involve the suspension or violation of the laws of nature. This is classically expressed in David Hume's thoroughly Newtonian and deeply problematic definition of a miracle as "a transgression of a law of nature by a particular volition of the Deity or by the interposition of some invisible agent."[102] Hume is here influenced as much by a mechanistic physics as by a reductionistic philosophy. If the physical world is to be considered as a causally closed, deterministic system, any action of a divine free agent must entail a violation of natural processes.[103]

Yet the Newtonian worldview now lies in the past, replaced by a complex and as yet not totally integrated understanding of things, shaped by quantum mechanics and relativity theory. It is no longer possible to declare that science has demonstrated either the causal closure of the universe, or the impossibility of divine providence acting within its boundaries.[104] The leading representatives of the "Divine Action Project" – a significant scientific and theological investigation of what it means to speak of God acting in nature, co-sponsored by the Vatican Observatory and the Center for Theology and the Natural Sciences in Berkeley, California, between 1988 and 2003 – may have failed to achieve unanimity concerning how God's action in nature can be related to either quantum or chaos theory;[105] nevertheless, they certainly succeeded in demonstrating that this possibility could be maintained with integrity against its critics.

We must reiterate that what is being demonstrated here is *not* that quantum mechanics itself creates or protects conceptual space for certain theological positions, but that certain ways of *interpreting* quantum mechanics have this outcome. Robert Russell, for example, interprets quantum theory metaphysically as being ontologically open.[106] This is a real possibility; but it is nevertheless a contested interpretation of quantum mechanics. There is a clear debate to be had about the metaphysical status of the objects of our consideration. Are we speaking about a physical theory, or a mathematical model? Both deterministic and indeterministic interpretations of quantum theory have been developed, each of equal empirical inadequacy. To make one particularly obvious point: if Bohmian determinism were to prove more convincing than Heisenbergian indeterminism, non-interventionist approaches to divine action at the quantum level would be called into question.

So how might such approaches to divine action relate to the evolutionary process? The possibility of accounting for evolutionary change by genetic mutation linked to quantum indeterminacy has been under consideration for some time. In 1958, the physicist William Pollard set out his defining view that an omnipotent God controls all events and acts at the atomic level by means of the Heisenberg Uncertainty Principle.[107] Though not an evolutionary biologist, Pollard argued that this physical principle had biological implications: genetic mutation was to be understood as arising from quantum indeterminacy.[108]

This approach was developed further by Robert Russell, who argued that genetic mutations represent an example of how what he terms a "quantum event" could give rise to a significant macroscopic consequence.[109] Russell argues that "God does not act by violating or suspending the stream of natural processes, but by acting within them."[110] This divine action affects "those genetic variations in which quantum processes play a significant role in biological evolution."[111] Russell's theology here runs somewhat ahead of the scientific consensus. While he is entirely right to emphasize the critical role that genetic mutation is regarded as playing in the evolutionary synthesis,[112] it is rather less clear how these genetic mutations could be said to be caused by "quantum events." Russell wisely concedes, with the graceful elegance of understatement, that "further scientific research is required for us to gain a clearer understanding of the relative importance of quantum processes and classical processes in variation." We don't really know what role "quantum processes" play here; in fact, it's not really clear what these "quantum processes" are in the first place. However, it is clear that the door has been opened to some potentially constructive explorations.

Others have explored alternative approaches, also of potential interest to evolutionary theism. Dissatisfied with approaches based on quantum indeterminacy, Arthur Peacocke moved away from his earlier "embodied" approach to divine causality,[113] and developed a notion of "top-down" causality, by which God's intentions and purposes are implemented in the shaping of particular events, or patterns of events, without any abrogation of the laws of nature.[114] John Polkinghorne, while conceding openness within natural processes at the level of quantum events, does not believe that that this can by itself provide a plausible account of divine action in nature.[115] The relationship between action at the quantum and macroscopic levels remains unclear. Although Polkinghorne recognizes the potential of chaos theory as a means of positing metaphysical openness within nature, the "grave and unresolved difficulties of relating quantum theory to chaos theory" cannot be overlooked. Polkinghorne himself has developed the theological category of *kenosis* as a means of affirming the autonomy of creation, the self-limitation of divine power, and the self-limitation of divine knowledge.[116] Unfortunately, Polkinghorne appears to misunderstand the Christological dimensions of this rich and fertile notion,[117] and interprets it essentially as God getting out of the way, so that natural processes (even if God-originated) may proceed without divine interference. The attempts of both Peacocke and Polkinghorne to explore possible scientific frameworks for accommodating our understanding of divine action are to be applauded,[118] even though their limits must be conceded.

This brief discussion of the possibility of divine action within the evolutionary process has implications for our earlier reflections on whether the evolutionary process may be considered to be teleological (185–202), and how the existence of such extensive suffering within it can be reconciled with the divine goodness (202–7). However, we must now move on to consider one of the most difficult and challenging questions raised for natural theology by evolutionary biology – namely, whether natural theology itself can be thought of simply as an evolutionary outcome.

239 The Concept of Creation

Notes

1   Dennett, Daniel C., *Darwin's Dangerous Idea: Evolution and the Meaning of Life*. New York: Simon & Schuster, 1995, 76.

2   Counterfactual history is, however, of importance in emphasizing the role of contingencies in shaping the course of history: see Hawthorn, Geoffrey, *Plausible Worlds: Possibility and Understanding in History and the Social Sciences*. Cambridge: Cambridge University Press, 1993, 1–37.

3   For what follows, see Pearson, John, *An Exposition of the Creed*. Oxford: Clarendon Press, 1877, 84–122.

4   Pearson, *Exposition of the Creed*, 88.

5   Pearson, *Exposition of the Creed*, 98.

6   Pearson, *Exposition of the Creed*, 111.

7   Pearson, *Exposition of the Creed*, 99.

8   Pearson, *Exposition of the Creed*, 122.

9   For a discussion, see Livingstone, David N., and Mark A. Noll, "B. B. Warfield (1851–1921): A Biblical Inerrantist as Evolutionist." *Isis* 91 (2000): 283–304, especially 299–300. Warfield was opposed to Darwinism primarily on two grounds: first, that it constituted a totalizing worldview; and second, on account of his understanding of its emphasis upon the decisive role of "randomness" within the evolutionary process.

10   Pearson, *Exposition of the Creed*, 122.

11   Augustine of Hippo, *De civitate Dei*, XII.11.

12   *As You Like It*, Act IV, Scene 1.

13   See Lightfoot, James, *A Few, and New Observations Upon the Booke of Genesis*. London: T. Badger, 1642, prolegomenon (unpaginated). Lightfoot dates the creation of the world to the equinox in September of 3928, using the Julian calendar. Lightfoot's calculations are often confused with those of James Ussher, as in the otherwise helpful study of Brice, William R., "Bishop Ussher, John Lightfoot and the Age of Creation." *Journal of Geological Education* 30 (1982): 18–24.

14   Barr, James, "Why the World Was Created in 4004 BC: Archbishop Ussher and Biblical Chronology." *Bulletin of the John Rylands University* 67 (1984–5): 575–608.

15   Middleton, Arthur, *Fathers and Anglicans: The Limits of Orthodoxy*. Leominster: Gracewing, 2001, 180–1.

16   A point emphasized by Mayr, Ernst, *The Growth of Biological Thought*. Cambridge, MA: Belknap Press, 1982, 309.

17   Bauman, Zygmunt, "On Writing Sociology." *Theory, Culture & Society* 17 (2000): 79–90, especially 79.

18   For his impact, see Kuznetsov, V. K., "Nicolaus Steno and Sessions of the International Geological Congress." *Lithology and Mineral Resources* 40 (2005): 483–6. For a popular account, see Cutler, Alan, *The Seashell on the Mountaintop: A Story of Science, Sainthood, and the Humble Genius Who Discovered a New History of the Earth*. New York: Random House, 2003.

19   Baxter, Stephen, *Ages in Chaos: James Hutton and the Discovery of Deep Time.*
      New York: Forge, 2004, 187–221.
20   Schopf, J. William, *Cradle of Life: The Discovery of Earth's Earliest Fossils.*
      Princeton, NJ: Princeton University Press, 1999, 35–70.
21   Buckland, William, *Geology and Mineralogy Considered with Reference to
      Natural Theology.* 2nd edn. London: Pickering, 1837, 8.
22   For Augustine's developing understandings of these passages, see Kim, Yoon Kyung,
      *Augustine's Changing Interpretations of Genesis 1–3: From De Genesi Contra
      Manichaeos to De Genesi Ad Litteram.* Lewiston, NY: Edwin Mellen Press, 2006.
23   It is important to distinguish the complete mature work *De Genesi ad litteram
      libri duodecim* (401–15) from the incomplete earlier work *De Genesi ad lit-
      teram imperfectus liber* (393–4). All references in this chapter are to the com-
      plete mature work. See further note 60.
24   Augustine, *De Genesi ad litteram*, V.xxiii.45.
25   For one of the best accounts of this notion, including discussion of its intellec-
      tual provenance and fecundity, see McMullin, Ernan, "Introduction." In
      Evolution and Creation, ed. Ernan McMullin, 1–58. Notre Dame, IN: University
      of Notre Dame Press, 1985, especially 8–16. See also McGrath, Alister E.,
      A Fine-Tuned Universe: The Quest for God in Science and Theology. Louisville,
      KY: Westminster John Knox Press, 2009, 95–108.
26   McMullin, "Introduction," 12.
27   See further McKeough, Michael J., *The Meaning of the Rationes Seminales in
      St Augustine.* Washington: Catholic University of America Press, 1926, 20–2.
28   Augustine, *De Genesi ad litteram*, V.iv.11.
29   Augustine, *De Genesi ad litteram*, VI.vi.11.
30   Augustine, *De Genesi ad litteram*, V.xxiii.44–6. For the appeal to both creation
      and conservation in medieval theological arguments against the eternity of the
      world, see Cross, Richard, "The Eternity of the World and the Distinction
      between Creation and Conservation." *Religious Studies* 42 (2006): 403–16.
31   Augustine, *De Genesi ad litteram*, V.xxi.42–xxii.43.
32   Augustine, *De Genesi ad litteram*, VI.x.17. "Sed etiam ista secum gerunt tam-
      quam iterum seipsa invisibiliter in occulta quadam vi generandi, quam extraxerunt
      de illis primordiis causarum suarum, in quibus creato mundo cum factus est dies,
      antequam in manifestam speciem sui generis exorerentur, inserta sunt."
33   Augustine, *De Genesi ad litteram*, VI.vi.10–11; IV.xvi.27: "alia quadam notitia
      colligitur inesse in natura quiddam latens."
34   See, for example, Augustine, *De Genesi ad litteram*, IV.xi.21; V.xx.40.
35   Augustine, *De Genesi ad litteram*, V.iv.11.
36   Augustine, *De Genesi ad litteram*, V.xx.41–2.
37   Augustine, *De Genesi ad litteram*, VI.xi.19.
38   Augustine, *De Genesi ad litteram*, VI.xi.18.
39   Augustine, *De Genesi ad litteram*, VI.xiii.23. "Ita enim certas temporum leges
      generibus qualitatibusque rerum in manifestum ex abdito producendis attribuit,
      ut eius voluntas sit super omnia."
40   For the subsequent use of significant phrases such as "quasdam certas leges,"
      see Ruby, Jane E., "The Origins of Scientific 'Law'." *Journal of the History of
      Ideas* 47 (1986): 341–59.

41 For Augustine's various attempts to reconcile these creation narratives, see Kim, *Augustine's Changing Interpretations of Genesis 1–3*, 131–61.

42 Augustine saw time as an aspect of God's creation, and was thus able to integrate the role of time in the actualization of potentiality within his overall doctrine of creation: Knuuttila, Simo, "Time and Creation in Augustine." In *The Cambridge Companion to Augustine*, ed. Eleonore Stump and Norman Kretzmann, 103–15. Cambridge: Cambridge University Press, 2001. Note also Gross, Charlotte, "Augustine's Ambivalence About Temporality: His Two Accounts of Time." *Medieval Philosophy and Theology* 8 (1999): 129–48.

43 Augustine, *De Genesi ad litteram*, IX.xvii.32.

44 Augustine, *De Trinitate*, III.ix.16.

45 Augustine, *De Trinitate*, III.ix.16. For further comment, see Gioia, Luigi, *The Theological Epistemology of Augustine's De Trinitate*. Oxford Theological Monographs. Oxford: Oxford University Press, 2008, 239–59.

46 For this idea in other early Christian writers, see Dalmais, Irénée Henri, "La Théorie des 'Logoi' des créatures chez S. Maxime le Confesseur." *Revue des sciences philosophiques et théologiques* 36 (1952): 244–9; Edwards, Mark J., "Justin's *Logos* and the Word of God." *Journal of Early Christian Studies* 3 (1995): 261–80; Leonhardt-Balzer, Jutta, "Der Logos und die Schöpfung: Streiflichter bei Philo (Op 20–25) und im Johannesprolog (Joh 1, 1–18)." In *Kontexte des Johannesevangeliums: Das vierte Evangelium in religions- und traditionsgeschichtlicher Perspektive*, ed. Jörg Frey and Udo Schnelle, 295–319. Tübingen: Mohr Siebeck, 2004.

47 For a modern variant of relevance to this discussion, see Polkinghorne, John, "The Inbuilt Potentiality of Creation." In *Debating Design: From Darwin to DNA*, ed. William A. Dembski and Michael Ruse, 246–60. Cambridge: Cambridge University Press, 2004.

48 Thunberg, Lars, *Microcosm and Mediator: The Theological Anthropology of Maximus the Confessor*. 2nd edn. Chicago, IL: Open Court, 1995, 72–9.

49 Thunberg, Lars, *Man and the Cosmos: The Vision of St Maximus the Confessor*. Crestwood, NY: St Vladimir's Seminary Press, 1985, 137–43; Rossum, Joost van, "The *Logoi* of Creation and the Divine 'Energies' in Maximus the Confessor and Gregory Palamas." *Studia Patristica* 27 (1993): 213–17.

50 Bartlett, Robert, *The Natural and Supernatural in the Middle Ages*. Cambridge: Cambridge University Press, 2008, 4–7.

51 For its application and further discussion, see Carroll, William E., "Creation, Evolution, and Thomas Aquinas." *Revue des Questions Scientifiques* 171 (2000): 319–48; Carroll, William E., "At the Mercy of Chance? Evolution and the Catholic Tradition." *Revue des Questions Scientifiques* 177 (2006): 179–204.

52 Paley, William, *Natural Theology: Or, Evidences of the Existence and Attributes of the Deity*. 12th edn. London: Faulder, 1809, 427–34.

53 Kingsley, Charles, "The Natural Theology of the Future." In *Westminster Sermons*, v–xxxiii. London: Macmillan, 1874, xxv. Like Augustine, Kingsley saw this process as being directed by divine providence (xxiv–xxv).

54 Two questions need to be explored here, both lying beyond the scope of this study: first, the general Victorian awareness of Augustine's theology of creation,

as set out in *De Genesi ad litteram*; and second, Kingsley's own attitudes toward the ideas of "primitive Christianity" in general, and of Augustine in particular. Kingsley was fiercely anti-Catholic, and tended to see Augustine specifically as a fountainhead for Catholic thought. He was also hostile toward the Oxford Movement, and regarded an interest in patristic thought with suspicion as a result. Kingsley's attitudes to the patristic theological heritage are best explored through his novels, some of which deal with this period: see, for example, Dorman, Susann, "Hypatia and Callista: The Initial Skirmish between Kingsley and Newman." *Nineteenth-Century Fiction* 34 (1979): 173–93.

55 There is ample evidence that Victorian writers knew and made good use of Augustine's *Confessions*, which were readily available in translation: see, for example, Cotter, James Finn, "Hopkins and Augustine." *Victorian Poetry* 39 (2001): 69–82.

56 Mivart, St George, *On the Genesis of Species*. New York: Appleton, 1871, 281. Mivart appeals particularly to *De Genesi ad litteram* V.v.14: "Terrestria animalia, tanquam ex ultimo elemento mundi ultima; nihilominus *potentialiter*, quorum numeros tempus postea visibiliter explicaret." He also correctly noted the theological potential of evolutionary convergence. It should be noted, however, that Mivart was regarded as unorthodox by many in the Catholic church of his day. For discussion, see O'Leary, Don, *Roman Catholicism and Modern Science: A History*. New York: Continuum, 2006, 78–93.

57 England, Richard, "Natural Selection, Teleology, and the Logos: From Darwin to the Oxford Neo-Darwinists, 1859–1909." *Osiris* 16 (2001): 270–87, especially 278–81.

58 Moore, Aubrey, *Science and the Faith: Essays on Apologetic Subjects*. London: Kegan, Paul, Trench, Trubner, 1889, 176, citing Augustine, *De Genesi ad litteram* V.v.xxviii. Note also his comments about Augustine suggesting that the "germs of all things were at first created" (p. 228).

59 A point emphasized by O'Meara, John, "Saint Augustine's Understanding of the Creation and Fall." *Maynooth Review* 10 (1984): 52–62, especially 52–3.

60 This excellent translation was undertaken by John H. Taylor: *The Literal Meaning of Genesis*. 2 vols. Ancient Christian Writers No. 41–42. New York: Newman Press, 1982.

61 The concept of "continuous creation (*creation continua*)" is often used to refer to this notion: see Härle, Wilfried, *Dogmatik*. 3rd edn. Berlin: De Gruyter, 2007, 423–5. While the notion has found wide acceptance, it should be used with caution: see, for example, the critical comments of Oliver O'Donovan: "Classical Christian theology took trouble to distinguish between the ideas of 'creation' and 'providence' ... The modern faith in 'continuous creation' is merely the latest form in which forgetfulness of this dialectic between order and contingency betrays itself." O'Donovan, Oliver, *Resurrection and Moral Order*. Grand Rapids, MI: Eerdmans, 1986, 61.

62 Others, however, would use the notion during the scientific revolution of the seventeenth century. See, for example, the case of Pierre Gassendi (1592–1655): Osler, Margaret J., "Whose Ends? Teleology in Early Modern Natural Philosophy." *Osiris* 16 (2001): 151–68, especially 160–1.

63 Augustine, *De Genesi ad litteram*, II.xviii.38.

64 Augustine, *De Genesi ad litteram*, I.xviii.37.

65 See the analysis in Blackwell, Richard J., *Galileo, Bellarmine and the Bible*. Notre Dame, IN: University of Notre Dame Press, 1991.

66 See the poem of R. S. Thomas, "*Via Negativa*"; in Thomas, R. S., *Collected Poems 1945–1990*. London: Dent, 1993, 220.

67 See Davies, Paul, *The Goldilocks Enigma: Why Is the Universe Just Right for Life?* London: Allen Lane, 2006, 147–71. For a much more detailed theological engagement with such issues, see Holder, Rodney D., *God, the Multiverse, and Everything: Modern Cosmology and the Argument from Design*. Aldershot: Ashgate, 2004; McGrath, *Fine-Tuned Universe*, 109–201.

68 For an excellent introduction, see Silberstein, Michael, "Reduction, Emergence, and Explanation." In *Blackwell Guide to the Philosophy of Science*, ed. Peter Machamer and Michael Silberstein, 80–107. Oxford: Blackwell, 2002.

69 See Clayton, Philip, "Conceptual Foundations of Emergence Theory." In *The Re-Emergence of Emergence: The Emergentist Hypothesis from Science to Religion*, ed. Philip Clayton and Paul Davies, 1–31. Oxford: Oxford University Press, 2006; Clayton, Philip, "Toward a Constructive Christian Theology of Emergence." In *Evolution and Emergence: Systems, Organisms, Persons*, ed. Nancey Murphy and William R. Stoeger, 315–43. Oxford: Oxford University Press, 2007.

70 Kauffman, Stuart A., *Investigations*. Oxford: Oxford University Press, 2000, 127–8.

71 See the discussion in McGrath, *Fine-Tuned Universe*, 143–53.

72 As noted by Smuts, Barbara, "Emergence in Social Evolution: A Great Ape Example." In *The Re-Emergence of Emergence: The Emergentist Hypothesis from Science to Religion*, ed. Philip Clayton and Paul Davies, 166–86. Oxford: Oxford University Press, 2006.

73 Seeley, Thomas D., P. Kirk Visscher, and Kevin M. Passino, "Group Decision Making in Honey Bee Swarms." *American Scientist* 94 (2006): 220–9.

74 Bhalla, Upinder S., and Ravi Iyengar, "Emergent Properties of Biological Signaling Pathways." *Science* 283 (1999): 381–7. For the emergence of cellular networks, particularly feedback mechanisms, see Alon, Uri, *An Introduction to Systems Biology: Design Principles of Biological Circuits*. Boca Raton, FL: Chapman & Hall, 2007, 41–70.

75 Bechtel, William, and Robert C. Richardson, "Emergent Phenomena and Complex Systems." In *Emergence or Reductionism?*, ed. Ansgar Beckermann, Hans Flohr, and Jaegwon Kim, 257–88. Berlin: De Gruyter, 1992. See further Ricard, Jacques, "Reduction, Integration and Emergence in Biochemical Networks." *Biology of the Cell* 96 (2004): 719–25; Korn, Robert W., "The Emergence Principle in Biological Hierarchies." *Biology and Philosophy* 20 (2005): 137–51.

76 See the important discussion in Emmeche, Claus, Simo Koppe, and Frederick Stjernfelt, "Explaining Emergence: Towards an Ontology of Levels." *Journal for General Philosophy of Science* 28 (1997): 83–119.

77 Emmeche, Koppe, and Stjernfelt, "Explaining Emergence," 93–4.

78 Morowitz, Harold J., *The Emergence of Everything: How the World Became Complex*. Oxford: Oxford University Press, 2002, 25–38.

244 The Concept of Creation

79 The emergence of mind is one of the most significant and contentious issues to be discussed at present. See the useful review in Murphy, Nancey, "Emergence and Mental Causation." In *The Re-Emergence of Emergence: The Emergentist Hypothesis from Science to Religion*, ed. Philip Clayton and Paul Davies, 227–43. Oxford: Oxford University Press, 2006.

80 Gregersen, Niels H., "The Idea of Creation and the Theory of Autopoietic Processes." *Zygon* 33 (1998): 333–67.

81 Gregersen, "The Idea of Creation and the Theory of Autopoietic Processes," 347–62.

82 Gregersen, "The Idea of Creation and the Theory of Autopoietic Processes," 359. Brun's suggestion that Gregerson has here lapsed into "process thought" shows a lack of familiarity with the Christian tradition of reflection on creation: Brun, Rudolph B., "Does God Play Dice? A Response to Niels H. Gregersen, 'The Idea of Creation and the Theory of Autopoietic Processes'." *Zygon* 34 (1999): 93–100.

83 Important recent discussions of this question include Thomas, Owen, ed., *God's Activity in the World: A Contemporary Problem*. Chico: Scholars Press, 1983; Tracy, Thomas F., *God, Action, and Embodiment*. Grand Rapids: Eerdmans, 1984; Tracy, Thomas F., ed., *The God Who Acts: Philosophical and Theological Explorations*. University Park, PA: Pennsylvania State University Press, 1994.

84 The best discussion of the specifically scientific aspects of this is Saunders, Nicholas, *Divine Action and Modern Science*. Cambridge: Cambridge University Press, 2002.

85 For a good review of the primary and secondary sources on this point, see Fretheim, Terence E., "The God Who Acts: An Old Testament Perspective." *Theology Today* 54 (1997): 6–18.

86 The narrative of God's action is thus seen as disclosing or "rendering" God's character: see Kelsey, David, *The Uses of Scripture in Recent Theology*. Philadelphia: Fortress, 1975, 39–50.

87 For comment, see Craigie, Peter C., *The Problem of War in the Old Testament*. Grand Rapids, MI: Eerdmans, 1978; Lind, Millard C., *Yahweh Is a Warrior: The Theology of Warfare in Ancient Israel*. Scottdale, PA: Herald, 1980.

88 See the comments in Fretheim, "The God Who Acts," 7.

89 For a detailed examination of one such instance of divine action, see Johnson, William Stacy, "God's Ordering, Providing, and Caring for the World: Grace as 'Gift of Death'." *Theology Today* 54 (1997): 29–42.

90 See, for example, Wright, N. T., *The Resurrection of the Son of God*. London: SPCK, 2003, 20–8; Vanhoozer, Kevin J., *Remythologizing Theology: Divine Action, Passion, and Authorship*. Cambridge: Cambridge University Press, 2010, 33–80.

91 Ward, Keith, *Divine Action*. London: HarperCollins, 1990; Freddoso, Alfred J., "God's General Concurrence with Secondary Causes: Pitfalls and Prospects." *American Catholic Philosophical Quarterly* 68 (1994): 131–56; Tracy, *The God Who Acts*; Polkinghorne, John, "Natural Science, Temporality, and Divine Action." *Theology Today* 55 (1998): 329–43; Russell, Robert J., "Does the 'God Who Acts' Really Act? New Approaches to Divine Action in Light of Science." *Theology Today* 54 (1997): 43–65; Wildman, Wesley J., "The Divine

Action Project, 1988–2003." *Theology and Science* 2 (2004): 31–75; Smedes, Taede A., *Chaos, Complexity, and God: Divine Action and Scientism*. Louvain: Peeters, 2004.

92 Bartlett, *The Natural and the Supernatural in the Middle Ages*, 4–7.

93 For the distinction, see Wildman, "The Divine Action Project, 1988–2003," 37.

94 For an excellent historical survey of such developments, see Harrison, Peter, "The Development of the Concept of Laws of Nature." In *Creation: Law and Probability*, ed. Fraser Watts, 13–36. Aldershot: Ashgate, 2008.

95 See the analysis in Brooke, John Hedley, " 'Laws Impressed on Matter by the Creator'? The *Origins* and the Question of Religion." In *The Cambridge Companion to the "Origin of Species,"* ed. Michael Ruse and Robert J. Richards, 256–74. Cambridge: Cambridge University Press, 2009.

96 Cornell, John F., "Newton of the Grassblade? Darwin and the Problem of Organic Teleology." *Isis* 77 (1986): 405–21.

97 England, "Natural Selection, Teleology, and the Logos."

98 Moore, Aubrey, "The Christian Doctrine of God." In *Lux Mundi: A Series of Studies in the Religion of the Incarnation*, ed. Charles Gore, 57–109. London: John Murray, 1890, 99.

99 Gildea, William L., S. Alexander, and G. J. Romanes, "Symposium: Is There Evidence of Design in Nature?" *Proceedings of the Aristotelian Society* 1, no. 3 (1889–90): 49–76, especially 68–9.

100 Press, Joel, "Physical Explanations and Biological Explanations, Empirical Laws and a Priori Laws." *Biology and Philosophy* 24 (2009): 359–74.

101 See Carroll, William E., "Divine Agency, Contemporary Physics, and the Autonomy of Nature." *Heythrop Journal* 49 (2008): 582–602. Carroll notes how "too often, those who examine the distinction Thomas draws between primary and secondary causality, read Aquinas in the light of a Humean understanding of cause" (p. 597 n. 20). See further Carroll, William E. "Aquinas on Creation and the Metaphysical Foundations of Science." *Sapientia* 54 (1999): 69–91.

102 Hume, David, *A Dialogue Concerning Human Understanding*. Oxford: Oxford University Press, 1975, 90.

103 This theme dominates the somewhat disappointing account of divine action in Wiles, Maurice F., *God's Action in the World*. London: SCM Press, 1986.

104 Cushing, James T., "Quantum Theory and Explanatory Discourse: Endgame for Understanding?" *Philosophy of Science* 58 (1991): 337–58.

105 For a summary and evaluation, see Wildman, "The Divine Action Project"; Lameter, Christoph, *Divine Action in the Framework of Scientific Knowledge: From Quantum Theory to Divine Action*. 1st edn. Newark, CA: Christianity in the 21st Century, 2005, 153–96.

106 Russell, "Does the 'God Who Acts' Really Act?"

107 Pollard, William G., *Chance and Providence; God's Action in a World Governed by Scientific Law*. New York: Scribner, 1958. For an assessment of Pollard's significance, see Fagg, Lawrence W., "Remembering William G. Pollard." *Theology and Science* 8 (2010): 101–7.

108 Pollard, *Chance and Providence*, 56. Pollard (1911–89) was the first Executive Director of the Oak Ridge Institute of Nuclear Studies.

109 Russell, Robert J., "Special Providence and Genetic Mutation: A New Defense of Theistic Evolution." In *Evolutionary and Molecular Biology: Scientific Perspectives on Divine Action*, ed. Robert John Russell, William R. Stoeger, and Francisco J. Ayala, 191–223. Vatican City: Vatican Observatory, 1998. For alternative approaches of potential biological relevance, see Peacocke, Arthur, "God's Action in the Real World." *Zygon* 26 (1991): 455–76; Birch, Charles, "Neo-Darwinism, Self-Organization, and Divine Action." In *Evolutionary and Molecular Biology: Scientific Perspectives on Divine Action*, ed. Robert John Russell, William R. Stoeger, and Francisco J. Ayala, 225–48. Vatican City: Vatican Observatory, 1998.

110 Russell, "Special Providence and Genetic Mutation," 195.

111 Russell, "Special Providence and Genetic Mutation," 196.

112 Russell, "Special Providence and Genetic Mutation," 205–6.

113 On which see Peacocke, Arthur, *Creation and the World of Science*. Oxford: Oxford University Press, 1979, 142–207.

114 Peacocke, Arthur R., "God's Interaction with the World: The Implications of Deterministic 'Chaos' and of Interconnected and Interdependent Complexity." In *Chaos and Complexity. Scientific Perspectives on Divine Action*, ed. Robert J. Russell, Nancey Murphy, and Arthur R. Peacocke, 263–88. Vatican City: Vatican Observatory, 1995. See further Smedes, *Chaos, Complexity, and God*, 107–71.

115 Polkinghorne, John, "The Metaphysics of Divine Action." In *Chaos and Complexity. Scientific Perspectives on Divine Action*, ed. Robert J. Russell, Nancey Murphy, and Arthur R. Peacocke, 147–56. Vatican City: Vatican Observatory, 1995. See further Smedes, *Chaos, Complexity, and God*, 33–105.

116 Polkinghorne, John, "Kenotic Creation and Divine Action." In *The Work of Love: Creation as Kenosis*, ed. John Polkinghorne, 90–106. London: SPCK, 2001.

117 Note especially the recent analysis in Chapman, Mark D., "Charles Gore, Kenosis and the Crisis of Power." *Journal of Anglican Studies* 3 (2005): 197–218. See also the older study of Dawe, Donald G., "A Fresh Look at the Kenotic Christologies." *Scottish Journal of Theology* 15 (1962): 337–49.

118 Smedes regards both Peacocke and Polkinghorne as having incorporated significant "scientistic" assumptions with their approaches: Smedes, *Chaos, Complexity, and God*, 207–9. This somewhat improbable judgment, which both Peacocke and Polkinghorne vigorously contest, rests on a redefinition of scientism as a mode of thinking that influences our understanding of what is possible in the universe, which is so broad that it is of little value. Smedes's approach seems to me to lead to a distancing of theology from any constructive dialogue with the natural sciences, which is as unnecessary as it is lacking in value. See Barbour, Ian G., "Taking Science Seriously without Scientism: A Response to Taede Smedes." *Zygon* 43 (2008): 259–69.

9

Universal Darwinism: Natural Theology as an Evolutionary Outcome?

The present work focuses specifically on the relation between natural theology and evolutionary thought, rather than more general questions relating to the possible evolutionary origins of religion or ethics. The second part of this work was concerned with considering some historical aspects of the complex and shifting relationship between evolutionary thought and natural theology, culminating in the publication of Darwin's *Origin of Species* in 1859. The century following the publication of Darwin's work generated substantial debate on these and related questions, which is itself worthy of careful study.[1] It is impossible to discuss more recent debates on this topic without being drawn into their history, especially when it is recalled that "natural theology" designates a spectrum of possibilities. The debates of the nineteenth century may help identify certain positions within that spectrum as now being untenable; nevertheless, a gratifyingly wide range of options remains open.

Yet this discussion focuses on the *content* of natural theology. It engages the question of whether appeals to nature in support of religious belief can cope with the challenges raised by evolutionary thought. The evidence suggests that it can. But that is not the full story. What of the *enterprise* of natural theology itself? What if there is a fundamentally evolutionary explanation for why we wish to think about God at all? Is there a purely natural explanation for the human desire to do natural theology?

The present chapter focuses on the question of whether natural theology – which we shall interpret in a generously broad manner – is itself a by-product of the evolutionary process. Do we have a natural tendency to dream of the divine, which is itself demonstrably an unintended and unnecessary outcome of the evolutionary process?

Darwinism and the Divine: Evolutionary Thought and Natural Theology, First Edition.
Alister E. McGrath.
© 2011 Alister E. McGrath. Published 2011 by Blackwell Publishing Ltd.

Some recent studies have suggested that human beings resemble other animals more closely than had previously been realized. The design and use of tools is no longer regarded as being specific to humans.[2] Other animals possess the capacity for mental processes,[3] and advanced vocal communication,[4] even if this does not involve the use of words. The complexity of primate social behavior has been recognized, with political strategies such as deception, which parallel those used in human social contexts, apparently being developed.[5] Yet in one vital respect, human beings are different. "The propensity to have religious ideas appears to be both widespread among human beings, and quite unique to our species."[6]

So how is this to be explained? It must be made clear immediately that different levels of explanation of such observations are possible. An evolutionary explanation of how music developed,[7] for example, does not exhaust the question of its present value to individuals or its social utility. Nor do evolutionary perspectives adequately explain justified beliefs.[8] While it might seem reasonable to propose that evolution has "designed us to appraise the world accurately and to form true beliefs,"[9] the question of whether at least some misbeliefs might be adaptive remains open. "Natural selection does not care about truth; it cares only about reproductive success."[10]

The main scientific question to be considered here is whether belief in God can be explained persuasively in purely naturalist terms, without recourse to proposing the actual existence of God, as an evolutionary outcome. It is important to appreciate that a functional atheism is as much the presupposition as the conclusion of such approaches, which have a tendency to logical circularity. Four possible lines of argument might be considered.

1   Religious beliefs have no adaptive functions, so that their presence and success in human populations is to be explained by other means. The notion of the "meme," to be considered later, is an example of such a reductive evolutionary explanation of belief in God.
2   Religious beliefs can be considered as by-products of more fundamental and essentially adaptive features of human cognition.
3   Religious beliefs are to be considered as adaptations that play a positive role in enabling humanity to deal with environmental complexity.
4   Religious beliefs are essentially cultural adaptations that co-evolve and interact with natural adaptations.

The difficulty faced by all these theories is that it is still unclear whether religious belief is to be regarded as adaptive or not. While some writers have assumed that there is no obvious adaptive function to religious belief,[11] the evidence for this is far from secure. A good case can be made for religion being interpreted in adaptationist terms.[12] Yet any such conclusion must be regarded as insecure, resting on less than reliable evidential foundations.[13]

In this chapter, we shall consider some contemporary debates within evolutionary theory about the origins of religion, and their relevance for natural theology.

The Darwinian Paradigm and Cultural Development

An appropriate starting point for our reflections concerns whether Darwinism is essentially a theory about the factors that control evolutionary change in the biological world, or whether it has wider validity. There is no doubt that Darwin himself envisaged his theory of natural selection as having applicability in other fields, most notably the evolution of language.[14] In the *Origin of Species*, Darwin penned a paragraph that cautiously proposed an isomorphism between the descent of language and the descent of humanity.[15]

> If we possessed a perfect pedigree of mankind, a genealogical arrangement of the races of man would afford the best classification of the various languages now spoken throughout the world; and if all extinct languages, and all intermediate and slowly changing dialects, had to be included, such an arrangement would, I think, be the only possible one.

This thought, however briefly expressed, generated much discussion.[16] For our purposes, it points to the possibility of the wider cultural applicability of Darwin's theory of natural selection.

One particularly significant development within western cultural history during the twentieth century has been the assimilation of the idea of cultural and intellectual change to a Darwinian evolutionary paradigm.[17] This contrasts with the situation at the beginning of that century, when the notion of "cultural evolution" temporarily began to lose its appeal. However, in the period following the Second World War, the neo-Darwinian synthesis began to emerge, and proved intellectually resilient.[18] This created new interest in the possibility of developing a cultural evolutionary theory.[19] The application of paradigms drawn from evolutionary biology to cultural development has led to cultural evolutionary theory expanding, drawing upon various aspects of the Darwinian paradigm to illuminate cultural change.[20]

Yet difficult questions remain. Can any aspect of cultural or intellectual development legitimately be analyzed on the basis of a Darwinian model of evolution?[21] Can an approach developed to deal with the evolution of biological species find wider validity, and be applied to long-term changes within human culture? There are some obvious and fundamental differences between biological and cultural transmission. Individuals are exposed to cultural influences from a range of sources, not limited to their biological parents; they can choose which culture, or which cultural entities, they adopt; and they, in turn, can transmit their own experiences and behavior to others, thus allowing *acquired* cultural characteristics to be inherited.[22] It is clearly important to explore whether the development of ideas or culture in general can be accounted for on such a mechanism, before turning to deal with its relevance for a series of questions related to natural theology.

Some – most notably, Richard Dawkins and Daniel Dennett (see 34–6) – have argued for what they call "Universal Darwinism." Dennett playfully imagines his detractors (of whom there seem to be many) demanding that Darwinism be kept on a tight rein:[23]

> Cede some or all of modern biology to Darwin, perhaps, but hold the line there! Keep Darwinian thinking out of cosmology, out of psychology, out of human culture, out of ethics, politics and religion!

For Dennett, there are limitless applications for the evolutionary algorithm. Darwinism is an algorithm that can operate on anything – a notion Dennett expresses in terms of Darwinism's "substrate neutrality." This, he argues, is the universal mechanism that explains the origins and substance of human culture, not merely of biological species. On such an approach, the evolution of human culture can be explained in terms of a process in which the key variables and mechanisms are identical to, or at the very least directly analogous to, those observed within biological evolution.

The social sciences have tended to appropriate biological models or paradigms in two different manners.[24] The first emphasizes the biological roots and origins of human behavior. Sociobiology and evolutionary psychology frequently make an appeal to human evolutionary history in accounting for physiological and behavioral traits of an organism – such as altruism – as evolutionary adaptations.[25] Sociobiologists tend to see cultural evolution as being very closely controlled by biological evolution, and cultural traits as being selected on account primarily of their biological functionality.[26] Others have argued that cultural evolution is better seen as a truly autonomous evolutionary process in which a form of Darwinian selection operates on cultural traits, favoring those traits that are more capable of generating replicas of themselves, irrespective of whether they contribute to the reproductive success of their carriers.[27] We shall return to this approach presently, as it is of no small importance for some questions relating to natural theology.

The second approach, however, is more cautious and nuanced. It is conceded that there are potential viable analogies between biological and cultural evolution and that cultural entities can be argued to exhibit variation, competition, and cumulative modification.[28] Yet analogy is not the same as identity. Biological and social systems are here recognized as complex systems that share some general properties but differ in important respects – such as the time frames over which change and development take place.[29] The most fundamental notion is that of change. Social and biological systems alike are recognized as being subject to change in principle, and in practice. Human institutions and natural systems are both in the process of changing, even though the time frames are radically different. Change is characteristic of such systems, and these changes are open to empirical investigation and theoretical analysis, using the narrative framework afforded by the concept of "evolution" as an interpretative tool.

The suggestion that common mechanisms might underlie both biological and cultural evolution has attracted some support. Some have noted that such a possibility was envisaged by Darwin himself,[30] while recognizing that this idea required some considerable development if it was to engage with the phenomena of human culture. Yet to speak of human culture as "evolving" is not necessarily to commit oneself to a Darwinian paradigm. If biological evolution can indeed illuminate its cultural counterpart, it must then be asked whether the better evolutionary paradigm is Darwinian or Lamarckian. Darwinism consists of two elements: random variation within a generation, which is subjected to the process of natural selection. Lamarckism denotes a family of views associated with the French evolutionist Jean-Baptiste de Lamarck (1744–1829), who proposed that changes acquired during the lifetime of an organism were passed on to its offspring.[31] The idea that phenotypic changes can be passed on to the genotype is now widely discredited as a mechanism for explaining biological evolution. But what about cultural evolution?

A crucial issue here is that of *intentionality* in cultural development. Although Lamarck gave priority to habit rather than conscious will in giving rise to biological adaptation, he clearly held that adaptation could result from intentions and inclinations. Habits are here understood to be the outcome of intention or volition. Later writers in the Lamarckian tradition gave greater emphasis to this aspect of Lamarck's thought, leading to the perception that evolution could, at least in some respects and to some extent, be considered as a consciously directed process. The term "Lamarckian" is now generally used, not to designate the original views of Lamarck himself, but to denote an approach to evolution that includes or embraces the volitional acquisition of characteristics.

The application of evolutionary ideas to social development was pioneered in the late nineteenth century by writers such as Joseph LeConte (1823–1901), Lester F. Ward (1841–1913), and John Fiske (1842–1901). Ward and Fiske both worked within a recognizably Darwinian paradigm, accounting for social change in terms of competition;[32] LeConte, however, clearly adopts an approach that includes more Lamarckian elements.[33] In particular, LeConte emphasized the importance of "the conscious voluntary cooperation of man himself in the work of his own evolution." Evolution is about environmental pressures; it is also about the human response to those pressures. For LeConte, to speak of cultural development in Lamarckian terms is to recognize the role of human volitional activity in the process of evolutionary change.

The problem that "Universal Darwinism" faces in confronting social and economic evolution is the absence of any cultural equivalent of a "Weismann barrier." Since the pioneering work of August Weismann in the late nineteenth century, it is virtually universally accepted that there is no biological mechanism by which the acquired characteristics of an organism can be transmitted to its progeny. Yet there are no reasons for believing that there is any analogue to the "Weismann barrier" in the case of cultural or social development. "Universal Darwinism" rests upon the implicit and untested assumption that there is a direct analogy or correlation between the mechanisms of biological and cultural evolution at this critical point. There is no reason to suppose that such a correlation exists.

A study of key episodes in human cultural evolution suggests that it is problematic to propose a direct correlation of cultural and biological evolutionary paradigms. While human culture may be subject to sporadic, unpredictable, or episodic developments, it is also open to manipulation and direction by power groups. The Italian Marxist cultural theoretician Antonio Gramsci (1891–1937), for example, asserted the malleability of culture, and identified means by which the evolution of culture could be shaped and directed by those in appropriate positions of influence.[34]

For Gramsci, culture is fundamentally a human creation, shaped and fashioned by those with positions of power and influence. It is directed intentionally and purposefully by those with the necessary motivation and capacity to do so. While Gramsci's theory does not correspond directly to any biological evolutionary paradigm, it is clearly much closer to Lamarck than to Darwin. Gramsci's approach can, for example, be correlated with conceptualizing culture as a transformational system.[35] Cultural evolution can thus be understood in terms of change arising from intentional selection through conscious or unconscious choices made by individuals within the system.

Those committed to "Universal Darwinism" are implacably opposed to any idea that the Lamarckian paradigm might offer a superior account of cultural evolution.[36] Dennett, for example, dismisses Lamarckian accounts of cultural evolution as "confused,"[37] although it is far from clear what evidentiary considerations lead him to draw this conclusion. The problem for "Universal Darwinism" is that its totalizing aspirations mean that it is defeated by exceptions. Those wishing to challenge its hegemony are not required to demonstrate the operation of a universal alternative to Darwinism within nature or culture; they are simply obliged to show that alternative mechanisms operate. The evidence suggests strongly that this is the case with cultural evolution. It is possible to argue that cultural evolution is shaped by happenstance as much as by human intentions and endeavors; nevertheless, this observation merely contextualizes the intentional element within human cultural evolution, rather than negating it.

A familiar case study will help illuminate these points. The Renaissance is widely regarded as one of the most remarkable developments in the evolution of western culture. Its origins are widely agreed to lie in Italy during the thirteenth century, although its full blossoming would take place during the following two centuries.[38] The movement gradually spread from Italy into northern Europe, causing significant changes wherever it took hold. Its impact on the worlds of ideas, architecture, literature, language, and the arts was immense. To note one example: the Gothic style of architecture gave way to the classical style, impacting significantly on western European urban landscapes.[39]

The European Renaissance was a brilliant, multifaceted movement, whose scintillating cultural dynamics were determined by the interactions of a complex series of interacting communities and individuals. Recent research has demonstrated the importance of networks of humanist writers – often referred to as "sodalities" – in coordinating the spread of the ideals of the Renaissance, and placing them on a secure intellectual foundation.[40] Yet there is little doubt about the overall intellectual basis of the Renaissance. Since the pioneering work of Paul Oskar Kristeller (1905–99), the fundamental agenda of the Renaissance has been widely accepted to be the critical reappropriation of the culture of ancient Rome (and, to a lesser extent, Athens).[41] The Renaissance was about the pursuit of eloquence, with classical norms and resources being seen as integral to this task.[42]

Perhaps stimulated by the presence of the remains of classical civilization in Italy, Renaissance theorists advocated the recovery of the rich cultural heritage of the past – the elegant Latin of Cicero; the eloquence of classical rhetoric; the splendor of classical architecture; the philosophies of Plato and Aristotle; the republican political ideals that inspired the Roman constitution.[43] Renaissance writers set about deliberately and systematically adopting these principles, and applying them to their own situation, rebuilding and reappropriating the ruins of the past.[44]

So what is the relevance of this case study for our theme? The key point is that of the intentional reappropriation of the past as a means of transforming the present. The historical development of the Renaissance was unquestionably subject to happenstance; yet many fundamental themes of the Renaissance were concerned with the intentional remolding of western European culture after classical models. The interplay of historical accidents and human intentions is of considerable interest and importance; it cannot, however, be fully accounted for by a Darwinian model of cultural evolution. Such a model needs to be modified to take account of the historical evidence.

For such reasons, there is growing sympathy for the view that cultural evolution is sufficiently distinct from biological evolution to create difficulties for its accommodation within a purely Darwinian paradigm. While Dawkins and Dennett continue to defend "Universal Darwinism," mainline opinion is clearly crystallizing around four alternative approaches to cultural evolution.

1 Cultural evolution is best considered as a Lamarckian process;[45] or
2 Any viable theory of cultural evolution must contain Lamarckian elements;[46] or
3 If a Darwinian paradigm is held to offer the best explanation of the evolution of cultural entities, it requires considerable expansion or modification to accommodate the observational evidence.[47]
4 Cultural evolution is best described using models drawn from other sources, such as disease epidemiology,[48] learning theory,[49] or cognitive psychology.[50]

These options are not mutually exclusive; it is not difficult to see how Darwinian elements could be incorporated into the approaches noted in the fourth category. Yet while social and cultural evolution might indeed be argued to be "broadly" Darwinian, this does not entail the strict "Universal Darwinist" claim that they are *solely* Darwinian. Darwinism can illuminate cultural development; nevertheless, considerable additional light is required from other sources.

So what is the relevance of this analysis for the theme of this work? In this chapter, we shall consider a series of arguments, grounded to a greater or lesser extent on the extension of Darwinism to cultural development, to the effect that religious belief is the outcome of evolutionary pressures. These arguments clearly raise significant difficulties for natural theology, and they must therefore be considered carefully.

The God-Meme: Natural Theology and Cultural Replicators

One of the most characteristic features of "Universal Darwinism" is its proposal for cultural replicators, by which both the general patterns and specific outcomes of cultural development may be explained. In 1976, Dawkins introduced the notion of the "meme" as the basis of a Darwinian explanation of the origin and spread of beliefs through society. "Memes" are held to constitute the fundamental units of civilization that replicate themselves to design culture – and the minds that make it. Memetics – the approach to the origins and diffusion of ideas in culture founded on the notion of the "meme" – was initially hailed as marking the beginning of a "new science of culture," based on "Universal Darwinism."[51]

The concept of the meme has come to be seen as essential to "Universal Darwinism."[52] This point was emphasized by Stephen Jay Gould, no friend to what he regarded as exaggerated or inflated Darwinian accounts of social development.[53]

Figure 9.1 American paleontologist Stephen Jay. Gould, January 1982.

Dennett, following Dawkins, tries to identify human thoughts and actions as "memes," thus viewing them as units that are subject to a form of selection analogous to natural selection of genes. Cultural change, working by memetic selection, then becomes as algorithmic as biological change ... thus uniting the evolution of organisms and thoughts under a single ultra-Darwinian rubric.

The core idea of memetics is that memes differ in their degree of adaptedness to the sociocultural environment in which they propagate. Mutations and recombinations of existing ideas will produce a variety of memes that compete with each other. Fitter memes will be more successful in being communicated, "infecting" more individuals and thus spreading over a larger population. The resulting evolutionary dynamics are fundamentally Darwinian, consisting of an initial *variation* creating new meme variants, followed by a process of *natural selection*, which retains only those that are best adapted to their environment. One of the most fundamental arguments of "Universal Darwinism," evident in the "New Atheism" that emerged in the period 2006–7, is that belief in God is spread by a well-adapted "God-meme," which propagates itself within a population by a process of thought contagion.[54]

Although alternative notions of cultural replicators had been around for some time,[55] the idea of the "meme" rapidly achieved cultural dominance. As noted earlier, it was introduced in 1976 by Dawkins as part of his argument that both biological and cultural evolution could be accounted for by "units of replication" or "units of transmission."[56] Dawkins appears to suggest that a Darwinian process absolutely needs replicators analogous to genes, and posits the meme as a result of his prior conviction that cultural evolution is an essentially Darwinian process. The prior belief or commitment is that cultural evolution is Darwinian; the consequence is the invention of the meme.

The choice of the word "meme" merits comment. Dawkins recalls how he wanted a word for a "cultural replicator" that sounded like "gene" – thus stressing the analogy between cultural and genetic transmission – and came up with "meme"[57] – an abbreviation of the term "mimeme," derived from the Greek *mimesis* ("imitation"). The meme was proposed as a hypothetical replicator – "a unit of cultural transmission, or a unit of *imitation*" – to explain the process of the development of culture within a Darwinian framework.[58]

> Just as genes propagate themselves in the gene pool by leaping from body to body via sperm or eggs, so memes propagate themselves in the meme pool by leaping from brain to brain by a process which, in the broad sense of the term, can be called imitation.

As examples of what he has in mind, Dawkins points to such things as tunes, ideas, catchphrases, fashions, aspects of architecture, songs – and belief in God.

Yet there is a clear difficulty with this definition of the meme. In Dawkins's account of the neo-Darwinian synthesis, it is the *gene* that is the unit of selection, even though it is the *phenotype* that is actually subject to the process of selection. The gene is the replicator, or the set of instructions; the phenotype is the physical manifestation of the organism, the visible characteristics or behavior resulting from that set of instructions. However, all the examples of "memes" that Dawkins offers in *The Selfish Gene* are the *result* of such instructions, not the instructions themselves. While Dawkins proposed an analogy between *meme* and *gene*, he actually illustrated this by appealing to the cultural equivalent of *phenotypes*, not genes.

Dawkins recognized this problem, and modified his ideas in his next major popular work – *The Extended Phenotype* (1982). His original account of the meme, he conceded, was defective; it required correction.[59]

> I was insufficiently clear about the distinction between the meme itself, as replicator, and its "phenotypic effects" or "meme products" on the other. A meme should be regarded as a unit of information residing in a brain ... It has a definite structure, realised in whatever medium the brain uses for storing information ... This is to distinguish it from phenotypic effects, which are its consequences in the outside world.

This new definition of the meme identifies it as the fundamental unit of information or instruction, which gives rise to cultural artifacts and ideas. A meme is a set of instructions, the blueprint rather than the product. What Dawkins originally defined as memes – things like "catchy tunes" – are now to be regarded as "meme products."[60] Yet this confusion over two quite different conceptions of the meme – namely, meme-as-behavior and meme-as-instructions – causes difficulty in evaluating both the scientific plausibility of the meme, as well the evolutionary paradigm within which it is located. As Susan Blackmore, widely regarded as one of the more enthusiastic advocates of the notion, points out, whether memetic evolution is considered to be Lamarckian or not depends on whether it is meme-as-behavior or meme-as-instructions that is being replicated.[61] Blackmore argues that a memetic approach based on copying-the-product opens the way to a Lamarckian understanding of the inheritance of acquired modifications, whereas copying-the-instructions does not, in that it is the instructions, rather than their outcomes, that are being replicated.[62] Dawkins's 1976 definition of the meme was thus Lamarckian, whereas his 1982 redefinition was Darwinian.

There is a further point that needs consideration here. Dawkins portrays humans as essentially passive recipients of memes. But what of human agency? This question was raised by philosopher Mary Midgley, a perceptive critic of the meme-hypothesis.[63]

> If memes really correspond to Dawkinsian genes they must indeed be fixed units – hidden, unchanging causes of the changing items that appear round us in the world. But all the examples we are given correspond to phenotypes, not genotypes. They are the apparent items themselves. Moreover, most of the concepts mentioned [as examples of memes] cannot possibly be treated as unchanging or even as moderately solid. Such customs and ways of thinking are organic parts of human life, constantly growing, developing, changing, and sometimes decaying like every other living thing. Much of this change, too, is due to our own action, to our deliberately working to change them.

Midgley here points to the volitional and intentional aspects of the evolution of human culture, which many would take to point to a more Lamarckian understanding of evolutionary mechanism. Her point is that, whereas people can act as passive carriers of biological viruses, they cannot be regarded as passive "vehicles" or "carriers" of ideas and beliefs. As psychologists have pointed out from the time of William James (1842–1910) onwards, individuals actively interpret the information they receive in the light of their existing knowledge and values, and on the basis of that may decide to reject, accept, or modify the information that is communicated to them.[64] In other words, individuals and groups actively participate and intervene in the formulation and propagation of culture. In that sense, cultural evolution must be considered to be Lamarckian, or to have Lamarckian elements, rather than being purely Darwinian.

Defenders of the meme, such as David L. Hull, hold that the replication and spread of memes is comparable to an epidemiological infection or contagion, in which individuals passively receive and carry viruses.[65] Yet this is a highly questionable, not to mention psychologically simplistic, account of the process of the human acquisition and transmission of ideas.[66] Psychological issues – overlooked by the more aggressive advocates of memetics – play a critical role in cultural development. "Culture is shaped by both psychological processes that determine how people think and feel, and social processes that determine how people interact."[67] Progress in understanding social and cultural evolution thus requires exploration of how innate human cognitive structures interact with social processes, and the behavioral outcomes of this interaction.

From what has been said already, it will be clear that the concept of the meme is controversial, being widely regarded as underdetermined by the evidence on the one hand, and explanatorily redundant on the other. The meme remains a hypothesis, constructed by analogy with the gene, on the basis of the (highly contestable) assumption that, since cultural evolution is a Darwinian process, there must be a cultural replicator analogous to the genetic replicator. Yet genes can be "seen," and their transmission patterns studied under rigorous empirical conditions. But what about memes? The simple fact is that they are, in the first place, *hypothetical constructs*, inferred from observation rather than observed in themselves, and in the second place, *unobservable*. This makes their rigorous investigation intensely problematic, and fails to enable a *meme* and an *idea* to be satisfactorily distinguished.[68]

Memes cannot be observed, and the evidence can be explained perfectly well without them. The "exasperated reaction of many anthropologists to the general idea of memes" reflects the apparent ignorance of the proponents of the meme-hypothesis of the discipline of anthropology, and its major successes in the explanation of cultural development – without feeling the need to develop anything like the idea of a "meme" at all.[69]

The process of replication has also come in for close examination. Much criticism has been directed against the potential reliability of such a process, with three particularly significant concerns being identified.[70]

1   Cultural transmission processes are usually incomplete and imperfect, so, unlike genetic systems, accurate replication rarely occurs. Replication, in the precise sense of the term, is thus the exception, rather than the rule.

2   Second, inferential processes "transform" these cultural representations during their transmission and reconstruction, in marked contrast to the process of RNA replication. This could be argued to point to *mutation-like* processes being much more important than *selection-like* processes in shaping cultural variation.

3   Unlike genes, cultural representations are rarely discrete units, suggesting that the idea of a "replicator" (such as the meme) makes little sense for most types of cultural representations.

Furthermore, neither ideas nor cultural artifacts can conceivably be said to be, or to contain, a self-assembly code. They are not "replicators," as required by the accounts of cultural transmission and development offered by Dawkins and Dennett.[71] Indeed, since there is no compelling scientific evidence for these entities, some have playfully – though not without good reason – concluded that there might even be a meme for believing in memes.

There are also serious doubts as to whether the meme can be considered to be a viable scientific hypothesis, when there is no clear operational definition of a meme, no testable model for how memes influence culture and why standard selection models are not adequate, a general tendency to ignore the sophisticated social science models of information transfer already in place, and a high degree of circularity in the explanation of the power of memes.[72] There is "standard codification of the concept,"[73] making a serious scientific research program impossible.

The fundamental analogy between gene and meme has been widely questioned. Dan Sperber, Pascal Boyer, and Scott Atran have argued that the flow of cultural information cannot be held to be directly analogous to genetic information.[74] For example, genetic information is passed specifically and uniquely from parents to offspring; it is not shared with a wider group of individuals. Cultural information is passed more generally between individuals and groups, and lacks the specificity of genetic information. A child's ideas will typically be constructed from many sources and through many exposures, extending far beyond any specific and unique informational relation to its biological parents. Those ideas cannot be thought of as a "copy" of some original set of parental ideas, analogous to genes.

Furthermore, while it is easy to identify the primary locus of competition between genes, the same is not true of hypothesized memes.[75] Genes compete with other alleles at the same locus on a chromosome, in that they give rise to differences in the organism's phenotypes. Both the locus and mechanism of gene competition are relatively well understood. So what is the equivalent in the case of the supposedly analogous memes? Such is the force of such points that Susan Blackmore has even questioned the analogy on the basis of which Dawkins originally developed the notion: "Memes are best thought about not by analogy with genes but as new replicators, with their own ways of surviving and getting copied."[76]

Some have resolved these serious difficulties by adopting an instrumentalist account of the meme.[77] There is no such thing as a meme; it is, however, a useful theoretical construct, which plays a valuable heuristic role in explaining observational evidence. "For us, the pertinent question is not whether memes exist … but whether they are a useful theoretical expedient."[78] It is quite possible that such an understanding of the meme may underlie Dawkins's characteristically confident statement: "Memes can sometimes display very high fidelity."[79] This is a creedal statement posing as a statement of scientific fact. What Dawkins is doing is to restate an observation into his own theoretical language, which is not spoken anywhere else within the scientific community. The *observation* is that ideas can be passed from one individual, group, or generation to another; Dawkins's *theoretical interpretation* of this observation – which is here presented simply as fact – involves attributing fidelity to what most regard as being a non-existent entity.

We see here an example of what most of its critics regard as the greatest failing of memetics: its "achievements" are limited to simply *redescribing* a host of phenomena in memetic terms, while persisting in presenting this as an "explanation" of those phenomena. Yet even the capacity to "explain" belief in God by locating it within a Darwinian evolutionary context must be called into question. In his careful study of the role of the "meme" in forms of atheism inspired by "Universal Darwinism," Joseph Poulshock makes the point that the appeal to the meme in debates about God is essentially circular.[80]

> If one can propose a Darwinian explanation that (1a) belief in God evolved as a maladaptive trait and that (2a) Darwinism shows that theistic belief does not correspond to reality, one can just as easily argue in Darwinian fashion that (1b) faith evolved as an adaptive trait and that (2b) some god-memes actually correspond to reality, supporting the idea that God exists.

One telling indication of the failure of the "meme" to garner academic support can be seen in the history of the online *Journal of Memetics*, launched in 1997, arguably at the zenith of the cultural plausibility of the meme.[81] The journal folded in 2005. Why? The answer can be found in a devastating critique of the notion of the meme, published in the final issue of this ill-fated journal.[82] Dr Bruce Edmonds makes two fundamental criticisms of the notion of memetics, which he believes have undermined its claims to plausibility in the scientific community.

1 The underlying reason why memetics has failed is that it "has not provided any extra explanatory or predictive power beyond that available without the gene-meme analogy." In other words, it has not provided any "added value" in terms of providing *new* understanding of phenomena.
2 The study of memetics has been characterized by "theoretical discussion of extreme abstraction and over ambition." Edmonds singles out for special criticism unrealistic and overambitious attempts, often developed in advance of evidence, "to 'explain' some immensely complex phenomena such as religion." Yet for many of its more uncritical and enthusiastic advocates, this is precisely the point of memetics – to explain away belief in God.

Edmonds ends his incisive dismissal of the meme with its obituary: Memetics "has been a short-lived fad whose effect has been to obscure more than it has been to enlighten. I am afraid that memetics, as an identifiable discipline, will not be widely missed."

Yet despite its widespread abandonment in mainstream science, the meme lingers on in one constituency – the "New Atheism." Indeed, it has paradoxically become one of the most significant weapons in the movement's critique of religion, making its severe evidential underdetermination a matter of no small importance. Faith in God is regularly attributed to memetic processes within the canonical writings of the "New Atheism," often being compared with infection with a virus. The naive reader might gain the impression that she is being presented with a synopsis of cutting-edge scientific research, when she is really being offered a distillation of speculative moonshine.

For example, in *The God Delusion*, Dawkins sets out the idea of memes as if it were established scientific orthodoxy, making no mention of the inconvenient fact that the mainstream scientific community views it as a decidedly flaky idea, best relegated to the margins. The "meme" is presented as if it were an actually existing entity, with huge potential to explain the origins of religion. Dawkins is even able to develop an advanced vocabulary based on his own convictions – such as "memeplex."[83] Belief in God may be attributed to a well-adapted meme, whose potency is inversely proportional to the grounding of this belief in reality. Dawkins thus posits, without evidence, a meme for "blind faith,"[84] opening himself to the charge that such a belief in memes is itself a form of "blind faith."

Daniel Dennett takes a similar view in *Breaking the Spell*, arguing that human brains provide shelter for "toxic memes," which proceed to create human minds.[85] Dennett had developed similar ideas earlier. In *Darwin's Dangerous Idea* (1995), he asserted that, far from being "godlike creators of ideas" who can manipulate, judge, and control ideas from an independent "Olympian standpoint," human beings are who they are, and think what they think, on account of "infestations of memes."[86] The idea of a human mind that somehow transcends both its genetic and memetic creators is nothing more than an outmoded myth.[87] For this reason, the human mind is particularly prone to being manipulated by these "new replicators."

In *Breaking the Spell*, Dennett sets out a naturalist account of religion, based largely on an appeal to the meme. His highly developed account of the meme makes up for its lack of empirical foundations by a highly flamboyant account of its metaphysical importance, above all in spreading beliefs – such as belief in God. So are *all* beliefs spread by what Dennett terms "toxic memes"? Or just the ones that anti-religious critics don't like? Is there a meme for atheism? Dennett's "Simple Taxonomy of Memes" certainly suggests so.[88]

Yet the empirical evidence for memes is underwhelming, putting Dennett in the somewhat difficult position of having to resort to the use of aggressive rhetoric to cover up the manifestly inadequate evidential underpinnings of his approach.[89] His atheist apologetic at this point rests on the assumption that belief in God is demonstrably the outcome of memetic influence. However, neither the notion of the meme, nor its alleged influence on religious beliefs, is scientifically proven; indeed, it has not even been stated in a form capable of scientific verification or falsification. Dennett, like other memeticists, has no answer to the question of why a "toxic" or "maladaptive" meme such as religion seems to be much more contagious than "adaptive memes" such as science.[90]

As noted earlier, the meme is hypothesized by analogy with the gene. Yet scientific arguments based on analogy can be deeply flawed, even if they possess a certain intuitive plausibility. A good example of this lies to hand in the fruitless search for the luminiferous ether in the late nineteenth century, based on the supposed analogy between light and sound. The celebrated Michelson–Morley experiment demonstrated that there was no evidence for this so-called "ether."[91] It was analogically plausible, but evidentially non-existent. Dawkins conceded some years ago that "memes have not yet found their Watson and Crick; they even lack their Mendel."[92] It seems much more likely that memes are waiting for their Michelson and Morley to deliver the final death blow to an unsatisfactory and unnecessary theory, of questionable relevance to the debate about God, and the relation of evolutionary theory to natural theology. For the moment, the meme seems to be taken seriously only by the advocates of a "Universal Darwinism," within which it has assumed an iconic role.

Religion: Evolutionary Adaptation or Spandrel?

While there is some agreement that the human religious imagination emerged naturally and spontaneously in the course of the evolution of human cognitive systems, there is a clear divergence over whether religious perceptions are to be explained reductively or realistically. Are religious ideas to be explained on a purely natural level, or do they represent an informed response to a transcendent reality? This binary framework is clearly inadequate for the purposes of such a significant discussion: it must be expanded to include the possibility of our knowledge of a transcendent reality being modulated or "filtered" by cultural and psychological factors – a point made by the school of philosophy generally known as "critical realism."[93]

The suggestion that Darwinism might offer an evolutionary account of the origins and development of religion can be traced back to the beginning of the twentieth century. The Oxford anthropologist Robert Marett (1866–1943) famously declared that "anthropology is the child of Darwin."[94] Marett and his colleagues argued that Darwin's idea of the common descent of all humanity entailed that there was a common, basic psychology that was essentially the same, irrespective of ethnicity or geography.[95] However, psychology was then in its infancy, and Marett and others found themselves unable to pursue their research without imposing or projecting their own ideas, values, and assumptions on early humanity.[96]

The idea that religious beliefs or behavior might be explained on evolutionary grounds was noted by Darwin himself. Although emphatic that "there is no evidence that man was aboriginally endowed with the ennobling belief in the existence of an Omnipotent God,"[97] Darwin noted that a more general definition of "religion" opened the way to a very different conclusion.[98]

> If, however, we include under the term "religion" the belief in unseen or spiritual agencies, the case is wholly different; for this belief seems to be universal with the less civilized races. Nor is it difficult to comprehend how it arose. As soon as the important faculties of the imagination, wonder, and curiosity, together with some power of reasoning, had become partially developed, man would naturally crave to understand what was passing around him, and would have vaguely speculated on his own existence.

Darwin's comments suggest that religion might be seen as the outcome of a process of human evolutionary development, arising from the emergence of certain human faculties. The two main schools of thought to emerge in recent years hold either that religion evolved through natural selection and confers some selective advantage, or that religion is an evolutionary by-product of other mental adaptations.

The adaptive character of religion is suggested by a number of lines of argument,[99] including social solidarity. On this approach, religion encourages social cohesion and discipline, giving the group a greater capacity to survive and reproduce. It has long been recognized that one of the primary functions of religion is the promotion of this type of group solidarity, which is often strengthened through rituals, expressing both the fundamentals of group identity and the dangers that attend it. This enhanced social bonding within a group is not to be seen as an end in itself; by increasing solidarity, religion facilitates cooperation within the group, thus enhancing its survival prospects.

There are some obvious difficulties in asserting that religion possesses adaptive value. For example, traits are adaptive only with respect to a particular set of selective pressures. It has yet to be shown that any specifically religious trait can be said to confer maximal reproductive benefit. More importantly, most of the studies emphasizing the importance of religion in fostering group solidarity focus on ethnographic studies of communities whose cohesion is enhanced by religion. However, this raises the question of whether it is possible to extrapolate from present-day situations to the past, particularly the distant past. Many would argue that patterns of religious behavior have undergone significant change over our evolutionary history. This point was made by the anthropologist E. E. Evans-Pritchard, who argued that changes in religious behavior were so substantial that it was virtually rendered impossible to generalize about the social functions of religion over time.[100] Furthermore, as Sosis and Alcorta point out, religion has a marked capacity and propensity to respond to the selective pressures of diverse ecological contexts, which may help explain its universality and endurance.[101] Religion itself possesses a capacity to adapt in response to environmental changes.[102]

Alternatively, some have argued that religion is to be seen as an evolutionary by-product, an unintended consequence of the evolutionary process. Stephen Jay Gould popularized the visual metaphor of the "spandrel" as a way of conceiving an outcome of evolution that appeared to be an adaptation, but was actually an "exaptation" – namely, a feature that now enhances fitness, but was not built by natural selection for its current role.[103] According to Gould, spandrels are non-adaptive secondary and unintended consequences of different adaptive traits. It is not possible to say that they themselves have been "selected." The view that religion is a by-product of the workings of normal, cognitive mechanisms – mechanisms that have evolved for reasons unrelated to religion – has attracted some support.[104]

Nevertheless, the idea of "exaptation" is deeply problematic. Gould and Vrba hold that a development can only be described as an adaptation if it evolved specifically for that purpose. Yet given that the evolutionary process is fundamentally blind in terms of its intentions, the distinction between "adaptation" and "exaptation" seems purely semantic. How can one speak of a by-product of evolution, without being able to speak of, let alone know about, the *intended* outcomes of this process? Furthermore, while Gould specifically identifies religion as an example of such an "exaptation" or spandrel, he fails to identify a specific trait that he believes was actually acted upon by natural selection.

On this approach, the emergence of religion is not to be regarded as a particularly important evolutionary event, in that it is an essentially predictable by-product of evolved human mental capacities.[105] Religion is to be seen as a cognitive parasite, in the sense that all the systems involved in its acquisition and its mental effects would be in place within the human mind, even if religion itself were not. The human cognitive processes that give rise to religion were evolved for other reasons; religion is an accidental by-product of these processes.

Natural Theology and Evolutionary Theories of the Origins of Religion

Any attempt to explore the evolutionary origins of religion remains deeply problematic, in that it inevitably rests upon speculative interpretation of ambivalent and limited historical evidence on the one hand,[106] and potentially contested definitions of religion on the other. Although religion is traditionally defined in terms of belief in supernatural agents, any evolutionary account of religion must engage with the level of human behavior if an explanation of its development is to be based on the assumed operation of the process of natural selection.[107] Natural selection operates at the level of behaviors, rather than beliefs or attitudes. It makes no distinction between someone who cares for her neighbors on account of her belief in God, and someone who behaves identically, but without any theistic motivation.

To speak of religion in terms of belief in "supernatural agents" may well help to identify some aspects of religious belief that distinguish it from ordinary perceptual experience; yet this does not help distinguish supernatural beliefs associated with ritual practices from unverifiable paranormal beliefs that do not elicit such behavioral responses. Indeed, sociological or anthropological approaches to religion often emphasize its social dimensions – as, for example, in Durkheim's functional definition of religion as "a unified system of beliefs and practices relative to sacred things."[108] Furthermore, Durkheim pointed out that to define religion in terms of the "supernatural" made sense only within the context of a modern European paradigm of scientific explanation for "natural" phenomena; for most of the world's peoples, including pre-modern Europeans, religious phenomena were seen as perfectly natural.[109]

For such reasons, evolutionary approaches to religion often focus on its social impact – for example, in encouraging pro-social behavior within groups, which is held to confer a selective advantage upon them.[110] Such processes appear to continue to operate today. Studies comparing religious communities to analogous secular ones suggest that, in general, those with religious foundations tend to be more socially cohesive and enduring than their secular counterparts.[111] Yet such explanations are better at explaining the maintenance, rather than the origins, of religious beliefs. The question of how the *origins* of religion are to be accounted for remains elusive, on this approach.

At present, the research literature has focused on the importance for the evolution of religion of the development of the human capacity for abstract thought and representation, particularly through the use of symbols, and increasing socialization.[112] Four general lines of inquiry are thought to be of importance to an understanding of how religion has developed:[113]

1   The idea of "agency detection" and causal attribution;
2   The social and emotional commitments of social existence;
3   Narrative formation and the emergence of existential anxieties; and,
4   Ecstatic or mystical experience.

Although each of these is significant, the approach that is of greatest relevance to natural theology is the first. We shall therefore consider it further.

A number of workers in the field of the cognitive science of religion have proposed that humanity is generally characterized by possessing a "Hyperactive Agency Detection Device (HADD)." An early statement of this idea can be found in Stewart Guthrie's *Faces in the Clouds* (1993), which set out the idea of "agency detection" as a human perceptual function.[114] The idea, however, is developed in cognitive terms by writers such as Justin Barrett, who is widely credited with establishing the discipline of the cognitive science of religion:[115]

> Part of the reason people believe in gods, ghosts and, goblins also comes from the way in which our minds, particularly our agency detection device (ADD) functions. Our ADD suffers from some hyperactivity, making it prone to find agents around us, including supernatural ones, given fairly modest evidence of their presence. This tendency encourages the generation and spread of god concepts.

The argument here, deriving from evolutionary psychology, is that human beings have a naturally selected agency-detection system, which is wired to respond to fragmentary information in the environment that might point to a looming threat from an agent – such as a predatory mammal or hostile human being. This "device" thus detects agencies in the environment on the basis of potentially ambivalent sensory information. A noise in the woods might be nothing more than the wind rustling leaves; it might, on the other hand, be an agent who is a potential source of food, or an agent who is a potential threat. Pascal Boyer thus argues that this "detect" facility is likely to give false positives, in that it is better to be needlessly alerted than to miss the possibility of food or the threat of being devoured by others. The origins of belief in God may thus be attributed to an inbuilt and oversensitive human tendency to detect agencies, which gives rise to false positives. God is, in effect, an imaginary agency inferred from the environment by an oversensitive agency detector – the "Hyperactive Agency Detection Device."

The original evolutionary function of the HADD was thus to detect and evade predators; the evolutionary by-product of this device is a susceptibility to infer superhuman beings from noises and movements in the environment. Selection pressures, whether operating on groups or individuals, thus lead to the emergence of various dispositions or propensities in human minds that happen to (but were not *intended* to) give rise to religious belief. Religious beliefs are thus accidents or by-products of the evolutionary process. Religious beliefs themselves do not confer any selective advantage on groups or individuals; they are essentially the unintended outcomes of beliefs and behaviors that do confer advantages.[116] It remains unclear how one can speak meaningfully of "unintended" outcomes of the evolutionary process (what exactly *does* evolution "intend"?), or of "by-products" of that process.

Conclusion to Part III

So what are the implications for natural theology of the ideas explored in these chapters? At first sight, the approach to the evolutionary origins of religion just considered seems to erode the legitimacy of natural theology, suggesting that this is to be seen essentially as an error or "false positive" arising from our evolutionary history. Yet on closer examination, the situation is not quite so simple.[117] As Justin Barrett points out, human civilization is characterized by a series of enterprises that could also be held to be accidental by-products of evolution, including the scientific method.[118]

> Many beliefs and values that the scientists of religion themselves hold dear likely would be weakened by the same argument if it applied to theistic commitments. Contemporary beliefs and behaviors bestowed by science and technology arose far too late in our history to have played a role in natural selection of humans. Evolution did not select for calculus, quantum theory, or natural selection. Are these beliefs then suspect for being "accidents" or "byproducts" of evolution?

Barrett's point is that beliefs that are held to be accidental or unintended outcomes of evolutionary processes are not invalidated for that reason. Evolution does not select for truth; but for what is helpful for survival in our ancestral environments. It is quite possible to argue that belief in God, mathematical calculus, music, the theory of evolution, and quantum theory all represent unintended by-products of evolution. The evolutionary origin of these human intellectual endeavors does not erode their significance.

Evolutionary theory, then, certainly does not invalidate natural theology, any more than it invalidates the "love of wisdom" we call philosophy, or mathematical calculus. It does, however, serve as the occasion for informed reflection on the nature and scope of natural theology. Evolutionary thought raises a series of questions, including the question of what form of natural theology is best adapted to deal with the complex understanding of nature that an evolutionary account of natural history suggests.

The analysis presented in these three chapters strongly suggests that a renewed natural theology is indeed capable of engaging with a Darwinian view of reality. Teleology, for example, may have been redefined; it has not been destroyed or invalidated. There is much work that still needs to be done, building on the foundations laid by recent writers. It is, I think, fair to suggest that some recent writing in the field of science and religion has not exploited the full potential of the riches of the Christian theological tradition. The recovery of the deep theological wisdom of the patristic era – such as Augustine's views on creation, to note one obvious example – has the potential to enrich and inform our present debate.

Notes

1 For some works that explore this development, see Moore, James R., *The Post-Darwinian Controversies: A Study of the Protestant Struggle to Come to Terms with Darwin in Great Britain and America, 1870–1900*. Cambridge: Cambridge University Press, 1979; Bowler, Peter J., *The Eclipse of Darwinism: Anti-Darwinian Evolution Theories in the Decades around 1900*. Baltimore, MD: John Hopkins University Press, 1983; Hodgson, Geoffrey M., "Generalizing Darwinism to Social Evolution: Some Early Attempts." *Journal of Economic Issues* 39 (2005): 899–914.
2 Boinski, Sue, Robert P. Quatrone, and Hilary Swartz, "Substrate and Tool Use by Brown Capuchins in Suriname: Ecological Contexts and Cognitive Bases." *American Anthropologist* 102 (2000): 741–61.
3 Byrne, Richard W., and Lucy A. Bates, "Why Are Animals Cognitive?" *Current Biology* 16 (2006): R445–8.
4 Owings, Donald H., and Eugene S. Morton, *Animal Vocal Communication: A New Approach*. Cambridge: Cambridge University Press, 2006, 1–47.
5 Byrne, Richard W., "Tracing the Evolutionary Path of Cognition: Tactical Deception in Primates." In *The Social Brain*, ed. Martin Brüne, Hedda Ribbert, and Wulf Schiefenhövel, 43–60. Chichester: John Wiley & Sons, Ltd, 2003.
6 Mithen, Steven J., "Symbolism and the Supernatural." In *The Evolution of Culture: An Interdisciplinary View*, ed. Robin Dunbar, Chris Knight, and Camilla Power, 147–69. Edinburgh: Edinburgh University Press, 1999, 148.
7 On which see Gray, Patricia M., Bernie Krause, Jelle Atem, Roger Payne, Carol Krumhansl, and Luis Baptista, "The Music of Nature and the Nature of Music." *Science* 291, no. 5501 (2001): 52–4; Mithen, Steven J., "The Music Instinct: The Evolutionary Basis of Musicality." *Annals of the New York Academy of Sciences* 1169 (2009): 3–12.
8 For a recent discussion of the issue, see McKay, Ryan T., and Daniel C. Dennett, "The Evolution of Misbelief." *Behavioral and Brain Sciences* 32 (2009): 493–561, and the subsequent discussion based on this article.
9 McKay and Dennett, "The Evolution of Misbelief," 494.
10 Stich, Stephen P., *The Fragmentation of Reason: Preface to a Pragmatic Theory of Cognitive Evaluation*. Cambridge, MA: MIT Press, 1990, 62.

11 For example, see Boyer, Pascal, *Religion Explained. The Evolutionary Origins of Religious Thought*. New York: Basic Books, 2001, 4–33; Atran, Scott, *In Gods We Trust. The Evolutionary Landscape of Religion*. Oxford: Oxford University Press, 2002, 12–13.

12 As argued by Alcorta, Candace S., and Richard Sosis, "Ritual, Emotion, and Sacred Symbols: The Evolution of Religion as an Adaptive Complex." *Human Nature* 16 (2005): 323–59.

13 Richerson, Peter J., and Lesley Newson, "Is Religion Adaptive? Yes, No, Neutral. But Mostly We Don't Know." In *The Believing Primate: Scientific, Philosophical and Theological Reflections on the Origin of Religion*, ed. Jeffrey Schloss and Michael Murray, 100–17. Oxford: Oxford University Press, 2009.

14 As noted by Richards, Robert J., *Darwin and the Emergence of Evolutionary Theories of Mind and Behavior*. Chicago: University of Chicago Press, 1987, 200–6.

15 Darwin, Charles, *On the Origin of the Species by Means of Natural Selection*. London: John Murray, 1859, 422.

16 See, for example, Gregorio, Mario A. di, "Reflections of a Nonpolitical Naturalist: Ernst Haeckel, Wilhelm Bleek, Friedrich Müller and the Meaning of Language." *Journal of the History of Biology* 35 (2002): 79–109.

17 See, for example, Wheeler, Michael, John M. Ziman, and Margaret A. Boden, *The Evolution of Cultural Entities*. Oxford: Oxford University Press, 2002. For the notion of "cultural entities," see Margolis, Joseph, *Culture and Cultural Entities: Toward a New Unity of Science*. 2nd edn. New York: Springer, 2009, 1–15.

18 The best study of this development is Depew, David J., and Bruce H. Weber, *Darwinism Evolving: Systems Dynamics and the Genealogy of Natural Selection*. Cambridge, MA: MIT Press, 1996.

19 See, for example, White, Leslie A., *The Science of Culture: A Study of Man and Civilization*. New York: Farrar, Straus, 1949; White, Leslie A., *The Evolution of Culture: The Development of Civilization to the Fall of Rome*. New York: McGraw-Hill, 1959; Steward, Julian H., *Theory of Culture Change: The Methodology of Multilinear Evolution*. Urbana: University of Illinois Press, 1963.

20 Boyd, Robert, and Peter J. Richerson, *Culture and the Evolutionary Process*. Chicago: University of Chicago Press, 1985; Durham, William H., *Coevolution: Genes, Culture, and Human Diversity*. Stanford: Stanford University Press, 1991.

21 Note the general points made by Sperber, Dan, and Nicolas Claidière, "Why Modeling Cultural Evolution Is Still Such a Challenge." *Biological Theory* 1 (2006): 20–2.

22 Boyd and Richerson, *Culture and the Evolutionary Process*, 11–16.

23 Dennett, Daniel C., *Darwin's Dangerous Idea: Evolution and the Meaning of Life*. New York: Simon & Schuster, 1995, 63. Similar ideas are expressed in Cziko, Gary, *Without Miracles: Universal Selection Theory and the Second Darwinian Revolution*. Cambridge, MA: MIT Press, 1995, 281–302.

24 Modelski, George, and Kazimierz Poznanski, "Evolutionary Paradigms in the Social Sciences." *International Studies Quarterly* 40 (1996): 315–19.

25 See, for example, Fletcher, J. A., and M. Doebeli, "How Altruism Evolves: Assortment and Synergy." *Journal of Evolutionary Biology* 19 (2006): 1389–93.

26   Most notably, Lumsden, Charles J., and Edward O. Wilson, *Genes, Mind, and Culture: The Coevolutionary Process*. Cambridge, MA: Harvard University Press, 1981.

27   For example, Cavalli-Sforza, L. L., and M. W. Feldman, *Cultural Transmission and Evolution: A Quantitative Approach*. Princeton, NJ: Princeton University Press, 1981.

28   For a detailed survey of the evidence, see Sperber, Dan, and Lawrence Hirschfeld, "Culture, Cognition, and Evolution." In *MIT Encyclopedia of the Cognitive Sciences*, ed. Robert Wilson and Frank Keil, cxi–cxxxii. Cambridge, MA: MIT Press, 1999.

29   Modelski, George, "Evolutionary Paradigm for Global Politics." *International Studies Quarterly* 40 (1996): 321–41, especially 322–3.

30   Mesoudi, Alex, Andrew Whiten, and Kevin N. Laland, "Is Cultural Evolution Darwinian? Evidence Reviewed from the Perspective of *The Origin of Species*." *Evolution* 58 (2004): 1–11.

31   On which see Burkhardt, Richard W., *The Spirit of System: Lamarck and Evolutionary Biology*. Cambridge, MA: Harvard University Press, 1977, 143–85. The French Jesuit paleontologist Pierre Teilhard de Chardin (1881–1955) mingles Darwinian and Lamarckian elements in his account of human evolution: see the analysis in Roberts, Noel K., *From Piltdown Man to Point Omega: The Evolutionary Theory of Teilhard De Chardin*. New York: Peter Lang, 2000, 115–18; Grumett, David, "Teilhard De Chardin's Evolutionary Natural Theology." *Zygon* 42 (2007): 519–34.

32   For Ward's careful consideration of the biological options, see Ward, Lester Frank, *Neo-Darwinism and Neo-Lamarckism*. Washington, DC: Gedney & Roberts, 1891. For their cultural application in what some termed Ward's "biologic sociology," see Rafferty, Edward C., *Apostle of Human Progress: Lester Frank Ward and American Political Thought, 1841–1913*. Lanham, MD: Rowman & Littlefield, 2003, 205–6, 247–55.

33   Stephens, Lester D., "Joseph Leconte's Evolutional Idealism: A Lamarckian View of Cultural History." *Journal of the History of Ideas* 39 (1978): 465–80. Note also his earlier study: Stephens, Lester D., "Joseph Leconte on Evolution, Education, and the Structure of Knowledge." *Journal of the History of the Behavioral Sciences* 12 (1976): 103–19.

34   Jones, Steve, *Antonio Gramsci*. London: Routledge, 2006, 24–41.

35   Durham, W. H., "Cultural Variation in Time and Space." In *Anthropology Beyond Culture*, ed. R. G. Fox and B. J. King, 193–206. Oxford: Berg, 2002.

36   See, for example, the hostile and not entirely fair account in Hull, David L., "The Naked Meme." In *Learning, Development and Culture: Essays in Evolutionary Epistemology*, ed. H. C. Plotkin, 273–327. New York: John Wiley & Sons, Inc., 1982. Happily, Hull later offers a more sympathetic evaluation of the possibility: Hull, David L., "Taking Memetics Seriously: Memetics Will Be What We Make It." In *Darwinizing Culture: The Status of Memetics as a Science*, ed. Robert Aunger, 43–67. Oxford: Oxford University Press, 2000.

37   Dennett, *Darwin's Dangerous Idea*, 355 n. 6. Dennett is unduly reliant on Hull's flawed analysis at this point.

38 There is a huge literature. For a useful introduction, see Nauert, Charles Garfield, *Humanism and the Culture of Renaissance Europe*. 2nd edn. New Approaches to European History 6. Cambridge; New York: Cambridge University Press, 2006.

39 See, for example, Huse, Norbert, Wolfgang Wolters, and Edmund Jephcott, *The Art of Renaissance Venice: Architecture, Sculpture, and Painting, 1460–1590*. Chicago: University of Chicago Press, 1990; Ackerman, James S., *Distance Points: Essays in Theory and Renaissance Art and Architecture*. Cambridge, MA: MIT Press, 1991.

40 Bernstein, Eckhart, "From Outsiders to Insiders: Some Reflections on the Development of a Group Identity of the German Humanists between 1450 and 1530." In *In Laudem Caroli: Renaissance and Reformation Studies for Charles G. Nauert*, ed. Charles G. Nauert and James V. Mehl, 45–64. Kirksville, MO: Thomas Jefferson University Press, 1998.

41 See the classic study of Kristeller, Paul Oskar, *Renaissance Thought: The Classic, Scholastic, and Humanistic Strains*. New York: Harper & Row, 1961. Kristeller's analysis has stood the test of time remarkably well: see Monfasani, John, ed., *Kristeller Reconsidered: Essays on His Life and Scholarship*. New York: Italica Press, 2006.

42 See the classic essay of Gray, H. H., "Renaissance Humanism: The Pursuit of Eloquence." In *Renaissance Essays*, ed. P. O. Kristeller and P. P. Wiener, 199–216. New York: Harper & Row, 1966.

43 For the general issue, see Witt, Ronald G., *In the Footsteps of the Ancients: The Origins of Humanism from Lovato to Bruni*. Leiden: Brill, 2000, 1–30.

44 Weiss, Roberto, *The Renaissance Discovery of Classical Antiquity*. Oxford: Blackwell, 1988, 59–72.

45 See, for example, Robson, Arthur J., "The Evolution of Strategic Behaviour." *Canadian Journal of Economics* 28 (1995): 17–41; Gould, Stephen Jay, *Life's Grandeur: The Spread of Excellence from Plato to Darwin*. London: Jonathan Cape, 1996, 217–30; Nelson, Richard, "Evolutionary Social Science and Universal Darwinism." *Journal of Evolutionary Economics* 16 (2006): 491–510.

46 See, for example, Knudsen, Thorbjørn, "Nesting Lamarckism within Darwinian Explanations: Necessity in Economics and Possibility in Biology?" In *Darwinism and Evolutionary Economics*, ed. John Nightingale and John Laurent, 121–59. Cheltenham: Edward Elgar, 2001.

47 Knudsen, Thorbjørn, and Geoffrey M. Hodgson, "Why We Need a Generalized Darwinism and Why Generalized Darwinism Is Not Enough." *Journal of Economic Behavior & Organization* 61 (2006): 1–19; Kronfeldner, Maria E., "Is Cultural Evolution Lamarckian?" *Biology and Philosophy* 22 (2007): 493–512; Kashima, Yoshihisa, "Globalization, Diversity and Universal Darwinism." *Culture & Psychology* 13 (2007): 129–39.

48 Cavalli-Sforza and Feldman, *Cultural Transmission and Evolution*, 46–53.

49 Boyd and Richerson, *Culture and the Evolutionary Process*, 81–131.

50 Lumsden and Wilson, *Genes, Mind, and Culture*.

51 See, for example, Brodie, Richard, *Virus of the Mind: The New Science of the Meme*. Seattle, WA: Integral Press, 1996; Lynch, Aaron, *Thought Contagion:*

How Belief Spreads through Society. New York: Basic Books, 1996; Poulshock, Joseph, "Universal Darwinism and the Potential of Memetics." *Quarterly Review of Biology* 77 (2002): 174–5.

52 See Aunger, Robert, *The Electric Meme: A New Model of How We Think*. New York: Simon & Schuster, 2003, 65–92; Gil-White, Francisco J., "Common Misunderstandings of Memes (and Genes). The Promise and the Limits of the Genetic Analogy to Cultural Transmission Processes." In *Perspectives on Imitation. From Neuroscience to Social Science*, ed. Susan Hurley and Nick Chater, 317–38. Cambridge, MA: MIT Press, 2005.

53 Gould, Stephen Jay, "More Things in Heaven and Earth." In *Alas, Poor Darwin: Arguments against Evolutionary Psychology*, ed. Hilary Rose and Steven Rose, 85–105. London: Jonathan Cape, 2001, 97.

54 The concept of the "meme" plays a prominent role in two prominent works of this movement: Dawkins, Richard, *The God Delusion*. London: Bantam, 2006; and Dennett, Daniel C., *Breaking the Spell: Religion as a Natural Phenomenon*. New York: Viking Penguin, 2006.

55 Note especially Campbell, Donald T., "Variation, Selection and Retention in Sociocultural Evolution." In *Social Change in Developing Areas: A Reinterpretation of Evolutionary Theory*, ed. H. R. Barringer, G. I. Blanksten, and R. W. Mack, 19–49. Cambridge, MA: Schenkman, 1965; Cloak, F. T., "Is a Cultural Ethology Possible?" *Human Ecology* 3 (1975): 161–81. More generally, see Jahoda, Gustav, "The Ghosts in the Meme Machine." *History of the Human Sciences* 15, no. 2 (2002): 55–68.

56 Dawkins does not engage with Boyd and Richerson's suggestion that particulate replication is not necessary for cumulative adaptations through selective processes – an assertion that, if true, seriously erodes the case for the meme. See Boyd and Richerson, *Culture and the Evolutionary Process*, 75; Boyd, Robert, and Peter J. Richerson, "Memes: Universal Acid or a Better Mousetrap?" In *Darwinizing Culture: The Status of Memetics as a Science*, ed. Robert Aunger, 143–62. Oxford: Oxford University Press, 2000, especially 153–8.

57 Dawkins, Richard, *The Selfish Gene*. 2nd edn. Oxford: Oxford University Press, 1989, 192.

58 Dawkins, *The Selfish Gene*, 192.

59 Dawkins, Richard, *The Extended Phenotype: The Gene as the Unit of Selection*. Oxford: Freeman, 1981, 109.

60 It should be noted that popular discussion of Dawkins's meme concept continues to be framed in terms of his 1976 definition, set out in *The Selfish Gene*, rather than its later revision, as presented in the less widely read *Extended Phenotype*.

61 Blackmore, Susan J., *The Meme Machine*. Oxford: Oxford University Press, 1999, 69.

62 For the critical issue of the reliability of this copying process, see Sperber, Dan, "An Objection to the Memetic Approach to Culture." In *Darwinizing Culture: The Status of Memetics as a Science*, ed. Robert Aunger, 163–73. Oxford: Oxford University Press, 2000.

63 Midgley, Mary, "Why Memes?" In *Alas, Poor Darwin: Arguments against Evolutionary Psychology*, ed. Hilary Rose and Steven Rose, 67–84. London: Jonathan Cape, 2001, 76–7.

64   See especially Sperber's complaint about the marginalization of human psychol-
     ogy in this discussion: Sperber, Dan, "Why a Deep Understanding of Cultural
     Evolution Is Incompatible with Shallow Psychology." In *Roots of Human
     Sociality: Culture, Cognition and Interaction*, ed. Nick Enfield and Stephen
     Levinson, 431–49. Oxford: Berg, 2006.
65   See Hull, "The Naked Meme"; Hull, "Taking Memetics Seriously."
66   Gabora, Liane, "Ideas Are Not Replicators but Minds Are." *Biology and
     Philosophy* 19 (2004): 127–43.
67   Henrich, Joseph, and Richard Boyd, "Culture and Cognition: Why Cultural
     Evolution Does Not Require Replication of Representations." *Culture and
     Cognition* 2 (2002): 87–112, quote at 87.
68   The recent debate on this matter between Susan Blackmore and William C.
     Wimsatt is of interest here. See Blackmore, Susan, "Memetics Does Provide a
     Useful Way of Understanding Cultural Evolution." In *Contemporary Debates
     in Philosophy of Biology*, ed. Francisco J. Ayala and Robert Arp, 255–72.
     Oxford: Blackwell, 2010; Wimsatt, William C., "Memetics Does Not Provide a
     Useful Way of Understanding Cultural Evolution." In *Contemporary Debates
     in Philosophy of Biology*, ed. Francisco J. Ayala and Robert Arp, 273–91.
     Oxford: Blackwell, 2010.
69   Bloch, Maurice, "A Well-Disposed Social Anthropologist's Problem with
     Memes." In *Darwinizing Culture: The Status of Memetics as a Science*, ed.
     Robert Aunger, 189–203. Oxford: Oxford University Press, 2000. See further
     Richerson, Peter J., and Richard Boyd, "Built for Speed, Not for Comfort:
     Darwinian Theory and Human Culture." *History and Philosophy of the Life
     Sciences* 23 (2001): 425–65. Richerson and Boyd's account of such approaches
     can easily be extended – for example, it does not include Sperber's "epidemiol-
     ogy of representations." For the original statement of this approach, see Sperber,
     Dan, "Anthropology and Psychology: Towards an Epidemiology of Repre-
     sentations." *Man* 20 (1985): 73–89.
70   For what follows, see Henrich and Boyd, "Culture and Cognition," 88. Henrich
     and Boyd here summarize the concerns of Scott Atran, Pascal Boyer, and Dan
     Sperber.
71   For a detailed analysis of the difficulties, see Gabora, "Ideas Are Not Replicators
     but Minds Are."
72   This point was made forcefully by Polichak, James W., "Memes – What Are
     They Good For?" *Skeptic* 6, no. 3 (1998): 45–54. See further the criticisms and
     concerns set out in Poulshock, Joseph, "Meme Schemes: Problems and Potentials
     in Memetics." *Journal of Psychology and Theology* 30 (2002): 68–80; Bennett,
     M. R., and P. M. S. Hacker, eds., *Philosophical Foundations of Neuroscience*.
     Oxford: Blackwell, 2003, 431–5.
73   Aunger, Robert, "Introduction." In *Darwinizing Culture: The Status of
     Memetics as a Science*, ed. Robert Aunger, 1–23. Oxford: Oxford University
     Press, 2000, 7.
74   See Sperber, Dan, *Explaining Culture: A Naturalistic Approach*. Oxford:
     Blackwell, 1996; Atran, Scott, "The Trouble with Memes: Inference Versus
     Imitation in Cultural Creation." *Human Nature* 12 (2001): 351–81; Boyer,
     Pascal, "Cognitive Tracks of Cultural Inheritance: How Evolved Intuitive

Ontology Governs Cultural Transmission." *American Anthropologist* 100 (1999): 876–89.

75 Dennett's discussion of this point is particularly unsatisfying: *Breaking the Spell*, 120–1.

76 Blackmore, *Meme Machine*, 61.

77 This seems to be the position of Jeffreys, Mark, "The Meme Metaphor." *Perspectives in Biology and Medicine* 43 (2000): 227–42.

78 Laland, Kevin, and John Odling-Smee, "The Evolution of the Meme." In *Darwinizing Culture: The Status of Memetics as a Science*, ed. Robert Aunger, 121–42. Oxford: Oxford University Press, 2000, 121.

79 Dawkins, *The God Delusion*, 196.

80 Poulshock, Joseph, "Evolutionary Theology and God-Memes: Explaining Everything or Nothing." *Zygon* 37 (2002): 775–88, quote at 787.

81 Website at http://jom-emit.cfpm.org. Accessed December 10, 2009.

82 Edmonds, Bruce, "The revealed poverty of the gene-meme analogy – why memetics per se has failed to produce substantive results." Published online in January 2005. At http://cfpm.org/jom-emit/2005/vol9/edmonds_b.html. Accessed December 10, 2009.

83 Dennett also enriches the vocabulary of memetics with terms such as "memosphere": Dennett, *Breaking the Spell*, 231.

84 Dawkins, *The Selfish Gene*, 212–13.

85 Dennett, *Breaking the Spell*, 328–33. Dennett's approach here is simply assertive, not evidence-based.

86 Dennett, *Darwin's Dangerous Idea*, 346. Dennett here also suggests that the human mind is "a sort of dungheap in which the larvae of other people's ideas renew themselves, before sending out copies of themselves in an informational diaspora," indicating that he expects his readers to find this an objectionable idea.

87 Dennett, *Darwin's Dangerous Idea*, 366, summarizing Dawkins's approach. See also 370–1: "If human minds are nonmiraculous products of evolution, then they are, in the requisite sense, artifacts, and all their powers must have an ultimately 'mechanical' explanation. We are descended from macros and made of macros, and nothing we can do is anything beyond the power of huge assemblies of macros."

88 See the discussion of the "new replicators": Dennett, *Breaking the Spell*, 341–57, especially the taxonomy of memes on p. 344.

89 The rhetorical devices used in his discussion of whether memes actually exist are of particular interest: see Dennett, *Breaking the Spell*, 348–53.

90 Note the points made by Sperber, "An Objection to the Memetic Approach to Culture"; Laland, Kevin N., and Gillian R. Brown, *Sense and Nonsense: Evolutionary Perspectives on Human Behaviour*. Oxford: Oxford University Press, 2002, 209–16.

91 For the original experiment, see Michelson, A. A., and E. W. Morley, "On the Relative Motion of the Earth and Luminiferous Ether." *American Journal of Science* 34 (1887): 333–45.

92 Dawkins, Richard, *A Devil's Chaplain: Selected Writings*. London: Weidenfeld & Nicholson, 2003, 124.

93 A point developed in McGrath, Alister E., *A Scientific Theology: 2 – Reality*. London: Continuum, 2002.
94 Marett, Robert, *Anthropology*. London: Williams and Norgate, 1912, 8. On Marett, see Bengtson, Dale R., "R. R. Marett and the Study of Religion." *Journal of the American Academy of Religion* 47 (1979): 645–59.
95 Marett, *Anthropology*, 11–12.
96 See, for example, Cole, Michael, *Cultural Psychology: A Once and Future Discipline*. Cambridge, MA: Belknap Press, 1998, 7–37.
97 Darwin, Charles, *The Descent of Man*. 2 vols. London: John Murray, 1871, vol. 1, 65.
98 Darwin, *The Descent of Man*, vol. 1, 65.
99 For a good summary and evaluation of the literature, see Sosis, Richard, and Candace S. Alcorta, "Signaling, Solidarity, and the Sacred: The Evolution of Religious Behavior." *Evolutionary Anthropology* 12 (2003): 264–74.
100 Evans-Pritchard, E. E., *Theories of Primitive Religion*. Oxford: Clarendon Press, 1965.
101 Sosis and Alcorta, "Signaling, Solidarity, and the Sacred," 272.
102 For the question of how such developments are to be conceptualized, see McGrath, Alister E., "The Evolution of Doctrine? A Critical Examination of the Theological Validity of Biological Models of Doctrinal Development." In *The Order of Things: Explorations in Scientific Theology*, 117–68. Oxford: Blackwell, 2006, 153–68.
103 For the metaphor, see Gould, Stephen Jay, and Richard C. Lewontin, "The Spandrels of San Marco and the Panglossian Paradigm: A Critique of the Adaptationist Programme." *Proceedings of the Royal Society of London* B 205 (1979): 581–98. For the notion of "exaptation," see Gould, Stephen Jay, and Elisabeth Vrba, "Exaptation: A Missing Term in the Science of Form." *Paleobiology* 8 (1982): 4–15.
104 See, for example, Boyer, *Religion Explained*, 95–135; Atran, *In Gods We Trust*, 43–5; Barrett, Justin L., *Why Would Anyone Believe in God?* Lanham, MD: AltaMira Press, 2004, 21–60.
105 See Sjöblom, Tom, "Spandrels, Gazelles and Flying Buttresses: Religion as Adaptation or as a By-Product." *Journal of Cognition and Culture* 7 (2007): 293–312, especially 300–1.
106 For example, consider the problems in tracing the evolution of the human mind, given that this is not to be equated with that of the human brain: see Mithen, Steven J., "How the Evolution of the Human Mind Can Be Reconstructed." In *The Evolution of Mind: Fundamental Questions and Controversies*, ed. Steven W. Gangestad and Jeffry A. Simpson, 60–6. New York: Guilford, 2007.
107 A point stressed by Steadman, Lyle B., and Craig T. Palmer, "Religion as an Identifiable Traditional Behavior Subject to Natural Selection." *Journal of Social and Evolutionary Systems* 18 (1995): 149–64.
108 Durkheim, Emile, *The Elementary Forms of Religious Life*. New York: Free Press, 1995, 46. For the development of this theory, see Pickering, W. S. F., *Durkheim's Sociology of Religion: Themes and Theories*. London: Routledge & Kegan Paul, 1984, 47–86.

109 Durkheim, *The Elementary Forms of Religious Life*, 26–31.
110 As, for example, in Wilson, David Sloan, *Darwin's Cathedral: Evolution, Religion, and the Nature of Society*. Chicago: University of Chicago Press, 2002, 125–88.
111 Sosis, Richard, and Eric R. Bressler, "Cooperation and Commune Longevity: A Test of the Costly Signaling Theory of Religion." *Cross-Cultural Research* 37 (2003): 211–39; Sosis, Richard, and Bradley Ruffle, "Religious Ritual and Cooperation: Testing for a Relationship on Israeli Religious and Secular Kibbutzim." *Current Anthropology* 44 (2003): 713–22.
112 See especially Huyssteen, J. Wentzel van, *Alone in the World? Human Uniqueness in Science and Theology*. Grand Rapids, MI: Eerdmans, 2006, 45–106; Mithen, Steven J., "The Inevitability of Religion. An Archaeologist's View from the Past." In *The Edge of Reason: Science and Religion in the Modern World*, ed. Alex Bentley, 82–94. London: Continuum, 2008; Mithen, Steven J., "The Prehistory of the Religious Mind." In *Theology, Evolution and the Mind*, ed. Neil Spurway, 10–41. Cambridge: Scholars Press, 2009.
113 Rossano, Matt J., "The Religious Mind and the Evolution of Religion." *Review of General Psychology* 10 (2006): 346–64.
114 Guthrie, Stewart, *Faces in the Clouds: A New Theory of Religion*. New York: Oxford University Press, 1993, 177–204. For developments of this approach, see Boyer, *Religion Explained*; Atran, *In Gods We Trust*; Pyysiäinen, Ilkka, *Magic, Miracles and Religion: A Scientist's Perspective*. Walnut Creek, CA: AltaMira Press, 2004, 7–11; Barrett, *Why Would Anyone Believe in God?*; Tremlin, Todd, *Minds and Gods: The Cognitive Foundations of Religion*. Oxford: Oxford University Press, 2006, 73–106.
115 Barrett, *Why Would Anyone Believe in God?*, 31.
116 See Sjöblom, "Spandrels, Gazelles and Flying Buttresses." Such an argument is central to Dawkins's *The God Delusion* (2006): for an assessment, see Markusson, Gudmundur Ingi, "Review of *The God Delusion*." *Journal of Cognition and Culture* 7 (2007): 369–73.
117 Barrett, Justin L., "Is the Spell Really Broken? Bio-Psychological Explanations of Religion and Theistic Belief." *Theology and Science* 5 (2007): 57–72.
118 Barrett, "Is the Spell Really Broken?", 63.

Part IV
Conclusion

10

The Prospects for Natural Theology

"It is the task of our theological generation to find its way back to a proper natural theology" (Emil Brunner).[1] In bringing this work to a conclusion, it is appropriate to consider whether its analysis has anything to contribute to the significant debates over the nature, scope, and future of natural theology within the Christian tradition. Brunner himself may have failed to win support for his own specific approach to natural theology; his call for its renewal and redirection, however, remains a live challenge to contemporary theological reflection.

As we have seen (15–18), natural theology can be conceived in a number of ways,[2] including the idea that there is a natural human propensity to seek and discover God. Natural theology does not propose itself as a scientific metanarrative, but as an important strand in a multilayered account of the human engagement with reality. The fundamentally theological notion that we are created to relate to God, and are thus disposed toward questing for the divine within the world of our experience,[3] is not a total account of the truth; it is nevertheless an important thread in the fabric of human self-understanding, offering a framework for engaging with fundamental questions such as "Why is the world intelligible to us?" and "Where do our notions of explanation, regularity, and intelligibility come from?".

The historical analysis set out in the second part of this work strongly suggests that the rise of evolutionary thought was the final of many nails in the coffin of William Paley's specific approach to natural theology. This, however, was itself a relatively late development, reflecting the cultural situation of England from about 1690, which was already being subjected to significant literary, philosophical, theological, and scientific criticism within its English homeland by 1850. Despite the severe erosion of

Darwinism and the Divine: Evolutionary Thought and Natural Theology, First Edition.
Alister E. McGrath.
© 2011 Alister E. McGrath. Published 2011 by Blackwell Publishing Ltd.

academic support for its core ideas, English physico-theology was still of importance in shaping the contours of popular debates about the religious implications of Darwin's theory of natural selection. The perception that Darwin's theory was subversive of religious belief was shaped to no small extent by the persistence of a "physico-theology" that accentuated the concept of contrivance. Darwin's naturalistic explanation of contrivance fatally wounded such approaches. Yet even at that time there were other approaches to natural theology – such as those that emphasized the orderliness and beauty of nature,[4] thus arguing from inference rather than deduction. Darwin is to be seen as exposing the vulnerability of "physico-theology," and thus catalyzing the re-evaluation of older approaches to natural theology and the formulation of alternatives (such as those hinted at, though sadly not fully developed, by Charles Kingsley and Frederick Temple).

Yet the enterprise of natural theology has, if anything, been given a new lease of life through the rise of evolutionary thought, partly by being liberated from the intellectual and spiritual straitjacket within which Paley's approach had unhelpfully confined it. For "natural theology" designates a family of approaches, each with its own history of development, application, and criticism within the Christian tradition. Paley's approach is one option among many; the rise of evolutionary thought supplemented an existing and vigorous theological critique of this approach, bringing this erosion of confidence to a point at which retrieval was no longer possible – or desirable. Natural theology needs to emerge from the lengthening shadows of Paley, and rediscover, retrieve, and renew alternative approaches. This concluding chapter therefore offers reflections both on the viability of natural theology in general, as well as an assessment of which particular style of natural theology seems best adapted to deal with the challenges raised by evolutionary thought.

It must be emphasized that while evolutionary thought does raise some new questions for Christian thought, most of the issues that arise from it can be seen as intensifications or recontextualizations of questions that are already well known to Christian theology, and to which answers had been developed within the Christian tradition. A theologically informed observer of the English Darwinian disputes of the late nineteenth century can only express intense frustration over the failure of many English religious writers of the age to appreciate the rich conceptual resources already present within the Christian tradition, which could have been brought to bear with considerable profit to the debates of that age – such as Augustine of Hippo's approach to creation through *rationes seminales* (222–9). While retrospective resolution of past debates is of little historical importance, it alerts us to the importance of engaging with contemporary scientific culture with a full knowledge of the theological resources of the Christian tradition.

We begin our final reflections on natural theology by considering whether it is reductively explained by evolutionary thought.

Natural Theology and the Human Evolutionary Past

Natural theology – like philosophy, quantum theory, and mathematical calculus – can be seen as the outcome of our past development and history, resting upon an evolved capacity to think, which is of relatively recent origin in comparison with evolutionary timescales. In one sense, Daniel Dennett is right: Darwinism is a "universal acid," which leaks out from its biological container to erode other fields of thought.[5]

Yet Dennett seems curiously reluctant to concede that this acid corrodes even the rational structures that he deploys in asserting and defending it. What if these ways of thinking and reasoning are nothing more than the vestiges of survival mechanisms, evolved to meet expediencies, rather than quest for truth? What if a fundamentally flawed reasoning process reassures us of its own validity, thus locking us into a cycle of delusion? The use of reason to confirm the trustworthiness of religion is to be compared to using biblical citations to prove the authority of Scripture, or papal pronouncements to confirm the ecclesiastical authority of the Pope. All three are self-referential and circular.

There is no reason to think that the evolution of the human mind is driven by truth; in fact, we do not fully understand the evolutionary history of the mind, so that we might identify possible hard-wiring leading to automatic patterns of reasoning. The philosophical defense of the validity of reason by reason is not merely intellectually circular and parasitic; it is confronted with the serious difficulty – happily unknown to the thinkers of the eighteenth-century Enlightenment – that the human mind may have evolved in such a way that false beliefs might turn out to be evolutionarily adaptive. As Michael Ghiselin rightly, though uncomfortably, observes:[6]

> We are anything but a mechanism set up to perceive the truth for its own sake. Rather, we have evolved a nervous system that acts in the interest of our gonads, and one attuned to the demands of reproductive competition. If fools are more prolific than wise men, then to that degree folly will be favored by selection.

"Universal Darwinism" has indeed the potential to become a "universal acid." Yet its more enthusiastic advocates seem reluctant to apply these conclusions consistently and thoroughly, instead applying it selectively against their opponents, while declining to concede its impact on their own ideas. It erodes facile confidence in systems – whether philosophical, scientific, theological, or ethical – that claim to be truthful, explaining their ideas and their origination as adaptive survival strategies. If all ideas and values are to be conceptualized in terms of strategies for survival in the intellectual world, there are no objective grounds for excluding the scientific account of the world from this ideological metanarrative.

As we noted earlier (32–6), this problem arises primarily from the improper inflation of Darwinism from a provisional scientific theory to a totalizing worldview. In the end, "Universal Darwinism" suffers from the intellectual hyperbole of certain forms of logical positivism. The declaration that "all metaphysical statements are meaningless" turns out to be self-referential and potentially self-refuting.[7] The exploration of the evolutionary origins and development of human thought has the potential to clarify; it also – when carelessly, polemically, and overambitiously applied – has the capacity to mislead.

There are no meaningful criteria by which a "Darwinian" view of the world can be proposed as an ultimate ideological system that is itself invulnerable to corrosion by its own universal acid. The ultimate circularity of the notion of the meme, especially when coupled with its notorious evidential under-determination, illustrates how the strategists of "Universal Darwinism" have managed to declare themselves to occupy a privileged intellectual "zone of invulnerability" from the corrosiveness of its own ideas. Happily, mainstream science has sidelined this metaphysical inflation of Darwinism, and demanded that it revert to its proper status as a *bona fide* scientific theory.

This welcome development does not invalidate the questions that need to be addressed. Are there evolutionary impulses that cause us to think in certain ways? Can these be identified and filtered out, to allow more balanced and reliable decisions? The evolutionary synthesis encourages us to operate a "hermeneutic of suspicion,"[8] which recognizes the possible bias of human thought, but equally recognizes that this bias can be identified and countered.

It is widely thought that humanity has a series of natural propensities, including an "impulse to natural theology."[9] There may indeed be an evolutionary component, dimension, or level to this impulse, just as partial evolutionary explanations might be offered for the human sense of longing for justice, the development of mathematics or music, or the intense intellectual curiosity about the natural world that is so powerful a motivation for the natural sciences. Yet while the evolutionary synthesis may suggest certain unverified and limited explanations of the impulse to undertake these quests, this does not invalidate their outcomes. It is entirely possible that a knowledge of human evolutionary history may help us understand something of why mathematics is able to map the real world so accurately; such a knowledge neither invalidates this characteristic of mathematics, nor diminishes its importance for the scientific method.

Natural Theology, Observational Traction, and the Best Explanation

Natural theology, however it is defined, has to do with borderlands – the threshold of Christian belief and experience of the natural world. It allows us to "see" the world in a manner that is grounded in the empirical, but is not restricted to it. Much has been written of the importance of natural theology as a means of giving access to the domain of the transcendent.[10] Yet it is also important to emphasize that natural theology gives the Christian faith traction with the natural world. The Christian vision of reality is such that it has the capacity to engage, interlock, and enfold – and hence *explain* – the complexities of the human experience of the natural world.[11]

There is an obvious parallel (though not an identity) with scientific theories at this point. Charles Darwin commented that his unprovable theory of natural selection must be judged "according as it groups and explains phenomena."[12] The point Darwin wanted to convey here was that the capacity of a theory to generate traction with observation was an important indicator of its truth. In judging a theory, we must consider both its evidential basis and its capacity to colligate data, weaving a web of coherence that unites and correlates otherwise disconnected and meaningless data.[13]

The American poet Edna St Vincent Millay (1892–1950) spoke of "a meteoric shower of facts" raining from the sky, lying "unquestioned, uncombined."[14] They are like threads that need to be woven into a tapestry, clues that need to be assembled to disclose the big picture. As Millay pointed out, we are overwhelmed with information, but cannot make sense of the "shower of facts" with which we are bombarded. There seems to be "no loom to weave it into fabric." The question that natural theology confronts is: how are these observations to be colligated (cf. William Whewell's "colligation of facts," Chapter 5 above)?[15] How are they to be woven together into a coherent pattern?

A worldview can be judged both by its internal consistency and coherence, and its external correspondence with reality.[16] The failure of a worldview to gain significant traction with the empirical worlds of human observation and experience inevitably raises serious questions about both its intellectual validity and existential relevance. Christianity is not fundamentally a religion of explanation; it is better characterized in terms of "transformation." Yet part of the envisaged transformation is a new way of "seeing" an ambiguous world – in other words, a natural theology.[17]

One influential way of conceiving natural theology, which achieved cultural hegemony at the time of the Enlightenment, interprets it as "proving" the existence of God on the basis of evidence gleaned from the natural world. This is the dominant theme of the approach of William Paley (91–7), whose influence continues to shape popular views of the discipline. Yet the term "evidence" requires careful consideration. Paley's approach depends upon a positivist approach to evidence, characteristic of his and earlier ages, which assumes that – for example – "contrivance" or "design" can be observed. They cannot; they must be *inferred* from what is observed.

As the great English debate over forensic evidence in the 1830s established beyond reasonable doubt, an observation only becomes "evidence" in the light of a framework of interpretation (115–19). Such an interpretative framework positions an observation so that it becomes evidence for or against a particular way of thinking.[18] Indeed, recent work in the philosophy of science has recognized the implicit role of such automatic processes of interpretation in the process of observation, now recognized as a "theory-laden" activity.[19] Whatever its other intellectual vulnerabilities might be, Paley's approach rests fundamentally on an outdated approach to evidence.

It is now clear that "evidence" is not an empirical given; it is a constructed notion, given its significance by the web of meaning of which it is alleged to be part, and whose validity it is held to endorse. To speak of "evidence for the existence of God" thus implicitly presupposes that nature is seen through an interpretative framework, which allows certain facts or observations to be *interpreted* as confirmatory of this belief. Talk about "proof" is thus really and fundamentally about affirming resonance or consonance between theory and observation.[20] How well does the theory accommodate observation? How good is the empirical fit between a proposed theoretical framework and what is actually encountered in the world? Whether explicitly acknowledged or not, any form of natural theology is dependent upon the interpretation of observations, and the adjudication of whether such observations are consonant with theory – whether the theory is atheist, deist, theist, or Trinitarian.

The analysis in the present work makes it clear that evolutionary biology is open to multiple interpretations – both theist and atheist. What the theist sees as evidence for God is equally open to being seen as evidence for the non-existence of God.[21] The same empirical observations are open to many possible interpretations. For example, the "laws of nature" are capable of being interpreted theistically (as representing "Laws impressed on matter by the Creator")[22] or atheistically (as demonstrating the autonomy of nature, and hence the absence of any meaningful role for God within it). This is not a new development. As Thomas H. Huxley rightly noted, Darwin's ideas were open to such multiple interpretations from the outset.

Loose talk about "proving" theism or atheism thus really misses the point; the critical question generally concerns which of an array of proposed explanations turns out to be most capable of accommodating the observational evidence. A failure to appreciate the contextual character of evidence has perhaps distracted theologians from appreciating the positive importance for natural theology of "inference to the best explanation" (whether this is interpreted following Charles S. Peirce, N. R. Hanson, or Gilbert Harman: see 197–200). Natural theology thus cannot be understood simply to concern "proving" God from nature, in that such a process invariably presupposes postulating hypotheses, which are then tested against observation for coherence and consistency. This process of testing possible explanations is more appropriately considered under the rubric of "inference to the best explanation."

This observation gives us further reason to insist that Christian theology should review those styles of natural theology that are conceptually wedded to the philosophies of science of earlier generations,[23] and take fuller account of the philosophies of explanation now regnant. Older styles of natural theology, sidelined by the Enlightenment, need to be given a higher profile. Charles S. Peirce, who is widely credited with developing the abductive approach, was clear about its potential for reaffirming the rationality of belief in God.[24] It is time it was properly incorporated into the Christian community's conception of natural theology.

A Community of Discernment: The Church and Natural Theology

Natural theology is not an individual undertaking; it is rooted in the life and ministry of the Christian community. Through faith, Christians develop habits of engagement with the natural world that allow it to be seen, understood, and evaluated in new ways. Such habits of thought are both generated and sustained by the Christian gospel, especially as this is proclaimed and embodied in the life of the church. It is a point that received classical expression in the writings of Augustine of Hippo. For Augustine, God is the intelligible sun who gives light to the mind and therefore brings intelligibility to what we see.[25] Yet the human eye must itself be healed by grace if the divinely illuminated landscape is to be seen properly: "Our whole business in this life is to heal the eye of the heart, so that God might be seen."[26] Augustine's point is that the Christian way of "seeing" reality is neither naturally acquired nor naturally endorsed. It comes about through the Christian revelation, which brings about a transformation of our perception of things.

Augustine's telling phrase "healing the eyes of the heart" suggests that the acquisition of such new habits of thought can be compared to a blind person being enabled to see the world for the first time. The reality of the world is hidden from us, until we are enabled to see it properly. It is a point familiar from the New Testament, which is perhaps unexpectedly developed further in the writings of Iris Murdoch, who emphasized the severe limitations of the human vision of reality. "By opening our eyes, we do not necessarily see what confronts us ... Our minds are continually active, fabricating an anxious, usually self-preoccupied, often falsifying *veil* which partially conceals the world."[27] This veil must be removed; our eyes must be healed; and as Augustine emphasizes, both these must be recognized as works of divine grace, not as a human skill or achievement.

God, then, is the ultimate enabler of the process of healing and renewal that allows us to see things as they really are. But how is this process of transformation mediated? Augustine sees the Christian community as playing a critical role in this process by reinforcing this way of seeing things in its proclamation and sacramental ministries, which both narrate and enact this vision of reality, correlating it with human experience. Stanley Hauerwas thus argues that the Christian church offers a framework or lens through which we may "see" the world of human behavior. This is provided and developed by sustained, detailed, extended reflection on the Christian narrative, which is articulated and enacted in the life and witness of the church: "We can only see the world rightly by being trained to see. We do not come to see just by looking, but by disciplined skills developed through initiation into a narrative."[28]

The Christian church thus embodies a way of seeing the world that is proclaimed and sustained by its controlling words, images, and actions. There is an obvious correlation here with Alasdair MacIntyre's insights on how communities maintain their identity through "habits" of thought and action, which are mediated through traditions.[29] We are thus called upon to see the world in its true light, by seeing and interpreting the world on the basis of a "mental map" that is grounded in the fundamental themes of the Christian tradition. This allows the shadows of the natural world to be softened and illuminated, and its ambiguities to be brought into sharper focus, so that it may be seen as it really is. This point was emphasized by Hauerwas, who argued that "the church serves the world by giving the world the means to see itself truthfully."[30]

Faith thus entails that the community of faith sees the world in a manner that differs strikingly from what Charles Taylor termed the prevailing "social imaginaries," a term he uses to designate "the ways people imagine their social existence, how they fit together with others, how things go on between them and their fellows, the expectations that are normally met, and the deeper normative notions and images that underlie these expectations."[31]

The church is thus called to be an active interrogator, not a passive endorser, of secular and secularizing visions of the world. It is called upon to proclaim, exhibit, and embody its own "social imaginary," deeply rooted in the gospel on the one hand, and with the capacity to transform reflection and practice on the other.

Such an imaginatively compelling and intellectually enriching vision of reality is mediated by the church, understood as a community of faith that is called into being by this vision of reality. We might think of the church as an "interpretive community," to use Stanley Fish's term,[32] which coalesces around and is characterized by a particular "point of view or way of organizing experience."[33] Fish developed the notion of the "interpretive community" primarily to account for a difficulty that emerged within postmodern explanations of the appearance of influential interpretations of texts, when no such interpretation could be regarded as "authoritative." Ecclesiologically, this can be reformulated in terms of the crystallization of a community around a particular interpretation of the texts of Scripture, history, and nature, set within a Trinitarian economy of salvation.[34]

While there is clearly more than this to any understanding of the nature and function of the church, it is important to appreciate how this aspect of the church's identity engages with the question of how the church can be distinct from other intellectual communities of discourse and reflection, while at the same time being able to connect up with the same realities that other people know and experience. The church and the world engage with the same empirical realities – what we might loosely call "the world" – but see (and hence understand and evaluate) them in very different ways.

Natural theology can thus be understood as the way in which the church "sees" the domain of nature. While beholding the same empirical realities as everyone else, the Christian community brings to this task its own distinct discipline of attention and framework of understanding. The community of faith is an "interpretive community" for the "book of nature," bringing its rich Trinitarian theological vision to bear upon the natural world. It does not seek to prove God from nature, but affirms and welcomes the resonance it observes between its vision of reality and what is actually observed. The intellectual capaciousness and fruitfulness of that interpretative lens does not prove its truth; it does, however, demonstrate its utility and reliability, while opening up further vistas of exploration and engagement.

One such outcome of this natural theology is the appreciation of the deeper context within which the natural sciences are to be located.[35] Natural theology complements the natural sciences by setting their outcomes in a wider framework of meaning, and corrects them by challenging them when they stray into metaphysically inflated interpretations of those outcomes. An obvious example of this defection is seen in the tendency to conflate Darwinism, understood as a scientific theory, with a rather different Darwinism, understood as an atheist metanarrative of origins and ends. Verbal identity here masks a profound conceptual divergence, which a rigorous natural theology can help identify and correct. Perhaps more significantly, a natural theology offers a conceptual framework that safeguards assumptions on which the scientific method must rely but cannot itself prove – such as the deep intelligibility of the universe, which humanity proves able to access and represent mathematically.

Yet there is one further point that must be made in bringing this section to a close. A Christian natural theology cannot purchase intellectual traction on the world of nature at the expense of losing its rooting in the narrative of Jesus of Nazareth – above all, the "word of the cross." A properly Trinitarian natural theology finds correlations between the suffering of the creator in Christ and the pain of the creation.[36] Where deist natural theologies portrayed God as the grand designer, immune from the pain and deficiencies of the created order, a Trinitarian vision of God declares that God entered into that created order, in order to inhabit and redeem it. The Trinitarian grammar of faith certainly offers a new way of making sense of the suffering of a Darwinian world. But perhaps more importantly, it also allows us to *cope* with it, by providing a framework of interpretation that enables suffering to be engaged both cognitively and existentially.

We find such a point developed in the writings of Simone Weil (1909–43). Weil, who discovered Christianity relatively late in her short life, doubted whether it was ever possible to offer a rational explanation for the presence of suffering, nor a means of evading it. Yet for Weil, "The extreme greatness of Christianity lies in the fact that it does not seek a supernatural remedy for suffering but a supernatural use for it."[37] Divine wisdom is known through human misery (*malheur*) rather than through pleasure. Indeed, "all pleasure-seeking is the search for an artificial paradise,"[38] which discloses "nothing except the experience that it is vain." Only the contemplation of our "limitations and our misery" raises us up to a higher plane. Weil's reflections point to the fundamental distinction that must be made between knowledge and wisdom – between making sense of things, and being enabled to live and develop meaningfully amidst the ambiguities of life and experience. We shall reflect further on this point, in bringing this work to a close.

In Quest of Meaning

Throughout this book, natural theology has been framed in terms of a quest for intelligibility. How can a Christian account of the natural world accommodate evolutionary biology, while at the same time challenging and correcting those who metaphysically inflate it? These are important questions, and this work has tried to make a contribution to their clarification. Yet the terms of the debate are a consequence of its history; the process of the "disenchantment" of nature, so distinctive a feature of the Protestant engagement with the natural world, inevitably led to the emergence of a strongly cognitive notion of natural theology as an attempt to "make sense" of the world, including arguing for the existence of God as an organizing and explanatory concept. The history of the English debate has shaped its character. Yet it is a strikingly inadequate and truncated vision of natural theology, which gives intelligibility priority over meaning.

Most of the approaches to natural theology considered in this work concern themselves primarily with intellectual accommodation. As William James once pointed out in his essay "Is Life Worth Living?", religious faith is fundamentally a "faith in the existence of an unseen order of some kind in which the riddles of the natural order may be found explained."[39] The apologetic situation confronted by Christianity in England since the Augustan age has made arguing the case for the reasonableness of faith of primary importance. Natural theology would seem to have a significant role to play today in the increasingly critical cultural dialogue concerning the intellectual roots and consequences of the Christian faith.

Yet, in concluding this work, it is important to point out that an authentic natural theology is concerned with the discernment of meaning in life, as much as the demonstration of rationality in faith. There is a fundamental and significant difference between intelligibility and meaning; the former does not entail the latter. "The more the universe seems comprehensible, the more it also seems pointless" (Steven Weinberg).[40] The quest for meaning lies beyond the empirical realm, which discloses a moral and aesthetic ambiguity that cannot act as the basis for a viable philosophy or ethic. Attempts to construct an ethic or philosophy based upon an appeal to nature and its processes have foundered. The natural sciences may clarify mechanisms; they do not determine meaning. Ultimately, questions such as "What are we here for?" or "What is the point of living?" have to be declared to lie beyond the scope of the scientific method.[41] This does not mean that they cannot be answered; it does, however, demand that we look beyond the scientific horizon if we are to find answers. The limits of science are often best understood when they are transgressed, and seen afresh from the far side of the empirical realm.

Christian theology offers an approach to nature that is grounded in its empirical reality, but transcends the limits of the empirical. It offers us theoretical spectacles, which allow us to behold things in such a way that we are able to rise above the limits of the observable, and move into the richer realm of discerned meaning and value. In doing so, it does not descend into fantasy, but makes warranted assertions that are grounded in its deep and rich Trinitarian vision of God. The natural world thus becomes God's creation, bearing the subtle imprint of its maker. We see not only the observable reality of the world, but its deeper value and true significance. A commitment to the empirical and observable is retained, but supplemented by a deeper level of understanding to which it leads – *when rightly interpreted.*

Nature is thus an "open secret"; though open to public gaze, its deeper significance lies hidden. A surface reading suggests that nature has "no design, no purpose, no evil and no good, nothing but blind pitiless indifference."[42] Yet the Christian tradition offers an interpretative lens, which illuminates nature's shadows and brings its features into sharper focus. Its many enigmas remain, but we see them in a new light. A Christian natural theology holds that the true meaning of nature is indeed capable of being unlocked; but this requires us to use a hermeneutical key that nature itself cannot provide. The Protestant approaches to natural theology that we have considered in this work presupposed the "disenchantment of nature" (57–9); the approach just outlined offers the possibility of a serious and informed re-engagement with the deeper questions of its meaning, which became sidelined through the Augustan emphasis upon natural theology as a "sense-making" activity.

This point was developed in a short poem by the German Romantic poet Joseph von Eichendorff (1788–1857), who pointed to the need for a "magic word" that unlocks nature, thus allowing its deeper meaning and beauty to be discerned beneath its superficial appearance.[43] Eichendorff argued for a renewed natural theology as a means of recovering a personal objectivity, which includes a right understanding of the human relationship with God.[44] It is a fitting point at which to end this study of natural theology in an evolutionary age.

> In all things a song lies sleeping,
> That keeps dreaming to be heard,
> And the world will rise up singing,
> If you find the magic word.

Notes

1 Brunner, Emil, "Natur und Gnade: Zum Gespräch mit Karl Barth." In *Ein offenes Wort. Vorträge und Aufsätze 1917–1934*, ed. Rudolf Wehrli, 333–75. Zürich: Theologischer Verlag, 1981, 375.

2 Note also the comments of the multiple interpretations of the concept found in Hutchinson, John, "The Uses of Natural Theology: An Essay in Redefinition." *Journal of Philosophy* 55 (1958): 936–44; Fischer, Hermann, "Natürliche Theologie im Wandel." *Zeitschrift für Theologie und Kirche* 80 (1983): 85–102.

3 For detailed discussion, see McGrath, Alister E., *The Open Secret: A New Vision for Natural Theology*. Oxford: Blackwell, 2008, 23–79.

4 See, for example, the approaches developed by Dutch writers: Jorink, Erik, *Het Boeck der Natuere: Nederlandse Geleerden en de Wonderen van Gods Schepping 1575–1715*. Leiden: Primavera Pers, 2006.

5 Dennett, Daniel C., *Darwin's Dangerous Idea: Evolution and the Meaning of Life*. New York: Simon & Schuster, 1995, 61–4.

6   Ghiselin, Michael T., *The Economy of Nature and the Evolution of Sex*. Berkeley, CA: University of California Press, 1974, 126. The impact of social factors in shaping belief, so rigorously explored by Marxist thinkers, should also be noted here. See, for example, Bhaskar, Roy, *The Possibility of Naturalism: A Philosophical Critique of the Contemporary Human Sciences*. 3rd edn. London: Routledge, 1998.

7   Cirera, Ramon, *Carnap and the Vienna Circle: Empiricism and Logical Syntax*. Amsterdam: Editions Rodopi, 1993, 32–6; 149–205.

8   For this helpful notion, see Stewart, David, "The Hermeneutics of Suspicion." *Literature and Theology* 3 (1989): 296–307.

9   Vidal, Fernando, and Bernard Kleeberg, "Knowledge, Belief, and the Impulse to Natural Theology." *Science in Context* 20 (2007): 381–400.

10 McGrath, *The Open Secret*, 23–79.

11 On explanation in such a context, see Malcolm, Norman, *Wittgenstein: A Religious Point of View?* London: Routledge, 2002, 24–39.

12 Darwin, Francis, ed., *The Life and Letters of Charles Darwin*. 3 vols. London: John Murray, 1887, vol. 2, 155.

13 See Kitcher, Paul, "Explanatory Unification and the Causal Structure of the World." In *Scientific Explanation*, ed. P. Kitcher and W. Salmon, 410–505. Minneapolis: University of Minnesota Press, 1989; Morrison, Margaret, "A Study in Theory Unification: The Case of Maxwell's Electromagnetic Theory." *Studies in History and Philosophy of Science* 23 (1992): 103–45; Glass, David H., "Coherence Measures and Inference to the Best Explanation." *Synthese* 157 (2007): 275–96.

14 Millay, Edna St Vincent, *Collected Sonnets*. New York: Harper, 1988, 140.

15 Whewell, William, *Philosophy of the Inductive Sciences*. 2 vols. London: John W. Parker, 1847, vol. 2, 36.

16 For the theological development of this point, see McGrath, Alister E., *A Scientific Theology: 2 – Reality*. London: Continuum, 2002, 14–52.

17 See McGrath, *The Open Secret*, 115–39.

18 Stanley Fish has thus rightly argued that the notion of "evidence" is often tautologically determined by such interpretative assumptions: Fish, Stanley E., *Is There a Text in This Class?: The Authority of Interpretive Communities*. Cambridge, MA: Harvard University Press, 1980, 272–4. See further Graff, Gerald, "Interpretation on Tlön: A Response to Stanley Fish." *New Literary History* 17 (1985): 109–17; Spaak, Torben, "Relativism in Legal Thinking: Stanley Fish and the Concept of an Interpretive Community." *Ratio Juris* 21 (2008): 157–71.

19 Adam, Matthias, *Theoriebeladenheit und Objektivität. Zur Rolle von Beobachtungen in den Naturwissenschaften*. Frankfurt am Main: Ontos Verlag, 2002; Brewer, William F., and Bruce L. Lambert, "The Theory-Ladenness of Observation and the Theory-Ladenness of the Rest of the Scientific Process." *Philosophy of Science* 68 (2001): S176–S186.

20 For the legal and forensic dimensions of this point, see Evett, I. W., G. Jackson, J. A. Lambert, and S. McCrossan, "The Impact of the Principles of Evidence Interpretation on the Structure and Content of Statements." *Science and Justice* 40 (2000): 233–9.

21   See Lustig, Abigail, "Natural Atheology." In *Darwinian Heresies*, ed. Abigail Lustig, Robert J. Richards, and Michael Ruse, 69–83. Cambridge: Cambridge University Press, 2004.

22   For the phrase in Darwin, see Darwin, Charles, *On the Origin of the Species by Means of Natural Selection*. 6th edn. London: John Murray, 1872, 428. For comment, see Brooke, John Hedley, "'Laws Impressed on Matter by the Creator'? The *Origins* and the Question of Religion." In *The Cambridge Companion to the "Origin of Species*," ed. Michael Ruse and Robert J. Richards, 256–74. Cambridge: Cambridge University Press, 2009.

23   This applies especially to "evidentialist" approaches to Christian apologetics, which often fail to appreciate the importance of observational interpretation.

24   Haldane, John, "Philosophy, the Restless Heart, and the Meaning of Theism." *Ratio* 19 (2006): 421–40, especially 425–9. Note also how William James's approach to natural theology inclines toward seeing it as the retrospective confirmation of an already existing faith: Hauerwas, Stanley, *With the Grain of the Universe: The Church's Witness and Natural Theology*. London: SCM Press, 2002, 43–86, especially 76–8.

25   For this Christianized version of Platonism, see Cary, Philip, *Augustine's Invention of the Inner Self: The Legacy of a Christian Platonist*. Oxford: Oxford University Press, 2000, 63–76.

26   Augustine of Hippo, *Sermo* LXXXVIII.v.5.

27   Murdoch, Iris, "The Sovereignty of Good over Other Concepts." In *Existentialists and Mystics*, ed. Peter Conradi, 363–85. London: Chatto, 1998, 368.

28   Hauerwas, Stanley, "The Demands of a Truthful Story: Ethics and the Pastoral Task." *Chicago Studies* 21 (1982): 59–71, 65–6.

29   See here Herdt, Jennifer A., "Alasdair MacIntyre's 'Rationality of Traditions' and Tradition-Transcendental Standards of Justification." *Journal of Religion* 78 (1998): 524–46; Porter, Jean, "Tradition in the Recent Work of Alasdair MacIntyre." In *Alasdair MacIntyre*, ed. Mark C. Murphy, 38–69. Cambridge: Cambridge University Press, 2003.

30   Hauerwas, Stanley, *The Peaceable Kingdom: A Primer in Christian Ethics*. Notre Dame, IN: University of Notre Dame Press, 1983, 101–2.

31   Taylor, Charles, *Modern Social Imaginaries*. Durham, NC: Duke University Press, 2004, 23.

32   Fish, *Is There a Text in This Class?*, 147–74.

33   Fish, *Is There a Text in This Class?*, 141.

34   McGrath, Alister E., *A Fine-Tuned Universe: The Quest for God in Science and Theology*. Louisville, KY: Westminster John Knox Press, 2009, 61–82.

35   A point frequently emphasized by John Polkinghorne: see, for example, Polkinghorne, John, *Theology in the Context of Science*. London: SPCK, 2008, 46–65.

36   Hauerwas, *With the Grain of the Universe*, 15–16; Southgate, Christopher, *The Groaning of Creation: God, Evolution, and the Problem of Evil*. Louisville, KY: Westminster John Knox Press, 2008, 28–35.

37   Weil, Simone, *Gravity and Grace*. London: Routledge, 2002, 81.

38   Weil, *Gravity and Grace*, 84.

39 James, William, "Is Life Worth Living?" In *The Will to Believe and Other Essays in Popular Philosophy*, 32–62. New York: Longmans, Green, 1897, 51.

40 Weinberg, Steven, *The First Three Minutes: A Modern View of the Origin of the Universe*. London: Andre Deutsch, 1993, 149.

41 Medawar, Peter B., *The Limits of Science*. Oxford: Oxford University Press, 1985, 66.

42 Dawkins, Richard, *River out of Eden: A Darwinian View of Life*. London: Phoenix, 1995, 133.

43 "Wünschelrute" (my translation); in Eichendorff, Joseph von, *Gedichte*, ed. P. H. Neumann. Stuttgart: Reclam, 1997, 32. For comment on the theological significance of this poem, see McGrath, Alister E., " 'Schläft ein Lied in allen Dingen'? Gedanken über die Zukunft der natürlichen Theologie." *Theologische Zeitschrift* 65 (2009): 246–60. The original German text reads as follows: "Schläft ein Lied in allen Dingen, / Die da träumen fort und fort, / Und die Welt hebt an zu singen, / Triffst du nur das Zauberwort."

44 Bormann, Alexander von, *Natura Loquitur. Naturpoesie und emblematische Formel bei Joseph von Eichendorff*. Tübingen: Niemeyer, 1986, 17–24, 48–73.

Index

abduction, as scientific reasoning
     process 198–9
Addison, Joseph 70, 72–3, 101
animals, status of 169–71
Aquinas, Thomas 69, 189, 191–2, 227
Arbuthnot, John 71
Aristotle 189
Athanasius of Alexandria 114
Atran, Scott 259
Augustan Age 49–50
Augustine of Hippo 15, 114, 220,
     222–9, 232, 280, 285
  on *rationes seminales* 222–8, 230,
     232–3
Ayala, Francisco J. 190–1

Bacon, Francis 75
Baer, Karl Ernst von 161
Barrett, Justin 267
Barth, Karl 18, 51
Barrow, Isaac 74
Bauman, Zygmunt 221
Beagle, H. M. S. 144–5
Bell, Charles 120, 122
Bentley, Richard 69–70
Berger, Peter 57
Black Beauty (1877) 170
Blackmore, Richard 70

Blackmore, Susan 257, 259
"blending inheritance" 151
Bohm, David 37
Bonaventura of Bagnoregio 17
Boyer, Pascal 259, 266
Boyle, Robert 65, 69, 91
Boyle Lectures 69–70
Bridgewater Treatises 5, 119–26
Brooke, John Hedley 16–17
Brougham, Henry Lord 112–15
Browning, Robert 130–3
Brunner, Emil 279
Buckland, William 110–11, 120, 221
Buffon, George Louis 100, 149

Chalmers, Thomas 120, 122
Chambers, Robert 166
Charleton, Walter 53
Cicero, Marcus Tullius 13–14
Clifford, William K. 153–4
contrivance, notion of 53–4, 63–70,
     91–7, 156–7
Cooke, Josiah Parsons 194
Copernicus, Nicolaus 28, 37
Cottingham, John 18
creation, doctrine of, and natural
     theology 61–3, 217–33
  in Augustine of Hippo 222–9

Darwinism and the Divine: Evolutionary Thought and Natural Theology, First Edition.
Alister E. McGrath.
© 2011 Alister E. McGrath. Published 2011 by Blackwell Publishing Ltd.

creation as process and event 230–7
and laws of nature 54–5, 60–1,
66–7, 159–60, 172, 234–5
special creation 156–7
Cudworth, Ralph 55
Cuvier, Georges 100

Darwin, Annie 158, 169
Darwin, Charles xii, 20, 100, 124,
143–70, 199, 249, 263, 279, 283
on adaptation 148
on animal emotion 169–71
and H. M. S. Beagle 144–5
on "blending inheritance" 151
on coexistence of theory and
anomaly 152–3
death of daughter Annie (1851) 158,
169
development of views on natural
selection 146–50
on distribution of species 148
and divine providence 166–70, 202
on extinction of species 147–8
Origin of Species (1859) 144–6,
150–1, 247
on pangenesis 151–2
and religion 157–60
on rudimentary structures 147
on "special creation" 156–7
on William Paley 155–7, 164
Darwin, Erasmus 96
Darwinism 27–40, 247–68, 287
applicable to cultural
evolution? 249–54
definitions of 28–32
as an ideology 32–6
metaphysical inflation of 36–40,
287
Neo-Darwinian synthesis 30–2
"Universal Darwinism" 247–68,
281–2
Dawkins, Richard 34–6, 38–9, 217,
250, 253–62
Deism 52–3, 60–1, 109–10, 159,
164–5, 235–6, 288
Dennett, Daniel 34–6, 217, 250, 261,
281

Derham, William 4, 70–1, 72, 75, 86,
90, 101, 115
Dickens, Charles 118
Dio Chrysostom 14
disenchantment of nature 4, 57–9
Dobzhansky, Theodosius 39–40
Dryden, John 49
Duhem, Pierre 200
Durkheim, Émile 265

Eberhard, Johann August 5
Edmonds, Bruce 260
Egerton, Francis Henry, Earl of
Bridgewater, 119
Eichendorff, Joseph von 290
Eliot, George 132
emergence, and creation 230–3
Essays and Reviews (1860) 133–4
Evans-Pritchard, E. E. 263
evidence, criteria of assessment 75–6,
102–3, 115–19, 283–5

Feuerbach, Ludwig 132
fine-tuning within nature 187, 194–7,
229–30
Fish, Stanley 287
Fiske, John 251
Freud, Sigmund 27–8

Galen of Pergamum 14, 65, 68
Gayon, Jean 28
geology, impact upon nineteenth-
century natural theology 110–12,
221–2
Ghiselin, Michael 281
God's action within nature 234–8
Gould, Stephen Jay 99–100, 156,
192–3, 255, 263–4
Gray, Asa 5, 160, 161, 163
Gregerson, Niels 233
Grew, Nehemiah 60
Guthrie, Stewart 266

Hale, Matthew 116
Hanson, N. R. 285
Harman, Gilbert 199, 285
Hauerwas, Stanley 286–7

Heisenberg, Werner 37
Helmholtz, Hermann von 161
Henderson, Lawrence J. 194
Hitchcock, Christopher 153
Hobbes, Thomas 74
Hooper, John 59–60
Hort, F. J. A. 11
Hoyle, Fred 196–7
Hull, David L. 257–8
Hume, David 87, 95, 96–7, 236–7
Hutton, F. W. 150
Hutton, James 221
Huxley, Thomas H. 4, 33, 160, 161–3, 165–6, 186–7, 202, 284
Hyperactive Agency Detection Device 266

induction, as scientific tool 152–4, 197–202, 283–5
inference to the best explanation 197–200, 283–5
Intelligent Design movement 33–5

James, William 18, 154, 257, 289
Jenkin, Fleeming 151–2

Kant, Immanuel 5, 87, 190
Kepler, Johannes 28, 54
Kidd, John 120
Kingsley, Charles 99, 100–1, 164–5
Kirby, William 120, 123
Kölliker, Albert von 161
Kristeller, Paul Oskar 253

Lamarck, Jean-Baptiste 32, 149, 251, 253–4
laws of nature 54–5, 60–1, 66–7, 159–60, 172, 234–5
Leclerc, Georges-Louis 149
LeConte, Joseph 251–2
Lewis, C. S. 16
Lewontin, Richard 33
Lightfoot, John 200
Locke, John 60, 134
Lombard, Peter 227
Lyell, Charles 125, 221

MacIntyre, Alasdair 286
Malthus, Thomas 168–9
Marett, Robert 263
Mayr, Ernst 39–40, 190, 191
meme, notion of 254–62, 282
Mendel, Gregor 152
Midgley, Mary 257
Mill, John Stuart 153
Millay, Edna St Vincent 283
miracles
    cessation of 4, 59–61
    and natural theology 66–8, 129
    Protestant approaches to 59–61
Mivart, St George 227
Monod, Jacques 192
Moore, Aubrey 146, 227–8, 235
More, Henry 55
Morowitz, Harold 232
Morris, Simon Conway 193–4
Murchie, Guy 203–4
Murdoch, Iris 11–12, 286

natural selection 146–50
natural theology 11–21
    during Augustan Age 49–76
    and the beauty of nature 72–3
    and the church 285–7
    in classical antiquity 13–15
    conceptual fluidity of 15–18
    and Deism 52–3, 60–1, 109–10, 159, 164–5, 235–6, 288
    and doctrine of creation 61–3, 217–33
    as evolutionary adaptation? 262–7
    and fine-tuning within nature 194–7
    future of 277–90
    and geology 110–12
    and inference of design 197–202
    and laws of nature 54–5, 60–1, 66–7, 172
    multiple definitions of 15–18
    and Newtonian physics 53–6
    during nineteenth century 85–103, 108–34
    as "physico-theology" 52–3, 63–71, 88, 91–7

and questions of meaning 288–90
resurgence of 18–20
and suffering within nature 169–71,
  202–7
and teleology 52–3, 63–71, 88,
  91–7, 160–6, 185–202, 202–8
Trinitarian dimensions of 3, 19, 195,
  201, 205–7, 235–6, 287
Needham, Joseph 193
Newman, John Henry 127–30, 197
Newton, Isaac 53–4, 60–1, 159, 200
Noble, Denis 39
Nieuwentyt, Bernard 86, 88–91

Origin of Species (1859) 144–6, 150–1,
  247
Otto, Rudolf 19
Owen, Richard 111–12

Paley, William xii, 4, 71, 85–103, 227,
  279–80, 283–5
  Cambridge career 86–8
  on chance in nature 191–2
  on contrivance 91–7
  Darwin's attitude towards 155–7,
    161–8
  Dependence on Bernard
    Nieuwentyt 88–91
  on intermediary causes in
    nature 97–9
  on observation of design in
    nature 91–7, 197–8
  preference of biological domain to
    physical 93–5
  on suffering within nature 203
  on teleology 91–7, 186,
  on the "watch" image 91–2,
    101–25
  Victorian critiques of 108–34, 166–7
Pattison, Hugh 133–4
Peacocke, Arthur 238
Pearson, John 62, 218–22
Peirce, Charles S. 198–9, 285
physico-theology, as specific form of
  natural theology 52–3, 63–71, 88
Platonic theory of Forms 12–13

Polkinghorne, John 23 n.36, 238
Pope, Alexander 49, 59
Poulshock, Joseph 260
Powell, Baden 56, 124
Protestant assumptions of Augustan
  natural theology 55–61
Prout, William 121, 122–3
providence, divine 61, 166–70, 191–4

quantum theory, metaphysical status
  of 37–8

rationes seminales 222–8, 230,
  232–3
Ray, John 4, 66, 86, 100, 101, 115,
  116, 221
religion, theories of the origins
  of 265–7
Rensch, Bernhard 39–40
Roget, Peter Mark 120, 122
Rolston, Holmes 206
Romanes, George 236
Russell, Robert 237–8

Sayers, Dorothy L. 143, 172
Schrödinger, Erwin 37
secondary causality 99, 233–5
Sewell, Anna 170
Shakespeare, William 130, 200
Sober, Elliott 153
Southgate, Christopher 205–6
Spandels 262–4
Spencer, Herbert 150
Sperber, Dan 259
Sprat, Thomas 66–7
Steno, Nicolaus 221
Strasbourg, Great Clock of 65–6
suffering, as theological issue
  concerning evolution 166–70
Sumner, John Bird 155

Taylor, Charles 286
teleology, in biological realm 52–3,
  63–71, 88, 91–7, 160–6,
  185–208
Temple, Frederick 164

Tennyson, Alfred Lord 166
Torrance, Thomas F. 204
Two Books of God 59

"Universal Darwinism" 247–68, 281–2
Ussher, James 220

Varro, Marcus Terentius 15
*Vestiges of the Natural History of
    Creation* (1844) 166
Virgil 14
Voltaire 110

Ward, Lester F. 251
watch analogy, in natural
    theology 65–6, 91–2, 101–25
Weber, Max 57
Whewell, William 4, 114, 118–19,
    120, 123–6, 149, 153, 199, 200
Weil, Simone 201, 288
Weinberg, Steven 289
Weismann, August 252
Weisman Barrier 252
Wilkins, John 4, 64–5, 90
Woolf, Clifford 204

CPSIA information can be obtained at www.ICGtesting.com
Printed in the USA
LVOW04s1516090415

433924LV00014B/122/P